TAKING SIDES: CLASHING VIEWS ON CONTROVERSIAL POLITICAL ISSUES
Third Edition

Where there is much desire to learn, there of necessity will be much arguing. . .

John Milton

"The man who pleads his case first seems to be in the right, then his opponent comes and puts him to the test."

Proverbs

STAFF

Jeremy Brenner — Managing Editor
Brenda Filley — Production Manager
Charles Vitelli — Designer
Libra VonOgden — Typesetting Coordinator
Jean Bailey — Graphics Coordinator
Dan Buop — Cover Photo

TAKING SIDES: CLASHING VIEWS ON CONTROVERSIAL POLITICAL ISSUES
Third Edition

Edited, Selected, and with Introductions by
GEORGE MCKENNA
City College, City University of New York
and
STANLEY FEINGOLD
Westchester Community College

The Dushkin Publishing Group, Inc.
Guilford, Connecticut

iii

To Fumiko and Sylvia

Library of Congress Catalog Card Number: 83-93817

Manufactured in the United States of America
Third Edition, First Printing

CONTENTS

Carl Cohen, a professor of philosophy argues that even well-intentioned
discrimination is unconstitutional and immoral. Thurgood Marshall, the
first black to be appointed to the high court, supports discrimination in
favor of blacks and other minorities as a means of remedying the long
history of discrimination against them.

Robert Carleson and Kevin Hopkins, Special Assistants to President
Reagan, argue that except for cases of physical survival, income should
belong to those who earn it. Former senator, George McGovern,
responds that society, through government, has a responsibility to those
at the lower end of the economic scale.

The late Jerome Frank, long a Judge of the U.S. Court of Appeals,
rejects the alleged dangers of obscenity and insists on the right to
advocate unpopular views. Political scientist Harry M. Clor holds that the
prohibition of obscenity maintains the public morality in essential ways.

Senator John Chafee outlines his view that the publication of the names
of C.I.A. agents is a threat to the lives of the agents, as well as the national
security and should be prohibited. Former Defense Department official
Halperin and legislative council Berman, contend that the names of
many agents are available from the government's own sources and that
to prohibit the publication of these names would violate the principles of
free speech.

Jeane Kirkpatrick, Ambassador to the U.N., suggests that we are injuring our own interests while doing nothing to promote human rights by failing to distinguish between authoritarian and totalitarian forms of government. Charles Maynes, editor of *Foreign Policy* magazine, points to our history of concern for human rights, and argues that we ignore violations at our peril, no matter what form of government commits them.

PREFACE TO THE THIRD EDITION

In the first edition of *Taking Sides* we said:

> The purpose of this book is to make a modest contribution toward the revival of political dialogue in America. What we propose to do is to examine some leading issues in American politics from the perspective of sharply opposed points of view. We have tried to select authors who argue their points vigorously but in such a way as to enhance our understanding of the issue.
>
> For each issue we have inserted a pair of essays, one pro and one con. We hope the reader will examine each position carefully, and then take sides.

The successes of the first and second editions have encouraged us to bring out this third, revised and expanded version. We have increased the number of issues to twenty, adding selections on the proposed limitation on the power of federal courts (Issue 7), gun control (Issue 11), President Reagan's welfare cuts (Issue 13), national security and civil liberties (Issue 15), abortion (Issue 16), public school prayer (Issue 17), nuclear deterrence (Issue 19), and human rights policies (Issue 20). Among the original issues we have made a number of improvements, bringing up to date our introductions to the selections and substituting new selections where appropriate. We have also extensively revised our introductory essay.

Despite these revisions, our basic thesis remains unchanged. We believe in public dialogue. We are convinced that the best way to protect against narrow-mindedness and fanaticism is to bring opposing views together and let them clash.

This does not mean that we consider all points of view to be equal. On the contrary, we encourage our readers to become partisans, as long as they support their positions with logic and facts, are able to make reasonable replies to opposing arguments, and are willing to revise their views if they are proven wrong.

The reader who has thoughtfully examined two antithetical views, each of which is expressed with all the evidence and eloquence that an informed advocate can bring to bear upon the argument, will also perceive what positions can be occupied both between and beyond the sharply-differentiated essays which he or she has read.

In one sense our approach resembles a series of formal debates, of the kind conducted by debating teams and moot law courts. In another and more important sense, however, the conflicting arguments of this book represent something quite different. A debate is an intellectual game, in which opposition is explicit but artificial. By contrast, the essays included here were rarely written in direct response to one another. More important, the form in which they are expressed is that of public consideration of real issues, in which both political participants and commentators seek the widest support for their positions. In every instance we have chosen what we believe to be an appropriate and well-reasoned statement by a committed advocate. If this often adds passion to reason, it is an element which the student of American politics cannot afford to ignore. But passion with substance is much different from empty rhetoric.

Although we have attempted (in the Introduction) to indicate the major alignments in American politics, a reflective reader of these essays is bound to realize that the mere ascription of a label will not dispose of the position. Every analysis presented here has merit—insofar as it reflects some sense of political reality and represents a viewpoint shared by some Americans—and each analysis therefore demands to be dealt with on its merit.

We hope that the reader who confronts lively and thoughtful statements on vital issues will be stimulated to ask some of the critical questions about American politics. What are the highest-priority issues with which government must deal today? What positions should be taken on these issues? What should be the attitude of Americans toward their government? To what extent, if any, does it need to be changed? How should it be organized in order to achieve the goals we set for it? What are these goals? Our conviction is that a healthy, stable democracy requires a citizenry which considers these questions and participates, however indirectly, in the answering of them. The alternative is apathy, passivity, and, sooner or later, the rule of tyrants.

ACKNOWLEDGMENTS

We wish to acknowledge the encouragement and support given to this project by Rick Connelly of the Dushkin Publishing Group. We are grateful as well to Jeremy Brenner for his very able editorial supervision. We also wish to thank Professors Jerry Yeric and Stanley Thames for their reviews and critiques of the second edition of this book. Finally, we thank our wives, Sylvia McKenna and Fumiko Feingold, for the support and understanding they showed during the period in which we prepared this book.

George McKenna
Stanley Feingold
New York City
October, 1982

INTRODUCTION: LABELS AND ALIGNMENTS IN AMERICAN POLITICS

Stanley Feingold

George McKenna

When the American people voted in the 1980 presidential election they were confronted with a variety of political labels. These were not only the political party designations—Democratic, Republican, and a host of others— but an assortment of terms purported to define political positions, terms like "liberal," "conservative," "moderate," "radical," and "pluralist."

The Republican nominee, Ronald Reagan, was considered to be one of the most "conservative" major-party candidates of recent times. President Jimmy Carter, the Democratic candidate, was also perceived as representing the more "conservative" elements in the Democratic party. John Anderson, known as a "conservative" during his twenty years in Congress, appealed to many voters who identified themselves as "liberals."

Do these labels have any genuine meaning? Beyond the single election, do they help us to understand opposing views on the major issues dividing American society? We believe that they do, but that the terms can also be abused, as when they are employed not to clarify thought but to substitute for it.

Our purpose in this introduction is to reexamine the basic meanings of some of these labels and apply them to current disputes, including the issues presented in this volume.

The underlying distinction between liberals and conservatives lies in their respective views of human nature. Liberalism tends toward optimism, conservatism toward pessimism (the conservative would say realism). Liberals

1

have in some historical periods gone so far as to believe in the perfectibility of humankind, and have thus placed great store in universal education, the closed ballot, and the direct primary as means of bringing about fuller participation in government. Although the hopes held for these reforms have proven excessive, liberals are undaunted in their championing of the rights and welfare of the poor and oppressed. The underlying belief is that there are virtually no limits to what a person can become if he or she is given a fair chance and a decent environment. Liberals are often secularists who see themselves on the side of the angels.

Conservatives scorn what they consider to be liberal illusions. They believe that the mass of people has a limited capacity for self-improvement, and if political practicality and democratic doctrine require that everyone shall have a voice in the government of society, we should not be gulled into believing that the mass of prejudices and half-truths that pass for the political opinions of most people constitute the collective voice of wisdom. Conservatism of the American variety does not imply a yearning for feudalism, slavery or absolute monarchy, but it does inveigh against those constraints which the majority might impose upon the most able and intelligent members of society.

The historical evolution of liberalism and conservatism as political creeds is worth studying because from this examination we can acquire both confidence that the terms have deep roots and caution against using them rigidly without reference to a particular political context.

CLASSICAL LIBERALISM

The etymological root of liberalism is the Latin *libertas,* meaning liberty or freedom. In the early nineteenth century, liberals dedicated themselves to freeing individuals from all unnecessary and oppressive obligations to authority, whether that authority came from church or state. They opposed the licensing and censorship of the press, the punishment of heretics, compulsory church taxes, religious establishments, and any attempt to dictate on matters of conscience. In economics liberals opposed state monopolies and regarded with great suspicion any attempt, however well-intentioned, to interfere with the development of private business. Liberalism at this point defined freedom principally as freedom *from,* and borrowed from the term *laissez-faire* from the French, literally "leave to be," that is: leave people alone. They believed that individuals by themselves could work best if government and church officials would stay out of their lives. Thomas Jefferson summed up the philosophy of classical liberalism when he said: "I am no friend of energetic government. It is always oppressive."

Insofar as classical liberals held a positive view of government it was in the area of suffrage, which they believed should be extended to every white male. (Women and blacks were added later—much later, and by then liberalism had itself undergone change.) Despite misgivings about "the tyranny of the majority," the mass of free men were sooner to be trusted than a permanent, entrenched elite. Liberal social policy was dedicated to fostering the fulfillment of the human personality. People are basically good, and a liberal commonwealth is one which removes those influences which repress or deform human good while nurturing those factors which contribute to the realization of our potential. Contemporary liberals have much the same objectives as classical liberals, but they are likely to hold that the means necessary to achieve those ends have greatly changed.

By the late nineteenth century the basic strategy of classical liberalism, with regard to its commitment to a *laissez-faire* state, was seriously questioned. The often harsh and unequal impact of industrialism led liberals to revise their views of both private enterprise and the state. Individual freedom still required opposition to repression by either secular or ecclesiastical authority, but this was no longer enough. Commerce and industry, often in the form of business monopoly, oppressed individuals by working them too long and paying them too little. Individuals acting individually could not protect themselves against concentrated economic power. The state was now perceived as having a positive function, enhancing freedom through its action. The state could— and liberals called upon the state to—educate the children, protect the health and safety of members of society, and assist them by subsidizing their welfare during hard times.

NEW DEAL LIBERALISM

In the United States the argument for state intervention did not win a truly popular constituency until after the Great Depression of the 1930s began to be deeply felt. The disastrous effects of a depression which left a quarter of the work force unemployed opened the way to a new administration—and a promise. "I pledge you, I pledge myself," Franklin D. Roosevelt said in accepting the Democratic nomination in 1932, "to a new deal for the American people." Roosevelt's New Deal was an attempt to effect relief and recovery from the Depression; it employed a variety of means, including welfare programs, public works and business regulation, most of which involved government intervention in the economy. The New Deal's claim to the title of liberalism was based upon its reliance on democratic government to liberate people from poverty, oppression and economic exploitation. At the same time, the New Dealers claimed to be as zealous as the classical liberals in defending political and civil liberties.

The common element in laissez-faire liberalism and welfare state liberalism is their dedication to the goal of developing the full potential of each individual. Is this best done by minimizing state involvement, or does it sometimes require an activist state? The New Dealers took the latter view, though they prided themselves on being pragmatic and experimental about their activism. During the heyday of the New Deal a wide variety of programs were tried and, if found wanting, abandoned. All decent means should be tried, they believed, even if it meant some dilution of ideological purity. The

Roosevelt Administration, for example, denounced bankers and business-men in campaign rhetoric but worked very closely with them in trying to extricate the nation from the Depression, and this set a pattern of pragmatism which New Dealers from Harry Truman to Lyndon Johnson emulated.

NEW POLITICS LIBERALISM

New Politics liberalism emerged in the late 1960s and early 1970s as a more militant and uncompromising movement than the New Deal had ever been. "Freedom Now," the civil rights slogan, expressed the mood. The Vietnam peace movement demanded "unconditional" withdrawal from Vietnam. The young university graduates who flocked into the New Politics had come from an environment where "non-negotiable" demands were issued to college deans by sit-inners. But there was more than youthful arrogance in the New Politics movement. There was a pervasive feeling that America had lost, had compromised away, much of its idealism. The New Politics sought to recover some of that spirit by linking up with an older tradition of militant reform which went back to the time of the Revolution. These new liberals thus saw themselves as the authentic heirs of Tom Paine and Henry David Thoreau, of the abolitionists, the radical populists, the suffragettes, and the great Progressive reformers of the early 20th century.

In terms of content, while New Deal liberals concentrated almost exclusively on bread-and-butter issues like unemployment and poverty, the New Politics liberals introduced into the political arena what came to be known as "social issues": the repeal of laws against abortion, the liberalization of laws against homosexuality and pornography, the establishment of affirmative action programs to ensure increased hiring of non-whites and women, and passage of the Equal Rights Amendment. In foreign policy, too, New Politics liberals departed from the New Deal agenda. With keener memories of the unpopular and, for them, unjustified war in Vietnam than of World War II, they became "doves," in contrast to the general "hawkishness" of the New Dealers. They are skeptical of any claim that the United States has to be the leader of "the free world," and they emphatically reject the notion that we must seek superiority in armaments over the Soviet Union. They are not isolationists (of all political groupings in America they are probably most supportive of the United Nations) and they claim to be as concerned as any other group that America's defenses be adequate, but they minimize the danger to the West of an outright Soviet invasion. The real danger, they emphasize, comes not from Soviet military advances but from mutual miscalculations that could lead to a nuclear holocaust. All of the above issues are touched upon in this book.

The political conflict between New Deal liberalism and New Politics liberalism was vividly demonstrated in the Democratic conventions of 1968 and 1972. In 1968 the Democratic Party nominated for the presidency Hubert Humphrey, an ardent New Dealer, at a tumultuous convention which

New Politics Democrats claimed was controlled by "bosses." The schism between the two branches of liberalism contributed to Humphrey's defeat. In the 1972 Democratic convention the tables were turned. This time, thanks to a number of changes in the procedures for selecting delegates, the New Politics forces were in charge. However, their triumph was short-lived. Whether the reasons were the shortcomings of standard-bearer Senator George McGovern, or the spite of New Deal Democrats (many of whom sat out the campaign or supported Republican incumbent President Richard Nixon), or inherent weakness in the New Politics ideology, the Democrats lost the presidential election by a landslide. In 1976 Jimmy Carter managed to avoid the crossfire of the two factions by de-emphasizing ideology; neither side was offered a clear profile of what kind of a liberal Carter was, if indeed he was a liberal.

CONSERVATISM

If liberalism has undergone historical transformation in America, so has conservatism. Just as early American liberals, symbolized by Thomas Jefferson, espoused less government, early conservatives, of whom Alexander Hamilton and John Adams were the earliest leaders, urged government support of economic enterprise and government intervention on behalf of privileged groups. By the time of the New Deal, and in reaction to the growth of the welfare state since that time, conservatives have strongly argued that more government means more unjustified interference in our lives, more bureaucratic regulation of our private conduct, more inhibiting control of economic enterprise, more material advantages for the less energetic and less able at the expense of those who are prepared to work harder and better, and, of course, more taxes—taxes that will be taken from those who earned the money and given to those who have not earned it.

Contemporary conservatives are not always opposed to state intervention. They may support larger military expenditures in order to protect society against foreign enemies, some intrusion into private life in order to protect society against internal subversion, and more zealous criminal prosecution in order to protect society against domestic violence. The point is that few conservatives and perhaps fewer liberals are doctrinaire with respect to the power of the state. Both are quite prepared to use the state for *their* purposes. It is true that "activist" Presidents such as Franklin D. Roosevelt and John F. Kennedy were likely to be liberals. However, Richard Nixon was also an "activist," and, although he does not easily fit any classification, he was far closer to conservatism than to liberalism. Lest we, all too easily, identify liberalism with statism and conservatism with anti-statism, we ought to recall that it was liberal Jefferson who counseled against "energetic government" and it was conservative Alexander Hamilton who designed bold powers for the new central government. (Hamilton wrote: "Energy in the Executive is a leading character in the definition of good government." See Issue 6: Is the President Too Powerful?)

NEOCONSERVATISM AND THE NEW RIGHT

Two newer varieties of conservatism have arisen to challenge the dominant strain of conservatism which served as the loyal opposition to the New Deal. Those who call themselves, or have finally allowed themselves to be called, "neoconservatives," are recent converts to conservatism. Many of them are former New Deal Democrats, and some of them like to argue that it is not they who have changed, but the Democratic Party, which has allowed itself to be taken over by the advocates of the New Politics. However true that may be, as neoconservatives they now emphasize themes which were largely unspoken in their earlier views. They recognize, as they did as New Dealers, the legitimacy of social reform, but now warn of carrying it too far and creating an arrogant bureaucracy. They support equal opportunity, as they always did, but now they underscore the distinction between equal opportunity and equality of result, which they identify as the goal of affirmative action programs. Broadly speaking, neo-conservatism shares with the older variety of conservatism a high respect for tradition and a "sober view," as political scientist James Wilson calls it, of human nature. (See Issue 9: "Will Tougher Sentencing Curb Crime?") Neo-conservatives, like all conservatives, are also deeply concerned about the Communist threat to America. They counsel us to shore up our defenses and to resist any movement which would lead us toward unilateral disarmament.

A more recent and more politically active variant of conservatism usually goes by the title of "the New Right." Despite the semantic resemblance between "New Right" and "neo-conservatism," the two differ in important ways. Neo-conservatives, as mentioned above, are usually lapsed liberals, while New Rightists tend to be dyed-in-the-wool conservatives, though ones who are determined to reach out to wider constituencies than the Old Right appealed to. Neo-conservatives tend to be academic types, who appeal to other similar elites through books and articles in learned journals. The New Right aims at grass-roots voters through a variety of vernacular forums, from church groups to direct-mail solicitation. Finally, where neo-conservatives customarily talk about politico-economic structures and global strategies, New Rightists reach down closer to the concerns of ordinary Americans by emphasizing what they call "family issues"—moral issues such as abortion, prayer in public schools, pornography, and what they consider to be a general climate of moral breakdown in the nation. The reader may have noticed that these "family issues" turn out to be much the same as the "social issues" introduced into the political arena by the advocates of the New Politics. This should not be surprising, since the New Right can be seen as a reaction to the previous successes of the New Politics movement in legitimizing its stands on "social issues."

In substance, then, spokesmen for the New Politics and the New Right stand as polar opposites: the former regard abortion as a woman's right, the latter see it as legalized murder; the former tend to regard homosexuality as a lifestyle which needs protection against discrimination, the latter are more inclined to see it as a perversion; the former have made an issue of their support for the Equal Rights Amendment, while the latter include large numbers of women who fought against it because they believed it threatened their role identity. The list of issues could be made longer, but by now it should be clear that the New Right and the New Politics are like positive and negative photographs of America's moral landscape. For all of their differences, however, their style is in some respects very similar. It is heavily laced with moralistic prose, it tends to equate compromise with "selling out," and it claims to represent the best, most "authentic," traditions of America. This is not to denigrate either movement, for the kinds of issues they address are indeed moral issues, and do not generally admit of much compromise. Nor can the issues simply be finessed or ignored, despite the efforts of conventional politicians to do so. They must be aired, and fought over, which is why we include some of them, such as pornography (Issue 14), abortion (Issue 16), and public school prayer (Issue 17), in this volume.

It is the conventional wisdom of American politics for presidential candidates to appear to be all things to all voters. In the White House, Presidents often guide the ship of state by trimming their ideological sails and moving with the prevailing winds. All the more surprising, then, is the fact that Ronald Reagan was an avowedly conservative candidate, and has also been a conservative President. To be sure, some conservatives have accused him of compromise on specific issues. For example, when in the summer of 1982 Reagan espoused increased taxes to reduce the federal deficit there were conservatives who accused him of compromising true conservative doctrine. In general, however, Reagan has managed to combine the Old Right's insistence upon economic independence from government interferences with the New Right's concern with moral issues. Liberalism has been put on the defensive, and a half-century after the inauguration of the New Deal it looks as though government is playing a different role than the one envisaged by liberalism.

RADICALS AND REACTIONARIES

The label "reactionary" is almost an epithet, and the label "radical" is worn with pride only by a few zealots on the banks of the political mainstream. A reactionary is not a conserver but a backward-mover, dedicated to turning the clock back to better times. Most of the rest of us harbor the suspicion that the reactionary would restore us to a time that never was except in political myth, and the repeal of industrialism or universal education or the twentieth century does not commend itself as a practical, let alone a desirable, political program.

Radicalism (literally meaning "from the roots" or "going to the foundation") implies fundamental reconstruction of the social order. Taken in that sense, it is possible to speak of right-wing radicalism as well as left-wing radicalism, radicalism which restores or newly inaugurates a hierarchical society as well as a radicalism which wants nothing less than an egalitarian society. The term is sometimes used in both of these senses, but most often radicalism is reserved to characterize more liberal change. Where the liberal would effect change through conventional democratic processes, the radical is likely to be skeptical as to the ability of the established machinery to bring about the needed change and might be prepared to sacrifice a "little" liberty to bring about a great deal more quality.

Both major parties in the United States know that it is suicidal to be identified by the public as either reactionary or radical. Sides are not to be sharply drawn. One reason is that many Americans are reluctant to choose. Reform? Yes, of course, but conserve too. Moderation is well-regarded in this country. Our self-image has both a progressive face and another of a preserved heritage. So we sometimes seek to make haste slowly, or as the Supreme Court once memorably put it, "with all deliberate speed." Why not have the best of both worlds, that which we possess and cherish, and also that which our ingenuity and idealism can bring into being? It is easier said than done. Those who insist we must choose sides unequivocally argue that the middle of the road is an unsafe lane of travel. On the other hand, some thoughtful Americans have chosen a political principle which seems to combine liberal and conservative elements. The principle is called pluralism, and it is important because it is embodied in the constitutional system of the United States.

PLURALISM

Pluralism espouses diversity, in a society containing many interest groups and in a government containing competing units of power. Because this implies the widest expression of competing ideas, pluralism expresses sympathy with an important element of liberalism. But pluralism, as Madison and Hamilton analyzed its sources in *The Federalist* commentaries on the Constitution, springs from a profoundly pessimistic view of human nature, and in this respect it corresponds more closely with conservatism. James Madison, who was possibly the single most influential member of the convention that wrote the Constitution, hoped that in a large and varied nation, no single interest group could control the government. Even if there were a majority interest, it would be unlikely to capture all of the national agencies of government—the House of Representatives, the Senate, the President, and the federal judiciary—each of which was chosen in a different way by a different constituency for a different term of office. Moreover, to make certain that no one branch exercised excessive power, each was equipped with "checks and balances" which enabled any agency of national government to curb the powers of the others. The clearest statement of Madison's, and the Constitution's, theory is to be found in the Fifty-first paper of *The Federalist:*

> *It may be a reflection on human nature that such devices should be necessary to control the abuses of government. But what is government itself, but the greatest of all reflections on human nature? If men were angels, no government would be necessary.*

This pluralist position may be analyzed in conflicting ways. It is conservative insofar as it rejects simple majority rule. It is liberal insofar as it similarly rejects rule by any single elite. It is conservative in its pessimistic appraisal of human nature. At the same time, pluralism's pessimism is a kind of egalitarianism, holding as it does that no one can be trusted with power, and that majority interests no less than minority interests will use power for selfish ends. It is at least defensible to suggest that in America pluralism represents an alternative to both liberalism and conservatism, in that where liberalism is majoritarian and conservatism is elitist, pluralism is anti-majoritarian and anti-elitist, and combines some elements of both!

Because a pluralist constitutional system makes change difficult to accomplish, it "tilts" toward conservatism. The *status quo* is not immovable, but it is never easily routed, at least not in the United States. The U.S. Constitution has been amended only fifteen times in the nearly two hundred years since the adoption of the Bill of Rights, and most of the amendments are technical in character. Nevertheless, liberals have derived advantages from the "flexibility" of our Constitution, or more precisely, the manner in which the Constitution has been interpreted by our courts. Although "strict construc-tionists" have prevailed in the sense that constitutional clauses have been given expanded meaning, leading to a growth in national power that the Framers could not have anticipated. At every point where the meaning of constitutional phrases has been stretched or enlarged, "strict constructionists" have cried that the Constitution was being undermined. In reality, positions on whether to interpret the Constitution strictly or loosely have depended more on conservative or liberal outlook than on some abstract theory of the nature of constitutions. Conservatism is identified with strict constructionism in the traditional defense of states' rights, and the preservation of that balance between national and state power which existed at the time of the Constitu-tion's adoption. The states' rights position was that of the *status quo*, tradition, inherited practice, and local elites resisting the nationalization of majority rule. At the same time, we must acknowledge that liberalism has been not less strict in its interpretation of the First Amendment defense of free speech. When "Congress shall make no law . . . abridging the freedom of speech" is held to mean *no* law against subversive, violent, peace-disrupting, or obscene speech, liberalism becomes literalism in constitutional interpretation.

The really formidable obstacle to change in the American constitutional system is the separation of powers among the three branches of national government; the legislative branch is itself composed of two houses, which are often deadlocked. A mere majority is thus unlikely to gain control of the government and to shape public policy. At the same time, the constitutional system is not traditionally conservative in thwarting the will of elite groups which are unlikely to gain sufficient influence to control governmental action. Perhaps pluralism comes closer to describing the governmental process, although it is not always of the kind that Madison envisaged. Determined minority interests, intent on influencing decision-making only in a confined area, seem to possess enhanced access to the places of power, thanks to the absence of party government and the presence of a fragmentation of power in Congress and the federal bureaucracy. A special interest will be content merely to reach and influence the ranking members of the appropriate congressional committees and the commissioners or other federal officials who deal with their interest on a regular basis.

SOME APPLICATIONS

Despite our effort to define the principal alignments in American politics, some policy positions do not neatly fit the categories. The reader of this book will reach his or her own conclusions, but we may suggest some alignments to be found here in order to demonstrate the variety of viewpoints.

In the debate on obscenity (Issue 14), Judge Jerome Frank adopts the liberal position that human beings are mature enough not to be harmed by what society happens to consider "obscene," while Harry Clor worries about the connection between obscenity and the darker, violent impulses in the human heart—a concern often voiced by the New Right. In a very different area of public policy, William J. Crotty defends party reform as a liberal measure that has made for more representativeness and "open" conventions, while it is opposed by Everett Carll Ladd, Jr. because it has diminished the conservative function of parties in mediating among candidates. (See Issue 2: Has Party Reform Succeeded?) Assessing the presidency (Issue 5), Theodore Sorensen echoes New Deal liberalism in stressing the positive features of the modern presidency, while Michael Novak would cut the presidency down to more controllable size, as some conservatives—and many New Politics liberals—would do.

The conflict between contemporary conservatism and liberalism is clearly expressed in the opposed approaches of David Bazelon and James Q. Wilson to the question of crime (Issue 9). Wilson proceeds from a "sober view of man" (which we noted earlier) to the conclusion that the best way to fight crime is to imprison criminals for a long period during which they cannot harm others. Bazelon, proceeding from a more optimistic appraisal of human nature, believes that crime is a desperate yet understandable reaction to intolerable social conditions, and that the best way to combat it is to reform society. More difficult to classify is the controversy considered in Issue 6: Does Government Regulate Too Much? Steven Kelman's argument in favor of regulation is compatible with either New Deal or New Politics liberalism, but Barry Crickmer's position is reminiscent of classical liberalism or libertarianism. His strictures against state paternalism have the flavor of classical liberalism, yet his position on regulation is identical with that taken by avowed conservatives from Barry Goldwater to Ronald Reagan.

Conservatism finds eloquent expression in Walter Berns's moral and constitutional defense of the death penalty (Issue 10: Is Capital Punishment Justified?), and the defense of President Reagan's welfare cuts by Carleson and Hopkins (Issue 13). Pluralism is championed by Andrew Greeley (Issue 1: Is America Ruled By an Elite?) and by Irving Louis Horowitz (Issue 3: Can Lobbying Endanger Democracy?), both of whom see legitimate power as the product of interest-group pluralism. Phyllis Schlafly, one of the best-known spokespersons for the New Right, argues in Issue 7 that the federal courts have become bastions of the New Politics and need to have their powers curbed, while federal judge Irving Kaufman defends the view, currently favored by liberals, that to tamper with the courts is to tamper with the Constitution. These characterizations hardly suggest the complexity and subtlety of the essays, but they indicate that there are philosophical reverberations beyond the immediate issues considered in the essays.

The thoughtful reader will independently assess the viewpoints in these essays in order to determine which are conservative or liberal or pluralist or otherwise, and which are right and which are wrong. The empirical evidence to support judgments of right and wrong is often scant. Does capital punishment deter criminals from commiting murder? Does obscenity contribute to a breakdown of morals and the commission of sex crimes? Even more often, right and wrong are matters of value judgment, so that at bottom one's position expresses a moral preference. (This is not to say that moral judgments are necessarily arbitrary or subjective, only that they ultimately take us outside the realm of politics and into philosophy—perhaps even into metaphysics and theology.)

Obviously, one's position on the issues in this book will be affected by circumstances. After Vietnam and Watergate, for example, many who had once championed the strong presidency have adopted the opposite view. But we would like to think that the essays in this book are durable enough to last through several seasons of events and controversies. We can be certain that the issues will survive, and the search for coherence and consistency in our use of political labels underlines the options open to us and reveals their consequences. The result must be more mature judgments about what is best for America. That, of course, is the ultimate aim of public debate and decision-making, and it transcends all labels and categories.

ISSUE 1

DOES AN ELITE
RULE AMERICA?

YES: Michael Parenti, from DEMOCRACY FOR THE FEW, 3rd edition
(New York, 1980)
NO: Andrew M. Greeley, from BUILDING COALITIONS: AMERICAN
POLITICS IN THE 1970'S (New York, 1974)

ISSUE SUMMARY

YES: Political Scientist Parenti holds the view that, in spite of symbolic
gestures, the centers of substantive power have changed little and the
notion of pluralistic democracy is an illusion.
NO: Sociologist Greeley is persuaded that there is no single, established
center of power, and points to the behavior of the system as evidence to
support his view.

Since the framing of the United States Constitution behind closed doors in
1787 there have been periodic charges that America is controlled, or in
imminent danger of being controlled, by a power elite. All representative
government is necessarily government by elites (i.e., small, selective ruling
groups), but those who raise the specter of a power elite are charging that
America is run by an *unrepresentative* elite, one which is unaccountable to the
majority of voters. Almost invariably, it is added that this elite is not just
political but economic as well. Although all industrial societies have gradations of wealth, democracy is supposed to counter the weight of money with
the weight of numbers. The basic contention of the elite-theorists, then, is not
simply that there are rich and poor in America but that the very rich—or a
small elite working in league with them—are making all the crucial decisions.

Fear of elitism has a long history in America. Richard Henry Lee, a signer of the Declaration of Independence, spoke for many "anti-federalists" who opposed ratification of the Constitution, when he warned that the proposed charter shifted power away from the people and into the hands of the "aristocrats" and "moneyites," those who "avariciously grasp at all power and property." Long after these fears were more or less quieted there still remained a residue of suspicion that the wealthy were manipulating the machinery of government for their own purposes. Before the Civil War, Jacksonian Democrats fulminated against Eastern merchants and bankers who, they charged, were usurping the power of the people. After the Civil War, a number of "radical" parties and movements revived this theme of anti-elitism. The ferment, which was brought about by the rise of industrial monopolies, government corruption, and economic hardship for Western farmers, culminated in the founding of the "People's Party" at the beginning of the 1890s. The "populists," as they were more commonly called, wanted economic and political reforms aimed at transferring power away from the rich and back to "the plain people." The populist assumption was that ordinary people had once possessed sovereign power in America, but that it had slipped away from them.

Since the 1930s American radicalism has probably been more influenced by Marxism than by populism. Like populism, Marxism emphasizes the domination of America by the rich; unlike populism, Marxism does not look back with nostalgia on some golden age of democracy in America. For Marxists, America has always been dominated by wealth, though the domination has taken different forms at different periods. Marxists also differ from populists in stressing the class basis of domination. Instead of seeing the problem of elitism as that of a conspiracy of a few evil men, Marxists view it more impersonally, as a tendency inherent in capitalism.

One of the best-developed arguments disputing the populist-Marxist thesis that America is ruled by an unrepresentative elite is the argument of *pluralism*. Pluralists are quite ready to admit that there are many elites in our society, for that is precisely their point: because America contains so many groups, each has a tendency to counterbalance the power of the others. Thus, no group or coalition of groups can become an "establishment" in America.

Andrew Greeley, a priest and sociologist who teaches at the University of Arizona, argues the pluralist position in the following debate on elitism. On the other side, arguing the elitist thesis, is political scientist Michael Parenti, who anticipates and tries to answer the pluralist argument from a perspective which appears to combine both populism and Marxism.

YES   Michael Parenti

DEMOCRACY FOR THE FEW

The United States is said to be a pluralistic society, and indeed a glance at the social map of this country reveals a vast agglomeration of regional, occupational and ethnic groups, and state, local and national governing agencies. If by pluralism we mean this multiplicity of private and public groups, then the United States is pluralistic. But then so is any society of size and complexity, including allegedly "totalitarian" ones like the Soviet Union with its multiplicity of regional, occupational and ethnic groups and its party, administrative, industrial and military factions all jostling for position and power.

But the proponets of pluralism presume to be saying something about how *power* is distributed and how *democracy* works. Specifically, pluralism means that

1. Power is shared among representative sectors of the population.
2. The shaping of public policy involves inputs from a wide range of competing social groups.
3. No one group enjoys permanent dominance or suffers permanent defeat.
4. The distribution of benefits is roughly equitable or certainly not consistently exploitative.

Thus Ralf Dahrendorf writes: "Instead of a battlefield, the scene of group conflict has become a kind of market in which relatively autonomous forces contend according to certain rules of the game, by virtue of which nobody is a permanent winner or loser." If there are elites in our society, the pluralists say, they are numerous and specialized, and they are checked in their demands by other elites. No group can press its advantages "too far" and any group that is interested in an issue can find a way within the political system to make its influence felt. Business elites have the capacity to utilize the services of the government to further their interests, but, the pluralists argue, such interests are themselves varied and conflicting. The government does many different things for many different people; it is not controlled by a monolithic corporate elite that gets what it wants on every question. Government stands above any one particular influence but responds to many. Power in America "is plural and fluid. . ." Not only is there "Big Government but also Big Business, Big Labor, Big Distribution, the Big Press, the Big Church and the Big Army."

PLURALISM FOR THE FEW

The evidence leaves us little reason to conclude that the United States is a "pluralistic democracy" as conceived by the pluralists. To summarize and expand upon some of the points previously made:

(1) Public policies, whether formulated by conservatives or liberals, Republicans or Democrats, fairly consistently favor the large corporate interests at a substantial cost to millions of workers, small farmers, small producers, consumers, taxpayers, the elderly and the poor. Benefits distributed to lower-income groups have proven gravely inadequate to their needs and have failed to reach millions who might qualify for assistance. Government efforts in crucial areas of social need have rarely fulfilled even the minimal expectations of reform-minded advocates. There are more people living in poverty today than there were ten years ago, more substandard housing, inflation and unemployment, more chronic insecurity, immiserization and social pathology, more crime, suicide and alcoholism, more environmental devastation and pollution, more deficiencies in our schools, hospitals and transportation systems, more military dictatorships throughout the world feeding on the largesse and power of the Pentagon, more people—from South Africa to Greece to the Philippines to Brazil to Mississippi—suffering the oppression of an American-backed status quo, more profits going to the giant corporations and more corporate influence over the institutions of society, more glut in the private commodity market and more scarcity and want in public services. Cities are on the verge of bankruptcy, and governors in almost every state are cutting back on assistance programs for low-income families, the elderly, the handicapped and the retarded. And in the midst of all this, presidents and other politicians mouth platitudes, urging us to regain "faith in ourselves" and in "our institutions."

(2) To think of government as nothing more than a broker or referee amidst a vast array of competing groups (these groups presumably representing all the important and "countervailing" interests of the populace) is to forget that government best serves those who can best serve themselves. That is not to say that political leaders are indifferent to popular sentiments. When those sentiments are aroused to a certain intensity, leaders will respond, either by making minor concessions or by evoking images of change and democratic responsiveness that are lacking in substance. Leaders are always "responding" to the public, but so often it is with distracting irrelevancies, dilatory and discouraging tactics, facile reassurances, unfulfilled promises, outright lies or token programs that offer nothing more than a cosmetic application to a deep social problem. The overall per-

1. IS AMERICA RULED BY AN ELITE?

formance of our political system even in times of so-called social reform might best be characterized as giving *symbolic* allocations to public sentiment and *substantive* allocations to powerful private interests.

Indeed, one might better think of ours as a dual political system. First, there is the symbolic political system centering around electoral and representative activites including party conflicts, voter turnout, political personalities, public pronouncements, official role-playing and certain ambiguous presentations of some of the public issues which bestir presidents, governors, mayors and their respective legislatures. Then there is the substantive political system, involving multibillion-dollar contracts, tax write-offs, protections, rebates, grants, loss compensations, subsidies, leases, giveaways and the whole vast process of budgeting, legislating, advising, regulating, protecting and servicing major producer interests, now bending or ignoring the law on behalf of the powerful, now applying it with full punitive vigor against heretics and "troublemakers." The symbolic system is highly visible, taught in the schools, dissected by academicians, gossiped about by newsmen. The substantive system is seldom heard of or accounted for.

(3) Far from the fluid interplay envisioned by the pluralists, the political efficacy of groups and individuals is largely determined by the resources of power available to them, of which wealth is the most crucial. Not everyone with money chooses to use it to exert political influence, and not everyone with money need bother to do so. But when they so desire, those who control the wealth of society enjoy a persistent and pervasive political advantage. Instead of being just

another of many interests in the influence system, corporate business occupies a particularly strategic position. On the major issues which determine much of the development of society itself, business gets its way with Congress, the president, the courts and the bureaucracy because there exists no alternative way of organizing the economy within the existing capitalistic structure. Because business controls the very economy of the nation, government perforce enters into a unique and intimate relationship with it. The health of the capitalist economy is treated by policymakers as a necessary condition for the health of the nation, and since it happens that the economy is in the hands of big companies, then presumably government's service to the public is best accomplished by service to these companies. The goals of business (rapid growth, high profits and secure markets) become the goals of government, and the "national interest" becomes identified with the dominant propertied interests. Since policymakers must operate in and through the private economy, it is not long before they are operating *for* it.

(4) The pluralists make much of the fact that wealthy interests do not always operate with clear and deliberate purpose. To be sure, elites, like everyone else, make mistakes and suffer confusions as to what might be the most advantageous tactics in any particular situation. But if they are not omniscient and infallible, neither are they habitual laggards and imbeciles. If they do not always calculate rationally in the pursuit of their class interests, they do so often and successfully enough.

It is also true that the business community is not monolithic and unanimous on all issues. The socialist economist Paul

Sweezy has pointed out some of the fissures within the business world: there are regional differences (Eastern versus Southwestern capital), ideological ones (reactionary versus liberal capitalism) and corporate ones (Ford versus General Motors)—all of which add an element of conflict and indeterminancy to economic and political policies. But these are the conflicts of haves versus haves and they seldom include the interests of the un-organized public. Nor, as Sweezy reminds us, should we exaggerate the depths of these divisions:

> Capitalists can and do fight among themselves to further individual or group interests, and they differ over the best way of coping with all the problems which arise from their class position: but overshadowing all these divisions is their common interest in preserving and strengthening a system which guarantees their wealth and privileges. In the event of a real threat to the system, there are no longer class differences—only class traitors, and they are few and far between.[1]

(5) If American government is not ruled by one cohesive, conspiratorial elite, there is ample evidence of continual collusion between various corporate and governmental elites in every area of the political economy. Though there is no one grand power elite, there are many fairly large ones. And these elites often conspire with and seldom restrain each other. A look at the politico-economic system shows that many of the stronger ones tend to predominate in their particular spheres of activity more or less unmolested by other elites and unchecked by government.

As we have seen, corporations are not merely beyond the reach of government;

1 Paul Sweezy, THE PRESENT AS HISTORY (New York: Monthly Review Press, 1970), p. 138.

they incorporate public authority in their own undertakings. Government does play a crucial role in redirecting sectors of the corporate economy that tend to become disruptive to the system as a whole: hence Teddy Roosevelt's occasional trustbusting, Franklin Roosevelt's opposition to holding companies and John Kennedy's attempt to force steel companies to hold back their prices. But such actions are usually limited in their range and are induced by a desire to protect the business economy in toto.

Most elitist conflicts, we noted, are resolved not by compromise but by log-rolling and involve more collusion than competition. These mutually satisfying arrangements among "competitors" leave out the interests of broad, unorganized sectors of the public and are usually harmful to public interests—as when the costs of collusion are passed on to the public in the form of higher prices, higher taxes, environmental devastation and inflation. The demands of the have-nots may be heard occasionally as a clamor outside the gate, and now and then morsels are tossed to the unfortunates—especially if private suppliers can make money on such programs. But generally speaking, pluralist group politics engages the interests of extremely limited portions of the population and only within a field of political options largely shaped by the interests of corporate capitalism.

Interest group politics is tiered or structured according to the scope and power of the contenders. Big interests, like the oil companies, banks and defense industry, operate in the most important arena, extracting hundreds of billions of dollars from private markets and the public treasure, affecting the well-being of whole communities and regions, and

1. IS AMERICA RULED BY AN ELITE?

exercising control over the most important units of the federal government. In contrast, consumer groups, labor unions and public interest advocates move in a more limited space, registering their complaints against some of the worst, or more visible, symptoms of the corporate system, and occasionally winning a new law or regulation that proves largely ineffectual in treating the endlessly proliferating ill effects of capitalism. Finally, the weakest interests, like welfare mothers and slum dwellers, are shunted to the very margins of political life, reminding us of their existence with an occasional demonstration in front of city hall, making a claim on the shrinking "nonessential" and often nonexistent human services budget.

It is worth repeating that *the diffusion of power does not necessarily mean the democratization of power.* A wide array of corporate groups is not indicative of a wide sharing of power in any democratic sense, for the sharing occurs among propertied interests that are becoming increasingly less competitive and more concentrated and collusive in both economic ownership and political influence. Decision-making power is "divided" in that it is parceled out to special public-private interest groups—quasiautonomous, entrenched coteries that use public authority for private purposes of low visibility. The fragmentation of power is the pocketing of power, a way of insulating portions of the political process from the tides of popular sentiment. This purpose was embodied in the constitutional structure by the framers in 1787 and has prevailed ever since. . . .

It is not quite accurate to presume that non-elites never win victories. The last century of intensive struggle between labor and management, continuing to this day and involving such groups as farm workers, hospital workers, teachers, and white-collar employees, brought notable advances in the working conditions of millions. But change, if not impossible within state-supported capitalism, is always limited by the overall imperatives of that system and is usually of a cosmetic or marginal nature. In most instances the acceptable changes prove to be supportive and even profitable to the larger capitalist interests. . . .

The government has any number of policy options which might be pursued: it could end its costly overseas military interventions, drastically cut its military expenditures, phase out its expensive space programs[2], eliminate the multibillion-dollar tax loopholes for corporations and rich individuals, increase taxes on industrial profits, cut taxes for lower- and middle-income groups, prosecute industries for pollution and for widespread monopolistic practices, end multibillion-dollar giveaways and legislate a guaranteed minimum income well above the poverty level. Government also could distribute to almost 2 million poor farmers the billions now received by rich agricultural producers, and it could engage in a concerted effort at conservation and enter directly into nonprofit production and ownership in the areas of health, housing, education and mass transportation.

Such measures have been urged, but in almost every instance government has pursued policies of an opposite kind. It is not enough to scold those who resist change as if they did so out of obstinance or ill-will; it is necessary to understand the dynamics of power that make these policies persist in the face of all appeals and

2 The space shuttle program and the B-1 bomber together cost more than the entire Vietnam war. [Eds. Note]

18

human needs to the contrary. Those who bemoan the "warped priorities" of our society assume that the present politico-economic system could produce a whole different set of effects. But the question is: *Why* have new and more humane priorities not been pursued? And the answer is twofold: First, because the realities of power do not allow for fundamental reform, and second, because the present politico-economic system could not sustain itself if such reforms were initiated. Let us take each of these in turn:

(1) Quite simply, those who have the interest in fundamental change have not the power, while those who have the power have not the interest. It is not that decision-makers have been unable to figure out the technical steps for change; it is that they oppose the things that change entails. The first intent of most officeholders is not to fight for social change but to survive and prosper. Given this, they are inclined to respond positively not to group *needs* but to group *demands,* to those who have the resources to command their attention. In political life as in economic life, needs do not become marketable demands until they are backed by "buying power" or "exchange power," for only then is it in the "producer's" interest to respond. The problem for many unorganized citizens and workers is that they have few political resources of their own to exchange. For the politician, as for most people, the compelling quality of any argument is determined less by its logic and evidence than by the strength of its advocates. And the advocate is strong if the resources he controls are desired and needed by the politician. The wants of the unorganized public seldom become demands—that is, they seldom become imperatives to which political officials find it in their own interest to respond, especially if the

changes needed would put the official on a collision course with those who control the resources of the society and who see little wrong with the world as it is.

(2) Most of the demands for fundamental change in our priorities are impossible to effect within the present system if that system is to maintain itself. The reason our labor, skills, technology and natural resources are not used for social need and egalitarian redistribution is that they are used for corporate gain. The corporations cannot build low-rent houses and feed the poor because their interest is not in social reconstruction but in private profit. For the state to maintain whatever "prosperity" it can, it must do so within the ongoing system of corporate investments. To maintain investment, it must guarantee high-profit yields. To make fundamental changes in our priorities, the state would have to effect major redistributions in income and taxation, cut business subsidies, end deficit spending and interest payments to the rich, redirect capital investments toward non-profit or low-profit goals and impose severe and sometimes crippling penalties for pollution and monopolistic practices. But if the state did all this, the investment incentives would be greatly diminished, the risks for private capital would be too high, many companies could not survive and unemployment would reach disastrous heights. State-supported capitalism cannot exist without state support, without passing its immense costs and inefficiencies on to the public. The only way the state could redirect the wealth of the society toward egalitarian goals would be to exercise total control over capital investments and capital return, but that would mean, in effect, public ownership of the means of production—a giant step toward *socialism.*

19

NO

Andrew M. Greeley

POWER IS DIFFUSED
THROUGHOUT SOCIETY

It is important that all of us who are concerned about politics realize that only on occasion can we legitimately blame a vague and shadowy "them" for our problems. Admittedly, it would be much easier if we could; then we could just sweep "them" out of office and replace them with some of "us." But one of the melancholy results of a democratic society in which power is widely diffused is that "they" turn out in the final analysis to be "we.". . .

There is a good deal to be said for the elitist viewpoint, and anyone who approaches American society with the naive notion that power is equally distributed in the population and that mere persuasive argumentation will mobilize the power in favor of social change is simply asking for trouble.

1. Some people have more power than others. The president of General Motors, for example, is likely to have more influence on decisions that are made in Washington than the assembly-line worker. The archbishop of Chicago is likewise going to have greater impact on what the Catholic Church does than the parish priest. Compared to Mayor Daley or County President George Dunne or Governor Walker or the president of the Chicago Board of Trade or of Marshall Field and Company or the *Chicago Sun-Times* I am relatively powerless about what happens in my native city. Indeed, a member of the United Steel Workers of America probably has more power than I do, because he is at least able to bring pressure on city events through his union that I am not able to bring because I lack some sort of intermediate pressure group standing between me and the city.

2. Because of the way power is distributed in American society, certain groups of men, either because of their position or because of the support they can command from large organizations, can have decisive power on specific issues, no matter what anyone else thinks. While it is rare that the combination of these

powerful men can override the strongly felt convictions of a majority of the population, it is generally unnecessary for them to try. On most issues the majority of the population, is relatively indifferent. Thus if the *Chicago Tribune* determines that there is to be a lakefront exposition hall named after their late beloved publisher, it is likely to succeed because it needs only the support of a few city leaders, and opposition to it is likely to be limited to a small segment of the population. A majority of Chicagoans probably don't care much one way or the other about the lakefront hall; if asked, they may be vaguely for it. It will be virtually impossible for the opposition to organize massive antagonism toward the idea among the general population.

3. Some extremely critical decisions are made in American society by a handful of men. For example, the decision to go ahead with the Bay of Pigs invasion and the subsequent decision to respond to the Russian intrusion of missiles into Cuba by a blockade were made by a handful of men in secret. So too, apparently, have most of the decisions in the Indochina war been made by a small group operating in secret. These men obviously do not make their decisions in complete isolation from the pressures of the wishes and opinions of the rest of society, and they also eventually run the risk of being ejected from political office if what they do displeases at least a majority of those who vote in an election. Nevertheless, most of us do not have much power in the making of foreign policy. Our influence on foreign policy is limited to what the political leadership thinks our limits of hostile response are and to our plebiscite on election day.

4. Well-organized pressure groups do exercise an influence on American society all out of proportion to the size of their membership and the representativeness of their opinions. Even though there is strong national support for gun control legislation, for example, the National Rifle Association has been successful in limiting gun control laws and in punishing senators who have dared to push too vigorously against the association. This is but one example of an incredible number of pressure groups that zealously watch social events to make sure that the well-being of their members—judged, of course, by the professional staff of the organization—is not harmed by what goes on among the political leaders.

5. David Riesman and others have called these pressure groups (which run all the way from the United States Catholic Conference to the National Education Association and include the United Steelworkers of America, the American Chamber of Commerce, and a vast variety of other thoroughly reliable and respectable institutions) "veto groups," that is, their power is most effective in preventing things from happening than in causing them to happen. The American Medical Association, for example, has effectively vetoed national health insurance for several decades, but it has not displayed much power in getting positive legislation for its own benefit. The veto groups may occasionally join forces with one another and rally around some common cause, but under normal circumstances they are much better at saying no than at saying yes.

6. But when all these concessions are made to the accuracy of the elitist analysis, one is still faced with the fact that they miss the most critical obstacle to social reform in the United States, and that obstacle is not the existence of an establishment but the relative nonexistence of one. To put the matter somewhat differently, it is the lack of concentration of power that is the real obstacle to social reform.

21

1.   IS AMERICA RULED BY AN ELITE?

Let us take two examples. First of all, if there were an establishment of business, military, intellectual, and political leaders who did in fact exercise political control over the country, they would have gotten us out of the Vietnam war long before they did. The war was bad for business, bad for education, bad for government, bad for everyone in sight. It combined inflation with recession, alienated the youth, split the college campuses wide open, and had a rending effect on the whole fabric of American society. Furthermore, American business did not profit from the war, American political leaders did not profit from it (they generally lost elections because of it), and the American people, whose sons were killed, did not profit from it. Almost all the influential national journals were against it, and even the military muttered that it was trapped into the war by intellectual advisors of the president against their better judgment. Nevertheless, though it may have been desirable for all concerned to get us out of the war, there never existed a powerful establishment that could convene itself and announce that the war was over. The young people who vigorously demonstrated against the war were frustrated and angry because they could not communicate with the establishment to make it end the war. They might have considered the possibility that if there were an establishment, it certainly would have ended the war. The reason they can't communicate with an establishment is that there isn't one.

One can also take it as well established that the best way to cope with housing pressures in America's large cities is to distribute substantial segments of the black population in the suburban fringe that rings these large cities. Political leaders, business leaders, research experts, community leaders, virtually everyone would agree that the desegregation of the suburbs is absolutely essential for coping with problems of urban housing. Yet there does not exist in American society a group of men powerful enough to enforce such a decision over the collective opposition of all the suburban veto groups. If there were an establishment with a base of power, we would certainly have blacks in the suburbs.

The implication of the previous paragraph is that an establishment should be capable of benign as well as malign activity. Many benign actions would be very much in the self-interest of any establishment worthy of the name. That these benign things do not get done is, I think, conclusive evidence that, alas, there is no establishment. Things would be much simpler and neater if there were.

Implicit in radical criticism of the establishment is the strategy that argues that if one replaced the existing establishment with a new one composed of radical elitists and representing "the people," then one could institute benign social reforms. Professor [C. Wright] Mills* was quite explicit about that. He did not so much advocate the abolition of the power elite as making it responsible—responsible to intellectuals. But obviously it could not be made responsible to all intellectuals, so Mills decided that the power elite should be responsible to those intellectuals who happened to have the same ideas on foreign policy that he did. The power elite, in other words, will become "responsible" when it is willing to do what C. Wright Mills and his colleagues tell it to do. On the whole, I am not sure I would have liked to be governed by Professor Mills or any of his successors. I very much doubt that we could have worked out an arrangement whereby they would have been willing to

*Late professor of sociology at Columbia University and author of THE POWER ELITE (Oxford, 1956). [Eds.]

stand for reelection. It would be interesting to see what those critics of the establishment would do if they became it. They would discover, of course, as do all government leaders, how limited their powers really are. They would probably suspect some sort of conspiracy on the part of shadowy forces still existing in the society bent on frustrating their noble plans. Like most other Jacobins before them, they would probably use force to destroy the conspiracy, only to discover that even force has its limitations as a means of effective government.

The most important obstacle to social change in the United States, then, is not the concentration of power but its diffusion. If power was concentrated sufficiently, those of us who wish for change would merely have to negotiate with those who hold the power and, if necessary, put pressure on them. But power is so widely diffused that, in many instances, there is no one to negotiate with and no one on whom to put pressure. American society has been organized from the beginning around two premises:
(1)"The central guiding trend of American constitutional development has been the evolution of a political system in which all the active and legitimate groups in the population can make themselves heard at some crucial stage in the process of decision."* The second principle is a corollary of the first: (2) The larger society cannot ignore for very long what a given group considers to be its fundamental self-interest. No group, in other words, can be expected to assume the role of the permanent loser. . . .

One can fault this system of pluralism in two respects. First, one can say that it has

*Robert A. Dahl, PREFACE TO DEMOCRATIC THEORY (Chicago: University of Chicago Press, 1956), p. 137.

failed according to its own principles; that certain disadvantaged groups are not given an adequate hearing or that society does not recognize its obligation to facilitate the development of political power in these groups. The criticism is certainly a valid one. The very nobility of the political ideal implied in American pluralism makes departures from it unfortunate and ugly, but if this is the only criticism one has to make, then the strategy is obvious: one must bargain to persuade the rest of society that its consensus must be broadened sufficiently to admit these other groups as valued and equal participants in the enterprise.

The second criticism is that given the complexities and difficulties of the modern world, the diffusion of power that exists in American society is dangerously inefficient. If one has to bargain with Polish surgeons, Latvian truckdrivers, red-necked farmers, Irish politicians, conservative black clergymen, Jewish garment makers, Swedish computer operators, Texas oil barons, Portuguese fishermen from Fall River, and cattle ranchers from Montana in order to win support for absolutely imperative social changes, then these changes will be delayed, perhaps for too long, while the evil and injustice continues. It is demeaning, degrading, and immoral to have to bargain for the elimination of clear and obvious injustice. Racism is obscene, war is obscene; both should go away without our having to bargain on the subject. A political system that distributes power so that bargaining is necessary to eliminate obscene immorality is in itself not merely inefficient but immoral. It is not proper that those who are moral and wise should be forced to negotiate with those who are immoral and stupid.

This is a logically and consistently coherent case; in effect, it advocates the

1. IS AMERICA RULED BY AN ELITE?

abolition of the pluralistic bargaining, co-alition-forming polity that we currently have. It advocates taking the slack out of the political system and placing it in the hands of a ruling elite that would be both virtuous enough and powerful enough to accomplish quickly those social changes deemed urgent or imperative. One supposes that a strong case can be made for issues like pollution, population control, and racial injustice not to be made subject to the bargaining process, that wise and virtuous ruling elites should enforce by legislation and by police power, if necessary, the regulations that cope with these problems. The issues are so critical that there is no time to bargain with those whose intelligence and sensitivity is so deficient that they cannot see how imperative it is that action be taken with utmost speed. One can, I say, make a convincing case for such a political system, but let it be clear that it is an elite-establishmentarian system with a vengence, that it bears no similarity to what normally has been considered democracy, that it is completely at odds with the American political tradition, and completely objectionable to most Americans. . . .

If this model of American society is correct, the appropriate political strategy for those who wish to accomplish social change is not to tear down the establishment but rather to seek allies to form coalitions of various individuals and groups with some commonality of interest. These coalitions will represent an amassing of power that will be stronger than the power of those whose behavior we think is socially injurious. Thus, for example, a coalition was finally put together to force both safety and antipollution devices on the American automobile industry. It took a long time to put such a coalition together—indeed, much too long. Coalitions must be formed more rapidly if we are going to be able to cope with the critical problems that constantly arise in advanced industrial societies. The alternative to winning allies for one's cause is to impose it on the majority of one's fellow citizens whether they like it or not. Not only would this mean the end of political freedom, but it also might be extremely risky, because once we have begun to impose our will as a minority we run the risk that they may start counting noses and in full realization of our minority position, impose their will on us.

There was one thing clear in the summer and fall of 1972. Practitioners of the New Politics were as capable of misusing power as were the "corrupt bosses" whom they supposedly replaced. It did not, however, appear that they were substantially superior to the bosses in their capacity to use power intelligently. Indeed, a persuasive case could be made that as power brokers, the New Politicians were as inept as they were at everything else. Those who wish to rebuild the Democratic coalition can ill afford to be naive about the position of power in American society. Neither can they afford the naivete of raging against mythical dragons like "the establishment." There may well be certain concentrations of power in American society that the reconstructed Democratic coalition will want to break up, but it must first amass for itself a sufficient concentration of political power to be able to have a reasonable chance of winning an election and implementing its program. The builders of the new Democratic coalition must understand what their predecessors of 1972 apparently did not: One builds political power not by excluding people but by including them.

POSTSCRIPT

IS AMERICA RULED BY AN ELITE?

Though Parenti and Greeley are clearly opposed to one another, both are careful to qualify their positions. Greeley freely acknowledges that America is a society with gradations of power. Just as a parish priest does not have the same power as a bishop, so it is with ordinary citizens in comparison with political office-holders, or assembly-line workers at General Motors as compared to the corporation's president. Father Greeley's analogy to the government of the Roman Catholic Church raises questions. The Church, after all, does not claim to be democratic; it is frankly hierarchical. Does he mean to suggest that hierarchy is inherent in all political relationships? What, then, becomes of the concept of popular sovereignty? As for Parenti, he states that "it is not quite accurate to presume that non-elites never win victories." When we let all the negatives in that statement cancel each other out, the statement amounts to an admission that the little people sometimes get their way in an America supposedly dominated by elites.

The literature of political science and sociology contains many confrontations between elite-theory and pluralism. In his refutation of elite-theory Greeley makes reference to C. Wright Mills' THE POWER ELITE (Oxford, 1956), which is a classic statement of it. As for pluralism, Greeley cites with approval Robert Dahl and David Riesman. Dahl's PREFACE TO DEMOCRATIC THEORY (Chicago, 1956) and WHO GOVERNS? (Yale, 1961) are elaborate defenses of the pluralistic thesis. Reisman's THE LONELY CROWD (Yale, 1961) deals with a number of aspects of American society, including what he calls "veto groups." One of the most prolific writers defending the theory of elite dominance is G. William Domhoff. His WHO RULES AMERICA (Prentice-Hall, 1967), and THE HIGHER CIRCLES (Random House, 1970) are attempts to prove it by reference to empirical data.

One way of evaluating the pluralist and elitist perspectives on who rules America would be to study them in terms of concrete examples. We might ask, for example, what significant events have occurred in America over the past twenty years. The list would probably have to include the civil rights revolution, the Vietnam War, the rise (or reappearance) of feminism, Watergate and its exposure and repercussions, and the activity of the new regulatory agencies in Washington. Were all these the work of one elite "establishment," or did they result from an interaction of groups in the political arena? Greeley, who specifically cites Vietnam as an example of the lack of elite control, would probably consider the rest of these developments as further proof that our system is pluralistic. Parenti would no doubt insist that those cases which seem to reflect broader participation are really cases of "symbolic" victories by non-elites, victories which left the real substance of power just where it had been all along.

ISSUE 2

HAS PARTY REFORM SUCCEEDED?

YES: William J. Crotty, from DECISIONS FOR THE DEMOCRATS: REFORMING THE PARTY STRUCTURE (Baltimore, 1978)

NO: Everett Carll Ladd, from WHERE HAVE ALL THE VOTERS GONE? (N.Y., 1978)

ISSUE SUMMARY

YES: Crotty demonstrates his contention that reform has opened up the political process, and has given unprecedented influence to the rank and file party members.
NO: Carll Ladd documents his view that since the era of reform began, the political parties have become less able to perform their primary task of providing acceptable candidates for elective office.

The present two-party alignment of Democratic and Republican parties became fixed shortly before the Civil War, a century and a quarter ago. Until recently the parties enjoyed great popular support. People tended to identify themselves—and their families, regions and ethnic groups—with one of the major parties. A striking change has taken place in recent years. One-third of all adult Americans consider themselves independent, refusing to identify with either party, and that proportion is increasing among young people coming of voting age.

The decline of parties relates to Vietnam and Watergate, and the ways in which these recent events reflected unfavorably upon the parties. Party decline may also stem from television's increasing influence. Television makes party politics look either suspicious or ridiculous. It also focuses upon the personality of the campaigner, weakening the tie of party loyalty. The increasing mobility and sophistication of Americans weaken their ties to family, birthplace and social class, all of which once supported party bonds as well.

Liberals and Conservatives alike often deplore the absence of meaningful ideological choice between the major parties. Liberals have additionally bemoaned what they perceived as the undemocratic processes by which the parties chose their candidates, particularly the candidate for President. Simmering resentment came to a boil at the Democratic convention in

Chicago in 1968. Bitterness within the convention, protests in the streets outside it, and the use of excessive force against the demonstrators broke the party apart, and it was unable to completely put itself together before the presidential election. However, the ill-fated convention adopted a mandate for procedural reform whose impact has changed the presidential nominating process and with it the character of the national parties.

Reforms initiated by a party commission went into effect at the Democratic convention in 1972. One of the major reforms called for proportional representation of women, blacks and young people in the state delegations. This was nearly achieved in the 1972 convention, but at the price of excluding many party leaders, including prominent elected officials, from seats in the convention. Another major reform required apportionment of delegate votes in accordance with the support each candidate received in the caucus or primary at which the delegates were chosen.

The Democratic reforms induced many states to abandon convention and caucus methods of delegate selection in order to comply with the national party's requirements, and the change was felt in Republican delegate selection as well. One result is that where seventeen states held primaries in 1968, thirty-seven did so in 1980. As the reformers had predicted, the changes opened up party meetings and reduced the influence of party bosses, rules for delegate selection were made specific where they had previously been vague, and minority points of view received a hearing in party councils previously denied them. Because primaries were more numerous and receiving more attention, voter turnout was higher.

Perhaps the most significant consequence of the changes was the diminished importance of the convention. It had been reduced to a mere ratifying body for the candidate who was chosen in the primaries. That candidate, as was the case with the Democrats in both 1972 (McGovern) and 1976 (Carter), might receive fewer than half of the primary votes but more than any other single candidate. In 1980, widespread dissatisfaction with the nominations of Jimmy Carter and Ronald Reagan suggested that within both parties there were leaders who might have commanded broader support both within party ranks and with independent voters. Believing that the give-and-take of the nominating convention was more likely to result in the designation of a nominee who was at least not unacceptable to most groups within the party, the Democrats set about to reform the reforms. The likelihood is that the 1984 conventions will contain more elected party leaders who are not bound by primary votes. The old convention system is unlikely to be restored, but it is bound to play a more significant role than it has in the last decade.

On balance, William J. Crotty defends the reforms as the beginnings of party democracy. Everett Carll Ladd, Jr. opposes them as having contributed to the decline of the political parties.

YES
William J. Crotty

DECISION FOR THE DEMOCRATS

The year 1968 seemed predestined for sorrow. It suffered from the accumulated grievances of the preceding years, which were exacerbated by two assassinations, riots, and an administration hellbent on pursuing a major war while denying that this was its intent. It experienced a government out-of-touch with its public and neglectful, to the point of being scornful, of any and all dissent from its policies, and it witnessed a frustration born of attempting a challenge through conventional means destined to be mocked by a system unresponsive at best, closed at worst, to its pressures. The result was the explosions that shook the nation during the Chicago convention.

The "why" of Chicago is relatively easy to document. Far more difficult is tracing and evaluating the response of the political parties. The reaction of the parties, and especially the Democratic party, to the upheavals was unprecedented by any standard: it resulted in nothing less than an attempt to reshape fundamental structural mechanisms to better accommodate a diversity of views, to provide a fully representative and "open" convention, and to modernize, in line with democratic principles, procedures notoriously unreceptive to change. Whether these ambitious goals were achieved, and at what price, is another story. It is possible, though, that the reforms emanating from the convention are of far greater substantive importance than anything to emerge from that fateful election year. . . .

Party reform took second place to a lackluster general election campaign in the fall. The Humphrey campaign meandered, spiritually and organizationally, toward a November decision. The Nixon drive concentrated on packaged media presentations, carefully worded slogans designed to reassure an anxious electorate, and the presentation of a low political profile engineered to take advantage of the divisiveness within the Democratic ranks and the schisms in a tired electorate. The voters did not appear inclined to award any of the contenders with a decisive plurality. Everyone appeared relieved when

From, DECISION FOR THE DEMOCRATS: REFORMING THE PARTY STRUCTURE. ©1978; The Johns Hopkins University Press. Reprinted by permission.

the unhappiest of election years finally drew to its inevitable close.

While the victorious Republican candidate readied himself for his oath of office, another inauguration of sorts was being prepared for January, though this one received considerably less press and public attention. The efforts of a broken and dispirited party to reexamine its unhappy immediate past and to remedy its ways to insure, in the words of George Mc-govern, that the events of 1968, and particularly the gross abuses that occurred at the Chicago convention, would never happen again, do not constitute an especially interesting story. Yet defeat—especially after an election year so debilitating for a party—can lead to a period of profound change and, in time, to a spiritual regenesis. This had happened to the Republicans after a bitter defeat in 1912, and, on a more superficial level, after their loss in 1964. In a different manner, a defeat was about to trigger a profound transformation of Democratic party procedures, one without precedent in the history of the American two-party experience. . . .

The reforms introduced a remarkable era to American politics. More was attempted, and accomplished, than can truthfully be said to have been envisioned in the decades since the Progressive movement of the early 1900s. Remarkably, the reforms had been initiated and executed by a political party that perceived itself to be in trouble. In contrast to earlier attempts at political change, the intent was to strengthen and preserve an institution of incomparable value to the American political system rather than to destroy or replace it.

The changes introduced were many. The traditional priorities of American party structure had been reversed. The

national party units had attempted, with some success, to establish a code of fair and decent behavior and to have it prevail in the conduct of party business. A sense of rationality had been introduced into an incredibly complex system, and an aura of openness and equity had begun to prevail in several areas—changes in the presidential nominating process, the most significant of the national parties' duties, appeared to be an excellent foreboding of future changes in all aspects of party operations. A series of organizational structures and institutional values, little changed since the formation of the political parties over a century and a quarter earlier, were giving way to a new sense of national purpose and, it was hoped, a relevancy and responsiveness to constituent pressures, responsibilities neither party had acquitted impressively over the years.

The political implications of what the reforms were attempting to accomplish were never far from mind. The work of the reformers would effectively open the party in two regards. First, it would permit new groups to enter and make their views as to policy or candidates felt without depending on the goodwill or sponsorship of party elders whose favor they would have had to curry. Second, it would develop the foundation for establishing a permanent set of rules that would treat all with an impartiality previously unknown in party circles. It is too much to argue that such objectives were achieved by the first, and more than likely the most decisive, of the reform bursts, but a substantial beginning had been made.

Party processes were given a new legitimacy at a time when parties had begun to appear increasingly irrelevant to the solution of the main problems besetting

2. HAS PARTY REFORM SUCCEEDED?

American life and when both party and the political system more broadly needed whatever support they could muster. In these terms then—and they are impressive—the reform movement, and most significantly the achievements of the McGovern-Fraser Commission, had accomplished a good deal. In its own way the reform era constituted a revolution in party operations, notable as much for its impact on traditional modes of thinking as on the structures it placed in question. One would be hard pressed to find comparable moments of achievement in the long history of political parties in this nation.

WHAT REFORM ACCOMPLISHED

The ramifications of the reform period were many. A listing of the accomplishments and their broader implications would include the following.

OPENING THE PARTY

The party was opened and, in the process, made more responsive to and representative of its rank and file. The new openness was meant to extend to all aspects of the party organization. The effort was made, for example, by the Sanford Commission, to extend procedural guarantees of fair play to party organizations from the local to the national levels. The party charter set standards and established guidelines for all manners of party deliberations. The Sanford Commision, in conjunction with the McGovern-Fraser, O'Hara, and, to a lesser extent, Mikulski commissions, attempted to restructure party institutions to make them more responsive to grassroots sentiments.

The most notable success in opening the party to influence from the rank and file was the transformation of the presidential nominating process. The work of the McGovern-Fraser Commission, of course, was responsible for turning a relatively closed nominating process, controlled primarily by the party regulars, into one directly reflective of the concerns of those party members who chose to participate in delegate selection.

REARRANGING POWER DISTRIBUTIONS WITHIN THE PARTY

In the process of opening presidential nominations, the power relationships within the Democratic party were rearranged. Gaining increased influence were the party activists and candidate supporters who worked during presidential election years to advance a cause, an issue, or a presidential contender with whom they identified. For the most part, these tended to be the professional people—lawyers, businessmen, teachers—and the young persons, blacks, housewives, and minority groups attracted to the party during the significant prenominating races. Losing influence were the power-wielders of the pre-1972 period: the party regulars, elected officials (governors, congressmen, senators, mayors, state legislators), party organizational personnel (state chairmen, national committee representatives, county chairmen), and the "fat cats," as they were called, of the business world who sought influence in politics by bankrolling candidates and campaigns and on whom the party had been heavily dependent. Also losing power in the new alignment favored by the reform procedures were the southern states and their parties, which were experiencing transformations, and the old-line factions and interest groups at the state and national levels, which had at least been consulted on nominations. These latter groups had held, in many cases, a negative veto over both candidates for the presidential nomination and the issues treated in the party platform.

The most dramatic example of the last category would have to be the labor unions. . . .The AFL-CIO continued to be a significant contributor to the congressional campaigns of Democratic candidates, but its concern with the national party affairs lessened. . . . .

THE NATIONALIZATION OF THE PARTY

. The reform movement altered the power distributions within the Democratic party in an even more fundamental way. The historic relationship between the national party and its local and state units was altered, and before reform had run its course, dramatically reversed. Traditionally, the national party exercised little real power in party matters. This role was reserved for the state and local units, the party agencies presumed to be closest to the voter. The national party appendages were relatively inactive. They occasionally provided skilled services to state and local parties in such areas as registration, polling, and getting-out-the-vote campaigns, but their contributions seldom went beyond the level of rudimentary back-up support. The national parties, of course, did hold their semi-annual national committee meetings, but these were uneventful gatherings of no particular significance to the parties at any level. The national party also supervised the arrangements for the quadrennial national convention. Here the power over the convention scheduling and agenda could be significant to the faction controlling the national chairmanship at the time. The national party, however, had little concern over such basic practices as delegate apportionment formulas, controlled by the state parties and influenced by local political customs and power arrangements.

All of this changed abruptly, and more than anyone could ever have predicted, because of the McGovern-Fraser Commission. Building on the precedent established by the (Richard) Hughes Special Equal Rights Committee, the McGovern-Fraser Commission required the state parties to enact changes demanded by itself, the offspring of the national party. . . .

EXTENDING THE RULE OF LAW TO PARTY AFFAIRS

Implicit in the proposals throughout the reform period was the effort to protect the interests of the individual party member and to extend and safeguard his influence in party deliberations. The intention was to remove, insofar as was possible, control over participation from the whim and caprice of individuals who happened to be in authority in a given place at a particular time. To a large extent, such an effort ran counter to the customary political efforts of using every available instrument to gain a political edge, however small, and certainly counter to the experience of the Democratic party. Traditionally, the party had resolved differences in a political give-and-take between contending party factions or candidates in any manner the combatants might devise. Manipulating rules or enforcing selective by-laws [were] among the many stratagems a party faction might use to gain its ends.

This effort to abolish the regulars' control over participation was not good enough for the reformers. They not only wanted an inclusiveness and an intra-party democracy in political decision-making, but they also sought an impartiality in party rules and procedures that was foreign to the historic practices of the Democrats.

The emphasis can be seen in all aspects of the reform movement. The McGovern-Fraser Commission's rules attempted to establish a model of fairness and openness in delegate selection that set the tone for future developments. The O'Hara Commission created elaborate procedures for resolving credentials committee challenges that assured clear standards of performance impartially assessed through a series of mechanisms similar to those employed by the courts. There would be briefs and counterbriefs, set times and dates for the selection meetings and for the various steps involved in adjudicating any disagreements, hearings of facts by qualified officers, and appeals made to a credentials committee and, potentially at least, to the national convention. The Credentials Review Commission carried the process a step further by attempting to provide a continuing assessment of the applicability and relevance of state party rules to the national party's reform guidelines.

Less successfully, the O'Hara Commission made efforts to open the flow of information to the individual delegates and to advance their control over presiding officials within the convention. Most dramatic of all, the Charter Commission wrote a party constitution for party affairs and established a judicial council, modeled after the Supreme Court, to codify and apply party rulings in all disputes brought before it. The Charter Commission's actions are perhaps the ultimate steps, if they prove to be feasible, in instituting the rule of law within party councils.

REFORM AS A CONTINUING PROBLEM

One other result of the reform movement may be less obvious. The reformers extensively reviewed party processes and then rewrote the rules of behavior for the totality of national party activities. As a consequence, the reform era opened questions, once presumed settled either for better or worse or at least removed from immediate political debate, to continual reassessment. The success of the reformers in overhauling party procedures within a very few years invites others to try. The public and the party membership have now been conditioned to such reassessments. Such activity is accepted as a legitimate national party function and the authority of the party to engage in such exercises—including the enforced implementation of its directives—is no longer a subject of contention. There is much to be gained by a restructuring of procedure by any party faction that might control the national party apparatus, a national convention, or simply a reform commission. The process invites attempts at duplication. In fact, because the impressive changes brought by the McGovern-Fraser Commission serve as a model of what could be accomplished, repeated attempts to introduce new reforms (in these situations, changes intended to favor one faction or candidate) may be difficult to avoid.

For the most part, the original review of procedures and the changes introduced by the reformers were badly needed. The presidential nominating process had evolved over generations, with little rationale or logic underlying the diverse procedures utilized in the states. The reformers contended that the process was closed and arbitrary and that it gave unfair advantage to the party regulars who controlled the processes. In this broad sense, the reformers' claims were not contested by the regulars (although, of course, the measures proposed by the reformers were less well received).

No particular rules governed the operations of the national convention and its management, and the procedures were open to gross abuse. The bylaws applying to local, state, and national party organs were complex, often unrecorded, and openly manipulated by those in power. Such problems demanded some type of ordering. The reform movement attempted to accomplish this task.

The work of the McGovern-Fraser Commission and, in the wake of the post-1972 election, the Mikulski and Compliance Review commissions, indicates that no area of presidential selection can remain off limits to reevaluation and potential modification. . . .

DEBATING THE MERITS

The controversies created by the reforms are not likely to abate. The reform movement raised fundamental questions about American political parties that are not easily answered and that go to the very essence of what political parties in the United States are, or should be, about. What is a political party for? Whom does it serve? What does (or should) it stand for? Whom should it represent (and *how* should these groups, interests, and individuals be represented?) Implicit in the controversy is the question of the adaptability and adequacy of political parties—institutions developed in another age—in dealing with the pres-

sures and problems of late-twentieth-century American life. Are political parties relevant to the major concerns of contemporary American Society? If not, can they be made relevant?

THE RESPONSE OF THE REGULARS

The answers that the Democratic party regulars and reformers would give to these questions should be clear enough at this juncture. The party regulars would contend that political parties are quite adequate to the demands made upon them. They would say that 1968 and its problems were exceptions to the long and basically successful exercise of party authority. If a little care is taken, the problems of that election year need not be repeated.

Political parties are electoral coalitions intended for winning elections. The achievement of this end is, by all odds, their most significant function, and all other obligations are secondary at best. The regulars would contend that a party should, of course, represent the best interests of its members, but they would go on to argue that the most effective way to do this is by winning elections. The way to pick the candidates most likely to be victorious is to give the decisive role in party affairs (including presidential nomination contests) to party and elective officeholders. These individuals have the greatest stake in the party's success as well as the knowledge and experience necessary to select the most formidable nominees representative of the party's long-run interests.

THE RESPONSE OF THE REFORMERS

Reformers would be more skeptical of the claims made on behalf of the political party. They would argue that the party has not served its membership well, that its procedures are out-dated and dis-criminatory, and that it has not adapted to a changing electorate and an evolving society. Their perception of the 1968 election year and its attendant difficulties would be quite different from that of the regulars. They would see that election year and the Democratic prenomination difficulties and national convention as symbolic of the internal decay that has been spreading within the party system. The 1968 election year was simply a manifestation of how serious the prob-lems have become.

The reformers have little faith in the party regulars. They openly question the breadth of the regulars' concerns and the extent to which they accurately reflect, or possibly even consider, the sentiments of the party rank and file. Reformers differ with the party regulars on where a party's major obligations lie, and they contest the wisdom, competence, and representa-tiveness of the party regulars. They see no particular value in entrusting the fate of the national party or control over its presidential decision-making process to an elite with which they have so little in common and which they believe to be out of touch with its constituency and with national political currents.

The reformers would argue that the grass-roots party members should be rep-resented in all party bodies and should, to the furthest extent possible, control their deliberations. To enlarge upon this belief, reformers feel that party members who participated in the presidential primaries and caucuses should have a controlling voice in the concerns of the process. The reformers believe in a participant-oriented party, accessible to those who cared to identify with it and take part in its activities, and open to influence from below. And they seek a

party that would best represent and im-plement as precisely as possible the views and wishes of its membership.

The conception of an open, participant-oriented party responsive to and dependent on the goodwill of its rank and file is at odds with the regulars' view of a quasi-closed organization led by a somewhat inaccessible and self-perpet-uating elite that would look out for the party's best interests. In fact, an open party that entrusts ultimate power over, for example, the choice of a presidential nominee to the individual party member acting in a primary or a caucus at the local level makes the need for indirect rep-resentation through local or state party organizations or elected officeholders extraneous. The reformers want a direct correspondence between the individual party member and national-level deci-sions, a relationship that deemphasizes the role and contributions of any inter-mediate agencies.

The reformers would also reject win-ning office as the sole end of a political party. Instead, they would contend that a party serves many functions and that perhaps its most important is adequately to represent the views of its members and to funnel these into governmental decision-making. Unless a political party responsively addresses its members' con-cerns about pressing social issues, its victories will be hollow. They believed that a political party has to be in direct touch with, and representative of, its grass-roots sentiments. Anything less means that the political party is not ful-filling its obligations.

The reformers would emphasize a broad set of party goals and activities (witness the party charter) than the regulars. They would argue that a party should attempt to fulfill a number of functions, from educating its membership on the issues of the day to campaigning for office, and that it should have permanent organizations active throughout the year with full-time professional staffs to serve the needs of its members. These party organizations should be open to direction from the rank and file.

While they favor a more ambitious program and a more highly institutionalized (and open) party structure, the reformers would be more skeptical of the party's operations and the adequacy of its contributions to contemporary society. They would want the party to engage in more activities while at the same time being more demanding in their assessments of the relevance and value of what the party undertakes. And they would insist (as they did) that to reach any of these goals, the Democratic party would have to be thoroughly restructured. The regulars, of course, would disagree on each and every point.

TWO MODELS OF REPRESENTATION

The two sides in the reform issues are operating from different models of political behavior. They are applying different standards of acceptable political conduct and accountability. The two models have little in common. The party regulars are advocating "a taking care of" (to borrow Hanna Pitkin's terminology) concept of representation that sees party regulars and the established interest group leaders within the Democratic coalition as the best conservators of the interests of the party and its members. . . .

The reformers would argue that a system that directly reflects rank-and-file views and allows the grass-roots participants control over party decisions, particularly over the critical choice of a presidential nominee, is not only preferable but is the only type of procedure that will meet their concept of democratic accountability.

To the extent that direct control over party decision-making is not feasible, the reformers would opt for an "agent" theory of representation. The representative chosen by the individual party members would be given limited independence. On the major issues facing the party, he would be carefully instructed on how to perform in order to best fulfill his sponsor's wishes.

The two conceptions of representation have little in common. The issues raised, both in theoretical and practical terms, are fundamental to one's definition of a political party and the relevance of its contributions to a society. They deal with the nature of the party and its continued existence. Add to these concerns the groups displaced by the turmoil caused by the reforms and the stakes being contested in the fight for control of a national party and its nominating processes, and it is not difficult to see why the debate over reforms has continued.

The reformers won the initial battle and much of what they accomplished cannot be reversed. Nonetheless, the basic differences between the competing conceptions of what a political party is (or should be) and the manner in which it should fulfill its obligations are essentially irreconcilable. At a minimum however, political parties in the future may be judged by stricter standards of performance than in the past. Political parties should be continually called upon to prove their relevance and justify their contribution by a public that is increasingly skeptical of their value.

The reform movement accomplished a

great deal in a short period of time. It managed to breathe new life into moribund party structures and to center debate on the operation of these agencies. Political parties are seldom the focus of public concern. They have grown episodically over the last century and a half to fill immediate needs. They are of immense concern quadrennially, when the various presidential contenders and their supporters attempt to bend them to their will. Between presidential elections a short-term interest is being replaced by a more customary apathy. It can be argued that during the interim between elections the hulking organizational monster that constitutes the remnants of the national party only fitfully serves any function of consequence to the electorate.

The reform movement attempted to resurrect an interest in party activities per se and to revitalize party structures and adapt them to modern concerns. . . .

Political parties had changed little in form or activity since their inception. One factor, however, had become increasingly clear: they had become spiritually exhausted and increasingly less relevant functionally to the operation of a modern democracy. The demand for organizations adequately executing the duties the parties are supposed to perform cannot be quarreled with. Critical concerns of any democratic nation include the mobilization of voters behind representative candidacies of similar policy persuasion; the selection and promotion of the most able within its ranks to positions of public responsibility; the effective representa-tion of the views of its members; the day-to-day scrutiny of the acts of those in office; and the provision of sensible policy and candidate alternatives to an electorate it educated to the implications of official behavior. Both parties performed these functions with increasingly less ability.

In truth the parties became fractious, warring tribes, divorced from their bases of support and slavishly dependent on a president chosen from their ranks. They responded more to organized pressures and financial strength than they did to the mass of their membership. A review of party history during the last few troubled decades would make it appear that the party supporters were an inconvenience to be suffered and catered to only during national election campaigns.

Such foreboding might never have arisen above the level of irrelevant speculation had it not been for 1968. The fury unleashed by the obvious abuse of official party machinery and the ugly picture of party operations that resulted convinced most people within and without the Democratic party that change was overdue. The forces that would propel reform had been set in motion, but the events of that election year proved the catalyst. Beyond a doubt, the immediate need for remedial action had been demonstrated. Change was required; the need had been dramatized in a manner that would create the necessary reform constituency, and people were available and willing to devote themselves to the effort. So began the attempt to democratize one of the nation's oldest and most significant political institutions. . . .

● ● ●

NO   Everett Carll Ladd, Jr.

WHERE HAVE ALL THE VOTERS GONE?

In October 1977 I shared with a group of civic leaders many of the complaints about the current condition of the U.S. parties. . . . Near the end of the discussion that followed my presentation, one member of the audience politely but pointedly inquired: "Do you really think that the American political system functioned better in the past than it does now, that everything is in decline?"

No, I don't. In many ways, the U.S. social and political system is now doing a better job responding to the needs of the entire citizenry than at any time in the past.

The fact remains, however, that Americans now feel notably dissatisfied with their primary public institutions. And this dissatisfaction—coming in the face of substantial achievements—seems to result in large measure from a breakdown in one critical institution designed to translate public expectations into public policy: the political parties. It is the argument of this volume that over the past decade and a half the parties have manifested a diminished capability. The party system is not functioning well. It is not doing a good job in performing those tasks which are uniquely its own. This failure carries with it serious consequences for popular confidence in the governing system. . . .

THE PERILS OF PARTY REFORM

Over the 1960s and 1970s the American party system has been performing strangely, yielding novel and all too often unfortunate results. For instance, in two of the past four presidential elections—1964 and 1972—the victors were beneficiaries of two of the greatest landslides in U.S. history. But the voters did not so much confer mandates on Lyndon Johnson and Richard Nixon as declare their opponents unacceptable. There is every indication that these negative landslides had adverse consequences for the political order. Large numbers of people felt they were without a proper choice.

Since 1964, American presidential nomination campaigns have been distinguished by the frequency of strong candidacies of a decided ideological

Selections are reprinted from WHERE HAVE ALL THE VOTERS GONE? by Everett Carll Ladd, Jr., with the permission of W.W. Norton & Company, Inc. Copyright ©1978, 1977 by W.W. Norton & Company, Inc.

character. Not popular with the mass constituencies of their respective parties, Goldwater, McCarthy, McGovern, and Reagan managed nonetheless either to command the nomination or come within an eyelash of doing so. And all of this happened at a time when both parties were implementing a series of momentous reforms designed to make themselves more representative!

Then, in 1976, with the Republicans at their post-Watergate nadir and presidential victory available to the opposition virtually for the asking, the Democrats— the American majority party and the oldest political party in the world— brought forth a candidate who was almost completely unknown and untried in national politics. Not more than 3 or 4 percent of the electorate could even identify Jimmy Carter six months before he was nominated for the most important of all offices. It is not surprising that the Carter campaign encountered persisting doubt and skepticism on the part of the public. The voters were dissatisfied with things as they were, but felt quite unsure whether they would be any better off with Carter in the White House. Partly for this reason, Carter's lead in the polls fell precipitously between July and October, and an election that had seemed destined to bring about the decisive retirement of a much-burdened incumbent became instead a near deadlock.

This series of strange electoral performances is chiefly the result of the pronounced weakening of American political parties that has taken place in recent decades—a process that by now has brought them to the point of virtual death as organizations. As a consequence of their increasing weakness, the parties are unable to perform a set of functions which are exclusively theirs,

and the whole political system has been rattled.

The enfeeblement of the parties has come to a head during the last decade, a span filled with partisan changes and experimentation that are conventionally billed as "reform." But if reform is understood to mean "the improvement or amendment of what is wrong," little of the sort has occurred. Reform proponents insist that the alterations have made the parties more democratic, more representative of the populace, stronger, more competitive, and generally better able to play their part in the governing process. In fact, the changes seem more to have deformed than reformed the parties. They have left the system on the whole less representative, less competitive, less able to govern.

The organizational weakness of U.S. political parties is in one sense an old story. Though Americans gave the world its first party system, they have always been highly ambivalent about the institution. Party leaders have been seen pejoratively as "bosses" and parties themselves as no better than "necessary evils." This approach to party follows in large measure from the culture's distinctive individualism, which prompts Americans to insist on their individual rights to determine electoral outcomes, and specifically on *their* rights, rather than those of party leaders, to control the nomination process.

The reform movements of the twentieth century, however, have carried the enfeeblement of parties way beyond anything required by the culture. In the early years of this century, the Progressives took a number of critical steps in that direction, particularly through their generally successful advocacy of the idea that nominations for state and local office be controlled by voters who turn out in primaries rather than by the party organization. The capacity of regulars to manage party life was decisively lessened and a theory of intraparty democracy, compatible with the old American emphasis on individual action and the suspicion of large organizations, took root to an extent not found in any other democratic system. The direct primary remains almost exclusively an American institution.

Over the last decade, a new burst of reform activity has picked up where the Progressives left off. It originated largely within the Democratic party, but in a less dramatic fashion it has engulfed the Republicans as well. And it has rendered the two great national parties unable to control the nominating process for the country's most important political office, that of president.

PARTY REFORM SINCE 1968

The current wave of party reform was set in motion by the tumultuous 1968 Democratic convention, which created two commissions, one headed by Senator George McGovern to examine and make recommendations bearing on delegates selection (a commission subsequently chaired by Representative Donald Fraser of Minnesota); the other led by Representative James O'Hara of Michigan to study convention rules and operations. Recommendations of the McGovern-Fraser Commission, implemented for the 1972 convention, proved particularly important and generated rancorous intraparty debate.

The commission insisted that *internal party democracy* was the primary value to be promoted. The changes which it was able to achieve required the state Democratic parties to "overcome the effects of past discrimination by affirmative steps" to assure the representation of blacks, women, and young people at the national conventions and other party-functions "in reasonable relationship to (the group's) presence in the population of the State." Minority views were to be represented in all slate-making sessions. Delegates were to be chosen almost exclusively through caucus and convention arrangements open to all party adherents and providing proportional representation for minority candidates, or through primaries. If a state Democratic party insisted on permitting its central committee to play a role in choosing delegates to the national convention, it was required to limit the number of delegates thus selected to not more than 10 percent of the total. Proscribed was the practice whereby "certain public or Party office holders are delegates to county, State, and National Conventions by virtue of their official position." Use of the unit rule—casting a state's delegate votes as a bloc, in the direction desired by the majority—was banned.

Party leaders in many states found the new stipulations involving the "democratized" caucuses and conventions for national delegates selection so complex and so unpalatable—the rules made these bodies available for easy manipulation by candidate supporters or issue enthusiasts and thereby greatly weakened the position of the regular leadership—that they opted instead for presidential primaries. The result was an explosion in the number of primaries, quite unforeseen by most McGovern-Fraser Commission members—from seventeen in 1968 to twenty-three in 1972 to thirty in 1976. Whereas less than half of all delegates to the 1968 convention were chosen by primaries, nearly three-fourths of the 1976 delegates were thus selected. . . .

OTHER PRECIPITANTS OF PARTY DECLINE

Reform has weakened the parties indirectly as well as directly. When nearly three-fourths of all Democratic convention delegates (and more than two-thirds of Republican delegates) are selected through primaries, for example, serious candidates have to create elaborate personal organizations to wage the costly and far-flung campaigns that are a precondition of winning. The victorious contender, once his nomination is in hand, is hardly about to disband the apparatus he put together for the primary struggle. He relies upon it and not on the party in the general election. Much attention has been devoted to the Committee to Reelect the President, the now-disgraced instrument of the Nixon forces in 1972. Yet for all its excesses, CREEP was in many ways the prototypical contemporary electoral organization: it was formed to serve the interest of one man; it placed these above the party's; and its substantial resources enabled it to disregard the party in contesting for the presidency.

Broad social changes have also helped to bring parties to the verge of organizational extinction. The populace is much more highly educated than ever, has many more sources of political information, clearly feels less dependent upon party as an active intermediary in the electoral process—and it is sharply and irreversibly more inclined to participate in an independent, nonpartisan basis.

The rise of the national press has also played a part in weakening the parties. Increasingly it has taken over important facets of the communications role that was once performed by party organizations. As journalist David Broder has observed, newsmen now serve as the principal source of information on what candidates are saying and doing. They act the part of talent scouts, conveying the judgment that some contenders are promising, while dismissing others as of no real talent. They also operate as race-callers or handicappers, telling the public how the election contest is going. At times they function as public defenders, bent on exposing what they consider the frailties, duplicities, and sundry inadequacies of a candidate; and in some instances they even serve as assistant campaign managers, informally advising a candidate, and publicly, if indirectly, promoting his cause.

With so much going against parties, one might have hoped for a modest dose of "countercyclical policy" to bolster a deteriorating but useful institution. Just the opposite, however, has been happening. For example, federal funding of presidential campaigns, voted into law as a means of "cleaning up" national politics, has reduced the dependency of candidates on party and on the interest groups that have served as prime building blocks of party organization. A number of proposals for further electoral reform now under consideration would have a similar effect. For example, there is strong support these days for a constitutional amendment to eliminate the electoral college and substitute direct election of the president. Whatever the proposal's overall merits, it would reduce the role of state parties by making state boundaries irrelevant to election outcomes. Candidates would become even freer to campaign without regard to the blocs, alliances, and structures that state party systems are built on.

There has been inadvertence and bad planning and just plain stupidity in all of this. But above all, the attack on political parties has come as a result of a straightforward and quite conscious pursuit of group interests. Senator McGovern for one has conceded that there are risks in "democratizing" the party, "opening it up," reducing the domination of "bosses" or "elites," and permitting "the people" to decide who the nominee will be. But he considers the risks to be worth it. "The alternative," he says, "is a closed system where you say the elite are better able to run the country than rank-and-file citizens."

THE PEOPLE AREN'T THE WINNERS

McGovern could not be more wrong in his notion that it is "rank-and-file citizens" who benefit from party "reform" and the elite who suffer; just the opposite is the case. For a century and a half, U.S. political parties, with all their faults, have been a force for extending democracy. Can there ever have been any real doubt that, were party removed from control over presidential nominations and the public invited to fend for itself in a lightly structured selection process, the winners would not be "the people"? In fact, it has been upper-middle-class groups, not the broad mass of Americans, who have confronted the party organizations, who have held them to be unresponsive to their policy perspectives, who have attacked the legitimacy of "bosses," who have urged "democratization." And it is these highly educated, well-informed, relatively prosperous groups who have primarily benefited from party "reform," for they tend to participate in more open nomination processes at a rate that far exceeds that of "rank-and-file-citizens."

That party reform serves the interests of the upper middle class can be seen in the statistics on voter turnout in primary elections. There has been much hand-wringing of late about low turnout in recent general elections, but participation in them is positively robust compared with that in the primaries. In 1976, for example, in the twenty-eight states that held presidential primaries and kept statewide data on them, just 28 percent of the voting-age population went to the polls, as compared with 54 percent casting presidential ballots from those states in the November election. . . .

On the Democratic side, much has been made of George McGovern's success in capturing his party's 1972 nomination in spite of the fact that at no time during the long primary and preconvention struggle was he popular with the rank and file of his own party. The convention that formally nominated McGovern was strikingly unrepresentative of the policy preferences of the mass of Democrats, as a study by Jeane Kirkpatrick so clearly shows. When he won the nomination, Senator McGovern declared that it was "all the more precious in that it is the gift of the most open political process in our national history." One must note that this "most open political process" produced one of the most unrepresentative outcomes in our national history.

And in 1976 things remained the same in some crucial respects. To be sure, the nominee that year was a man who had clearly established himself during the primary as a centrist, popular with the party's rank and file. Yet the convention itself was as unrepresentative as it had been four years earlier. The delegates may have nominated Carter and done his bidding on the platform and related matters, but they had little in common ideologically with him or the mass of Democrats. They resembled not the rank and file, but the New Class—the young, college-educated, professional and managerial groups who have been especially advantaged by the recent recourse to "open" selection mechanisms. They stood far to the left of the rank and file, particularly on the issues of the New Liberalism—such as whether the U.S. should have a softer foreign policy vis-a-vis the Soviet Union, whether defense spending should be cut, and various social and moral questions ranging from abortion to busing. . . .

The balance of America's political experience with party "reform," however, suggests the contrary. We do need the kinds of services that only strong, autonomous party organizations can provide. By substantially removing party from nominee selection almost everywhere, we have eliminated the one institution able to practice political planning. By removing party from governance, we have aided the already strong centrifugal forces working against coherence in public policy. And even in the area of representation, where the reformers have made their proudest claims, it is at least arguable that the machinery of party achieved results superior to those of the putatively more democratic procedures that have been created in their stead.

PROTECTING AN ENDANGERED POLITICAL SPECIES

So it is high time that the nation began rethinking public policy toward the parties. They have become an endangered species, and an all-out campaign ought to be launched to protect and revive them. Direct election of the president should not be established. It would deal too severe a blow to the already tottering state and national party systems. It is possible to take care of the problem of the "faithless elector"—and to remove any real possibility that a candidate without a plurality of the popular vote might win the presidency—within the structure of the electoral college. Federal funding of elections bypasses parties too much and encourages autonomous candidacies, and it should be ended. Looking to what are strictly intraparty decisions, the recent proposal by "strong-party" advocates on the Democrats' Winograd Commission to make all Democratic governors, U.S. senators, and congressmen voting delegates to the national convention by dint of their office should be revived. It is one concrete means of acknowledging and honoring the institutional aspects of party in the presidential-selection process.

The basic change that is needed, though, is simply a renewed appreciation of what useful things parties—as institutions and not just labels—are to have around. If this should somehow come to pass, it would then be relatively easy to rebuild the parties as instruments for planning and representation within what must be recognized as a now-irreversible feature of the U.S. nominee-selection process—the widespread use of direct primaries. Restoring the organized parties to vigorous health and giving them back their central role in the presidential-selection process should be the No. 1 reform objective of the next decade.

● ● ●

POSTSCRIPT

HAS PARTY REFORM SUCCEEDED?

Crotty's sympathetic account makes clear that advocates of reform wanted to increase participation by party activists, and there can be little doubt that this was accomplished. The objective was enhanced party democracy. Ladd's critical analysis argues that this was achieved at the cost of reduced influence by party leaders and regulars, and the consequence was diminished party responsibility. It sometimes seems as if these are incompatible values: If responsibility is stressed in party organization, it is to the detriment of democratic participation, and vice versa. Can these goals be reconciled?

No student of American politics has thought longer or written better on this subject than Austin Ranney, whose CURBING THE MISCHIEFS OF FACTION (California, 1975) expresses sympathy for the intentions of reform, criticism of the results, and skepticism as to our ability ever to foretell what the consequences of new reforms will be. The recent historical background to reform is examined in Everett Carll Ladd, Jr., with Charles D. Hadley, TRANSFORMATION OF THE AMERICAN PARTY SYSTEM, Second Edition (Norton, 1978). In the growing literature exploring the unique way in which the United States chooses its head of state, there are provocative insights in James David Barber, ed., CHOOSING THE PRESIDENT (Prentice-Hall, 1974) and Stephen J. Wayne, THE ROAD TO THE WHITE HOUSE (St. Martin's Press, 1980).

In the essay we have read, William J. Crotty concluded: "The reform movement constitutes but a beginning." Still other reforms have their advocates including establishment of a single nation-wide presidential primary (or, alternatively, four regional primaries to replace the numerous individual ones), and public financing of congressional elections. The critics of reform seek to restore an independent deliberative role to the national convention, and the Democratic Party has already begun to move in that direction.

ISSUE 3

CAN LOBBYING ENDANGER DEMOCRACY?

YES: Edward Magnuson, from "The Swarming Lobbyists," *Time Magazine,* August 7, 1978

NO: Irving Louis Horowitz, from "Beyond Democracy," *The Humanist,* Sept./Oct., 1979

ISSUE SUMMARY

YES: A senior writer of *Time* magazine raises the spectre of government by lobby, with the broader welfare being the victim.

NO: Sociologist Horowitz disputes the idea that single issue groups have replaced parties, and contends that, even if that were the case, it would simply be the basis for a new form of democratic government.

The very term "pressure group" has a negative connotation. If we do not always picture pressure groups in terms of lobbyists bribing congressmen, we do invariably think of them as "special interests" which subordinate the public good to their private advantage.

This way of thinking has deep roots in the United States. One of our Founding Fathers, James Madison, seemed to be referring to pressure groups when he wrote about the dangers of "factions." Madison defined "faction" as a group

united and actuated by some common impulse of passion, or of interest, adverse to the rights of other citizens, or to the permanent and aggregate interests of the community.

What is to be done about factions? In considering this question Madison introduced a rather mixed group of metaphors. "Liberty is to faction" he said, as "air is to fire." If we destroy liberty we smother faction. But Madison immediately rejected this harsh remedy, remarking that it would be "worse than the disease." Air may feed fire, but it is also "essential to animal life." So the question remained: if it is either impossible or undesirable to abolish factions, what can be done to limit their "mischiefs"?

Taken as a whole, Madison's philosophy pointed toward this solution: let every group participate in government—indeed, welcome the broadest participation of interest groups—and then enact into law whatever series of agreements these groups have been able to reach as they interact. If the groups broadly represent the spectrum of political positions in the society, their compromises and collective conclusions comprise for all practical purposes the community or national interest.

Insofar as Madison himself inclined toward such a view, he favored large republics over small ones because large republics "take in a greater variety of parties and interests," and he believed that the best society was one which was "broken into so many parts, interests and classes of citizens" that nobody's rights could be endangered.

This does not mean that Madison liked what we would today call pressure groups or interest groups. As we have seen, he regarded them as subversive of the public good or the rights of others. But he saw no alternative to tolerating them, hoping that if there were enough of them they would more or less cancel each other out and allow "the interests of the community" to shine through.

There are others today who regard interest groups in a more positive light. They call themselves "pluralists," and their vision of society focuses not so much on its wholeness as on its individual fragments or components. It is the various interest groups, they believe, which account for the richness and freedom of America. If we worry too much about "unity" and "national purpose," we may end up with repression and uniformity. Anyway, they often add, what *is* "the national interest" in a country so diversified as ours? The only safe answer is to define it as whatever results from the free play of interest groups.

Over the past fifteen years two developments which relate to the topic of interest groups have occurred. First, a number of ethnic groups have begun to emphasize their particularity to such an extent that their identification with the nation as a whole has become problematic. Second, the growth of federal programs, particularly spending programs, has encouraged all organized groups to come to Washington to lobby for "their share" without any great concern for what happens to the broader society. These are forces which by their nature are centrifugal and which unimpeded, tend toward fragmentation. Pluralists insist that the nation has more than enough centripetal counterforce to hold it together; their critics are not so sure.

In the following selections a report from *Time* magazine highlights the fragmentizing tendencies of the new "special interest" lobbies, while sociologist Irving Horowitz worries that the real danger may come from the other side, from advocates of "political monism" who, he believes, are attempting to turn back the clock to an earlier age of strident "Americanism."

YES
Edward Magnuson

THE SWARMING LOBBYISTS

Tax law reform. Killed. Labor law reform. Dispatched to die in committee. Consumer protection agency. Killed. Hospital cost containment. Gutted. The crude-oil tax in the energy bill. Stalled.

There is normally a complex of reasons for the failure of a major piece of legislation to emerge from Congress, and sometimes it is simply that there is no clear national consensus behind it. But in these five instances, and others like them, the force that proved decisive in blocking passage this year arose out of a dramatic new development in Washington: the startling increase in the influence of special-interest lobbyists. Partly because of this influence, President Carter has encountered serious difficulty in getting legislation through Congress; partly because of this influence, Congress itself is becoming increasingly balky and unmanageable.

The lobbyists have grown so able and strong that [in 1978] a mere handful of them was able to kill another bill, one of particular significance to them. It would have required the lobbyists to reveal who pays them, who they represent and what issues they have sought to shape. . . .

There was irony in the spectacle of some of the most sophisticated generals of the vast new army of lobbyists, so skilled at casting the special interests of their clients in terms of the broader national good, now pleading so persuasively to keep their own operations secret. It was evidence of the extent to which the increasingly independent members of Congress have let the clashing voices of a multitude of special interests obscure their own sense of the broader national good.

Lobbying as such is scarcely a sin. Quite the contrary. "Without lobbying," declared three Senators (Democrats Edward Kennedy and Dick Clark, Republican Robert Stafford) in a joint statement on the lobby disclosure bill, "Government could not function. The flow of information to Congress and to

From "The Swarming Lobbyists," *Time* Magazine, August 7, 1978. Reprinted by permission.

every federal agency is a vital part of our democratic system. But there is a darker side to lobbying. It derives from the secrecy of lobbying and the widespread suspicion, even when totally unjustified, that secrecy breeds undue influence and corruption." Chairman Ribicoff observes that "lobbying has reached a new dimension and is more effective than ever in history. It has become a big computerized operation in which the Congress and the public are being bombarded by single-issue groups." He adds: "The Congress and the public should be aware of who's trying to influence whom and why and for what."

The Connecticut Senator's concern is justified. Lobbyists approach their jobs with more intelligence, hard work and persuasive argument than ever before. While fewer than 2,000 lobbyists are registered with Congress under a largely ignored 1946 law, their actual number has soared from about 8,000 to 15,000 over the past five years. Their mass arrival has transformed Washington's downtown K Street into a virtual hall of lobbies. New office buildings springing up west of the White House along Pennsylvania Avenue fill up with lobbyists as soon as the painters walk out. It is estimated that lobbyists now spend $1 billion a year to influence Washington opinion, plus another $1 billion to orchestrate public opinion across the nation.

There is probably not a single major corporation that does not now employ Washington lobbyists. Ford Motor Co., which kept three representatives in the capital in the early 1960s, today maintains a full-time staff of 40 people. Among the airlines alone, 77 have separate lobbying staffs in Washington. More than 500 corporations, including some quite small firms, operate Washington lobbies, if only for the sake of what they consider prestige.

(Only 100 corporations were represented ten years ago.) Of the roughly 6,000 national trade and professional associations in the U.S., 27% are now headquartered for lobbying effect in Washington, which has overtaken New York City as a center for such groups.

Apart from business and industry, 50 labor unions maintain their separate offices in Washington, often working independently from A.F.L.-C.I.O. Chief George Meany's 300-member staff, which occupies an impressive stone and marble headquarters near the White House. Politically aware action groups also have their lobbyists in Washington, including 14 that pursue the special interests of the elderly and six that deal with air pollution. Even the Virgin Islands Gift Fashion Shop Association has a lobbyist. Large staffs are maintained by such broader public interest groups as Common Cause and the Ralph Nader organization. Grumbles House Speaker Tip O'Neill: "Everybody in America has a lobby."

Why? One major reason is obvious and ominous: the ever increasing influence of federal law and regulation over the lives of all Americans, as well as over the businesses they operate and the groups they join. The Federal Government now has rules ranging from the establishment of whisky tax rates to the placement of toilets on construction sites, from the design of atomic power plants to the milk content of ice cream, from foreign arms sales to childproof tops on aspirin bottles. A single clause tucked away in the Federal Register of regulations (this year's version has already grown to a mountainous 32,000 pages) can put a small-town manufacturer out of business or rejuvenate an industry that was on the brink of bankruptcy. The lobbyist who gets the clause removed, or puts it in, can be worth his salary for 100

3. CAN LOBBYING ENDANGER DEMOCRACY?

lifetimes. The very magnitude of federal spending—about $565 billion this year—reflects the stakes involved as competing groups try to get what they consider their fair share, or more.

As power has been centralizing in Washington, life in this technological age has grown increasingly complex. There is no way for each member of Congress, or even each specialized federal bureaucrat, to be sure of the precise impact of his decisions. Sometimes the consequences are far from what was originally intended. The ever watchful lobbyists are eager to point out such hazards, and they serve a vital function when they do.

Yet fundamental changes in the nature of Congress have not only brought more lobbyists to Washington but have also transformed the way in which they do their work. In its rebellion against the imperial presidency of Richard Nixon, Congress has reasserted itself as at least the equal of the White House in resolving basic issues of national policy. Congress now has its own budget committees with powerful influence over spending priorities. The lawmakers have decreed that when they pass an appropriations bill, the money must be spent; it is not an option, as Nixon and other Presidents often regarded it. In the aftermath of Viet Nam, Congress asserted its control over the authority to make war and insisted on a larger role in foreign policy. And as influence flowed toward Capitol Hill, the lobbyists followed.

At the same time, Congress has also reformed its procedures. It has stripped its once autocratic committee chairmen of their almost singlehanded ability to ram through a bill—or kill it. Power has been diffused to subcommittees, where even freshman Senators and Congressmen can wield considerable influence.

As the seniority system has broken down, all members have found their jobs more demanding—and many of the oldtimers have quit, complaining that Congress is "no fun anymore." This, in turn, has produced a remarkable turnover in membership (more than half the Representatives have been in office fewer than six years), attracting, young, aggressive lawmakers determined to make up their own minds on all issues. Often elected from districts with no strong party preference, they listen a lot to what the folks back home are telling them, and what their constituents are saying is increasingly inspired by lobbying campaigns initiated in Washington.

While all those changes offer today's lobbyist golden opportunities, they also vastly complicate the lobbyist's job. Instead of cozying up to a few key chairmen or a powerful Speaker, the lobbyist must do tedious homework on the whims and leanings of all the legislators; he can never be certain when some relatively obscure member may prove to be the key to passing, killing, or amending a bill. Lobbying now demands, as never before, highly sophisticated techniques, a mastery of both the technicalities of legislation and the complexities of the legislators' backgrounds, and painstaking effort. It is thus understandable that contemporary lobbyists relish tales of the simpler, if splashier, days in their trade. . . .

The new lobbyists in Washington have eagerly charged into the openings created by a weakened presidency and a more independent and less rigidly organized Congress. One of the most striking aspects of this new lobbying is the willingness of Big Business to join in. While corporations still somewhat squeamishly call their lobbyists "Government affairs specialists" or

"Washington representatives," the fact that the heads of multi-billion-dollar firms are now willing to plead their causes personally shows their awareness that Government is not going to retreat from its intrusion into their corporate lives. "Fifteen years ago, the businessman was told that politics is dirty, you shouldn't get involved," observes Albert Abrahams, chief lobbyist for the influential National Association of Realtors. "Now they know if you want to have a say, you've got to get in the pit."

The most visible symbol of the business world's new willingness to get into the trenches is the Business Roundtable, composed of nearly 200 top officers of the nation's most powerful corporations (among them: AT & T, Boeing, DuPont, General Motors, Mobil Oil, General Electric). The group's policy committee convenes monthly in New York to stake out positions on pending legislation and plot strategies to influence the outcome. Often invited to the White House, the executives get their views across to the President. While in Washington, some stay on to buttonhole legislators. Says one lobbyist: "A Congressman is impressed by the head of a corporation coming in to see him. Before, it was below a businessman's dignity to do that."

Yet some of the more aggressive new business lobbyists scoff at the Roundtable, contending that the corporate bosses flinch from a real fight out of fear of union retaliation. "The Business Roundtable is the most ineffectual lobby in Washington," contends Paul Weyrich, who heads a conservative lobby named the Committee for the Survival of a Free Congress. "They want to compromise before compromise is warranted. They never want to play hard ball." James McKevitt, a former Colorado

Congressman who is the Washington counsel for the National Federation of Independent Business, is similarly scornful. Says he of the top executives: "Too many of them suck eggs with the President."

The most broadly respected business lobby is the United States Chamber of Commerce, which has far surpassed the once influential National Association of Manufacturers as a pragmatic power in Washington. As long as a decade ago, the N.A.M. was dismissed by one expert on capital powerbrokers as being lost in "a faintly fusty aura of dignity, lavender and the Union League." By contrast, the Chamber, operating out of a stately marble and limestone headquarters facing Lafayette Park, has come on strong. Embracing 2,500 local affiliates, 1,300 professional and trade associations and 68,000 corporations, it threw its weight behind 61 legislative issues last year, among them labor law reform, a consumer protection agency and public financing of congressional campaigns. It won 63% of the battles it joined—an impressive record in a Democratic Congress. . . .

The local pressure is skillfully organized by the Chamber. Four of its lobbyists in Congress watch the progress of each bill that is worrying businessmen, then send an alert when a key legislative action is approaching. The word goes quickly to 1,200 local Congressional Action Committees with some 100,000 members. Through the Chamber's various publications, the alert soon reaches 7 million people. Thus when Washington headquarters signals an "action call"—the time for besieging members of Congress with letters, telegrams and phone calls—the membership is ready to move. The Carter bill that would have created a consumer protection agency was buried under just such an avalanche of Chamber-inspired mail early this year.

The Chamber also mans six regional offices in which some 50 operatives study the quirks and pressure points of Senators and Congressmen from their area. They pinpoint what the Chamber calls "Key Resource People," who have special local influence with a legislator. It might be a big campaign contributor, college classmate or law partner. At a critical moment, these regional staffs are told: "Get the K.R.P.s into the act." The regional offices also clip local editorials for pro-Chamber viewpoints and dispatch them to Washington. Two volumes of newspaper clippings were dumped on congressional desks with heavy impact in the Chamber's successful drive to stall passage of the labor reform bill. . . .

The key inside operator in the new conservative coalition has been Nevada Senator Paul Laxalt. Elected in 1974, he sensed that such conservative lobbies as the Right to Work Committee, with its large computerized mailing list, and a rejuvenated Senate Republican Steering Committe—unofficial counterpart to the liberals' Democratic Study Group—could combine to block passage of liberal legislation. He put that theory to work in 1975 in a coordinated conservative attack on labor's common situs picketing bill. To the astonishment of the labor lobbyists, the new combination stimulated enough grassroots pressure to persuade President Ford to veto the bill—with a certainty that the Senate would sustain the veto.

By far the most spectacular of the outside conservative lobbyists at the grassroots level is Richard Viguerie, 44 a Houston-born specialist in mass marketing, who has compiled a detailed list of some 4 million conservative activists. Operating out of a handsome office building in McLean, Va., Viguerie and his 300 employees man two IBM computers that can break out lists of likely contributors with details of how they stand on particular issues and what they have given to which candidates or legislative drives in the past. He considers his magnetic tapes of lists so valuable that they are guarded 24 hours a day—and duplicates are kept in a secret mountain hideaway. Indeed they are valuable. His company grossed an estimated $3 million last year from the use of his tapes to stimulate mass mailings.

Viguerie figures he will send out 100 million letters this year at a cost to his clients of about 22¢ a letter. His company nets at least three of those 22 pennies. More carefully targeted mailings go firstclass and include a stamped return envelope for contributions; the postage alone costs 30¢ a letter. The purpose of most Viguerie letters is to ask the recipients to send their own pleas (postcards and wording provided) to their local members of Congress to act for or against a bill—and to send a donation to cover the cost of Viguerie's mailing. Says Viguerie: "It's a self-financing lobbying system. If you can make a mailing of 3 million and break even, what a success!"

Although he lost the fight, Viguerie takes pride in having dispatched more than 2.5 million letters against the Panama Canal treaties. He estimates that he was responsible for Senate Republican Leader Howard Baker alone receiving more than 100,000 letters urging him to vote against the treaties. Baker suspected the mail did not represent sentiment in Tennessee, ordered a private poll of his state—and found that 60% of the voters favored the treaties. He not only voted for them but worked hard to enlist other Republican Senators to do the same. Viguerie concedes that many legislators pay more attention to self-generated appeals than to a flood of obviously lobbyist-inspired mail. Nonetheless, insists Viguerie, "when a Congressman gets 40,000 letters on a single issue, he ignores that at his folly."

Labor and liberal lobbyists have no similarly sophisticated computer mailing lists, although they believe they nearly matched the conservatives in inspiring mail on the labor reform law—millions of letters flowed from each side, probably the largest total outpouring of mail on any legislative issue in U.S. history. Labor drew on its decreasingly effective but still formidable network of union activists, especially retired members who have the time and zeal to respond to calls for action from the A.F.L.-C.I.O.'s headquarters. The federation has 51 state organizations and 740 local units it can muster into political action; in all, it has some 105 separate unions and 14 million members. Yet it takes at least two weeks to energize its political pressure, unlike the almost instantaneous capability of Viguerie's operation. Says Labor Lobbyist Biemiller about Viguerie's computerized propaganda, "It's a goddam scary thing."

The A.F.L.-C.I.O produced a film about the Viguerie system, with a narrator intoning: "This is a horror film, not the usual kind featuring haunted houses, creepy creatures, ghosts or ghouls. It's going on right now—and you are the target." Viguerie loves the film, has got a copy of his own—sends it out to conservative groups to drum up more business for himself. When opposing lobbyists argue that Viguerie's letters distort issues in an emotional way—the Panama Canal treaties were "a surrender" and "a giveaway"—he does not apologize. His view: "You have to grab an issue by the scruff of the neck."

While the conservatives are gaining in the ideological war among the lobbyists, the once influential public interest lobbies are losing ground. By arguing too self-righteously for too long on too wide a range of issues, Ralph Nader has lost his formerly considerable effectiveness on Capitol Hill. Perhaps his biggest mistake was to rush out a series of profiles of the members of Congress—sketches so full of errors and misconceptions that he lost credibility on other issues. Indiana Democratic Congressman Andy Jacobs ridicules Nader. In a formal report Jacobs filed this year on contributions, he listed among his assets: "Name-calling attacks by Ralph Nader." He rated their value as "priceless." Contends Jacobs: "Nader has become a legend in his own mind."

Common Cause still has influence, largely because its retired founder, John Gardiner, retains much public respect. Its current chief lobbyist, Fred Wertheimer, has offended many Congressmen with his public scoldings when they failed to vote as he wished, but another Common Cause lobbyist, Michael Cole, 34, maintains solid connections in Congress.

It is the new breed of bright and aggressive hired guns who typify the proliferation of lobbyists in Washington. Their approach to their jobs is individualistic and shrewd, their fields of specialization varied, and their specific results often difficult to document. Yet their ubiquitous presence has transformed the city. Speaker O'Neill, who does battle with many of these independent operators, does not resent them. Says he: "Give me a guy who has the smarts. That's what lobbyists are; they're smarts."

One of the brightest newcomers is Thomas Boggs, 37, whose clients include Mars, Inc., the candy manufacturer. Since Mars advertises to children on TV, Boggs was interested to hear that the Federal Trade Commission was considering a proposal to ban all television advertising aimed

51

at children on the ground that it is inherently deceptive. Boggs met with a group of lawyers to plan a lawsuit against the FTC regulation. Then he had a different idea: "Why don't we simply go to Congress and stop this silly law?"

Boggs went to the House Appropriations Committee, where he persuaded a few Congressmen who were already angry at what they considered bureaucratic distortions of congressional intent, to add an amendment to a pending bill to finance the FTC for the next year. It stipulated that none of the money could be used to pay the salary of any FTC employee who spent his time investigating advertising aimed at children. The amendment was approved in subcommittee by a 5-to-4 vote and by the full committee, 33 to 14. When the bill reached the House floor, the amendment was deleted—but the whole FTC appropriations bill was killed too. Boggs is confident that both the bill—and his amendment—will return.

Dean Burch, former chairman of the Federal Communications Commission, has switched sides and is now a lawyer-lobbyist specializing in issues that come before his former agency. His expertise enabled him to spot a seemingly harmless bill deceptively titled the Consumers Communications Reform Act as special legislation sponsored by AT & T, which would have effectively frozen out attempts by smaller telephone companies to give AT & T more competition. AT & T had proposed the bill under the aegis of a trade group called the U.S. Independent Telephone Association and had lined up 235 House sponsors, most of them unaware of how much it favored AT & T. Burch and a few colleagues, representing small communications companies, painstakingly sought out each of the 235 sponsors and explained what the bill actually would do.

AT & T's proposal died in committee. What turned it around? "We started walking the halls," said Burch.

The American Medical Association's John Zap, a onetime official at HEW, is similarly shrewd in using the practical impact of a bill to switch a vote. When Florida Democrat Paul Rogers, who heads a House subcommittee on health and the environment, proposed a tough bill to control hospital costs, Zap quickly secured statistics on just how hard the proposal would hit hopsitals in Rogers' district. Rogers then modified his own bill. Contends Zap: "That was a service to him as well as ourselves. He had not realized what would happen in his district if the bill became law.". . .

Contrary to alert lobbyists who make such useful clarifications of law, the National Rifle Association is an example of a very strong lobby that can aim concentrated pressure on a single issue so as to thwart majority public opinion. Despite polls showing broad support for gun controls, N.R.A.'s regular barrages of emotional mail have persuaded nervous members of Congress to reject gun-control bills 14 times in the past ten years. When the Bureau of Alcohol, Tobacco and Firearms proposed on its own to have all new guns marked with a 14-digit identifying number—without recording the owner's name —N.R.A. Executive Director Neal Knox alerted his lobby's sharpshooters. Result: the Senate compliantly decreed that none of the bureau's 1979 appropriations could be used on any such gun regulations.

Does Congress bow too meekly to the wizardry of the direct-mail lobbyists and their magical magnetic drums of computerized lists? Too often it does. It takes a self-confident Congressman to rely on his own assessment of whether the mail truly reflects the sentiment of the voters he represents. And while it is a cardinal rule of Washington lobbyists never to mislead a member of Congress in face-to-face argument, no such niceties limit the distortions many of the lobbyists deliberately stimulate at the local level. . . .

There may be more serious abuses in backroom dealings between lobbyist and lawmaker, as past scandals and the Korean bribery affair suggest. Yet on balance the relationship between the governors and the governed, even when the lobbyist does represent one of the nation's many special-interest groups, is often mutually beneficial, and perhaps indispensable, to the fullest workings of democracy. The increasingly knowledgeable and competent Washington lobbyist supplies a practical knowledge vital to the writing of workable laws. He does it at no public expense—and at only the cost of being sure his own interests get the fullest of hearings. All in all, that may not be a bad bargain, but it does represent a major change in the way the Government goes about the difficult task of trying to balance competing interests against the Constitution's demand to "promote the general Welfare."

● ● ●

NO

Irving Louis Horowitz

BEYOND DEMOCRACY

If there breathes a red-blooded American who has not been consistently plagued by fourth-class mailings representing one of thousands of special-interest groups, he or she should step forward and report immediately as a relic or heirloom. Whether such special-interest groups are the cause or effect of issue-oriented politics remains to be determined. What is clear is that such groups claim to have caused everything from the relative success of anti-abortion campaigns to the extension by Congress of an additional period of time for the passage of the Equal Rights Amendment. We have now reached the point at which nearly every special interest promotes itself as operating in the name of the general interest. Typical of this new trend is the worthy Natural Resources Defense Council—an anti-nuclear, pro-environment group, staffed by thirty-one lawyers, scientists, and environmentalists (unnamed defenders of the public), who live off of a paper membership of forty thousand. They exclaim in their promotional packet: "Thank God! . . . Somebody who does not represent any governmental or special interest." But not only is this a special-interest group, but one not above cribbing from its own promotional copy. For what Judge Richey in testimony before the Senate Judiciary Committee actually said was: "Everytime I see somebody . . . like the NRDC come into my court, I say 'Thank God!' because I know I am going to have competent counsel . . . that does not represent any governmental or proprietary interest." But in a world of sophisticated mailing techniques, this is a little murder—one replicated on a daily basis by more than one thousand lobbying efforts, who are doing right by doing good, even if they must say so themselves.

This transformation of pluralism into the massification of self-interest has now been subjected to a veritable barrage by the defenders of the public faith. What makes the current assault on special-interest groups so intriguing is that, for the most part, it has gone unanswered. One gets the distinct impression that

From Irving Louis Horowitz, "Beyond Democracy: Interest Groups and the Patriotic Gore," *The Humanist.* September/October 1979, pp. 4, 7-10. Copyright ©1979 by The Humanist. Reprinted by permission.

liberalism has come to accept, or at least acquiesce, in the conservative theory of government. Even staunchly liberal writers and politicians speak fervently of a rebirth of patriotism and a renewed concern for nationhood. Dialogue has by default turned into a monologue. The only differences now seem to be which interest groups or lobbying efforts deserve to be supported or suppressed. What we are now privy to are liberal variations upon the conservative theme. With only slight differences of language, from scholarly journals through popular weeklies, the theme being echoed is the same: the decline of American national government and the rise of single-issue interest groups. . . .

There can be little doubt that the current wave of interest-group politics has had serious impact on the executive branch of government no less than on the legislative or electoral processes. In a recent series of articles, "Governing America," John Herbers reports that "The United States is becoming increasingly difficult to govern because of a fragmented, inefficient system of authority and procedures that has developed over the last decade." Right, Left, and Center seem to concur in this judgment. Representative Philip M. Crane, Illinois Republican and chairman of the Conservative Union, views such failure as the "natural result of fifty years of big government." Tom Hayden, a major political voice of the Left and now a California figure of some note, reports: "You can take any issue you want, and the system isn't delivering. There is no glue holding the country together.". . .

Perhaps the best way to illustrate these cries and alarms is a recently cancelled, major White House Conference on families. The reason for the cancellation was because a decision could not be reached on whether a "white, Catholic male" stemming from an "intact family" should be appointed as assistant director to offset the fact that the director was a "divorced black woman." Quite apart from the subject matter that the conference was to discuss was the panoply of organizations (American Home Economic Association, United States Catholic Conference, the National Association of Social Workers, the Italian-American Foundation—among others) that were all determined to register their claims and hence affect the findings and recommendations. Rather than permit this "potential land-mine" as one participant called the conference, the meetings themselves were jettisoned. (Spencer Rich, "Touchy Issues Sank Conference on Families," *The Washington Post.* June 24, 1978.)

It remains a moot point whether any serious, operational policies could have been pursued given the depth of pre-existing interest-group rivalries. What is not moot is the power of such groups in determining, not only political goals, but the structure of American policy-making as a whole – if there is such a whole.

There are, in fact, large numbers of lobbying activities: five hundred corporate lobbies, fifty-three lobbies for minority groups, thirty-four for social-welfare agencies, thirty-three for women, thirty-one for environmental issues, fifteen for the aging, and six for population control. Add to this, overseas lobbyists such as Japanese business interests being pushed by sixty-one lobbies, and Israeli political interests by ten—to name only two—and it is apparent that interest-group forces appear to be of a magnitude far greater than anything known in the past.

In addition, considerable numbers of people can be mobilized on an issue-by-

3. CAN LOBBYING ENDANGER DEMOCRACY?

issue basis. John Gardiner's Common Cause and Ralph Nader's Congress Watch exist to make sure that their interests are properly represented and monitored. Conservative groups are no less adroit than their liberal counterparts. Thus a group like Robert Kephart's National Taxpayers Legal Fund seeks to offer nothing short of personal freedom from the "powerful bureaucracy itself" in exchange for a modest fiscal contribution. The ordinary citizens, nearly half of whom absent themselves from national presidential elections, clearly prefer to vote with their dollars rather than their feet.

In a world of political oversimplification, in which sophistication becomes the enemy of the slogan, it is little wonder that a cry for national patriotic revival is heard. As Charles Peters puts the case:

> For most of the twentieth century, patriotism has been strong in America. Large numbers of people from all classes volunteered for service in World Wars I and II. As one who worked on the staff of the Peace Corps in the early sixties, I know many of our volunteers were motivated by patriotism – they were ashamed of the Ugly American and wanted to show the good side of their country to the world. But Vietnam changed all of that. First it killed the patriotism of the educated youth who resisted the war from the beginning. Then even more viciously it destroyed the patriotism of the poor who went to Vietnam and realized they had been suckers. (Charles Peters, "The Solution: A Rebirth of Patriotism," *The Washington Monthly.* Vol. 10, No. 7, October 1978, pp. 37-38.)

This dilemma and disunity of government, defined as a ceaseless round of conflict and interest groups, has reached sufficient proportions to elicit a one-million-dollar program on conflict resolution sponsored by the Ford Foundation. In the administrative prose of McGeorge Bundy,

interest groups in America are the centerpiece of issue-related conflicts.

> America in recent years has been swarming with conflicts and disputes of all sorts. The issues range across the entire social spectrum – for example, racial equality, energy allocation, environmental protection, consumer rights, and equal educational opportunity. Conflicts over these matters arise among interest groups, between interest groups and government, between levels of government, and between individuals. Thousands of administrative agencies and other decision-making bodies have had great difficulty in attempting to resolve such large numbers of conflicts efficiently and fairly. And, the quantitative problem is compounded by the growing complexity, technological sophistication, and interdependence of society's problems. (McGeorge Bundy, Ford Foundation Press Release, June 21, 1978. Commentary on Sanford M. Jaffee, NEW APPROACHES TO CONFLICT RESOLUTION, New York: The Ford Foundation, 1978.)

The objectives of this new foundation effort are to strengthen the capacity of existing formal institutions, to find better ways of handling disputes outside the formal political apparatus, and to identify reforms that may help either to avoid or to simplify conflicts in the future. But seemingly no funds are allocated to discuss the possiblity that conflict-resolving mechanisms already in place are the problem, whereas conflict situations may be the essence of democratic procedures.

What do we make of this? The nub of the argument is, in the first place, empirical. What alternatives are there? Second, ethical: What are the implications of the present situation? On the analytic side, there seems to be a considerable confusion of the growth of special-interest politics with the decline of national politics or national patriotism. In point of fact, at the very time interest-group politics grow larger, so too has the power of the national government. Many claims of special interest groups are intended to redress that national power. What really has declined in post-war America are intermediary forms of political structure: the collapse of local politics, the weakening of voluntary political associations, the decline of mass participation in the political process. The political party system itself has failed to represent these interests. The intermediary structures have declined, not the national system. Hence the chief imagery of the conservative arsenal, the description of the way in which interest groups sap national goals, is profoundly inaccurate. What has been sapped are intermediary forms of mass participation, not the political power system as such.

A critical factor has been the rise of the mass-communications media as a device for expressing public opinion. Television in particular, by virtue of its special qualities, has focused solely on issues, promoting focus on people rather than ideas. Television generally has had an easier time focusing on specific issues than providing a context of general political concerns. Interest-group politics is the handmaiden of the mass media. But the mass media do little to weaken a sense of national allegiance or national loyalty. They do weaken a sense of local and community participation.

Another element that has not been addressed is the crosscutting impact of special-interest groups. Because the political process and the political system remain too powerful, the need for compromise and coalition becomes greater rather than smaller in the current situation. Coalitions are continually made between advocates of civil rights and gay activists, or between feminists and environmentalists.

For the most part, the power of interest-group politics has been the defeat of a candidate rather than his or her election. It is true that mobilization around a special interest or single issue can defeat Representative Don Fraser or Senator Dick Clark. It is not true that the groups that mobilized against them have the capacity to elect representatives and senators.

The lobbying efforts of industrialists have always been recognized as a legitimate part of American politics, from MR. SMITH GOES TO WASHINGTON to ADVISE AND CONSENT. A theme in American letters has been the honest politician versus the grafting lobbyist. What tends to be new is not the lobbying effort or even the single-interest group, but the social sources of those groups: the phenomenon of black power, red power, or gay power. In fact these new movements, measured by corporate expenditures, tend to be pathetically weak and not nearly as effective as the older lobbying effort. Much of the current rebellion against interest-group thinking seems in part a reaction to these new types of groups. With the exception of Matthew Josephson, and some earlier "muckrakers," it was rarely perceived that business lobbyists splinter America. What, then, minority-group lobbyists do is hard to fathom, unless one assumes the utter naturalness of business lobbying in a business civilization, and the deviance of all other forms of registered political claims.

It still remains difficult to ascertain the quality of these single-issue groups. Their strength often derives from living in an age of mass marketing and mass mailings. The possiblity of having an organizational base of thirty, forty, or fifty thousand people is simply a function of dollars invested. One or 2 percent returns on selected mailing lists can generate such numbers with relative ease. But there are no studies that show that these mailing-list respondents can actually be mobilized for political ends beyond giving an occasional donation. The numbers involved in interest-group politics, while initially appearing frightening, are in fact relatively modest indicators that the party apparatus, not to mention the political process, remains intact. In a sense, such single-issue groups provide sensitizing elements to political networks and a focus of a more traditional sort..

The assumption that single-issue politics in any way contributed to the breakdown of the two-party system is subject to serious examination. Political parties still carry within themselves, lower voting participation notwithstanding, the base of political continuity in America. Further, many interest groups have in fact become absorbed by one or the other party. For example, one finds the Democratic Party a strong supporter of gun-control legislation and the Republican Party a strong supporter of the National Riflemen's Association. Parties continue to express a wide variety of interests, both in their party platforms and in bloc-voting patterns. This is not a uniform condition: Congressional crossings do take place. But that precisely is the legitimate role of an interest group: to influence individuals within each party to break ranks on the basis of an issue important enough to do so.

Interest groups vary considerably. Sometimes we are referring to an interest-group issue that has a specific organization, such as the National Riflemen's Association or Common Cause. Other times, interest groups are identified broadly, as the Sunbelt versus the Snowbelt. But whether one should use such broad demographic characteristics as examples of single-issue politics, or simply a transformation in national demographic or urban patterns, is difficult to pinpoint. The Sunbelt as an organizing premise is deeply limited by differences in state boundaries, state political systems, and local needs. There is slender correlation between voting patterns and select political variables either in the Sunbelt or in the Snowbelt for that matter. There are precious few ideological signs to distinguish the two except the high cost of petroleum in the Snowbelt and the relatively easy access to petroleum in the Sunbelt. A secondary differentiation might be the power of trade unions. But even this varies considerably from state to state, locality to locality. Whether geography constitutes an interest group is dubious; and whether it constitutes a constellation of new political forces is doubtful.

There is another confusion between interest groups and the process of communication. In part, American society is undergoing not so much fragmentation as professionalization. The growth of specialized fields and the division of labor means that it is not enough to be identified as a middle-class professional. New terms arise in terms of being doctors, lawyers, dentists. Dentists themselves fragment into specialized areas, as do lawyers and accountants and others as well. This is not necessarily a consequence of interest-group politics, but of specialization of knowledge and the transference of that knowledge to an audience that must use it in the public domain.

Hence, the empirical distinction of single-issue politics, or the rise of fanatic factions or Balkanization; all come upon some extremely difficult factual issues. Rather than prove beyond a doubt that democracy is ailing, such views tend to prove the contrary—namely, that there is a continuation of vibrant political life in American society.

What then of the values that are being inculcated by this new conservative theme? There can be no doubt of the authenticity, the sense of anguish, about special interests. There also can be no question that there is a growing concern not only as to whether this nation can adhere or endure, but what the quality of this nation will be in a world of special-interest groups. We now inhabit a society in which, even the basic language of the nation is subject to challenge, and the forms of our political, cultural, and economic life are also subject to polarizing tendencies.

Is there a threat to the survival of the country, and is there a breakdown of national sensibility and patriotism that heralds this collapse? Rather than take this issue head-on, perhaps we should turn the question around: What would a world look like without interest groups, or more pointedly what interest groups, are to be sacrificed in the name of national unity? Once posed in this way, the elemental threat to democracy implied by the neo-conservative revival becomes clearer. For it is not simply an attack on factionalism and interest groups but on the presumed high costs of democracy that is being addressed. The neoconservatives are eyeing democracy itself as a source of inflation. The very cacophonous sound of competing interest groups becomes a source of conservative anger because of its high "costs" and low "benefits." But which groups should be sacrificed—black power, red power, gay power? Is it to be business lobbyists or lobbyists of foreign nations? To even pose the question in this way, by seeking an answer based on sacrificing one or more of these groups, is to be confronted

with an attack on democracy. It is an attack on the rights of people to use the machinery of government and the power of organization to insinuate their collective will. After all, a political party that has been enshrined by custom over time has no more legal standing than a lobbying or interest group. Neither are constitutionally mandated, nor are either constitutionally subject to abolition by fiat. So what we have at the normative level is a fear that these interest groups are somehow eroding the basis of American national purpose.

But what is that purpose? How is it defined? Here one finds the attack on single-interest politics exposed as an assault on pluralism pure and simple. Purpose itself has tended to get the United States into trouble in the post-war world. The exaggerated sense of manifest destiny and national purpose made the Vietnam War a programmed monstrosity. The imposition of political monism in place of pluralism is the elemental goal of those who consider democracy some sort of medical disaster. The sensibility that is spoken of by this attack on single-issue politics is a sensibility of an older age, in which presumably everyone knew his or her place and everyone was willing to accept the preeminence of America in world affairs.

The situation in representative government has been transformed over time. When representation meant one legislative figure standing for every two hundred fifty or every twenty-five hundred persons, the relationship of the governed to the governor was well known and easily identified. When two senators represented states of less than one-half million people, the sense of responsibility to the constituency was high. When those same two senators represent twenty million, there is a corresponding weakening of that sense of identification with the public. The rise of interest-group politics in America may be viewed, not as a function of decay, but of growth. The demographic transformation of a colonial nation to a major world power brought in its wake new ways to express discontent, even rebellion. The interest group of today is closer to the Town Hall of yesterday than the political apparatus it supposedly has superseded. It is responsive in ways that are more natively American than the current political climate. The relationship of dollars to demagogues, of donors to recipients, is much clearer in single-issue organizations and group associations than in the political party structure as it currently exists.

In short, the current frontal assault on single-interest politics and special-interest groups is part of the Madisonian belief that liberty is to factionalism what oxygen is to fire. It is part of the federalist inheritance over and against the democratic persuasion. The Jeffersonian persuasion organizes the polity in favor of the diffusion and division of authority as the source of national strength.

In the long pull of time, in terms of our two-hundred-year national history, what we are witnessing is the struggle between Jeffersonian and Madisonian claims, only in more complicated and complex conditions. But the Jeffersonian position, while silent in theory and having few overt adherents, continues to gain strength at the expense of the more sophisticated Madisonian viewpoint, not by virtue of any theoretical genius, but rather by virtue of the fact that America is a mass-democracy nation and that the forms for expressing that democracy have changed and have become less a matter of elites who have time for the party life, and more a matter of participating-interest-group life. One thing is clear to all: individuals must organize if they are to gain any measure of strength or security. The argument of parties versus groups is therefore a discussion over what kind of organizational life America is to have, not a false choice between them. Seen this way, the current emphasis on group life is by no means a categorical evil and, quite the contrary, may yet turn out to be the basis of a twenty-first-century American democracy.

● ● ●

POSTSCRIPT

CAN LOBBYING ENDANGER DEMOCRACY?

Horowitz's interpretation of James Madison is an unusual one. Madison is usually labeled a pluralist, but Horowitz calls "Madisonian" the "current frontal assault on single-interest groups." By citing Madison's remark about liberty being to faction what oxygen is to fire, Horowitz may leave some readers with the impression that Madison favored extinguishing liberty in order to extinguish faction. What we must remember is the rest of Madison's analogy: liberty is as essential to political life as oxygen is to biological life.

For a book which paints pressure groups—and particularly their representatives in Washington—in extremely lurid colors, see Robert N. Winter-Berger, THE WASHINGTON PAY-OFF (Dell, 1972). The style is sensational, but, since the author was once a lobbyist and claims to write from first-hand experience, the content cannot be dismissed out of hand. At the other extreme, see Lester Milbrath, THE WASHINGTON LOBBYISTS (Rand McNally, 1963), a book which pays homage to "the ordinary, honest lobbyist and his workaday activities." On a more theoretical level, a defense of pressure-group politics is found in David B. Truman, THE GOVERNMENTAL PROCESS (Knopf, 1951), while a broad-scale critique is supplied by Theodore J. Lowi in THE END OF LIBERALISM (Norton, 1969).

Those who defend interest-group politics are often criticized for failing to distinguish between "public" interests—interests which are supposed to be good for the nation as a whole—and strictly "private" or selfish interests. The usual reply of those defending interest-group politics is that it is impossible to make a valid distinction between the two, since virtually every group can rationalize its selfish interests as being altruistic. To that reply the late political scientist E.E. Schattschneider proposed the following rejoinder. "Is it possible," he asked, "to distinguish between the members of the National Association of Manufacturers and the members of the American League to Abolish Capital Punishment?" It certainly is, he answered, for *"the members of the A.L.A.C.P. obviously do not expect to be hanged."*

ISSUE 4

IS CONGRESS OBSOLETE?

YES: Tad Szulc, from "Is Congress Obsolete?" *Saturday Review,* March 3, 1979

NO: Gary Orfield, from CONGRESSIONAL POWER: CONGRESS AND SOCIAL CHANGE, (New York, 1975)

ISSUE SUMMARY

YES: Political commentator Tad Szulc supports his contention that Congress as an institution has become overburdened and has lost control of its own processes, depending upon staff members and lobbyists for important decisions.

NO: Brookings Institute member Gary Orfield argues that Congress does a good job of reflecting the attitudes and trends in the electorate as a whole. If Congress seems unresponsive, it is not the fault of the institution, but a comment on the priorities of the country at the moment.

Can Representative Government Do the Job? was the question posed in the title of a thoughtful 1945 book, and many Americans remain uncertain as to the answer. Putting the question another way, we may bluntly ask: Is Congress strong enough?

There is a widespread feeling that Congress isn't strong. The structure of Congress impresses—or depresses—its critics as being a horse-and-buggy vehicle in a jet age. Power is fragmented among many committees in the absence of national parties which might impose discipline on legislators and coherence on legislation. Within the committees, power is concentrated in the chairmen who, until recently, were chosen strictly on the basis of seniority (length of service) rather than leadership capacities. Woodrow Wilson called it "a government by the chairmen of standing committees of Congress," and if much power has shifted since to the President, within Congress the chairmen remain subject to few checks.

President Truman campaigned against what he characterized as a Do-Nothing Congress. The criticism that Congress doesn't do much good leads even incumbent congressmen to run against Congress's record and to promise reform.

Perhaps the decline of Congress in this century is partly due to its outmoded structure, but it is easy enough to see the cause in two World Wars, Korea and Vietnam, the Great Depression, and economic and other issues that transcend national boundaries. Increasingly, we have looked to the President rather than to Congress for inspiration, initiative, and leadership. He is after all an individual and we can personalize his power; we can identify him and identify *with* him, while Congress remains a faceless abstraction.

The President can act with promptness and decisiveness not available to two houses with 535 members. He alone is nationally elected and may therefore come closer to being a tribune of the people. He alone possesses life-and-death power as the negotiator of international relations and Commander-in-Chief of the armed forces.

It was not surprising therefore that liberals looked to the President for the bold action that was not forthcoming from a lethargic and leaderless Congress. But many who had prayed for presidential dominance remained to warn against the Imperial Presidency as a result of Watergate, the abuse of power, the evidence of unnecessary presidential secrecy and calculated deceit, and a new awareness of unchecked presidential decision-making.

The fear that presidential power may be abused has kindled the hope that representative government can be improved. Toward that end, the seniority system is (at least for Democrats) no longer a certain route to committee chairmanships, the requirement of open committee meetings and increased access to once-confidential files has increased public (and particularly press) scrutiny of governmental behavior. Congress has set up its own budget committees, and the War Powers Act was designed to inhibit presidential war-making in the absence of a congressional declaration of war.

Perhaps what is necessary is not technical reform but political will, that is, a public desire to have Congress exercise its power more vigorously. Reformers cannot fairly criticize Congress for not adopting programs which most Americans have not indicated they want Congress to adopt. On the other hand, it might be argued that reformers are simply incapable of strengthening Congress, even if they have the American people behind them, because the presidency today is beyond the reach of legislative checks and balances.

To these obstacles, political correspondent Tad Szulc adds the burden of too much legislative business and the influence of too many lobbyists. Recognizing the obstacles, Brookings Institution analyst Gary Orfield argues that there isn't much that Congress cannot do, at least domestically, if it really wants to.

YES

Tad Szulc

IS CONGRESS OBSOLETE?

Emerging from the Capitol shortly before eight o'clock on a Sunday morning last October, a red-eyed and exhausted senator stopped to talk to a friend before getting into his car for the drive home. In a hoarse whisper, he said: "You know, I've been in the Senate for 14 years, but I have never seen anything like the last 24 hours. This just can't be allowed to happen again." What the lawmaker didn't wish to see repeated was the paroxysm of wild, last-minute legislating that had held congressmen captive on the floor of both houses since early Saturday morning, with the midterm elections only three weeks away. In the course of an around-the-clock closing session, the Senate had passed 22 bills, and the House of Representatives 14, spending hours on countless amendments to such crucial legislation as those governing taxation and energy.

But this Congress, the 96th (in session since January 15), may very well conclude with the same eleventh-hour frenzy. The staggering volume and complexity of legislation, which was primarily responsible for its predecessor's last-minute snarl, is a problem that will not go away. The legislative burden, however, is only one cause of the disease with which Congress is now afflicted. The recent establishment of a vast system of subcommittees, intended to reduce the power of committee chairmen, has so diffused authority that crucial legislation is continuously being bottled up for months in subcommittees before emerging in barely recognizable form. Meanwhile, this same fragmentation is repeated in the members' ties to party and to ideology. On several occasions President Carter has found himself in the embarrassing position of depending on Republican votes to avert defeat, despite heavy Democratic majorities in both houses. And the one-issue candidate, with his nonchalance toward the broad ideals that have defined the two parties, has become a commonplace of political analysis. Finally, and perhaps most insidious of all, congressmen have become ever more dependent on lobbyists

From, "Is Congress Obsolete?" *The Saturday Review* March 3, 1979. ©1979, *The Saturday Review.* Reprinted by permission.

and special-interest groups for advice—even including instructions on how to vote—and for underwriting the skyrocketing costs of campaigns.

These problems, by and large, are not matters of happenstance; they are embedded in the structure of Congress and American politics. Looking toward the future with this in mind, one cannot avoid asking a fundamental question: Is Congress an obsolete institution? Without a radical change in the way that it governs, can Congress act as an efficient law-making body in the Eighties and beyond?

A midwestern senator sums up the situation in dismal tones: "We are losing control of what we are doing here . . . there isn't enough time in a day to keep abreast of everything we should know to legislate responsibly, dealing with so many bills, having to attend so many committee and subcommittee meetings, listening to the lobbyists, having to worry about problems of constituents, and, of course, keeping a close eye on politics back home. You know, one *has* to get reelected. . . ."

An analysis of Congress's basic problems must begin with the incredible legislative burden that it now tries to shoulder. The numbers alone are overwhelming. In the 1977-78 session, congressmen introduced 22,313 public and private bills and resolutions. The House took 1,810 seriously enough to file reports on them, the Senate, 1,413. In the end, they passed 3,211 bills and resolutions, with 804 bills finally enacted into law. These figures included fundamental lawmaking, as well as such matters as providing for the display of the U.S.S. *Wyoming's* nameplate, bell, and silver service at the Wyoming State Museum. And as if that weren't enough,

the Congress had to act in the last two years to confirm 124,730 military and civilian nominations submitted by the President.

The problem of overwork is aggravated by the complexity of legislation, which has come more and more to embrace highly detailed, technically difficult issues. The 1978 tax bill, for example, was 814 pages long, though it was an amendment to the 1954 Internal Revenue Code rather than a new piece of legislation. Few congressmen could honestly claim to understand every ramification of the bill that they ultimately passed. Since every member of the Congress cannot be an expert in every field—most will carve out a specialty or two—the majority come to depend on the judgment of the recognized experts, their staffs, lobbyists, and representatives of special interests.

"I don't know what the answer to this problem can be," a young southern representative commented. "I try to do my homework, but, say, on taxes, I will be guided by the views of Al Ullman (chairman of the Joint Internal Revenue Taxation Committee) or Russell Long (chairman of the Senate Finance Committee). I have a legislative assistant boning up on taxation, and, like everybody else, I get my ear bent by lobbyists. In the end, I'm not sure if I vote intelligently every time, especially on the more complex issues."

Congressmen have taken to appointing more and more staff members in order to stem this vast tide of information. A full 5,000 staffers are now attached to congressmen, committees, and subcommittees. Their influence may be pernicious or benign; but in any case it is expanding rapidly, so that staffers have become the unacknowledged legislators

4. IS CONGRESS OBSOLETE?

of the Congress. Some are counted among the most powerful figures in Washington on particular topics. For example, Richard Perle, Senator Henry Jackson's (D-Wash.) principal adviser on defense issues, is credited with substantially influencing key arms-control thinking in the Senate, and has been called "the quintessential Washington operator." Many Capitol Hill experts give the credit for the 1978 energy compromise not to Speaker Thomas P. O'Neill, Jr., but to his 25-year-old legislative assistant, Ariel Weiss. But whether staffers even fulfill their original purpose of saving their boss's time is open to doubt, since staff members are themselves responsible for more and longer bills, more hearings, more reports, more unfathomable issues.

Other efforts to deal with the flood of legislation have proved no more successful. The subcommittee system, greatly augmented by the post-Watergate "freshman class" of 1974, has smothered or splintered legislation more often than it has expedited it. The 96th Congress has inherited 29 standing committees and 151 subcommittees in the House, 21 committees and 112 subcommittees in the Senate (outnumbering the 100 senators), four joint committees, and seven joint subcommittees. The House also has six Democratic and Republican partisan committees, while the Senate has seven. The average representative sits on three subcommittees, the average senator, five. Not only do these groups-within-groups keep legislation holed up for as long as a year, but the tendency of their interests to overlap further adds to the confusion.

Most congressmen find themselves unable to devote adequate time and thought to their various assignments; Instead, they flit in and out of hearings, spending an hour in a committee, and minutes in some of the subcommittees. "I can't be everywhere at the same time," a New York congressman said. "And I also have to race to the floor for quorum votes or votes on bills whenever that damned bell rings. It's insane."

A further attempt to deal with the huge volume of work is the so-called "suspension calendar." Under this procedure, originally intended to dispose rapidly of lesser legislation, the House sets aside part of Monday and Tuesday for floor votes without allowing amendments. But this aim is often subverted by the inclusion of important money bills that sneak past unwary congressmen on the suspension docket.

One of the most alarming aspects of the functioning of Congress is the new primacy of lobbyists. An estimated 15,000 of them currently spend $1 billion a year pursuing congressmen around Capitol Hill, and probably another $1 billion a year for related activities in the home districts. The growing reach of Congress into highly specific, detailed legislation touching on the interests of particular groups has made this new muscle necessary for them; and this same complexity, forcing congressmen into the hands of technical experts, has made it possible. Whether he represents a defense contractor, a labor union, the association of restaurant-owners (who campaigned successfully against President Carter's attempt to remove tax deductions from "three-martini lunches"), or a public interest group, the lobbyist is the master of his subject. He may know even more about it than a Hill staffer. In this sense, he becomes a "technical adviser" to the congressmen, many of whom gladly accept his assistance.

"There is obviously no bribing," a senator said, "because the lobbyists and congressmen are, by and large, too sophisticated for such crude business. But lobbyists can be enormously convincing politically, outlining for their targeted congressmen the pluses and minuses, in terms of political impact in their districts, of how a vote is cast. And, believe me, it works."

It is a common sight in the lobbies of the House and Senate—literally—for groups of lobbyists to congregate before a vote and indicate with thumb-up or thumb-down signals what a member should do on the floor. Others do it from public galleries. William S. Cohen, the Maine Republican who was elevated last November from the House to the Senate, says that he developed the habit of hunching his shoulders and lowering his head as he made his way through clusters of lobbyists from the front door to the elevator. "I just didn't want to see their signals," he says.

A more recent innovation is the political action committee (PAC). Under the 1974 election law, corporations and unions can contribute $5,000 to as many PACs as they wish. Formed by corporate employees, trade groups, or stockholders, as well as by unions, close to 1,900 PACs contributed over $64 million to congressional candidates in the 1978 elections.

Though business PACs have been accused of giving to front-runners no matter what their affiliation, most of the giving is anything but indiscriminate. A study of federal election returns shows that committee chairmen received especially lavish gifts, and that the industries or professions for which the chairman legislated led the list of donors. The average House chairman received $45,000 from political committees, double the 1976 total. Thomas Foley (D-Wash.), chairman of the House Agriculture Committee, took in $145,000 from special interests, 57 percent of his campaign treasury. Rep. John M. Murphy (D-N.Y.), chairman of the Merchant Marine Committee, received nine contributions of $2,500 or over from maritime and transportation groups. Few of these congressmen even needed the money, since they were already outspending their opponents, and almost all won handily.

There is no question that lobbyists and special interests affect legislation. The most spectacular display of their power was mustered around the tough energy-conservation package that President Carter submitted to the Congress on April 20, 1977. It sought to curb the use of oil by taxing it at the wellhead and other measures. The bill was approved by the House in autumn of 1977, but it came unraveled in the Senate a year later, when special interests—oil and natural-gas companies and oil and gas-producing states among them—arrayed a formidable army against the Carter proposals.

The lobbyists advocated the deregulation of the price of natural gas, which the White House (at least at the outset) and consumer goups opposed, and the removal of the tax features of the bill. The legislation remained stalled for a year in Senate committees, then in House-Senate conferences, and finally in a House Ad Hoc Committee on Energy. The committee reached a compromise on the deregulation issue in early October, but the House didn't complete voting on the energy package until 7:30

67

4. IS CONGRESS OBSOLETE?

AM on the last day of the session. (The Senate acted a few days earlier.) Though oil and gas interests professed dissatisfaction, they got what they wanted.

The session's other major piece of legislation, the tax reform bill, was just as badly mauled. The legislation that finally emerged after a year's struggle in Senate and House committees and on the floor of both houses provided precious little relief for the average American family— and the rise in Social Security levies, particularly in a time of inflation, meant that most Americans would be even worse off than before. Only the powerful fared well: Rich taxpayers got a break on capital gains, while business received a cut in the maximum corporate tax rate.

While members of Congress lose sight of central concerns amid the vast welter of legislation and the badgering of lobbyists, consensus becomes an ever more evanescent ideal. Appeals to loyalty, either to basic principles or to the party that is supposed to embody those principles, simply do not carry the strength that they used to. President Carter's difficulty in gaining support for such issues as the energy and tax reforms, or the two Panama Canals treaties, was due not only to his lack of personal magnetism or shrewdness, but also to the growing resistance of congressmen to being mustered along party lines. The Canal treaties, for example, were ratified by exactly the required two-thirds majority only because Senate Minority Leader Howard Baker of Tennessee and a number of moderate Republican leaders concluded that the United States—and not the Carter administration—should be spared the foreign policy embarrassment of a rejection. Meanwhile, nine Democrats voted against the treaties.

On such issues as budget-cutting, tax reform, and defense spending, the distinction between the two parties has been blurred beyond recognition. This has led, paradoxically, to less cohesion rather than more, since loose ideological coalitions can form and dissolve around specific issues when parties fail to dictate clear and opposing points of view. "I'm no longer sure whom the Congress represents," says a veteran California representative. "It's getting to be more and more atomized. On lots of issues, we go for the lowest common denominator so that we can legislate at all."

Is it any wonder, then, that congressional elections rouse so little enthusiasm in the public? Only 37.9 percent of eligible voters went to the polls to elect the 96th Congress, the lowest midterm turnout since 1942. As recently as 1970, 43.5 percent of eligible Americans queued up at polling stations. A further depressing discovery is the massive number of young voters who declined to vote, a scant six years after the much-heralded lowering of the voting age to 18.

Nor is enthusiasm within the Congress itself running at a very high pitch. Fifty-eight members of the House, a record number, chose not to seek reelection in 1978. Three senators did likewise. The reasons ranged from frustration over a member's inability to influence legislation constructively, to just plain overwork, the sacrifice of family life, and—often—the realization that a congressman, particularly if he is a lawyer, can earn more money in private life.

In the end, there is no reason to expect that the 96th Congress will behave or perform any better than its predecessor. Aware as members are of all the short-comings in the functioning of the

Congress, there is no outlook for any serious changes or reforms. The truth is that few congressmen are prepared to upset the applecart: Their personal interests are, by and large, well served by the status quo.

One reform mentioned periodically is the extension of the House term from two to four years, so that congressmen can spend a smaller percentage of their terms worrying about reelection or mollifying the special-interest pressures emanating from the home district. But the extension of congressional terms can be accomplished only through a constitutional amendment, an idea received very coolly in Washington.

The sorry spectacle of a Congress unable to legislate has led some thinkers to advance truly radical proposals for reform. Retired Massachusetts congressman Michael Harrington has proposed "a distinctly American parliamentary setup," in which the President and the Cabinet would be selected by the Congress and serve concurrently with it. The Cabinet would take on many of the lesser responsibilities of Congress, which would then be free to engage in the kind of serious policy debate so rarely heard in its chambers. The executive and legislative branches would cooperate, of course, far more closely than they do today.

Whatever the merits of this system, however, it is certain to be ignored by a body incapable even of minor reform.

Calls for change have been lukewarm at best. Meeting early in December, the Democratic Caucus agreed to limit service on House subcommittees to five panels per member, a minute improvement, and to reduce the time-wasting number of roll-calls (a suggestion since accepted by Congress). There are no other proposals to win action.

With the next presidential and congressional elections less than two years away, the harsh realities of politics combined with the inertia already paralyzing Capitol Hill should prevent Americans from expecting too much from their beleaguered lawmakers. It would be a near-miracle if a sensible compromise emerges on national health legislation, one of the priorities in the 96th Congress. Action may be required to cope with the worsening energy crisis, but it could be just a rerun of the 1978 stalemate. The same may apply to possible anti-inflation legislation. The Senate ratification of the new arms agreement with the Soviets is a toss-up. The legislative logjam shows no sign of unclogging. Leaders will go on with uphill battles to corral majorities.

It looks like bad business as usual for the 96th Congress.

● ● ●

NO

Gary Orfield

CONGRESSIONAL POWER

POPULAR STEREOTYPES OF CONGRESS

Americans continually proclaim their pragmatic flexibility and realism. Yet they maintain the oldest set of stable political institutions in the world and repeatedly describe the operations of that structure in terms of seldom challenged myths. These myths include a view of Congress as a declining and hopelessly fragmented body trying with little success to cope with the expansive and even dangerous power of a stronger institution, the Presidency.

Even in early 1974, when, with the deepening of the Watergate crisis, respect for Presidential authority approached its modern low point Congress was seen in even more intensely unfavorable light. While the polls showed that only a fourth of the public approved of the job President Nixon was doing, they also showed that Congress had the respect and approval of only one American in five. Even Congress's impressive performance in the impeachment proceedings, which forced President Nixon's resignation, has produced little confidence that Congress can play a major positive role in the formation of national policy.

The assumptions about the sorry state of Congress have often been so pervasive that observers don't even bother to look at the evidence. This book will argue that the popular stereotype is fundamentally wrong. Congress is alive and well, at least in the field of domestic policy. If it is not progressive, it is usually reasonably representative and responsive. As public opinion changes, as Presidents define their constituency in different ways, and political circumstances gradually alter the membership of the House and Senate, Congress has been moving away from its traditional conservative or passive role in the development of national policy. This change became quite apparent with the beginning of the Nixon Administration. As the President moved sharply to the right on social policy, and the Supreme Court was largely neutralized by a series of four conservative appointments, Congress often remained the most progressive of the three branches in dealing with social policy issues.

The early 1970s did not see Congress become a seedbed for liberal activism. Although the legislative branch was now often more responsive to new social needs than the other principal institutions of government, there were still very broad and important areas of inaction and stalemate in domestic policy. This analysis will show that there is nothing in the institutional structure of Congress which renders the legislative branch either weak or conservative. In fact, Congress regularly exercises more power than it is credited with, and the ideological impact of its participation shifts from issue to issue and from political circumstance to political circumstance.

Our political system's lack of responsiveness to some of the very real social crises that preoccupy many intellectuals is not inherent in the Congressional process. Congressional reformers are simply wrong when they claim that institutional changes will produce "good" responses to the environmental problem, to inequitable taxation, irrational urban policies, and other major difficulties. The basic problem is more fundamental, and arises from the fact that the major progressive political force in this society, the activist liberal wing of the Democratic Party, is almost always a minority. Reformers spread the illusion that different procedures within Congress would produce answers to problems most Americans simply don't want to face. So long as Congress is a representative body, it is highly unlikely to produce decisive answers to controversial questions before public opinion accepts the necessity of action. . . .

THE CHANGING PRESIDENCY

The Presidency, political scientists have often said, is inherently progressive because the Presidential election system has a built-in liberal bias, while Congressional power grows out of an electoral structure that magnifies local concerns. A number of Presidential campaigns during the past several decades have been organized around competition for the big blocks of electoral votes in the large urbanized states. At the same time Congressional malapportionment over represented rural areas in the House, while the lightly populated nonindustrial states have always been greatly over-represented in the Senate.

Most political scientists have argued that the great importance of the big, closely divided states in Presidential elections has magnified the political influence of the urban minorities concentrated in these states. The political situation, analysts argued, made the President the natural spokesman for minority and urban needs. This very argument was used by some Congressional liberals in 1969 against adoption of a Constitutional amendment for direct election of the President.

Whatever the historical validity of these assertions, they no longer hold. In the 1964, 1968, and 1972 Presidential campaigns the GOP candidates wrote off the black vote and operated on the assumption that the real swing vote was in the suburbs. The Republican nominees saw the black vote, not as a swing vote, but as an integral locked-in element of the Democratic Party base. Turning their backs on the declining central-city electorate, they looked to the suburbs. In dramatic contrast to previous elections, the GOP adamantly refused to concede the South to the Democrats. By following a strategy that ignored the urban ghettos and put primary importance on the Southern and Border states, the Republicans were altering the Presidential political base from a source of liberal leverage to a collection of forces desiring to slow and reverse social changes already underway. . . .

THE DECLINE OF CONSERVATIVE POWER IN CONGRESS

While a new interpretation of the Presidential constituency was taking hold in the minds of many, something quite the opposite was beginning to become evident in Congress. As the 1970s began, the big cities enjoyed reasonable representation and growing seniority power within Congress. As political competition in the South spread and produced real challenges in former one-party districts, a growing proportion of the safe, stable, one-party districts that remained were located in the central cities, where Democratic voters frequently constitute overwhelming majorities. Given the continuing decline in central city population and the ten-year time lag before a new reapportionment, the relatively liberal central-city constituencies were destined to have increasing overrepresentation in the House as the 1970s advanced. . . .

The Senate was now seldom in the control of the old, rigidly conservative coalition of Southern Democrats and Republicans. On a number of issues it was now possible to form a moderate-liberal majority in support of social policy proposals.

THE UNCHANGING CRITICISM OF CONGRESS

Congress was changing, but perceptions of Congress remained largely fixed. Denunciations of Congressional ineptitude and legislative stalemate continued to proliferate. Inside and outside of Congress, critics said that only basic reforms could preserve Congress's intended role as a major force in American government. Even while they were sending their local incumbents back to Washington in great numbers, the American people expressed extremely low regard for Congress as an institution.

Characteristically, both the criticisms of Congress and the proposed cures are usually stated in institutional terms. We are told that the Congressional structure is inefficient or unresponsive, or that the rules screen out the competent and stifle innovation. Implicitly, however, the criticisms are political. When a critic says that Congress is not responsive, he obviously has in mind some set of national needs he believes Congress should respond to. Often these are the needs of an oppressed social group or of important decaying public institutions like the central cities and their school systems. The reform proposals often implicitly assume that procedural changes would release a suppressed progressive majority, likely to take a far more activist role in the provision of governmental services. This assumption may well be incorrect.

While the claim that certain major institutional features of Congress imposed a conservative bias on the legislative process has considerable historic validity, the recent picture is unclear. With a few notable exceptions, which run in both liberal and conservative directions, recent Congresses have rather accurately reflected the values and the confusion of the public in dealing with major issues of social change.

If the interpretation offered here is correct, liberals are unlikely to accomplish much by reforming Congressional procedures. The sobering reality is that the real obstacles are not so much on Capitol Hill as in the society as a whole. While tinkering with legislative arrangments may permit some minor improvements, basic social reforms probably require a political movement able to change public values.

Most of the time, we have the Congress we really want and the Congress we deserve. We send the same members back to Washington time after time. Congress is inherently neither liberal nor conservative. Its political tendencies change with the times, with political circumstances, with the delayed responses of the seniority system, and with tides of public opinion. In social policy battles of the early 1970s, Congress became relatively more progressive and activist than the Presidency.

RECENT AREAS OF CONFRONTATION

The interplay of Presidential and Congressional influences can be examined by closely looking at the development of policy in three broad areas—civil rights, education, and employment—during the period from the late Johnson Administration through the early portion of President Nixon's second term. These issues, analyzed in the central portion of this study, and others discussed in less detail thereafter, obviously cannot adequately represent the whole sweep of domestic social policy. Each, however, is a prominent and long standing political question on which there were relatively clear progressive and conservative positions. By looking at the development of several issues through a large number of legislative battles spanning several years, one obtains a more realistic portrait of the policy

process than by merely examining the legislative history of one or a few bills.

The civil rights section will underline the limits of Presidential authority and the power of the Congressional veto when the President tries to reverse reforms that are already part of established law. Though he invested considerable time and prestige and intensely pressured his Congressional supporters, the President met a series of costly defeats. Even though he drew on his leadership role to deepen and exploit racial polarization, the President encountered successive frustrations.

In education policy the President's main objectives were to reduce the federal support for education and to renounce most of the existing federal leverage on state and local school systems. Congress, on the other hand, pressed each year for higher funding and retention of the federal requirements in the Great Society legislation. It was Congress that prevailed—only modestly in the financial struggle, but much more clearly in the protection of the legislative framework.

While the civil rights and school policy battles often involved legislative vetoes of conservative White House initiatives, the development of a new jobs policy is best seen as an important Democratic Party effort to initiate a new domestic policy from a Congressional base, in the face of strong Presidential opposton. Study of this effort provides an opportunity to reflect on both the possibilities and the limitations of Congressional policy initiation during a period of executive hostility. . . .

THE NEED FOR REASSESSMENT OF CONGRESS

We must stop thinking in terms of

institutional stereotypes and unexamined assumptions. Both scholars and activists need to devote more attention to reassessing the contemporary reality and future possibilities of Congressional policy initiatives. They need to think less in terms of a handful of visible new bills, and more in terms of the whole array of Congressional influences that help shape policy in a given area. It is time for critics to rethink their wildly overoptimistic promises about Congressional reform, and to recognize that Congress often only reflects the indecision or contradictory desires of the local publics and the local political structures.

It is a delusion for liberals to think that there is a hidden majority for basic social reform somewhere inside Congress that could be liberated by a few institutional reforms. Activist liberals must begin with the realization that they have only a minority in Congress, particularly in the House. On some issues, in fact, a more democratic House might be an even less progressive House. If strong progressive programs are to prevail in Congress, their supporters must first prevail in elections.

CONGRESS AND SOCIAL POLICY: A SUMMARY

The United States has been passing through a period of massive social and economic change during the past decade. Congress has played an extremely important role in shaping the uneven governmental responses to those changes. Contrary to popular cliches, the nation has not entered a period of an imperial Presidency and a passive Congress, nor has deadlock totally paralyzed action in most areas of policy.

The past decade has brought profound changes in the position of blacks, women, and young people in the social and political system. The major civil rights laws were a powerful response to the central shame of American democracy, governmental enforcement of the racial caste system of the South. After decades of resistance, Congress not only passed these laws, but strengthened them and then protected them from a hostile President. Congressional action has been crucial to the women's movement's attack on concepts of female status ingrained in Western culture. Congressional action making eighteen-year-olds full citizens has had little visible immediate impact, but will surely make the political system more open and responsive to young people.

After Congress approved the vast expansion of the federal role in domestic programs in the 1960s, the determined efforts of a conservative President to reverse the trend tested the real dispositions of the Democratic Congress. The period found even the more conservative elements of the legislative branch operating more progressively than the President. This was very apparent, for example, in the massive Social Security boosts approved by the Ways and Means and the Senate Finance committees, and in the continual rejection of the President's meager education and health budgets by both Appropriations committees. In most cases Congress led the executive branch in responding to new ecological issues and in creating new tools for control of the economy.

The period of the late 1960s and early 1970s witnessed simultaneously the advance of sweeping claims of Presidential powers, and the decline of the real strength of the Presidency. During the period between the end of the Second World War and the late 1960s, Presidents enjoyed great latitude in the conduct of foreign policy and military affairs. This freedom of action, and the bipartisan Congressional support that sustained it, began to erode when rising opposition to the Vietnam War destroyed the Johnson Presidency. At first it affected the margins of international power, such as foreign military assistance, but by the early 1970s it had produced serious Congressional pressures to restrain the military apparatus and to subject Presidential action to legislative control. War powers legislation—passed over a Presidential veto—and some reductions in the defense and foreign aid budgets began to cut into the muscle of executive leadership; 1973 saw the extraordinary spectacle of Congress forcing the end of military action in Cambodia by cutting off funds, and Congress rejecting trade legislation central to the policy of detente with the U.S.S.R.

The Nixon period witnessed the resurgence of some long neglected legislative powers in domestic affairs, and the most striking Congressional rejection of a President's domestic program in decades. In the major Supreme Court nomination fights, Congress resumed an active role in the constitution of the highest Court, a power that had lain dormant for most of the twentieth century. When the early phases of the Watergate scandal indicated grave improprieties in the executive branch, Congress acted both through a massive investigation and through insistence on an independent special prosecutor to force revelation of the most serious corruption in American history. When the investigation came under Administration attack, very heavy Congressional pressure persuaded the President to retreat. Eventually he was forced to leave office.

The success of the legislators in resisting a sustained, intense White House fight against serious investigation of the scandals and in helping the press educate the public, and forcing the President to yield unprecedented personal records was a tribute to the vitality of Congress. The experience seemed certain to increase both Congressional power and Congressional vigilance for some time to come. Anyone who doubts the continuing reality of Congressional power need only read the transcripts of the extraordinary White House tapes that President Nixon was forced to release by pressure from the House Judiciary Committee. Amid all the plots and the bitter, candid criticisms of men and institutions, it is evident that President Nixon and his chief advisors retained a fear of Congressional power. While their discussions are full of plans to thwart the independence and manipulate the operations of various governmental institutions, the mass media, and the criminal justice system, there is a continual recognition of the limited power the White House can exercise over Congress.

In 1974 the House Judiciary Committee began the impeachment process for the second time in American history. The process had been virtually forgotten since Congress failed to impeach Andrew Johnson after the Civil War, but now it worked. Only when impeachment and conviction seemed certain did the President resign. The revival of Congress's ultimate weapon surely lends strength to the legislative branch, and diminishes the power and autonomy of future Presidents.

Presidential power rests to a substantial degree on the sense of respect and legitimacy accorded to the office of the

4. IS CONGRESS OBSOLETE?

President. One certain effect of the Watergate scandal and the President's resignation has been to weaken that respect for some time to come, thus increasing the relative power of Congress.

While the Watergate disaster dramatized Congress's investigatory power and resurrected the idea of impeachment, its drama often obscured more mundane facts about the period. In the long and often unpublicized domestic policy struggles of the period, Congress responded to intense and singleminded White House pressure without yielding its role.

The period of Presidential reaction on social policy under President Nixon showed that the close tie between Congress and various organized constituencies could have liberal as well as conservative consequences. Coming to office with the belief that he had a mandate to reverse many of the domestic innovations of the Great Society, the President encountered determined resistance from Congress. Congress responded by rejecting a higher portion of Nixon legislative proposals than those of any recent President, even though Nixon presented a relatively slim set of innovations. Only by stretching executive powers and spending his political authority in bitter confrontations with Congress over vetoes and impoundments was the President able to slow the momentum of those programs. Eventually, the price to be paid was strong Congressional attempts to cut back on the powers of the executive branch.

In arguing that Congress possesses a substantial capacity to initiate new national policies, and that those policies may well be more "progressive" or "responsive" than positions taken by a

President, this book certainly does not mean to support another false view of Congress. While Congress may be *relatively* more activist than a conservative President, it can hardly be described as a liberal institution. The major liberal force in American politics is the Northern and Western wing of the Democratic Party. Only when political circumstances give that wing of the party an operating majority in Congress (a rare circumstance) or predominant influence in the executive branch (a more common occurrence) does that institution become the primary focus for policy innovation.

During the Nixon Administration Congress succeeded in putting a few major new social issues on the national agenda, and in protecting much of the Great Society framework. On many other issues, however, its record was far more mixed. Design of new housing policies, for example, was long stalled by a stalemate within Congress, as well as by one between Congress and the White House. Congress delegated vast powers over the economy to the executive branch without making basic policy decisions. Congress preserved existing civil rights laws, aimed primarily at the classic Southern forms of discrimination, but proved incapable of developing policies to cope with the intensifying racial separation of the urban North. There were few significant new ideas in education policy in the legislation of the early 1970s, and the intense national discussion of health care needs yielded little on Capitol Hill. Efforts to reform the tax structure or to alter the basic assumptions of welfare policy were largely barren. The list goes on and on.

Judged against the national goals of activist liberal groups, or even against the Democratic Party platform, the record of

Congress was fundamentally inadequate. Congress has not responded forcefully to a number of evident social needs. The obstacle has been sometimes the President, and sometimes Congress itself.

The important thing to remember is that the failings criticized by activists are usually not failings produced by the structure or procedures of Congress, but by the vision of its members. The shortcomings—and many of the achievements—result from reasonably effective Congressional representation of widely held and often contradictory values of the public and of the members' active and important constituents. The unwillingness to move forward in some significant areas of social policy reflects far less the inadequacies of Congress as an organization than the failure of middle-class Americans to recognize that any social crisis exists. The basic reason why neither Congress nor the President is truly liberal is that liberalism normally represents a minority position in the United States—a fact often obscured by the assumption that the Democratic Party is a liberal party, rather than an exceedingly broad coalition.

Much of the national movement for extensive Congressional reform is based on false assumptions. Reform and rationalization of committee jurisdiction, chairmen's powers, the budget process, Congressional staff capacity, etc., may produce a more efficient legislative body, more equitable to individual members, and perhaps better able to compete with the executive branch. These are worthwhile goals, but they are not likely to transform the substance of Congressional decisions. Reformers who promise an institutional answer to a political question are likely to be disappointed. There are no shortcuts. Probably the only way to build a new Congress is to undertake the hard political work necessary to send new men and women to Capitol Hill.

Although Congress is neither the liberal institution some would wish, nor the conservative institution many believe it to be, it is a powerful force in the construction of national policy. While the political circumstances of depression, wars and international crises, and a burgeoning executive branch have often served to magnify the Presidency, the remarkable fact is that Congress has preserved the Constitutional model of fragmented power through an era of serious parliamentary decline in most Western nations. If anything, the political scandals of the early 1970s have only reinforced this model, increasing public support for the assertion of Congressional authority....

In a society experiencing rapid social and political change, the major democratic institutions reflect shifting constituencies and evolving political alliances. At the present time these forces tend to be moving Congress away from its very conservative past, and the Presidency away from the historical circumstances that once made the White House the powerful spokesman for urban minorities. The very heavy dependence of GOP Presidential candidates on Southern support and the growing power in the House of liberal Democrats from safe one-party urban seats are two signs of these changes. Nothing suggests, however, that there is anything permanent or historically inevitable about these changes. The time has come for students of American politics to recognize the limits of institutional generalizations based on the political circumstances of the recent past.

The abuses of Presidential power

4. IS CONGRESS OBSOLETE?

revealed by the Watergate scandals have tended to replace the popular image of the beneficience of Presidential power with a popular fear of the abuse of executive authority. The long established tendency of progressives to look to the White House for responsive leadership is being replaced by a judgment that the President is excessively powerful, and by a tendency to look to Congress for salvation. Both images assume that the President possesses vast, even excessive powers. While this is surely true in the fields of foreign policy, military affairs, and national security, it is not true in the development of the nation's social policy. Thus, for example, institutional changes intended to reduce the power of a corrupt executive branch may have the consequence of constricting the already limited power of a future liberal President to initiate and implement major social reforms.

It has been a disservice—and one currently conducive to a crushing disillusionment with politics—for academics to spread the belief that Presidential power is better than Congressional power. (What they actually meant was that during the period between the early 1930s and the mid-1960s, the Presidency was usually controlled by the Democratic Party, and that the President tended to respond to a more liberal constituency than that of the Congressional leadership.) It would, of course, be equally misleading to assume that Congressional power is better, more progressive, or less corrupt.

It is vital to realize that the making of national domestic policy takes place in a context of genuinely divided power, and that the Congress as well as the President possesses both the ability to initiate and the power to veto major policy changes. The system works well when there is a clear consensus in the country, or clear control of both branches by the dominant wing of either party. Usually these conditions are not present and the system is biased either toward compromise and incremental change, or toward confrontation and inaction. The Nixon period clearly shows that the modern Presidency can be quite as efficient an engine of negative social policy as was Congress during certain earlier progressive Administrations.

It is only fair to recognize that much of the criticism that has been aimed at Congress has been misdirected. It is really criticism of the inefficiencies and delays built into the American Constitutional system, and of the nebulous and often contradictory ideological bases of the alliances that constitute the national political parties. Failure to correctly identify these underlying causes leads one to misjudge the solutions.

The people of the United States generally have the kind of legislative body they want and deserve. It is a Congress that has the power to take decisive action, but most of whose members rarely believe the public demands such change. It is an evolving institution and an increasingly representative one. It has great power but rarely selects leaders who use that power with energy, skill, and imagination. With a few significant exceptions, the altering of its internal rules will not change its decisions much. Congress is likely to be a moderately progressive institution in the next years. If it is to be much more than that—or less—its membership must be significantly changed.

POSTSCRIPT

IS CONGRESS OBSOLETE?

The consideration of congressional efficiency and representativeness is rarely very far removed from a partisan perspective as to the public policies which Congress should adopt. Thus Szulc's criticism of congressional weakness is not simply a reflection of legislative organization but also an explanation of congressional vulnerability to special interests, particularly those that do not represent larger public concerns. Orfield contends that Congress is changing and can continue to change, even in the absence of substantial procedural or structural reform. He maintains that the national legislature is less conservative than it once was, but less liberal than many reformers wish it might be—because the American people by and large do not wish it.

It is clear that, even after the scandals of the Nixon presidency, most Americans look to the President and not to Congress for leadership and policy direction. This is also true of students of American politics. Books on Congress are far fewer than those on the presidency. Among the most stimulating and insightful recent books on Congress are David Mayhew, CONGRESS: THE ELECTORAL CONNECTION (Yale, 1974), which assumes that the principal motive of the member of Congress is reelection, and Eric Redman, THE DANCE OF LEGISLATION (Simon and Schuster, 1973), which, in focusing upon a single Senate bill (the National Health Service Act of 1970), gives a vivid and particularized portrait of the legislative process. Mark Green, WHO RUNS CONGRESS? (Bantam / Grossman, revised 1975), is a muckraking survey that dwells upon what's wrong, and depressingly concludes that a great deal is. For a student seeking up-to-date information on Congress and legislative issues, *Congressional Quarterly Weekly Report* and the annual *Congressional Quarterly Almanac* are sources of reliable information.

Nearly all analyses of Congress emphasize the way in which Congress works. Szulc believes that we must reform—reduce the volume of legislation, simplify the committee system, curb the lobbyists, and strengthen party alignments—but we are most unlikely to do so. Orfield asserts that change is not only possible, but constantly takes place. In fact we generally get the kind of Congress we deserve. Critics and defenders might agree that the caliber of Congress depends in large part on the concern of the electorate. We should then consider how to motivate the American people to desire and demand a better Congress.

ISSUE 5

IS THE PRESIDENT TOO POWERFUL?

YES: Michael Novak, from CHOOSING OUR KING (New York, 1974)
NO: Theodore Sorensen, from WATCHMEN IN THE NIGHT (Cambridge, Massachusetts, 1975)

ISSUE SUMMARY

YES: Writer Novak proposes that the presidency be broken down into two separate functions in order to lessen the impact of a single person on our society.
NO: Author Sorensen argues that there are great dangers in a presidency without the power to respond to fast-changing events, and to command the allegience of the people.

"Energy in the executive," said Alexander Hamilton in 1787, "is a leading character in the definition of good government." Hamilton dreamed of a vast American "empire" of manufacturing and commerce. An energetic executive was to be the lynchpin of the empire. Defense against foreign and domestic enemies would require "decision, activity, secrecy, and dispatch," which only a single powerful executive could provide. The President was to be "the bulwark of national security."

Nearly two centuries later, Hamilton's vision seems to have acquired a life of its own, growing into something which Hamilton himself could not have dreamed of. As chief executive and commander-in-chief, the President today commands six million employees and carries a sword which would surely startle a Caesar or a Bonaparte. He has also been called our chief legislator, chief of state, chief diplomat, chief of party, and manager of our prosperity. But even this litany does not take the full measure of his powers. Hamilton was deeply suspicious of popular government, but it has turned out to be the greatest spring of all for "energy in the executive." Today's President is more than just a manager; he has become an embodiment of popular sovereignty, a "steward of the people," as President Theodore Roosevelt called himself—or, in the words of a more recent admirer of the office, a "republican king."

After Vietnam and Watergate some Americans became less sanguine about the powers of the presidency. Hamilton considered "decision, activity, secrecy, and dispatch" to be the unique virtues of the executive, but some observers now wondered whether "decision" could not at times resemble arrogance, "dispatch" recklessness, and "secrecy" furtiveness. Hamilton's invocation of "national security" also sounded hollow to those who remembered how far that claim was stretched during the Johnson and Nixon administrations—far enough to cover everything from unilateral warmaking to domestic spying and burglary.

Some of the more recent critics of the executive branch had once been promoters of the activist presidency. From the early days of the New Deal to the middle of the 1960s American liberals tended to regard the President as the people's tribune, and the Congress as a patchwork of special interests. But as President Johnson led the nation deeper into Vietnam, many of these same liberals began to worry about "the arrogance of power" in the White House. And by the time of the Watergate revelations it was Congress, not the presidency, which seemed to them the authentic voice of the American people. The President, formerly the people's tribune, was now an ominous "imperial" figure.

Gerald Ford and Jimmy Carter did their best to divest the presidency of its kingly aura—Ford by his relaxed and easy-going manner, Carter by his "populist" touches, which included everything from participating in radio call-in shows to carrying his own luggage. These were symbolic changes, but they may have reflected an underlying change in the powers and pretensions of the modern presidency. By 1980 there were questions about whether Carter had overcorrected. Had the presidency now become too weak? The national humiliation over the American hostages in Iran sharpened the issue and helped bring Ronald Reagan into office on the promise to restore leadership and decisiveness to the White House.

In the following selections Theodore Sorensen, a former top aide to President Kennedy, warns against allowing the pendulum to swing too far away from Presidential power, while political analyst Michael Novak states the case for limiting the President's power.

YES
Michael Novak

CHOOSING OUR KING

Every four years, Americans elect a king—but not only a king, also a high priest and a prophet. It does not matter that we are a practical and sophisticated people, no longer (we think) influenced by symbols, myths, or rituals. To what our president represents, we react with passion.

The president of the United States is no mere manager of an insurance firm. The way he lives affects our image of ourselves. His style and his tastes weigh upon our spirits. Eisenhower encouraged a "silent" generation, Kennedy an "activist" decade, Nixon at first made some feel solid and appreciative and others, even in the beginning, heavy and ashamed. Intimate and personal feelings are affected by our experience of various presidents.

The symbolic power of the president is real. Ten million police officers, heads of boards of education, lawyers, judges, realtors, union leaders, and local officials calibrate their daily decisions according to the support or the resistance they expect from the White House. What will the Justice Department do, or fail to do? The president is able to make his own views felt in every town and village of the nation, by compulsion and enforcement, by imitation and antipathy. On the local level, if ultimately one expects support far up the line, great risks can be taken. If one is left to one's own resources merely, one must confront the local balance of powers.

Some speak of the "moral leadership" of the presidency as though what we need is a moral man out in front, like a cavalry officer lowering his saber. Yet moral leadership in the presidency is not something habitually "out in front" of us, but something that infiltrates our imaginations and our hearts. The president, whoever he is, affects our *internal* images of authority, legitimacy, leadership, concern. By his actions, he establishes a limit to national realism. What he *is* drives us away from America and makes us feel like exiles—or attracts our cooperation. Cumulatively, the presidents under whom we happen to live influence our innermost attitudes.

For this reason, the election of a president is an almost religious task; it intimately affects the life of the spirit, our identity. Who the man is determines in real measure who we are. Thus, the swirling, otherwise inexplicable passions of many presidential elections. Not only power or money are at stake, important as these are, but our own inner life. The presence of one man rather than another, the ascendance of Nixon (say) rather than the ascendance of McGovern, has great power to depress or to elate, to liberate energies or to shrink them.

Eugene McCarthy said we must "depersonalize" the presidency, "demystify" the office. Without separating kingship from administration, that can scarcely be accomplished. Today the symbolic role inheres in the office. It is enhanced by the nation's bigness, diversity, and tightening networks of power.

Dostoevsky once wrote that an invisible filament of humble charity covers the entire earth. An act at any one point on the earth, he imagined, reverberates until it touches every other person. In our day, on television, a single act simultaneously inhabits the fantasy of millions of humans everywhere, *becomes* them, obliges them to accept or to reject, enters immediately into the structures of their psyche. We do not know what the truth is, but if on television the president says our ships were attacked in the Gulf of Tonkin, then that attack (even if it did not occur) occupies our attention and demands that we refute it or accept it or dismiss it. Whatever we do, there stands the president's assertion, solid until painstakingly disproved. This power over our attention, over our power to structure issues, is so enormous that it dwarfs all others. . . .

Hands are stretched toward him over wire fences at airports like hands extended toward medieval sovereigns or ancient prophets. One wonders what mystic participation our presidents convey, what witness from what other world, what form of cure or heightened life. The president arouses waves of "power," "being," "superior reality," as if where he is is history. It is true that the president's hand is on the button of destruction. Life and death are in his hands; honor and dishonor too. What he does affects the daily life of each of us in ways witch doctors could scarcely even dream. His office is, in quite modern and sophisticated form, a religion in a secular state. It evokes responses familiar in all the ancient religions of the world. It fills a perennial vacuum at the heart of human expectations. . . . It would be much easier for the president if he were a prime minister, called simply to manage the affairs of government in as practical and unadorned a way as possible. Yet, in American politics what critics refer to as "the cult of personality" arises. It arises not because it is willed either by the citizenry or by the presidents themselves, but because of the nature and the limits of the human imagination.

Causes, institutions, and administrative processes must be personified before humans can passionately engage them. Humans are flesh and blood, and they understand best what is flesh and blood. Thus, Martin Luther King made black civil rights a cause that it has ceased to be since his death. Thus, Eugene McCarthy in 1968 observed that antiwar sentiment in the United States needed to be personified in order to be a political force, and he agreed to step forward as the person. McCarthy's deed was a great one and it catalyzed a great new force in American politics, the new politics of the "new class." Yet, great as that force is in American life, it is not stronger than its ability to personify itself in a leader able to

5. IS THE PRESIDENT TOO POWERFUL?

command the dedication of a wide range of people. Leaderless, it is ineffective . . . .

Thus, talk about "doing away with the cult of personality" or "demythologizing the presidency" must be taken as gestures toward an unrealistic rationalism. The president dominates not only the news, but also the language of policy, the shape and pace of legislation, and the spirit of appointments to the federal courts. His idiosyncrasies, ambitions, and failures dominate more conversations than those of any other citizen—as truly if he is unpopular as if he is popular. Let us be as skeptical as may be, we are living in a symbolic world over which the president has unparalleled power. To cease believing in his power will not make it go away. To say we must not vest our hopes or fears in him runs counter to the plain fact that he has nuclear power at his fingertips, more police power than any sovereign in history, more power to dominate the organs of public opinion than any other human, more power in defining who are the nation's enemies, more power over the military and the making (if not the declaring) of war than any citizen or group of citizens.

Thus, the president is rather more like a shaman than we might wish. Our lives *do* depend on him. A person with power over life and death is raised above a merely pragmatic level. He is surrounded, as it were, with a nimbus of magic. He necessarily lives on a level that must seem to him "above" that of other humans. The fact that he *is* human gives a sort of reassurance about which we endlessly read—that he eats breakfast food, prefers mysteries, listens to Bach or Lawrence Welk. But our survival is linked to his deeds. Our lives participate in his. His nerves, his wisdom, his panic, his steadi-

ness make us vulnerable. Even if we have contempt for him, he has power over the shape and direction of our lives. If he decides that the great moral conflict of our time is permissiveness or the need for individual selfishness, not only must those who disagree fight against the ordinary tides of evil, they must also fight against the respectability the president gives their opponents. If he symbolizes an America we despise, he divides our own hearts against themselves.

The president also affects the cultural tone of the entire nation. It makes a difference if he prefers Bach to Welk or John Wayne to Dustin Hoffman or enjoys the company of Pablo Casals rather than Bob Hope and Billy Graham. Such choices on his part send out a signal either that discrimination is worth an effort, or else that it is well to glory in what happens to be popular.

Thus, the president enters into the innermost symbols by which we identify ourselves. We do not think about him all the time; on many days we give him not a thought. It is the property of basic symbolic forms to influence us even when we are not conscious of them. When the president acts as president, he acts in our name. He is us. If he goes by a way we do not approve, he uses us against ourselves. This alone is a remarkable power. . . .

The presidency has in recent decades acquired symbolic power far beyond that of Congress. Television, above all, places at his disposal a highly personal medium. It magnifie[s] individuals, picking them out from crowds, lifting out a single face for intense and gripping presentation. Television cannot do equal justice to the Congress. Humans participate easily in the drama of persons; we have only a pale comprehension of social forces and institutional processes. To this fundamental human imbalance, television adds the harsh individualism of the camera.

The camera is metaphysically biased. It cannot reveal everything about human life. It selects only those features that suit its nature: personal drama rather than abstract, underlying causes; facial surfaces rather than movements of the spirit and the mind. It is a powerful instrument, often unsparing and ruthless in its revelations, suggestive, quick to capture certain quicksilver movements of emotion behind the texture of a face or the radiance of an eye. But it is not a good instrument for rendering those kinds of complexity that require many words.

Television fixes on the president and makes him the main symbolic representative of the government. Symbolically, it dwarfs the Congress and the courts. There may be a balance of powers in the government; but no such balance exists on television.

Thus, television places in the president's hands enormous metaphysical powers not provided for in the Constitution—powers over reality, powers over appearances, powers over perception, powers over the imaginative matrix within which issues are presented. The Constitution did not intend for the president to have powers of speech and presence beyond that of other citizens. It envisaged that he would argue as a man among men. Now television takes his face, as it takes no other face in politics, into every living room. Not merely his *words*—in a speech barely audible to a distant audience or on the cold printed page—but his *presence* dominates the attention of citizens who sit in silence and only listen.

For nine months after June, 1972, the vast majority of newsmen assigned to

Washington merely reported what the White House told them regarding Watergate, with little further inquiry. One reason they were comfortable in doing so is that television lets the president establish the underlying sense of reality within which all citizens live and move. The medium is insidious. It is a holistic medium, a purveyor of "wholes." It sets "facts" in "contexts." It provides images which block necessary insights and prompt misleading ones. It deflects attention. It sets up appearances as persuasive as reality itself. Television is not a good instrument for complicated, remote investigative reporting. It requires the "big story." It lacks the patience available to a daily newspaper, and it cannot accommodate the mass of tiny details by which a lengthy investigation proceeds. Most profoundly of all, it silently suggests what is the "reasonable," "calm," "moderate" attitude to assume. Television is a *total* guide. That is why watching it is effortless.

If we are to reform the presidency, the heart of the matter is the president's power over reality, his symbolic power. The social reality of the United States cannot be left to definition by one man alone. Whoever names a problem gains power over it; to set the terms of debate is to narrow possible resolutions. There are at least four reforms that might be taken, by Constitutional amendment if necessary, in order to restore a balance of powers in symbolic realities.

First, Congress, and in particular the opposition party in the Congress, must have a single spokesman who can personify the Congress of the United States, just as the president personifies the executive branch. . . . He (or she) need not be the *leader* of the opposition, although obviously the public prominence he or she would gain would yield considerable power. He or she need not supplant the majority leaders of the Senate or the House, for example. It would not necessarily follow, either, that the Opposition Spokesman would be the next presidential nominee of his party. He might be selected, indeed, precisely because he could not or would not be the nominee. His utterances would then be uniquely free of the taint of personal ambition. . . .

Second, the range of executive power has such enormous sweep that the president should be obliged on a biweekly basis to come before leaders of the opposition for a public, hour-long accounting of his policies. These conferences would be in addition to press conferences. Their purpose would be to allow opposition leaders to bring questions of fact, goals, priorities, and procedures into public view. Without such power, how will the Congress and the people learn in what entanglements the 2,500,000 employees of the executive branch are involving them? Agents of the executive branch have often implicated the United States in unexamined military and commercial practices. Executive policies, out of public view, mired the nation in Vietnam long before the people knew how deeply. Executive impenetrability encased President Nixon in the scandals of his election campaign more foolishly and for a longer time than the public should have endured.

The executive branch does not come *under* the Congress. But it is accountable to the people. As representatives of the people, the leaders of the opposition party in Congress would function as public interrogators of the president. In such a forum, the separation of powers would not be impugned. The obligatory question periods would not be "hearings." They would not be official functions of the Congress, *qua* Congress. They would be modeled on press conferences, except that elected officials of the opposition rather than newsmen would raise the questions. The site could be alternated between the White House and the Senate caucus room. Congressmen would here be functioning as surrogates of the people's right to facts and information. The president might bring with him various cabinet officers, to help him with precise replies. It would not be permissible for him to absent himself. The president is at present accountable to the people almost solely on election day. He would now become so on a regular basis, in respect to truthfulness and fact, under questioning, at such biweekly conferences. . . .

Third, the president's cabinet should always, perhaps by force of law, include a proportion of members of the opposition party. A paramount need of the president is a unified executive branch. But a second, indispensable need is for counselors close at hand who have a political base outside his own party. Better that he should know in his own councils the questions troubling the opposition than face them only *ex post facto* and across Capitol Hill. Telling the truth to the president is difficult for persons around him, even in the best of times. In the worst of times, an institutional device for providing the president with a built-in opposition may well be his salvation, as it might have been at several junctures in the last three administrations.

Fourth, we must begin to think of a step we have for two centuries avoided—the separation of the presidency into two functions: the head of state and the chief executive. I realize that this suggestion is not immediately practical; it is too radical, too shocking to our tradition. But thinking about it illuminates our present dilemma. And perhaps one day it will seem obvious and practical. For our present arrangement flies in the face of human nature. Human beings are symbolic animals. We are not "rational" in the sense that we respond or should respond, solely to pragmatic calculation.

A president may hold all the powers and responsibilities for foreign affairs and domestic management now in his possession, while being stripped of his role as personifier of the national identity, and be greatly liberated, not impeded, in his performance of his daily duties. It is true that he would lose some of the magic and mysticism surrounding his present office. It is true that, living outside the White House and working in closer proximity to the working offices of the Senate and the House, he would not be held in quite the awe his present eminence now affords him. But his actual administrative authority would remain clear and untrammeled; his access to radio, television, and the press would be uninhibited; his capacity to conduct foreign affairs—even his authority over nuclear weapons—would remain intact.

There would be one change in the presidency, and one only; but it would be a substantive one. No longer would the president be the personification of the nation and no longer could he derive from that personification a cloak for his administrative failings, a moral stature to which his deeds did not entitle him. His stewardship of government, naked and undisguised, would be easier to measure. His pretenses would necessarily be fewer.

Moral leadership would still be open to him. For on him would still fall the task of defining what in each season is significant for the nation's attention, and what commands its capacity for action. He would define the goals, priorities, and practices of political administration. He would take to the people the courses of action he felt they should embrace. He would wrestle with the Congress even as he does now.

He would lose, it is true, that power to tame men and to awe them by the honors he can bestow; for he would no longer bestow such honors. But he would not lose his capacity to telephone private persons for advice or to invite them to his offices or to be photographed with them—so that some sense of central importance and proximity to power might be shared with them.

A chief of state, meanwhile, would be elected at the beginning of each decade. By his prior career and his personality he would furnish to that decade part of its symbolic character. He would be charged with reinforcing ceremonially all those qualities among citizens that make a nation civilized, accomplished, and creative. He would be the organizer of scientific academies and prizes, of artistic performances and certificates of honor, of such studies and commissions—on violence or urban needs or pornography or education—as national perplexities might make appropriate. A sizable budget would be available to him for these activities. Although he had no powers of military command, the chief of state would be the Ceremonial Marshal of the Armed Forces, charged with review of their fitness and their readiness. He would preside at launchings and reentries of ventures into outer space and other scientific-technical initiatives. His intellectual creativity and personal enthusiasms would become a major source of public dialogue about national priorities.

Chief of state and president would compete in the public mind as symbols of prestige, as establishers of trends, and as directors of opinion. A chief of state of one political party and a president of the other might, quite subtly, wage war for the support of public opinion, not so much over individual policies (over which the chief of state would have no jurisdiction) but rather over the "tone" and "style" and "direction" of the government. Each would no doubt find it to his advantage not openly to bait the other for each would need the other's support, a divided public not being of assistance to either. The longer term of office of the chief of state would yield him some independence from the president; the actual Constitutional powers of the presidency would yield the president more than sufficient independence of the chief of state. Yet for symbolic reasons it would be to the interests of both to work in significant harmony. By conferring honors, by speeches, by establishing official commissions, the chief of state could strengthen —or weaken—the authority of the president. By opposing in the Congress the budget requests (beyond a fixed base) the chief of state would annually present to pay for his cultural activities, the president would have a weapon in reply.

Suppose, for example, that from 1960 to 1970, Averell Harriman or Adlai Stevenson or Dwight D. Eisenhower or Margaret Mead or Loren Eisely or Kingman Brewster or John D. Rockefeller III had been chief of state. In electing a chief of state, the people would be electing a person to represent them to the world and to preside over their cultural life. The election could be held after a national primary. The two candidates who finished highest in the primary would then oppose one another in the general election, such election being held in the odd-numbered year before a new decade opens (an anniversary year of the Constitutional convention of 1789).

The main point of this proposal is not to suggest that the roles of chief of state and head of government can in fact be separated with maximum practical gain both for the presidency and for the nation. The main point is to emphasize the unforeseen aggrandizement of the office of the president, when television and the course of world affairs exalted his symbolic power without providing any safeguards for the people's liberty and free perception of reality. If this proposal does not provide a way to restrain the president's swollen symbolic power, while keeping intact an energetic executive power, some other proposal will have to be better designed to meet the same two purposes.

The path of dictatorship lies through symbolic power—through propaganda. If once a president gains monistic power over the nation's symbols, his ability to override and circumvent and dominate the Congress seems now quite evident. If a president is restrained by symbolic pluralism, the danger of dictatorship is largely overcome. For a president not supported by the citizenry can scarcely intimidate the Congress, the courts, and other centers of opposition.

Power flows from the energy of symbols. A wall of separation to block the president's power over the nation's symbols is the most important self-defense we must . . . now erect.

●　●　●

NO

Theodore Sorensen

WATCHMEN IN THE NIGHT

The weak Nixon Presidency, masquerading as a strong and powerful Presidency, obscured the fact that this country today requires strong presidential leadership. Not unaccountable leadership, not a monopoly on leadership, but strong leadership nevertheless. Our only nationally elected executive most possess the flexibility and strength necessary to provide this country with responsible direction. We have survived caretaker Presidents in the past, but the price of those deceptively quiet periods in our history has always had to be paid later.

It is not altogether bad and certainly not coincidental that the flow of power to the Presidency has accelerated at times of major international crisis. Within his lawful authority, the Executive—and only the Executive—can move with the speed, energy and flexibility such crises usually require. Now the problems we face are global, affecting all peoples: the critical shortages of food, fertilizer, fuel, and certain other basic commodities; the twin failures of arms control and population control; the spread of world-wide inflation and the spectre of world-wide depression. Within the last two years the leaders of virtually every major democracy on earth found themselves replaced or in political trouble because of their inability to cope effectively with these and other problems. I would not go as far as Senator J. William Fulbright (of all people) went in the 1961 Stevens Memorial Lecture at Cornell, when he argued:

> that the price of democratic survival in a world of aggressive totalitarianism is to give up some of the democratic luxuries of the past . . . (through) the conferral of greatly increased authority on the President.

But the present critical hour of mounting crises and leadership vacuum is a most unlikely time to seek a passive or powerless President in the most powerful nation on earth.

Nor was it coincidental that the other quantum leap in permanent

5. IS THE PRESIDENT TOO POWERFUL?

presidential power was spurred by the Great Depression. A single point of responsiblity, speaking for the whole people, representing in egalitarian fashion the interests of the powerless as well as the powerful, was indispensable in the 1930s to pull this country through spiritually as well as economically.

Now our economic crisis again requires someone willing to make tough, unpleasant, and unprecedented decisions. Solutions to the problems of unemployment and laggard economic growth were never easy. But they were child's play in comparison with the search for politically acceptable and effective answers to our current problems—inflation in the midst of recession, quadrupled energy prices, a series of shortages—answers that are also consistent with our democratic framework, our global responsibilities, and our simultaneous need to reduce poverty and racial discrimination.

The President may in fact have *too little* power today to tackle fast-changing economic problems effectively. He cannot adjust taxes or spending without long congressional debate and approval, and by then it is often too late to apply a slow-acting fiscal stimulus or brake. He cannot openly control the Federal Reserve Board's policies on money and credit. He cannot veto excessive items in an appropriations bill or (as of this writing, with some cases still pending) impound the funds authorized thereunder. His powers over exports, imports, stockpiles, prices, wages, housing, debt, and government employment are all strictly limited by Congress and by the willingness of the bureaucracy to accept and implement his politices. He has few facilities for effective, long-range economic planning. He has no power to put into one enforceable package a "social contract" on taxes,

wages, prices, interest rates, and spending that could enlist the support of all elements of the economy—as distinguished from merely holding an economic summit meeting.

A dozen years ago President Kennedy pointed out that he and Prime Minister Macmillan both sought the fiscal stimulus of a tax cut at about the same time. Macmillan's was enacted in six weeks. Kennedy's was still pending months later at his death.

Even the.New York Times, recently in the forefront of those favoring a dispersal of White House powers, advised President Ford, with regard to inflation:

> Successful prosecution of the job will require vigorous Presidential command of his own department and agency heads (who too often behave like interest-group representatives and spokesmen, rather than as servants of all the people).

Unfortunately only editorial writers can enjoy the luxury of calling for more "vigorous Presidential command" of the executive branch one day and a more rapid dispersal of presidential power the next. There is no doubt that any increase in presidential discretion to meet the increased complexity and pace of our economic problems would involve an increased risk. There is always risk in giving any official any power. But there is also risk in denying ourselves the machinery to master our economic problems.

By definition, inclination, and long training, Congress cannot provide executive leadership. An issue such as the 1973 Middle East oil embargo produced separate legislative hearings in 40 separate committees, several inconsistent "emergency" bills to cope with the embargo—some not enacted until months after the embargo was ended—frequent statements of goals that had no prospect of fulfillment, and little in the way of meaningful congressional policy initiatives or in-depth research. Even while loudly protesting the practice of impoundment in late 1972, both houses passed bills leaving it to the President to decide which programs beyond his arbitrary budget ceiling would be cut.

While the role of Congress should be strengthened to restore constitutional balance, that cannot be accomplished by weakening the Executive. Pennsylvania Avenue, it has been rightly said, is not a seesaw.

Nixon's abuse of power to grant clemency, or to hire and fire employees, or to set milk support prices—to cite only three minor examples from the Watergate annals—does not mean that those powers could be better exercised by Congress. When the legislative branch tried to run the executive branch after the Andrew Johnson-Ulysses Grant era, it was not a period of greatness in Washington.

Those liberals, soured by Vietnam and Nixon, who desire a transfer of authority from the Presidency to Congress, appear to be acting on the basis of one or more assumptions—that most members of Congress are consistently less "hawkish" than the President on matters of war and peace, or less subject to the influence of the military-industrial complex, or more liberal on civil rights and civil liberties, or less responsive to the pressures of special-interest elites and short-term politics, or more ethical, open, nonpartisan, credible, and pure in deed and motivation. The overall record does not support a single one of those assumptions.

Nor can a collective legislative body, any more than a weak and passive President, convey the sense of dedication needed to redirect our energies and restore our sense of discipline and worth, and thus end our national crisis of the spirit, as Franklin Roosevelt did in 1933.

The single largest difficulty with curbing executive authority is that the power to do great harm is also the power to do great good.

● To have denied, as some would deny, any "implied constitutional authority" in the Presidency might have blocked some of Nixon's wiretaps; but such an approach would also have blocked Kennedy's first Executive Order in which, without express statutory authority, he expanded the surplus food distribution program for the poor, using funds from Customs reserves.

● To have eliminated, as some would eliminate, all secrecy in presidential foreign affairs operations unrelated to troop movements and intelligence sources might have prevented not only Nixon's bombing of Cambodia, but also his opening of relations with China.

● To have required, as some would require, advance congressional approval of any Executive Order which resembled legislative rule-making might have stopped both the Huston covert intelligence program and certain LBJ civil rights directives on housing and employment.

● Permitting the effectuation of no international agreements or understandings other than those submitted to the Senate, as recently proposed, might have blocked not only dubious deals with South Vietnam, but also the resolution of the Cuban missile crisis.

● A recently suggested constitutional or statutory amendment might have made possible a new presidential election

5. IS THE PRESIDENT TOO POWERFUL?

when a firestorm of protest greeted Nixon's firing of Archibald Cox; but, under such an amendment, Truman might have lost his post for firing Douglas MacArthur.

● Had there been no White House Special Projects Fund providing every President since 1956 with $1.5 million for contingencies (and Congress has recently considered its abolition), Nixon would have had to look elsewhere to finance some of the plumbers' activities, but Kennedy would have been unable to establish in the face of an unconcerned Congress an emergency guidance counselor program to ease youth unemployment in the summer of 1962.

We cannot endlessly add to the powers of the Presidency with a Lincoln in mind without increasing a Nixon's opportunity to do harm. But we cannot unduly weaken the office with a Nixon in mind without hampering a law-abiding President's power to do good.

PROPOSED STRUCTURAL CHANGES

With the aforementioned parallels in mind, I see no merit in the various structural and institutional changes in presidential power arrangements proposed or revived as suggested statutes or constitutional amendments in the wake of the Nixon Presidency. Most are Maginot lines designed to fight the last "war," the last crisis to confront the country, Watergate, without any thought as to their effect on the next one. These proposals will be only briefly mentioned here.

Some are merely gimmicks substituting ill-considered action for thought, thrown onto the floor in response to the cry of "do something." Those voiced to me, not all seriously, range from the perennial suggestion of a national ombudsman with no power base in the system, to an unworkably rigid apparatus for greater Cabinet participation, to novelties such as prohibiting public relations men in political campaigns or having the President periodically travel about listening in disguise like the ancient caliphs of Baghdad. . . .

Such thoughtful observers as Michael Novak would have us imitate those countries ·which separate the head of state from the head of government, enabling our President as latter to avoid both the burden and the glory that come with ceremonial duties. I want to see less pomp and grandeur surrounding our Presidents. But neither our traditions, our politics, nor our concepts of efficiency neatly divide the head of state and head of government functions. The President would still need to dine with foreign leaders. He would still want to meet the 4-H Club chairmen whose parents are voters. He would still be revered for his power, even if a head of state lived in the White House and gave out the medals. And in the light of justifiable concern over every President's isolation, we should not now cut back on the speech-making, delegation-greeting, and dam-dedicating that may keep him at least in some slight contact with the citizenry. It is a mistake to exaggerate the amount of time wasted by Presidents in needless ceremonial functions that they have no wish to attend.

This is only one of many proposals borrowed from other systems of government, with no evidence that those systems have proven more successful than our own in stemming the flow of power to the executive. The parliamentary system with merged legislative and executive power, and all members of Parliament including the Prime Minister and other ministers standing for office simultaneously, appears to have worked best in smaller, less diverse countries than ours —countries where the states are creatures of the national government, centralized national parties can discipline errant legislators, and senior civil servants dominate the ministries. None of these conditions applies here or is likely to be adopted here. Nor do all proponents of our accepting such a system realize the extent, under most parliamentary systems, to which a Prime Minister is becoming more and more a chief executive with centralized powers and can generally dominate Parliament for legislative purposes more readily than many an American President can dominate Congress.

In this country, the power to bring the executive branch down with a legislative vote of "no confidence" would introduce utter confusion. Many congressmen, fearful of the cost of campaigning, would not support such a motion when merited. But many with safe seats who are about to seek reelection anyway would support it regardless of merit; and given the recently volatile nature of the electorate's emotions and pressures, Presidents might be shuffled in and out before they could rearrange the furniture in the Green Room. At the very least every President would be forced, far more than at present, to gratify the demands of a variety of special factions, cliques, and pork barrel interests. . . .

Like the vote of no confidence, other recent proposals are aimed at a quicker gratification of the public desire to get rid of an unpopular President: special elections, recall elections, or a less rigid standard for impeachment. Without doubt our system is slower than many others in responding even to legitimate

needs to change Chief Executives; and the ordeal of Richard Nixon struck many as unnecessarily prolonged and traumatic. Yet in the end it is clear that quicker ouster would have left questions of guilt unresolved and the country bitterly divided.

It is best that Presidents, like containers, not be too easily disposable. Some unpopular acts (like John Adam's refusal to go to war) may turn out to be in the long-run national interest; some serious mistakes (like the Bay of Pigs) may constitute the experience from which wisdom comes; and, in the absence of some extraordinary occurrence such as dual vacancy in the Presidency and Vice Presidency, fixed elections are a stabilizing tradition we should not quickly cast aside. As previously noted, tampering with the system conceived by the framers has not always been successful.

The final group of proposed structural curbs would, in various forms, pluralize presidential decision-making: require him to obtain the concurrence of an Executive Council, the Cabinet, or of Congress or its leaders; or divide his duties, with separate executives for foreign and domestic affairs, or for policy and administration; or substitute government by Cabinet or committee. "The only way to defuse the Presidency," wrote Barbara Tuchman, "is to divide the power and spread the responsibility."

But making the President less responsible is not an answer to irresponsible Presidents. Plural bodies can, after some delay and fragmentation, produce a legislative decision acceptable to the lowest common denominator. But they cannot produce the kind of executive leadership this nation's problems require.

No matter whom a President is formally required to consult, he can still informally

5. IS THE PRESIDENT TOO POWERFUL?

meet with a "kitchen cabinet" of his own choosing. Adding another structural layer of advice can increase delay and indecisiveness, but rarely safety. Advice is cheap, but it can be expensive for the country. For it is the President, because he is the one held responsible if policies go wrong, who is likely to be more cautious. Advisers, as JFK observed, can always "move on to new advice." (The Joint Chiefs of Staff recommended new military initiatives to him, he said, "the way one man advises another one about whether he should marry a girl. He doesn't have to live with her.")

Moreover, foreign and domestic, or policy and administrative, burdens are less separable now than ever. There is no need to reopen the framers' deliberate decision that a single Executive is best.

None of these structural or institutional reorganizations would have prevented Watergate. All would provide corrective action, if at all, only after the fact—as our present system already does. None would solve the political and operational problems at the heart of the matter. . . . Many would carelessly curb or reshape an office that over the long haul has served us well.

Unfortunately these ill-considered if well-motivated proposals that would harm the Presidency are part of the Nixon legacy. "Support the Presidency" proclaimed the buttons his organized devotees distributed during the impeachment proceedings. Support the Presidency. I still do. He did not.

By now, my basic conclusion should be clear: instead of punishing or weakening the Presidency for the sins of Richard Nixon, its powers should be renewed but held accountable—more closely watched, more precisely defined, more carefully kept within constitutional bounds, and more clearly answerable to the electorate, Congress, and our other institutions.

● ● ●

POSTSCRIPT

IS THE PRESIDENT TOO POWERFUL?

Once again it is the task of Americans to weigh the considerations on both sides. Do we need further checks on the executive branch, or is the risk too great that such checks will not only weaken the Presidency but the nation itself? As President Lincoln framed the question: "Must a government of necessity be too strong for the liberties of its own people, or too weak to maintain its own existence?"

Arthur Schlesinger, Jr., once a rather uncritical promoter of the activist presidency, later recanted and offered his *mea culpa* in THE IMPERIAL PRESIDENCY (Houghton Mifflin, 1973). George Reedy, former secretary to President Johnson, wrote a small classic on the "monarchical" White House and what it does to its chief occupant (THE TWILIGHT OF THE PRESIDENCY, New American Library, 1970). In defense of the presidency, Clinton Rossiter argued in THE AMERICAN PRESIDENCY (Harcourt Brace Jovanovich, 1960) that the President is adequately checked but hardly needs to be, since only decent men are elected to the office. This last contention may raise some eyebrows today, but Rossiter's basic theme—"Leave your presidency alone!"—is still arguable.

James David Barber emphasizes the man rather than the office in THE PRESIDENTIAL CHARACTER, 2d. ED. (Prentice-Hall, 1977). Barber ranked the modern Presidents as active or passive with respect to the energy they brought to the office, and positive or negative in terms of their reaction to the job. Barber's categories remind us that man makes the office as much as the office makes the man.

Our last words are not intended to resolve any issue but simply to remind the reader that the presidency and its power are subject to changing fortunes. In 1885 Woodrow Wilson wrote: "The presidential office . . . has fallen from its first estate of dignity because its power has waned; and its power has waned because the power of Congress has become predominant." In 1908 Wilson reached a radically different conclusion: "If he (the President) rightly interprets the national thought and boldly insists upon it, he is irresistible. . . . His office is anything he has the sagacity and force to make it."

ISSUE 6

DOES THE GOVERNMENT REGULATE TOO MUCH?

YES: Barry Crickmer, from "Regulation: How Much Is Enough?" *Nation's Business,* March 1980

NO: Steven Kelman, from "Regulation That Works," *The New Republic,* November 25, 1978

ISSUE SUMMARY

YES: Editor Barry Crickmer argues that the interests of citizens and consumers could be better served by the forces of the profit motive than by government intervention.

NO: Political scientist Steven Kelman supports the notion of government regulation as the only viable counterbalance to the power of business.

Government regulation of economic decision-making is as old as the Interstate Commerce Commission, which was established in 1887 to regulate railroad rates. The Sherman and Clayton Antitrust Acts of 1890 and 1914 respectively, and the law establishing the Federal Trade Commission in 1914, were also designed to outlaw unfair methods of business competition.

Congress later established regulatory agencies to set standards for natural (or socially useful) monopolies, such as electric power and radio and television. Between 1920 and 1940, it set up the Federal Power Commission, the Federal Communications Commission and the Civil Aeronautics Board. The national government has also regulated the investment of capital in industry and banking practices generally, with the creation of the Federal Reserve System in 1913 and the Securities and Exchange Commission in 1934, after the great stock market crash.

Although governmental regulation of commerce on behalf of the public interest was introduced as early as the Pure Food and Drug Act of 1906 (now administered within the Department of Health and Human Services), most activity within this area is relatively recent. The Equal Employment Opportunity Commission was established in 1965; the Environmental

Protection Agency, the Occupational Safety and Health Administration, and the National Highway Traffic Safety Administration were all created in 1970; the Consumer Product Safety Commission was set up in 1973, and the Office of Surface Mining Reclamation and Enforcement (within the Department of the Interior) came into being in 1977. With these and other newly-established agencies, the federal government assumed a wide-ranging responsibility to protect all persons against certain hazards that unrestrained private economic enterprise might otherwise create.

The rules written by these regulatory bodies have changed our lives in many ways, altering the food we eat, the cars we drive, and the air we breathe. Their defenders have applauded the protection that has been provided against profit-motivated predators who would otherwise adulterate our food, endanger our safety, and pollute the environment, all in their single-minded pursuit of profits.

On the other hand, many investigators have joined businessmen in condemning government's movement into these areas, making the following arguments. One: Regulation inhibits production by suppressing innovation and discouraging risk-taking, resulting in declining employment. Excessive regulation has been blamed for the economic reverses of the Chrysler Corporation. Two: Regulation invariably overregulates by setting standards for every aspect of manufacture when it could set overall objectives which businesses could meet in whatever ways they devise. Some economists maintain that government would accomplish more by assessing fees or taxes to discourage certain activities rather than fixing rigid standards. Three: Regulation costs too much in business compliance expenditures which are passed on to the consumer, and in increased government payrolls. If government regulation drives a company out of business, the standard of living for those affected will go down. Simply put, the costs outweigh the benefits. Fourth: Regulation doesn't really work. Most of the progress against fatal accidents, including motor vehicle deaths, occurred long before the relevant regulatory agencies were established.

"The Reagan Administration has dismantled some areas of regulation and challenged others, arguing that deregulation "gets government off our backs" and encourages economic enterprise. Among proposed restraints on regulatory agencies are periodic review of their activities, allowing either house of Congress to veto proposed new regulations, and the requirement of economic impact analyses before new rules go into effect."

The lines are clearly drawn in the following essays. Barry Crickmer argues that the objectives of safety and health, as well as productivity, will be better achieved in the absence of government regulation. Steven Kelman defends the social regulation of the past decade as having contributed significantly to a better society.

YES

Barry Crickmer

REGULATION: HOW MUCH IS ENOUGH?

Federal regulation is often called inflationary, irritating, costly, and even farcical. But that's not the worst that can be said of it. The worst is that it isn't working.

The development, methodology, philosophy, and results of federal intervention in the marketplace fit Sir Ernest Benn's definition of politics as "the art of looking for trouble, finding it everywhere, diagnosing it wrongly, and applying unsuitable remedies."

For all the billions of dollars the regulatory agencies have spent and the billions more they have caused to be spent, there is surprisingly little evidence that the world is any better off than it would have been without federal tinkering.

NEEDLESS EXPENSE

Economist Murray Weidenbaum observes that "virtually every study of regulatory experience from trucking to pharmaceuticals to pensions indicates both needless expense and ineffective operations or, worst yet, counterproductive results."

For the old-line, economic regulatory agencies, the evidence of ineffectiveness has convinced even liberals to favor trimming or abolishing their powers. Presidential candidate Edward M. Kennedy (D-Mass.) points proudly to his role in deregulating the airlines. Even Federal Trade Commission Chairman Michael Pertschuk has been extolling the virtues of free market incentives.

But the newer, health-safety-social-environmental regulators still have vigorous defenders, although the defense is of necessity based more on what it is hoped they will do than on what they have done so far.

TYPICAL PROBLEMS

The first to document the failure of health and safety regulation may have been University of Chicago economist Sam Pelzman. He is certainly one of the pioneers in the field.

Dr. Peltzman did a cost-benefit analysis of the more stringent drug regulations that followed the thalidomide tragedy in Europe.

The Food and Drug Administration was an appropriate target for this seminal work published in 1973-74. Historically, the FDA belongs with the older single-industry regulators; by mission, it resembles the newer health and safety agencies. Further, some of its key problems are typical of most health and safety regulation.

Dr. Peltzman found that the new drug rules were costing American consumers three or four times as much as the economic benefits they produced. He also suggested that a too-cautious approach to approval of new drugs might foreclose or delay lifesaving advances in pharmaceutical technology.

Following Dr. Peltzman's work came a study by William M. Wardell, professor of pharmacology, toxicology, and medicine at the University of Rochester.

Dr. Wardell compared post-thalidomide drug development in the United States and Great Britain, which has fewer restrictions on new drugs. He demonstrated that lives were being saved in Britain and lost in the United States because of the more conservative U.S. policy toward new drugs. The British benefit not only from the more rapid introduction of valuable new drugs, he found, but also from the development of safer substitutes for potentially hazardous drugs in use.

It is easy to understand the FDA's caution. The damage done by a drug that should have been banned is visible and dramatic. The suffering and death that could have been prevented by a drug that was never developed are invisible and conjectural. Bureaucrats can hardly be blamed for trying to minimize known risk at the expense of unknown benefit. This dilemma is endemic to public-sector health safety regulation.

AUTO SAFETY

After making his point about drug regulation, Dr. Peltzman turned to auto safety. In a study published in 1975, he found that "essentially nothing in the post-1965 behavior of the total death rate can corroborate the idea that safety devices provide the kind of lifesaving suggested in safety literature."

A year later, the General Accounting Office reported that auto safety equipment mandated between 1966 and 1970 seemed to have reduced the risk of death and injury significantly, while that required after 1970 has produced no further improvement.

Other critics charge that federal auto safety regulations raise repair costs and waste gasoline.

It appears that the National Highway Traffic Safety Administration didn't know when to stop, stopped too soon, or should never have started.

In its seven years of existence, the Consumer Product Safety Commission has produced a handful of standards dealing with such threats as matchbook covers and swimming pool slides, inadvertently put a company out of business because of a typographical error in a list of hazardous toys, and arrested nine allegedly unsafe trash bins at a

99

shopping center outside Washington, D.C.—in a daring daylight raid, as crime reporters say.

The trash cans went peacefully, if not quietly.

The incident prompted commission officials to search for a less cumbersome way to enforce their safety standards.

The Occupational Safety and Health Administration, like the traffic safety agency, is a very active agency with little to show for its activity. At least four major studies—including one by the Chamber of Commerce of the United States—failed to find any significant OSHA impact on the existing trend of industrial fatalities. Unlike the traffic safety agency, however, OSHA does not even try to subject its rules to cost-benefit analysis.

Similar evidence could be cited concerning the failures of the Environmental Protection Agency, the Energy Department, and other major and minor federal regulators. "The history of regulation is a history of disappointment," Harvard professors Albert Nichols and Richard Zeckhauser observe in a *Public Interest* article.

WHY DOES REGULATION FAIL?

The question is, why? Why has the direct and indirect expenditure of more than $100 billion a year on federal regulation failed to produce results commensurate with the effort? Or in some cases, any positive results at all?

Is the federal government trying to do the impossible? Or is it trying to do the possible in an impossible way? The answer is probably a little of both.

Many of the newer regulatory programs were ill-conceived and ill-considered. Typically, each got started after a single-interest pressure group

succeeded in creating a wave of hysteria over an alleged crisis.

When this happens, most members of Congress quickly jump on the reform bandwagon. Those who don't may get crushed under its wheels. Says Rep. George Hansen (R.-Idaho): "It's very hard in Congress to vote against mother and home. And how do you vote against something labeled clean meat, safety, and health?"

The news media—especially television—build pressure for quick fixes because they tend to focus on problems that can be presented dramatically, rather than on the comparatively dry analyses of possible solutions. Also, representatives of single-interest groups always have something quotable to say, so they get lots of publicity. Through such exposure, special-issue crusaders develop what Mr. Weidenbaum calls the power of arrogance. Soon, as authors Nichols and Zeckhauser put it, "the appetite for favorable results is . . . so enormous that the probability of success seems almost irrelevant," and the most far-reaching laws are passed with little thought to the consequences.

When OSHA was formed, they point out, no evidence was presented that even relatively modest gains could be achieved.

A similar pattern prevailed during adoption of the tough auto emissions standards of 1970. Congress passed that bill with little debate. And yet, "few people seem to have had any idea of what was in the legislation," said Howard Margolis, a research fellow at the Massachusetts Institute of Technology, writing in *Public Interest*.

"Even a superficial examination of available information" would have shown that the costly new standards could make very little difference in air pollution levels.

The same phenomenon is discussed by economists Dorothy Tella and Paul MacAvoy in an analysis written for the U.S. Chamber's Council on Trends and Perspective:

"The rapid growth of health, safety, and environmental regulation in the late 1960s and early 1970s is not easy to explain. The market failures cited to justify new regulation did not show up then for the first time, and at least some of the indicators . . . that prompted Congress to regulate . . . were explained almost wholly by demographic factors beyond the reach of the regulatory process. . . .

"In every case where Congress chose to regulate, there were alternatives—court penalties for polluters, tax penalties for employers with poor safety records, government-funded information programs. In general, better arguments could have been made for the alternatives than for agency controls."

If the health and safety regulators were created in response to nonexistent crises, it is not surprising they have made little impact on mortality rates.

SAFER AND HEALTHIER

Certainly, health and safety problems do exist and will continue as long as human beings remain fallible. Even so, statistics confirm that the American public is far safer and healthier today than in past years.

Moreover, the same statistics show that most of the progress occurred well before the advent of the health and safety agencies. The general accident rate, for example, peaked at 94.1 fatalities per 100,000 people in 1907, then began a long, steady decline until leveling off at about 20 per 100,000 after 1957.

This long-term improvement in safety suggests another hypothesis to explain the poor record of federal regulators. The private sector is motivated by profits to seek safer working conditions and products. That profit incentive will reduce the accident and disease rate to the lowest level consistent with an efficient allocation of resources.

The federal government is then left with trying to achieve dramatic safety gains when fine-tuning is all that can reasonably be expected.

The theory is difficult to prove because, as long as any hazards remain, they can always be attributed to business misfeasance. But it is not hard to demonstrate the stong profit incentive in improving safety.

Unsafe working conditions can deprive an employer of trained workers, increase insurance costs, and raise wages for dangerous work. Unsafe products expose the manufacturer to civil suit, higher insurance costs, and loss of patronage to competitors.

However, there is no free market incentive for pollution control. Control costs raise prices without increasing the value of a product to the consumer, and a manufacturer who bears the costs of pollution control voluntarily suffers a competitive disadvantage. Consequently, there is agreement on the need for government action to limit pollution. The disagreement comes over the means.

In passing, though, government itself does not show in its own activities a concern for the public interest superior to that of the private sector. Federal facilities are among the worst polluters, from the Tennessee Valley Authority to the Capitol Power Plant. OSHA's offices have violated OSHA's standards. The Equal Employment Opportunity Commission has been found guilty of racial discrimination. Government and private employees alike were exposed to asbestos dust before its harmful effects were known.

People will make mistakes, whether they are in public or private enterprise. But neither pleas of human fallibility nor complaints about cost deter some health and safety regulators from demanding perfection.

"Every worker has a fundamental human right to a safe and healthful workplace," asserted Labor Secretary Ray Marshall in a speech (in 1979). Absolutely safe? Perfectly heathful? On the previous page of his text, the Labor Secretary sagaciously observed that "it is much easier, when dealing with environmental and occupational health, to fall back upon demagoguery. . . ."

Joan Claybrook, administrator of the traffic safety agency, shows a similar lack of perspective.

Accused of requiring more safety than the consumer wants to buy, she replied in *Regulation* magazine that "producers who know how to make a product safer have an obligation to do so, and if they do not fulfill that obligation, then government must take it on . . . the sanctity of life has the highest value in our society."

That statement, praiseworthy on its surface, is the kind of mother-and-home phrase that troubles many legislators. There are many ways to save lives and improve health, but, unfortunately, the government has no rational, established method for choosing among them.

"Why should the government spend almost $30,000 per year to keep a kidney patient alive," University of Virginia professor Steven E. Rhoads asked in *Public Interest*, "and yet not pay for mobile cardiac units that can provide an additional life-year for as little as $1,765?"

At the other end of the scale, the chemical industry has calculated that OSHA's proposed limits on worker exposure to benzene would eliminate one case of leukemia every six years, at a cost of $300 million each.

CURIOUS INCONSISTENCIES

A society never has enough resources to do everything that everyone would like to do. But OSHA and its brethren are not responsible for weighing their own plans against alternative uses of resources outside their spheres of influence. Thus, OSHA's efforts to save lives, like the FDA's, may result in a net loss of lives. This lack of a guiding philosphy and a coordinating authority also results in some curious inconsistencies.

Consider the CAT scanner, a very effective and expensive type of X-ray machine.

Federal health planners say physicians and hospitals are acquiring more of these devices than are needed, thereby wasting money. So the government wants to limit their number. In this case, cost-effectiveness is considered more important than the comfort, convenience, and perhaps even safety of the patients affected.

Contrast that policy with OSHA's proposed factory noise controls. OSHA wants employers to silence noisy machinery at great cost, rather than require workers to wear protective earplugs at modest cost.

The protective ear gear is uncomfortable, and workers might not wear it, says OSHA.

So in the case of noise standards, comfort and convenience are more important than cost-effectiveness.

PHILOSOPHICAL CHOICE

Beyond the economic trade-offs, there is a difficult philosophical choice between freedom and safety. Is an adult citizen a peer of the realm or its ward?

Sometimes society permits informed adults to participate in hazardous activities, vocational and avocational. And sometimes the law is used to limit or forbid such decisions.

"Why . . . do we find ourselves serenely contemplating a person's plan to climb a dangerous Himalayan peak at the same time that we propose making it illegal for her to buy a can of Tab?" asked University of California geneticist William R. Havender in a *Regulation* article.

There is little government objection to test pilots, firefighters, police, military personnel, and athletes accepting the risks of their trades.

Yet, industrial workers must apparently be protected from all risk, regardless of cost and their willingness to accept those risks in return for high pay and other benefits. In personal behavior, the government has attempted to force motorcycle riders to wear protective helmets on the ground that deaths and injuries impose costs on society. But if medical authorities are correct, far higher costs are imposed on society by those who smoke, eat, and drink to excess.

PERSONAL COMPULSION

Why do the regulators pick on the motorcycle riders? Perhaps because the motorcycle vote is relatively small.

"The resort to personal compulsion is a last resort when politicians fear that the public will not pay the cost of programs pushed on behalf of abstract principles," said Harvard Law School professor Charles Fried in *Regulation.* And he deplores "the moral obtuseness that treats people as public utilities."

Prof. Fried is not alone in his concern that freedom is endangered by well-meaning regulators. That point is often made.

But the regulators also raise some troubling questions. Are citizens always aware of the risk inherent in a product or occupation? If not, how can they make rational decisions? Dare we take chances with potentially hazardous environmental contaminants that may cause irreversible damage that does not show up for decades? And where environmental or genetic risk is involved, who represents the interests of future generations?

Americans need to make some painful choices about the priority of first principles. Until there is an agreed-upon basis for making trade-off decisions, it will remain impossible to know how much or how best to regulate.

In the words of Washington Gov. Dixie Lee Ray, a former federal regulator herself: "The reality is that zero defects in products plus zero pollution plus zero risk on the job is equivalent to maximum growth of government plus zero economic growth plus run-away inflation, That's what we have."

● ● ●

NO
Steven Kelman

REGULATION THAT WORKS

The last decade has seen the dramatic restrictions in the freedom of action society chooses to allow to business firms. A series of laws in areas like environmental protection, occupational safety and health, consumer product safety and equal opportunity has restricted the prerogatives of business firms to pursue production, hiring and marketing practices that would have continued without these laws. Business and conservatives have now launched a counterattack against these changes. Cleverly exploiting various popular resentments, the counterattacking forces seek to lump "excessive government regulation" together with themes as diverse as high taxes and school busing to generate an all-embracing demand to "get the government out of our hair." To hear the critics of the new government regulatory programs tell it, nothing less fundamental than our very freedom is at stake in the battle against meddlesome bureaucrats. And now, with national concern over inflation growing, we are being told that the new regulatory programs are an important cause of the increased cost of living, and must be reduced for that reason as well.

One fact it is important to get clear from the beginning is that the alleged popular ground swell against government regulation of business does not exist. A recent Louis Harris survey asked Americans, "In the future, do you think there should be more government regulation of business, less government regulation, or the same amount there is now?" By 53 percent to 30 percent, those polled favored either more regulation or the same amount as now, over less regulation. In fact, almost as many respondents (24 percent) favored more regulation as favored less regulation (30 percent). Repeated polls have shown wide popular support for measures to make workplaces safe, and to clean up the environment.

This absence of any ground swell against the new regulatory thrust of the last decade is reassuring because the conservative and business counterattack

From "Regulation that Works," Steven Kelman, in The New Republic, November 25, 1978, pp. 16-20.

is, I believe, largely wrong. New regulatory programs neither threaten freedom nor contribute significantly to inflation. On the whole, the new regulation is a good thing. Certainly there have been excesses by bureaucrats, but what is more impressive than these excesses is the unfinished work the new agencies still have before them to deal with the injustice that prompted their creation in the first place.

There are two kinds of activities often lumped together as "government regulation." When denouncing the "costs of government regulation," opponents of the new regulatory agencies tend to forget this distinction. An older generation of liberals, fond of asserting that regulatory agencies always get captured by those they regulate, also ignore this distinction.

Most of the regulatory agencies established before the last decade were set up to regulate prices and conditions of entry in various industries. The grandfather of such agencies was the Interstate Commerce Commission, established in 1887, to regulate railroads. There is a lively dispute among historians about whether the ICC, when it was established, was an attempt to tame a powerful and oppressive industry, or a government-sanctioned effort by the railroads themselves to set up a cartel to avoid price competition. It is much clearer, however, that other agencies regulating market conditions in various industries such as the Civil Aeronautics Board and the Federal Communications Commission, *were* originally established at the behest of industries seeking to avoid "excessive" competition. These agencies, by maintaining artificially high prices in various industries, have been very costly to consumers and to the economy as a whole. But you do not hear the voices of business complaining about them. Indeed, when proposals are made to deregulate surface transportation, airlines, or television, the main opponents of such proposals have been the industries being "regulated."

The situation is very different, both politically and conceptually, for the regulatory agencies—which have blossomed especially during the last decade—intended to regulate non-market behavior by business firms. Usually they regulate acts that injure third parties. These "social" regulatory agencies include the Environmental Protection Agency, the Occupational Safety and Health Administration, the National Highway Transportation Safety Board, the Consumer Product Safety Commission, and the Equal Employment Opportunity Commission. These agencies generally came into being despite genuine business resistance. Business representatives certainly have ample opportunity to participate in developing the regulations these agencies promulgate, but there are other organized constituencies interested in their work as well (environmentalists at EPA, trade unions at OSHA, civil rights and women's groups at EEOC, for instance). Few reasonable people believe the social regulatory agencies have been "captured" by business—least of all, as the current attacks demonstrate, business itself.

The conceptual basis for the social regulatory agencies also is different from that of agencies intended to limit or replace the free market. In any society, one of the basic tasks of government and the legal system is to decide which acts of individuals are so harmful to others that they cannot be freely permitted (and which harmful acts may rightfully be per-

105

formed, even though others are indeed harmed). A common dictum has been that people may act freely as long as their actions concern only themselves: "My freedom to move my arm ends where your face begins." But clearly this dictum is unsatisfying. Virtually everything we do affects others. Even acts as trivial as appearing at work with a blue shirt, or consuming a bottle of Perrier water in a public place, injure the person who despises the color blue, or who is offended to see people buy products from France. Anything we do that damages our own welfare hurts those who hold us dear. What the legal system must do is to determine *which* acts affecting others should be allowed, and which should be proscribed. The social regulatory agencies are engaged in this age-old task. There is nothing conceptually new about their activities. What *is* new is that they have redefined certain acts by business firms previously regarded as acceptable, and determined that they are henceforth unacceptable.

Government has never left businessmen "unregulated," as business spokesmen now wistfully, but erroneously, imagine. The voluminous case and statute law of property, contracts and torts along with large chunks of the criminal law, comprise an elaborate system— far more complex and intricate than any OSHA standard—regulating acts that injure property holders, as well as acts by property holders that injure others. A starving person does not have the freedom to injure a rich man by appropriating the rich man's money in order to buy food. People do not have the freedom to injure a landowner by trespassing on his land. (Richard Posner, a professor of law at the University of Chicago, argues that traditional commonlaw rules merely re-

produce what would have occurred through market transactions, if the costs of negotiating such transactions were not too high, and that modern social regulations, by contrast, subvert expected market outcomes. Even if this statement were true, and it is subject to much debate, it is still not obvious why legal rules *ought* to mimic the outcomes of market transactions.) Furthermore, the process by which these older rules were elucidated and enforced through litigation was much more cumbersome and arbitrary than the rulemaking of today's regulatory agencies.

The plethora of regulations regarding property that has grown up over the centuries is not some sort of natural order, onto which new regulations of business behavior in areas like safety, health, environmental protection, consumer fraud, and discrimination represent an unnatural intrusion. As long as the regulations were restricting the freedom of non-property-holders to injure *them*, businessmen raised no chorus of complaints about an oppressive government stifling freedom. The chorus of complaints from business has begun only as regulations have begun increasingly to restrict the freedom of business firms to injure others.

The harms that social regulations of the last decade were intended to curb were not insignificant. Urban air had become unhealthy as well as unpleasant to breathe. Rivers were catching on fire. Many working people were dying from exposure to chemicals on their jobs. Firms were selling products of whose hazards consumers were ignorant. And the nation faced a legacy of racial and sexual discrimination. Frequently the harm was borne disproportionately by the more disadvantaged members of society, while the more advantaged produced the harm. The social regulation of the past decade grew largely, then, out of a sense of fairness—a view that people, frequently disadvantaged people, were being victimized by others in unacceptable ways.

The impact of the new agencies in alleviating these injuries has begun to be felt. Racial and sexual discrimination have decreased, partly thanks to broader social trends, but partly thanks to government efforts. There has been a vast increase in the amount of information manufacturers are required to tell consumers about their products, and surveys indicate that many consumers use this information in making purchasing decisions.

Since the much-maligned OSHA and its sister agency regulating coal mining safety have come into existence, the number of accidental workplace deaths has been cut almost in half. Worker exposure to harmful amounts of coal dust and chemicals like vinyl chloride, asbestos and lead have been reduced, and this will reduce the toll of occupational sickness and death in the years to come. Improvements in emergency medical care and some changes in workforce composition since 1970 may be partially responsible for the dramatic reduction in workplace deaths. But today's figures don't even reflect the reduction in deaths due to occupational disease, which will be felt mainly in future years because of the frequently lengthy period separating exposure to harmful levels of a chemical and death or illness due to that exposure.

Environmental regulation has produced significant improvements in the quality of air in the United States. (Without regulation the situation would have gotten worse because economic growth tends to increase the level of pollution.) Carbon monoxide levels in eight representative cities declined 46 percent between 1972 and 1976. Carbon monoxide levels that had been found in urban air were enough to increase the incidence of heart attacks and of painful angina attacks among people with heart disease. There has been a major decline in heart attack deaths in the United States during the 1970s. No one yet knows why, but I predict that studies will show that improvement in air quality has played a role in this decline. Another common air pollutant, sulfur dioxide, which definitely causes respiratory illness and death and is suspected of causing cancer, has now declined to a point where almost every place in the country is in compliance with EPA standards.

Water pollution has been reduced as well. There are rivers and lakes around the country—from the Pemigewasset River in New Hampshire through the Mohawk River in New York to the Wilamett River in Oregon—previously badly polluted, that are now opened in parts for fishing and swimming. Levels of various pesticides in streams and rivers, as well as of phenol—an organic waste considered a good indicator of the presence of toxic industrial wastes—have declined dramatically during the 1970s.

Lives have been saved by other regulatory actions. The introduction of childproof containers on household poisons appears to have reduced accidental poisoning significantly. Highway deaths declined by almost 15 percent between 1965 and 1972, even before the post-OPEC speed limit reductions. Some of this decline may be due to factors other than new auto safety regulations, such as fewer teenagers on the road. But the decline in traffic fatalities has occured despite an enormous increase in the number of bicycle and motorcycle fatalities caused by the new popularity of these vehicles.

The critics ask: have the benefits outweighed the costs? Are they feeding inflation, for example? Allegations that health, safety, environmental and antidiscrimination regulations are a major cause of inflation are little short of grotesque. Much of the business thunder about regulation begins by citing some overall figure for the "cost of regulation," and then goes on to zero in on agencies like OSHA and EPA. These agencies are chosen, however, only because business dislikes them especially, not because they are major contributors to the "cost of regulation." Most of the cost of regulation is imposed by the market-fixing agencies, like the ICC, that the business world likes. Murray Weidenbaum, director of the Center for the Study of American Business and an adjunct scholar at the American Enterprise Institute, estimated that in 1976 federal regulation in the areas he examined cost $62.3 billion to comply with. But of this sum, approximately $26 billion—or 42 percent—was the estimated impact on consumer prices of tariff protection against imports and of price and entry regulations by the ICC, CAB and FCC. (The largest figure in this category was the cost of ICC regulation of transportation.) Another $18 billion— 29 percent of the estimated total cost— represented the alleged cost of federal paperwork. Certainly there are plenty of pointless federal paperwork requirements. But few of these relate to what would normally be thought of as "government regulation." Much federal paperwork takes the form of reports for statistical purposes and of requirements for federal contractors or other citizens receiving federal benefits.

Only five percent of Weidenbaum's estimated total—$3.2 billion in 1976— was spent on complying with OSHA regulations. Another $7.8 billion allegedly was spent to comply with EPA regulations —less than 13 percent of the total. (Weidenbaum also estimated a $3.7 billion retail cost for auto safety and emissions requirements.)

Even those modest figures do not reflect the direct savings that result from some of these regulations. The actual monetary cost of pollution abatement measures, for example, is the cost to firms of capital equipment, energy and maintenance, *minus* the savings in medical bills, damaged crops, premature corrosion of property, laundering expenses, and so forth, that would otherwise be borne by victims of pollution. Most accounts of the "inflationary impact" of government regulation do not calculate such savings.

More fundamentally, these estimates of the "cost" of regulation ignore widespread benefits that do not have a direct monetary value, but are real nonetheless. In the case of pollution control, for example, the air smells a bit better for five million people; 100,000 people get to see mountains in the distance which they would not have seen had the air not been as clean; and 50 lives are saved. There is no way of objectively determining whether these non-priced benefits justify the new monetary costs. Economists have come up with different ways to assign dollar values to benefits like clean air that are not traded on markets which would then allow us to weigh all the benefits against all the more concrete costs. But there are philosophical difficulties, as well as technical ones, with these efforts.

In deciding whether a given act that injures a third party should be allowed, one relevant factor is how much a third party suffers as a result of the behavior, as compared to the benefits the perpetrator gains from the behavior. The greater the benefit, and the more the inconsequential the injury suffered by the third party, the stronger the case to allow the behavior to be exercised freely.

But since the costs of injury are borne by its victims, while its benefits are reaped by its perpetrators, simple cost-benefit calculations may be less important than more abstract conceptions of justice, fairness and human dignity. We would not condone a rape even if it could be demonstrated that the rapist derived enormous pleasure from his actions, while the victim suffered in only small ways. Behind the conception of "rights" is the notion that some concept of justice, fairness or human dignity demands that individuals ought to be able to perform certain acts, despite the harm to others, and ought to be protected against certain acts, despite the loss this causes to the would-be perpetrators. Thus we undertake no cost-benefit analysis of the effects of freedom of speech or trial by jury before allowing them to continue. As the steelworkers union noted in commenting on an OSHA regulation of coke oven emissions, no anaylsis of its inflationary impact was performed before the Emancipation Proclamation was issued. This notion of individual rights that supersedes a neutral cost-benefit analysis is ordinarily dear to the hearts of American conservatives. Yet when it comes to the regulation of business activities that intrude on the lives of individual consumers or workers, they perversely see the government regulation itself as an intrusion on individual rights.

The costs and benefits of the business behavior now coming under regulation have not been distributed randomly. Much of the new social regulation benefits more disadvantaged groups in society. To put it somewhat simply—but not, in my view, unfairly—those who argue, say, that OSHA should "go soft" on its health regulations in order to spare the country the burden of additional costs, are saying that some workers should die so that consumers can pay a few bucks less for the products they purchase, and stockholders can make a somewhat higher return on their investments. It is hard to see why workers exposed to health hazards should be at the front lines of the battle against inflation, however the overall costs and benefits tally up.

There are, to be sure, those sudden friends of the poor who allege that environmental regulation has significantly added to unemployment, or who point out that regulation-induced price increases weigh most heavily on the poor. But studies have concluded that, on balance, environmental legislation has probably created many more jobs than it has cost. And one must wonder whether there aren't more direct ways to help the poor than to eliminate the health, safety, and environmental regulations that slightly increase the cost of goods they buy.

(Some economists argue that workers are compensated for working at risky jobs by receiving risk premiums [higher pay]. To the extent this is true, occupational safety and health regulation amounts to in-kind benefits redistributed to workers, over and above what they are able to bargain for on the market. Some economists argue that workers themselves bear the primary cost of such regulations, in foregone wage increases in the long run. There is no real empirical evidence that safety regulations actually have this effect. But even if this *were* true, it would reduce the cost burden such regulations imposed on the economy, because the cost of the regulations would be counteracted by lower wages paid to workers.)

There is a final reason to doubt the calls to subject everything to cost-benefit analysis. Many of the benefits of social regulations, as noted earlier, have no ready dollar value because they are not traded on markets. To economists this is an unfortunate obstacle to analysis, and economists are forever scurrying around, trying to come up with measures of people's "willingness to pay" for clean-smelling air, living in a quiet environment, recreational benefits, or reduced risks of premature death. But the very fact that there is no dollar value assigned to those benefits is one reason many people celebrate them in a special way. Most reasonable people agree that there is a place for markets in society, but most reasonable people also agree that market relationships have their costs as well. Dealings in the market promote certain undesirable personal attitudes and interpersonal relationships. Few are even the economists (although there are some!) who would wish market relationships to dominate within families, or among friends. An obsession with the calculative mindset of market relationships and cost-benefit analyses would itself recover something of what is special about the social regulatory agencies as expressions of a desire to keep market relationships in their place.

None of this means that every regulation promulgated by social regulatory agencies in the last few years is justified. In some instances, as with some affirmative action requirements, regulations may have gone beyond their conceptual justifications. Affirmative action requirements may be an example. In other instances the administrative burden, the paperwork requirements or the monetary costs of regulating may be too great to justify the benefits, however real, received by those whom the regulations are intended to protect. Offhand, for example, it appears to me that the costs of retrofitting older urban subway sytems to accommodate the handicapped, only a small number of whom could be expected to use these systems anyway, appear unjustified, even though failure to retrofit does indeed injure some disadvantaged people. Questions like this should be considered case-by-case, but with sympathy for those people injured by the failure to regulate.

The thrust of the current movement against social regulation in the United States is a wish by the strong to regain prerogatives whose disappearance, for the most part, is one of the most welcome events of the past decade. Individual regulations can and should be criticized. But the assault on the concept of regulation must be resisted if we are to continue to be a decent people living in a decent society.

● ● ●

POSTSCRIPT

DOES GOVERNMENT REGULATE TOO MUCH?

Any consideration of social regulation by government must assess both costs and benefits. Society must ask how much it is willing to pay to avoid a given risk, just as workers will demand increased wages for running a greater risk. Most people are likely to agree that there are some benefits that merit the cost, and some costs that outweigh the benefit. Crickmer does not make many concessions, but he does acknowledge that pollution controls are necessary and that earlier automobile safety requirements did make a difference in reducing deaths and injuries. On the other side, Kelman recognizes that "the monetary costs of regulating may be too great to justify the benefits." If neither author is an absolutist, they nevertheless remain very far apart. This is true even when they quote the same economist on the cost of regulation.

That economist, Murray L. Weidenbaum, has written a comprehensive account of government regulation, BUSINESS, GOVERNMENT, AND THE PUBLIC (Prentice-Hall, 1977). Weidenbaum's survey and case studies cover consumer products, the environment, and job and automobile safety. Harold Seidman, in POLITICS, POSITION AND POWER, 2d ed. (Oxford, 1975), maintains that conflicts between the regulatory agencies and the elected branches rarely turn on questions of substantive reform or administrative efficiency, but are essentially political conflicts between opposed interests. Herbert Kaufman, RED TAPE: ITS ORIGINS, USES, AND ABUSES (Brookings Institution, 1977), clearly and briefly explains why bureaucratic institutions, including regulatory agencies, create so many obstacles to compliance.

The world is a dangerous place. The supporters of governmental regulation believe that in the absence of such controls we will face greater hazards and dangers loosed upon us by unscrupulous entrepreneurs. The opponents hold that we will more surely be strangled by red tape and impoverished by the regulatory costs which make prices higher when they do not actually make production unprofitable. It is tempting to counsel moderation between the extreme principles, but it is difficult to apply moderation in actual practice. Take the debate on the peaceful development of nuclear energy. Neither side will be happy with a compromise that means small-scale utilization of atomic power. Such a policy will not fulfill the hopes of those who see nuclear energy as a solution for the energy crisis, and it will not allay the fears of those who see it as a threat to the lives of millions of people living near nuclear plants. Yet it is possible that, in this field as in others, the give-and-take of politics will dictate solutions which satisfy neither side and which keep the issue of regulation alive.

ISSUE 7

SHOULD WE CURB THE POWER OF THE FEDERAL COURTS?

YES: Phyllis Schlafly, from "It's Time to Reform the 'Imperial' Judiciary," *The Phyllis Schlafly Report,* September 1981

NO: Judge Irving R. Kaufman, from "Congress vs the Court," *New York Times Magazine,* September 20, 1981

ISSUE SUMMARY

YES: Conservative activist, Phyllis Schlafly, argues that the courts are abusing their power, and that jurisdiction over sensitive social issues should be withdrawn from them.
NO: Judge Irving Kaufman contends that the framers of the Constitution saw the judiciary as the best arbiters of these social issues.

Although the Supreme Court has declared fewer than one hundred Acts of Congress unconstitutional, judicial review (the power to exercise this judgment) is a critical feature of American government. It extends to all law, not simply federal law, and not only statutes, but the actions of all agents of governmental power.

The power of judicial review consists not only of a negative power to invalidate acts contrary to the Constitution but equally, and far more frequently, of a positive power to give meaning and substance to constitutional clauses and the laws enacted in accordance with constitutional power. Finally, individual cases have impact and reverberation which may profoundly influence the future direction of law and behavior. To take a prominent example, when the Supreme Court reinterpreted the equal protection clause of the Constitution's Fourteenth Amendment in 1954, it changed forever the legal and social patterns of race relations in the United States.

Some limitations on judicial review are self-imposed, such as the Court's refusal to consider "political questions," that is, questions better decided by the elective branches rather than the courts, but it is the Supreme Court which decides which questions are political. The Supreme Court has been notably reluctant to curb a President's extraordinary use of emergency power in wartime, and has done so rarely.

Still other limitations on judicial review derive from the judicial process, such as the requirement that the party bringing a case to court (any court) must have sufficient "standing" as an aggrieved party to be heard. Some laws do not appear to give any contesting party the basis for bringing a suit. Other laws rarely present themselves in an appropriate form for judicial decision, such as the ordinary exercise of presidential power in foreign relations. These exceptions qualify yet do not really negate the spirit of Alexis de Tocqueville's observation nearly a century and a half ago that "scarcely any political question arises in the United States that is not resolved, sooner or later, into a judicial question."

Judicial review is exercised by state courts and inferior federal courts as well as by the U.S. Supreme Court, but the last word is reserved to it. When a power so vast is exercised in areas so controversial as those cited, the judiciary cannot claim immunity from criticism, and it does not receive it. Critics have argued that the framers of the Constitution did not intend that so great a power should be possessed by so unrepresentative (i.e., unelected) an organ of government. The Court has been chided for going too far, too fast (law-enforcement agencies on the rights of accused persons) and for not going far enough, fast enough (civil rights activists on racial equality). In the 1930s, liberals castigated the Nine Old Men for retarding social progress in invalidating major New Deal measures. In the 1950s, conservatives pasted "Impeach Earl Warren" (Warren was then Chief Justice) stickers on their car bumpers, and they bemoaned the Court's coddling of communists and criminals. "In recent years, most of the six appointees of Republican Presidents may have turned the tide again, and critics view the Supreme Court headed by Chief Justice Warren Burger as being less sympathetic to enforced integration, women's rights, the defense of accused persons, and the protection of socially disapproved expression.

Other critics of judicial activism, such as conservative political activist Phyllis Schlafly, believe that the Court's power has become entrenched and that it subverts the democratic principle of elected rulers. Judge Irving R. Kaufman argues that our constitutional system requires an independent judiciary and that the courts protect liberty."

Whether the framers intended that the courts exercise the power of judicial review or not, they now possess it, they are not going to relinquish it, and it is unimaginable that Congress will ever take it away. The issue is therefore not whether judicial review, but how much? Should judges act on issues of social policy where legislatures have failed to act? Do courts perform a democratic function in upholding the rights of minorities, which are ultimately the rights of all, even against the power of a majority? Or do they serve democracy better by leaving questions of social change to be decided by the people's representatives?

YES

Phyllis Schlafly

IT'S TIME TO REFORM THE "IMPERIAL" JUDICIARY

A few years ago, we heard a lot of talk from the Watergate reporters about the danger to democracy from the "Imperial Presidency" — that is, from a President and White House staff who thought they were above the law and could do whatever they pleased. After many months of hammering by the media, a President resigned, dozens of Federal employees went to jail, and all threats from that source were thoroughly eliminated.

We don't hear anything in the national media about "the Imperial Judiciary," yet the Supreme Court has forced decisions down the throats of the American people which could never be approved in the democratic process, notably in the areas of forced busing and prayer in public schools.

Over the past 40 years, the Supreme Court has set itself up as a super-legislature and handed down many decisions which offend the majority of Americans. These include ordering forced busing, abolishing prayer and the Ten Commandments from the public schools, unleashing pornography, abolishing capital punishment and other deterrents to crime, interferring with the election process, and dismantling our internal security. The most shocking of all such decisions was *Roe v. Wade* in 1973 which invented the "constitutional right" of a woman to kill her unborn baby.

Some lower Federal courts have become even more carried away with delusions of their own power. The Supreme Court itself had to overrule such extreme Federal district court usurpations as ordering the registration and drafting of women when men are registered and drafted (overruled in *Rostker v. Goldberg*) and ordering the payment of tax funds for abortions even though Congress had forbidden it (overruled in *Harris v. McRae*). Other tyrannical Federal district courts have gotten away with taking over the day-to-day running of a public school system, and of a prison system, and of the political reapportionment of legislative districts.

Although the Constitution assigns "all" Federal legislative power to the Congress, and reserves to the states and to the people all powers not delegated to the Federal Government, the Federal courts have presumed to legislate in a wide range of areas in which they have no proper authority or competence. After some judges are appointed, they think they have been anointed. The problem is what to do about the activist Federal judges who have no respect for the restraints that are supposed to limit their power.

The greatness of our American system of constitutional government is that it is based on a unique and ingenious system of interlacing checks and balances. Laws are passed by a majority of both Houses of Congress, *but* can be vetoed by the President, *but* can be effectively repassed by a two-thirds majority of both Houses. Similar balancing mechanisms exist for treaties, appointments, constitutional amendments, etc.

But where are the checks on judicial usurpation? Where are the institutional balances? Can democratic government survive? Must we endure government by judges appointed for life — or can we once again have government by elected representatives?

A recent public opinion survey conducted by Sindlinger and Company of Media, Pennsylvania, for the Heritage Foundation shows that the American people are far ahead of the politicians on this issue. The people are ready and eager to cut the power of the Imperial Judiciary. Here are some of the startling results of the Sindlinger survey:

(1) 68 percent of Americans want Federal judges to run for election.
(2) 74 percent believe Federal judges should be reconfirmed periodically.
(3) 81 percent favor Congressional efforts to withdraw jurisdiction from Federal courts over cases involving issues such as busing.
(4) 62 percent would prefer to have a sensitive issue such as busing, abortion, and voluntary prayer decided in state courts rather than in Federal courts.
(5) 86 percent believe that Congress should review the rulings of Federal judges to ensure that they do not go beyond the bounds of the Constitution.
(6) 80 percent believe that only a two-thirds majority of the Supreme Court should be permitted to declare a Federal or state law unconstitutional.
(7) 55 percent believe that Congress should be allowed to overturn a Supreme Court ruling by a two-thirds majority vote.
(8) 64 percent favor limiting the authority of Federal regulatory agencies to initiate lawsuits against businesses and citizens.
(9) 77 percent say the Federal judiciary does not represent their personal views.

In the election of November 1980, the American people brought about landmark changes in the executive and legislative branches of the Federal Government. But the judicial branch remains untouched, even though it is the Federal courts which have done so many of the things about which voters are angry.

The reason why Supreme Court justices feel free to hand down pseudo-legislative, unpopular decisions and then ignore public outrage is that all Federal judges, including Supreme Court justices, enjoy life

7. SHOULD WE CURB THE POWER OF THE FEDERAL COURTS?

tenure. They do not have to run for re-election; they do not have to be reconfirmed; they have lifetime job security no matter how unwise or unpopular their decisions are.

The American voters repudiated Jimmy Carter's Administration and policies in the election of 1980. But President Carter appointed 265 Federal district and appellate court judges. That is 35 percent of the Federal court judges on the bench today, and they will be writing the Carter policies into our laws for the next 30 years.

If the American people disapprove of Ronald Reagan's policies they can throw him out of office after four years. We can change our Congressmen after only two years. But Supreme Court Justice Sandra O'Connor could be making unpopular law for the next 30 years. The nomination of Sandra O'Connor to the U.S. Supreme Court provides a perfect opportunity to arouse the nation to restore a proper balance of powers among the three branches of our Federal Government.

President Dwight Eisenhower appointed Earl Warren and William Brennan as Justices of the U.S. Supreme Court. Later, President Eisenhower told friends that he regretted the Warren appointment more than anything he ever did. If Eisenhower had lived longer, he would have regretted Brennan even more. Eisenhower had only eight years as President, but Earl Warren spent 16 years on the Court and Brennan has been there 25 years, wielding tremendous power against almost everything Eisenhower stood for.

How did President Eisenhower get conned into making such important appointments that he would regret all his life? The Warren appointment resulted from a rash political promise made during the Republican National Convention (because California Governor Warren controlled the largest single bloc of delegates). Eisenhower appointed Brennan on the basis of inaccurate information about Brennan's views.

The Sandra O'Connor appointment resulted both from a rash campaign promise and from false information about her long pro-abortion record. President Reagan was never told that Sandra O'Connor, when she served on the Defense Department advisory committee called DACOWITS, initiated and sponsored a resolution on April 6, 1975, urging the repeal of the laws that exempt women from military combat. In supporting the extremist goal of assigning women to combat duty, O'Connor placed herself contrary to the position of Congress, of the President, of the majority of the present Supreme Court, of the Republican Platform, and of the wishes of the overwhelming majority of the American people.

Justice William O. Douglas was appointed to the Supreme Court because President Franklin Roosevelt wanted to replace what he called the "nine old men" with youthful liberal justices. Douglas outlived Roosevelt and stayed on the Court for 36 years (writing 1,200 opinions), through the fourth term of President Roosevelt and the terms of Presidents Harry Truman, Dwight Eisenhower, John Kennedy, Lyndon Johnson, Richard Nixon, and Gerald Ford.

Douglas' prejudice against religion was so intense that he even questioned the constitutionality of chaplains in the armed services and the words "In God We Trust" on our money. His decisions and behavior were so objectionable that, at one time, Congressman Gerald Ford tried to have Douglas impeached because of his money dealings with Las Vegas gamblers. Ford's proposal was unsuccessful . . .

Five of the current Supreme Court

justices are over age 72. That's why many people are dismayed at the idea of giving life tenure in the Supreme Court to someone who is out of step with the pro-family, pro-life policies on which Ronald Reagan was elected.

As the American people have been confronted with one decision after another involving judicial usurpation of legislative functions, the usual response has been to try to overturn them by constitutional amendments. That has not been a satisfactory remedy. Amending the Constitution is a long-drawn-out procedure and requires super-majorities at each step of the process. Why should the people have to shoulder this burden when the fault was the abuse of power by the Federal judges?

Furthermore, resorting to constitutional amendments to overturn wrong Federal court rulings implies that the decisions were legitimate exercises of judicial authority. The court decisions should not be cloaked in that mantle of legitimacy when often they do not deserve it.

Nor is it a sufficient answer to say that the Constitution provides a process for impeachment of judges. That is a political impracticability. If Congress tried to impeach every Federal judge, or even every Supreme Court justice, who abused his power, Congress would have little time left for anything else.

The short-term solution for the problem of the Imperial Judiciary is for Congress to withdraw jurisdiction from the Federal courts in those sensitive areas where decisions have offended either the separation of powers principle or the majority of the American people, or both. The long-term solution for judicial usurpation is to cut the power of all Federal judges by eliminating their lifetime tenure which (like Samson's hair) is the source of their power.

The most effective remedy for bad Federal court appointments and decisions is to require all Federal judges and Supreme Court justices to stand for reelection as most state court judges do. This would require a constitutional amendment — but one amendment would take care of all the abuses at the same time. An amendment to Article III, that would require elections along the lines of the successful "Missouri Plan," would be a long, positive step toward ending judicial usurpation and restoring the proper balance of powers between the three branches of our government.

This constructive suggestion was made recently by Jules Gerard, professor of constitutional law at Washington University Law School in St. Louis. Gerard suggests that Federal judicial appointments be for a term of six years only. Each Supreme Court justice and Federal court judge would then be on the ballot every sixth year in the form, "Shall he be retained?" The elections would take place at the Congressional elections.

Supreme Court justices and judges of the circuit and district courts of the District of Columbia would be on the ballot nationwide.

Judges of other circuit and district courts would be on the ballot in the areas covered by their respective courts. A method would be devised to assure that not all of the judges of any multi-judge court would be on the ballot at the same election. Any judge who failed to be retained would be disqualified from holding Federal judicial office.

Another recommendation which Gerard puts forth for discussion would provide for the removal of any judge censured by two-thirds of both Houses of Congress, a short-form impeachment. There could also be some mechanism to discipline (short of removal) incompetent, lazy, abusive, or other misbehaving judges.

No doubt it will be argued that such proposals, if adopted, would deprive the Federal courts of their independence. But the constitutional role of the judiciary should not mean freedom from any restraint. Federal judges should not be in a privileged sanctuary where they alone, of all public officials, do not have to answer for abusing their power, or where they alone can wield that power for an undemocratic length of time (as Justice William O. Douglas did during the time period of seven presidential terms).

No state grants lifetime tenure to its judges. As Gerard points out, "there is no evidence that state judges [who must be elected] are less able to withstand improper pressures, or more likely to sell their souls to the devil, than Federal judges."

Strenuous efforts have been made in recent years to withdraw jurisdiction from the Federal courts on subjects on which the U.S. Supreme Court handed down highly unpopular decisions such as busing, pornography, internal security, or prayer in the public schools. In 1972, the effort led by Senator Robert Griffin to withdraw jurisdiction on busing failed in the Senate by only one vote. In 1980, the Jesse Helms Amendment to withdraw jurisdiction over prayer in public schools passed the Senate, but failed to come to a vote in the House because of the legislative chicanery practiced by Speaker Tip O'Neill.

The power of Congress to withdraw jurisdiction from the Federal courts comes from the U.S. Constitution, Article III. Section I gives Congress total power over all Federal courts except the Supreme Court, including the power to create them, to define their jurisdiction, and to abolish them altogether (thereby leaving judicial remedies to state courts).

Section 2 of Article III gives Congress the power to make "exceptions" and "regulations" to the Supreme Court's appellate jurisdiction. This is known as the Exceptions Clause.

Liberal Congresses have often withdrawn jurisdiction from the Federal courts on subjects and in periods when the liberals did not trust the Federal courts. Examples include the Norris-LaGuardia Act of 1932 (which withdrew jurisdiction over injunctions in labor disputes), the Hiram Johnson Acts of 1934 (which withdrew jurisdiction to enjoin the collection of state taxes and to interfere with the enforcement of state public utility rates), and the Emergency Price Control Act of 1942 (which withdrew jurisdiction over certain civil actions).

The Supreme Court ruled on Congress' power to withdraw Supreme Court jurisdiction in *Ex parte McCardle* (1868) stating, "we are not at liberty to inquire into the motives of the legislature. We can only examine into its power under the Constitution; and the power to make exceptions to the appellate jurisdiction of this Court is given by express words."

Congress' power to withdraw jurisdiction is an essential part of the unique American systems of checks and balances. Withdrawing jurisdiction from the Supreme and other Federal courts is the proper *check* by which Congress can *balance* the system when the judicial branch assumes too much power.

Some have argued that Congress' power to withdraw jurisdiction should not extend to the area of Supreme Court interpretation of "constitutional rights." But this argument makes no sense when applied to "rights" which the Supreme Court itself invented.

Professor Jules Gerard of Washington University Law School testified in the summer of 1981 before the Senate Sub-committee on the Constitution in support of Congress' exercising its constitutional power to regulate and make exceptions to the jurisdiction of the Federal courts. Sympathizing with the exasperation, even the despair, of those who are fed up with the Imperial Judiciary, Gerard concluded that "any step, however small, in the direction of alleviating the (intolerable) situation is to be welcomed."

In a scholarly and methodical way, without reference to any particular proposal to withdraw Federal court jurisdiction in a specific area (which most such legislative proposals try to do), Gerard showed that Congress power under Article III to make exceptions to the appellate jurisdiction of the Supreme Court, and to all jurisdiction of other Federal courts, is, on the whole "reasonably clear — clear from constitutional language, structure and history, and from prior Supreme Court decisions."

Some legal writers have asserted that today's Supreme Court would not permit the Congress to interfere with what they call the "essential functions" of the Supreme Court. This "essential functions" theory is flatly contradicted by constitutional text and history, as well as by dozens of Supreme Court opinions.

Those who assert the "essential functions" theory usually invoke the holy name of "checks and balances." But, as Professor Gerard so aptly pointed out in his testimony, "it surely is ludicrous to argue that the system of checks and balances can be maintained only by reading out of the Constitution the only explicit check on the judiciary that the Framers deliberately put there," namely, the Article III power to limit jurisdiction.

If there ever was a time for that constitutional check to be used, the time is now

because, as Gerard so eloquently stated, the Supreme Court today is "without allegiance to principle, except to the principle of being unprincipled. It regularly substitutes sophistry for logic, obfuscation for explanation, and personal predilection for reasoned analysis in its opinions, wherein day becomes night, and up means down. What it delivers in many cases are peremptory edicts rather than persuasive judgments."

What kind of persons should be appointed to the Federal courts, and whether some kind of a qualifying test should be applied, was one of the issues during the 1980 presidential campaign. Columns of newsprint were consumed in denouncing what was called the "litmus test" of the Republican Platform adopted in Detroit.

Contrary to such contrived, publicity-seeking outbursts, the Republican Platform did not require any "litmus test," but only expressed a pious hope. It said: "We will work for the appointment of judges at all levels of the judiciary who respect traditional family values and the sanctity of innocent human life."

President Carter, on the other hand, who personally appointed 35 percent of all Federal judges — more than any other President in history — made his judicial appointments on the basis of an ideological litmus test plus a race/sex quota. In 1978, he remarked, "If I didn't have to get Senate confirmation of my appointees, I could just tell you flatly that 12 percent of all my judicial appointments would be blacks, 3 percent would be Spanish-speaking and 40 percent would be women."

Carter required all his judicial appointees to be liberal, pro-abortion, pro-feminist Democrats. The American Judicature Society (the judges' equivalent of the American Bar Association) made a survey of

7. SHOULD WE CURB THE POWER OF THE FEDERAL COURTS?

Carter's appointees which showed that 48 percent considered themselves liberal, 44 percent moderate, and none conservative.

Carter made noisy boasts about his plan for "merit selection" of judges. The litmus test to be appointed to the merit selection commissions to choose the judges was "early Carter." A survey by the American Judicature Society found that virtually all members of Carter's merit selection commission were liberal Democrats, and nearly all were early Carter supporters. Hamilton Jordan selected the panelists and had final veto power over all who served.

The result of Carter's litmus test and quota selection can be seen in his four appointments to the Circuit Court of Appeals for the District of Columbia, the second most important court in the country because it handles most appeals from Federal regulatory agencies. Patricia Wald spent 25 years fighting for liberal causes, starting with the representation of Owen Lattimore (whom the Senate Internal Security Subcommittee unanimously called "a conscious articulate instrument of the Soviet conspiracy") and continuing later with her advocacy of "children's rights" (such as voting at age 13).

Abner Mikva, a left-wing Congressman from Chicago, was promoted to this important court after achieving a cumulative rating of 96% from the Americans for Democratic Action. Harry Edwards, a law professor from the University of Michigan, was a supporter of "affirmative action." Ruth Bader Ginsburg, a Columbia University law professor, was appointed because of her advocacy, in briefs and articles, of judicial activism to achieve the most extreme feminist goals.

The American people voted for a change on November 4, but they won't get a change in the judiciary for many years, if ever, because Carter's judges are locked into lifetime jobs. Yet it is the Federal judiciary, much more than the other two branches of government, which is principally to blame for the policies so offensive to the American people in the areas of crime and punishment, abortions, reapportionment, race relations, education policies, internal security against subversion, pornography, federal-state relations, land-use planning, and the environment.

Federal judges have more to say about the future of the United States, its laws, its schools, its morals, its internal defenses, its culture, than Congress. Federal judges are accountable to no one and have lifetime jobs free from the insecurities of elections, dismissals, and salary cuts.

Abram Chayes, Harvard law professor, summed it all up in a recent speech at Georgetown Law School. He said that "the legacy of [the Carter] Administration on the bench is superb, and ... will live long beyond the 1980 elections."

That is precisely why, if our constitutional democratic republic is to survive, the new Congress and the Reagan Administration *must* devise a way to shorten the life of that legacy. The Sindlinger survey proves that the American people will support the President and Congress if they exercise leadership in reducing the power of the Imperial Judiciary and overturning its wrong decisions.

• • •

NO

Irving R. Kaufman

CONGRESS VS THE COURT

The first Monday in October, the commencement of the new Supreme Court term, is normally one of the more exciting dates on Washington's calendar. The long summer recess over, the nine Justices don their black robes and enter the marble and oak courtroom where they will ponder questions of truth and justice. This year, however, [will also] be a time of no little concern for these esteemed jurists — as it should be for us all. The reason: The role of the High Court as a counterbalance to the legislative and executive branches of government — a fundamental pillar of the American system — is under attack. Congress currently has before it more than 30 bills designed to sharply restrict the authority of the Federal judiciary and limit its power to interpret the Constitution.

These bills have been introduced by members of Congress's new conservative coalition, individuals who have been profoundly disturbed by many of the decisions the Supreme Court has made over the last two decades. For example, the Court has forbidden mandatory prayer in public schools, upheld a woman's right to abortion during the first three months of pregnancy, and characterized busing as the only constitutionally adequate remedy in some instances of racial imbalance in public schools. These decisions, all formed on the basis of constitutional principle — and constitutional principle alone — undoubtedly appear as obstacles to the social changes the new legislative coalition intends to make in this country now that the political pendulum is swinging in its direction. The way the coalition proposes to overcome these obstacles threatens not only a number of individual liberties, but also the very independence of the Federal courts, an independence that has safeguarded the rights of American citizens for nearly 200 years.

The current legislative outlook is ominous. A subcommittee of the Senate Judiciary Committee has already approved a bill that would forbid the lower Federal courts to entertain challenges to state antiabortion legislation (even legislation that defined abortion as murder). In the last Congress, the Senate

7. SHOULD WE CURB THE POWER OF THE FEDERAL COURTS?

easily passed a proposal to withdraw lower Federal court jurisdiction in school-prayer cases. A discharge petition to move the bill from the House Judiciary Committee to the floor failed by only 32 votes. The bill has been reintroduced and its chances for passage are rated better in this year's Congress. Other bills which would take from the Supreme Court the power to revise state and lower Federal court decisions in school prayer, abortion and busing cases, are now wending their way through the Senate-House Judiciary Committees.

Legal experts from all sections of the political spectrum have begun stepping forward to denounce these proposals. The American Bar Association calls them a danger to the fundamental system of checks and balances. And Prof. Laurence H. Tribe, of the Harvard Law School, has gone so far as to characterize one of the bills as "too palpably unconstitutional to permit reasonable persons to argue the contrary." Still, the possibility that some of these bills may be enacted into law cannot be dismissed. If that should happen, the Supreme Court would either have to accept the Congress's mandate or adjudicate the constitutionality of the laws. If the Supreme Court then decided that the laws were, indeed, unconstitutional, it would be up to Congress either to back down or to permanently reduce the Court's power through constitutional amendment.

Such dilemmas have come close to occurring in the past. Today, it is the conservative wing that is attempting to circumscribe the Court's historical role. At other times in the past, the attack against the Court has been led by liberal reformers — while conservatives stood as sentinels guarding the sanctity of the Constitution. In the early 20th century, the Court struck down many pieces of legislation that sought to promote social change, including laws regulating child labor, setting minimum wages and maximum hours, forbidding the use of injunctions in labor disputes, and providing compensation for accident and illness. In response, liberals, and progressives led by Robert M. La Follette, attacked not only the concept of judicial review but the judges themselves. Statutes were introduced in Congress to require the votes of at least six justices to invalidate legislation, and some Congressmen supported constitutional amendments that would have mandated the popular election and recall of Federal judges.

Some years later, after the Supreme Court invalidated much New Deal legislation, President Roosevelt proposed a bill that would have allowed him to increase the Court's membership. Had that bill passed, Roosevelt would have been able to "pack" the Court with political allies, insuring that it would always decide as he saw fit. Fortunately, that plan died in the Senate Judiciary Committee.

Efforts to curb the courts have, if anything, become more frequent in recent years, and they have been proposed by politicians of almost all political stripes. After the Supreme Court's 1954 decision in Brown v. Board of Education, which declared an end to the purposeful segregation of public schools, a number of bills were introduced in Congress proposing to remove all Federal court jurisdiction in desegregation cases. At about the same time, the call for popular election of Federal judges was renewed. Later, in 1958, at the height of the cold war, serious and widespread support gathered for a bill that would have overturned Supreme Court decisions guaranteeing First Amendment freedoms to political dissidents by removing appellate jurisdiction in cases involving alleged subversive activity. And in 1964 the House of Representatives (but not the Senate) passed a bill that would have deprived the Supreme Court and the lower Federal courts of the power to hear cases regarding enforcement of the Court's new rule of one-man, one-vote for apportionment of state legislatures, a rule that was intended to redress inequities in voting strength caused by racial animus. The reapportionment decisions spurred a furious attack on the Court led by proponents of states' rights, some of whom went so far as to propose that a "Court of the Union," composed of the Chief Justices of all the states, be established to review the decisions of the Supreme Court.

All the bills under consideration this year invoke the concept of jurisdiction, the basic authority of a tribunal to decide a case. Sponsors of the bills cite Article III of the Constitution, which assigns to Congress the power to define and regulate the jurisdiction of all Federal courts including the Supreme Court. Using this power, the Congress has, for example, denied Federal judicial authority in some cases involving lawsuits for less than $10,000. No one questions the legitimacy of that restriction. So why, the sponsors ask, can Congress not also declare, as one bill does, that "the Supreme Court shall not have jurisdiction to review . . . any case arising out of any State statute, ordinance, rule or regulation . . . which relates to abortion?" The answer is not simple. It rests on an understanding of the scope of Congress's authority over the jurisdiction of the Federal courts, which, in turn, depends on an understanding of the Constitution and the role the Constitution mandates that the Federal courts play in the American system.

The framers and early expositors of the Constitution did not fear the power of the courts. With no innate authority either to enforce its own judgments or to control the purse strings, the judiciary was expected to be the weakest of the three branches of government. It was rather the legislative branch that the framers felt a need to restrain. Steeped in English parliamentary history, they knew the dangers of legislative tyranny. James Madison, the principal architect of the Constitution, observed: "The legislative department is everywhere extending the sphere of its activity and drawing all power into its impetuous vortex."

The framers set up the Federal court system as one means of checking the Congress. Using the power of judicial review, the courts would invalidate any legislative acts that were inconsistent with the strictures of the Constitution. The theory was, and still is, that Congress should exercise only a delegated authority, derived from the people. The Constitution, in contrast, was intended to represent the actual embodiment of the people's fundamental and supreme will. Thus, when presented with a case in which a legislative act contravenes the constitutional mandate, it is the duty of the courts to uphold the latter. "To deny this," said Alexander Hamilton, "would be to affirm that the deputy is greater than his principal; that the servant is above his master; that the representatives of the people are superior to the people themselves."

The Supreme Court has therefore struck down laws passed by Congress that conflict with the Constitution ever since the landmark 1803 case of *Marbury v. Madison*. For almost as long, the Court has invalidated constitutionally offensive state statutes as well. That duty, scholars insist, is grounded in Article VI of the Constitution, which commands: "This Constitution, and the laws of the United States which shall be made in pursuance thereof . . . shall be the supreme law of the land."

7. SHOULD WE CURB THE POWER OF THE FEDERAL COURTS?

It was inevitable that the judiciary, of the three branches of government, would be charged with the responsibility of assessing the constitutional validity of legislation. To insure the judiciary's ability to perform this sensitive duty faithfully and neutrally, the framers deliberately shielded the judges from political pressures by guaranteeing them, within the Constitution itself, life tenure, and by further providing that their salaries could not be diminished through legislative act. Their independence, to quote Hamilton again, would insure "that inflexible and uniform adherence to the rights of the Constitution, which we perceive to be indispensable in the courts of justice."

This is not to say that the Federal courts' judgments relating to the constitutionality of legislation — including legislation on such issues as abortion, school prayer and busing — cannot be overridden. An unpopular Supreme Court decision on a constitutional issue can be overturned through a constitutionally prescribed means: an amendment to the Constitution. In fact, three times amendments have been proposed and ratified as a way of nullifying controversial Supreme Court decisions. (The 11th Amendment, which forbids a suit in Federal court against a state without its consent, was adopted to overrule a 1793 holding that the Supreme Court had jurisdiction over a case brought by two South Carolinians against the State of Georgia. In 1868, during the Reconstruction period following the Civil War, the 14th Amendment was enacted. This amendment, which proclaims that all persons born in the United States are full citizens of the United States, with all "rights and immunities" of citizens, overruled the infamous Dred Scott decision of 1857, which had declared that black slaves, as no more than pieces of property, lacked the rights of citizens. Finally, in 1913 the 16th Amendment was adopted to overturn a Supreme Court decision holding that the Federal income tax was unconstitutional.)

Constitutional amendments, however, are not a means most critics of the Court are eager to employ to bring about the changes they seek. Their passage requires a cumbersome procedure of ratification — as supporters of the proposed equal rights amendment well know. The framers deliberately made the amendment process cumbersome because they did not want expediency to prevail over constitutional rights. They believed that any alteration of the fundamental law of the land should enjoy the overwhelming and sustained support of the citizenry. A simple majority in both Houses of Congress, sufficient to pass the ordinary statute, should not be enough to justify permanent changes in the nation's charter of basic freedoms.

Herein lies the tactical appeal of the withdrawal-of-jurisdiction strategem. Many supporters of the 30 or so divestiture bills now before Congress freely admit that they are attempting to bypass the amendment process. Their rationale is simple: Since the popular support to override Court decisions by amending the Constitution is difficult to garner, why not accomplish the same result with a simple statute restricting the power of the courts to consider the constitutional principles they dislike? In 1964, following the Supreme Court's landmark decision on legislative reapportionment, Senator Everett M. Dirkson introduced a bill to withdraw Federal court jurisdiction in apportionment cases. When asked whether he was attempting to enact a constitutional amendment in the form of a statute, he responded: "[There is] no time in the present [legislative] session to do anything with a constitutional amendment. ... We are dealing with a condition, not a theory." A candid and revealing response, then as now.

The rationale of our Constitution is not to be lightly ignored. It was designed to protect individual rights by vesting the Federal courts with the final, binding authority to interpret the fundamental law. The only way to override the Constitution as so interpreted is to amend it. The backdoor mechanism of withdrawing the Court's jurisdiction is clearly antithetical to the judiciary's role in the constitutional scheme. If the bills depriving the Court of the authority to hear cases on such topics as abortion, school prayer and busing are considered constitutional, Congress might just as well pass laws depriving the Court of the authority to hear constitutional claims based on such freedoms as speech and religion. The potential consequences are astonishing.

There is another contention being put forward by the proponents of the withdrawal-of-jurisdiction bills that needs to be discussed. These legislators note that the Constitution states that "the Supreme Court shall have appellate jurisdiction, both as to law and fact, with such exceptions, and under such regulations, as the Congress shall make." The "exceptions-and-regulations" clause, they argue, grants Congress wide-ranging authority to restrict the substantive categories of cases that may be appealed from the state and lower Federal courts to the Supreme Court. But to assert that the framers, who clearly intended the Supreme Court to exercise the power of judicial review, also intended to grant Congress plenary authority to nullify that power is to charge the framers with baffling self-contradiction. Indeed, the history of the exceptions-and-regulations clause suggests that it was never intended to carry the heavy constitutional baggage

with which the bill's supporters are now loading it.

The clause originated in the fears of some members of the Constitutional Convention that Supreme Court review of factual determinations (appellate review was to be "both as to law and fact") would impair the right-of-jury trial in the states. Hamilton stated: "The propriety of this appellate jurisdiction has scarcely been called in question in regard to matters of law; but the clamors have been loud against it as applied to matters of fact." Since the practices with respect to appellate review of factual determinations varied so widely from state to state, the framers decided to leave to Congress, in the exceptions-and-regulations clause, the authority to regulate the scope of Supreme Court review of facts.

The clause was never meant to confer a broad control over appellate review of substantive legal issues, including issues of Federal constitutional law. Indeed, the Convention considered and rejected proposed constitutional language that "the judicial power shall be exercised in such manner as the legislature shall direct." Far from a mandate to effectively abrogate the vindication of constitutional rights, the clause was intended merely as a way to give Congress the authority to regulate the Supreme Court's docket with reasonable housekeeping measures. Thus, in the Judiciary Act of 1789, Congress restricted the Court's appellate jurisdiction over cases coming from the United States Circuit Courts to those in which the amount in controversy exceeded a prescribed minimum.

On only two or three occasions in its history, has the Supreme Court passed upon the constitutionality of legislation seeking to limit its appellate jurisdiction. Both cases occurred over a century ago and both reveal constitutional defects in the current proposals relating to jurisdiction. In the first case, *Ex parte McCardle,* decided in 1869, the Court upheld a restriction on its appellate jurisdiction. Although relegated to a small niche in history, this case was enormously important in its day, for it involved a challenge to the post-Civil War Reconstruction program, in which Congress had placed 10 of the former Confederate states under military rule. McCardle had been imprisoned by the military government of Mississippi for the publication of allegedly libelous material. Pursuant to a Federal statute passed in 1867, he applied to a lower Federal court for a writ of *habeas corpus* ordering his release. He asserted that the Reconstruction Acts were unconstitutional. The court denied his application, and he appealed to the Supreme Court on the basis of that same Federal statute. Before the case was decided by the Court, however, Congress repealed that part of the 1867 statute which authorized appeals to the High Court. "We are not at liberty to inquire into the motives of the legislature," the Court held. "We can only examine into its power under the Constitution; and the power to make exceptions to the appellate jurisdiction of the Court is given by express words."

Despite this pronouncement, the McCardle case is not ordinarily read as authority for a broad Congressional power to restrict the enforcement of constitutional rights in the Supreme Court. Under the Judiciary Act of 1789, McCardle could still apply for an original writ of *habeas corpus* in the Supreme Court. Therefore, the repealing act actually cut off only one avenue of *habeas* relief. The Court concluded as much in the 1869 case of *Ex parte Yerger,* a case that was in many ways strikingly similar to *McCardle.* Yerger held

that the repealing statute did not affect the petitioner's right to apply for an original writ pursuant to the act of 1789. In contrast with the statute under consideration in *McCardle,* the bills that would forbid any Supreme Court review of busing, school prayer and abortion decisions would totally foreclose the possibility of a Supreme Court hearing on a claim of Federal constitutional right. Surely, *McCardle* cannot be considered a precedent for that.

This view is confirmed by *United States v. Klein,* decided in 1872, in which the Court struck down a limitation on its powers of appellate review. Klein administered the estate of a cotton plantation owner whose property was seized and sold by Union agents during the Civil War. Under legislation providing for recovery of seized property of noncombatant rebels upon proof of loyalty, Klein sued and won in the Court of Claims, proferring a Presidential pardon as proof of loyalty. The Court had previously interpreted a Presidential pardon as carrying with it a proof of loyalty. But pending the Government's appeal to the Supreme Court, Congress passed an act which legislated that acceptance of a pardon was, on the contrary, conclusive proof of disloyalty and one which, in addition, required the Supreme Court to dismiss for want of jurisdiction any appeal in which the claim for recovery was based on a pardon.

Invalidating that legislation, the Court concluded that Congress had unconstitutionally attempted to interfere with the Court's duty to interpret and give effect to a provision of the Constitution: "The language of the proviso shows plainly that it does not intend to withhold appellate jurisdiction except as a means to an end. Its great and controlling purpose is to deny pardons granted by the President the effect which this Court had adjudged them to have. The proviso declares that pardons shall not be considered by this Court on appeal. We had already decided it was our constitutional duty to consider them and give them effect, in cases like the present, as equivalent proof of loyalty."

In a similar manner, the current withdrawal-of-jurisdiction proposals do "not intend to withhold appellate jurisdiction except as a means to an end." And the end, in this instance, is precisely the same as it was in *Klein,* the circumvention of the Supreme Court's authoritative interpretation of a constitutional provision. As *Klein* demonstrates, Congress does not have the power to subvert established constitutional principles under the guise of regulating the Court's appellate jurisdiction.

Those who would read the exceptions-and-regulations clause broadly also argue that state courts, which frequently rely on the Federal Constitution in striking down state legislation, could adequately protect constitutional rights without review in the Supreme Court. The short answer to this contention is that a Federal constitutional right is of dubious value if it means one thing in Mississippi and another in Minnesota. State courts have at times differed profoundly on the meaning of constitutional provisions. To cite but one illustration, in 1965, the Supreme Judicial Court of Massachusetts concluded that the book "FANNY HILL" was unprotected by the First Amendment. At about the same time, the New York Court of Appeals found that it was. Obviously the need for uniformity in matters of Federal constitutional interpretation is essential, and the appellate jurisdiction of the Supreme Court was designed to meet that important need. Chief Justice John Marshall said in *Cohens v. Virginia:* "The necessity of uniformity as well as correctness in expounding the Constitution and laws of the United States,

would itself suggest the propriety of deciding, in the last resort, all cases in which they are involved. ... [The framers of the Constitution] declare that, in such cases, the Supreme Court shall exercise appellate jurisdiction."

In connection with this uniformity function, there is an interesting tale concerning one of the most eminent jurists in American history, Judge Learned Hand of the United States Court of Appeals for the Second Circuit. In 1958, at the ripe age of 86, Hand, still nimble of mind and capacious of spirit, was asked by Senator Thomas C. Hennings Jr. of Missouri, chairman of the Senate Judiciary Subcommittee on Constitutional Rights, to comment upon a then-current bill to remove Supreme Court appellate jurisdiction in cases regarding internal security. Hand promptly responded: "It seems to me desirable that the Court should have the last word on questions of the character involved. Of course there is always the chance of abuse of power wherever it is lodged, but at long last the least contentious organ of government generally is the Court. I do not, of course, mean that I think it is always right, but some final authority is better than unsettled conflict."

It should also be self-evident that the framers saw independent, tenured Federal judges — knowledgeable in Federal law, drawn from all over the country and, as prescribed in the Constitution itself, appointed by the President and confirmed by the Senate — as more appropriate arbiters of conflicts between constitutional and state law than elected state judges, many of whom are popularly elected and who might be partial to state law. The framers realized that only the Federal judges could insure the supremacy of Federal law. As James Madison said: "In controversies relating to the boundary between the two jurisdictions [Federal and state], the tribunal which is ultimately to decide is to be established under the general Government. ... Some such tribunal is clearly essential to prevent an appeal to the sword and a dissolution of the compact."

The argument for giving Congress the authority to determine the kinds of cases and the types of remedies that the inferior Federal courts may hear is a bit more complicated — if equally unpersuasive. It too is based on Article III of the Constitution, which gives Congress the right to establish "such inferior courts as the Congress may from time to time ordain and establish." Since this provision has been interpreted by many legal experts as giving Congress the right to establish or abolish the lower courts, does it not follow that it also gives Congress the authority to regulate the subject matter of their jurisdiction? The fallacy of this argument is that the framers predicated Congressional discretion on the assumption that litigants would in all cases be able to present their Federal claims or defenses to *some* Federal court, either in the district court or on appeal. And it was further assumed that, even if no lesser Federal courts were created, the Supreme Court itself would serve as the requisite forum by hearing all constitutional cases appealed from the state courts.

Throughout most of the 19th century, this was possible. The Court's docket was almost empty by today's standards and it could ordinarily hear a constitutional case any time one of the parties so desired. But beginning about 1875, the Supreme Court's case load began to grow enormously, giving rise to a series of acts, culminating in the Judges Bill of 1925, which gave the Court the discretion to decide which cases, within certain categories, it would hear. In the process, the Supreme Court was transformed from a general court of appeal into a court which would decide only cases of great constitutional moment or high precedential value.

As the Supreme Court has found itself deciding a progressively smaller percentage of the cases involving Federal, constitutional and statutory law, the role of the lower Federal courts in protecting constitutional rights has expanded to the point of practical and effective primacy. And over the last two decades, a period during which there has been an explosive growth of litigation, the inferior Federal courts have become, in most instances, the only forums in which a litigant could secure a decision on his constitutional claims by a judge life tenured under Article III of the Constitution. If Congress were now to abolish the lower Federal courts, it would effectively cut off almost all opportunity for Federal adjudication of Federal rights. And clearly, the framers did not wish to leave to the states final authority to decide matters of Federal constitutional law. For this reason, the argument that Congress can withdraw jurisdiction over certain classes of Federal cases or rights because it has discretion to abolish the lower courts does not hold up under examination.

Authoritative precedent also strongly suggests that even if Congress had the power to abolish some or all of the lower Federal courts, it may not use its power over lower court jurisdiction to thwart the vindication of constitutional rights. The Court of Appeals for the Second Circuit said in Battaglia v. General Motors Corporation, decided in 1948, that, "while Congress has the undoubted power to give, withhold and restrict the jurisdiction of courts ... it must not so exercise that power as to deprive any person of life, liberty, or property without due process of law."

The conclusion that can be drawn from all of these arguments is this: Congress does indeed have broad discretion to withdraw jurisdiction from lower Federal courts — where no substantive constitutional rights are at issue. The statutory rights that owe their existence to Congress, as distinguished from constitutional rights, may be taken away either by a repealing statute or by a provision withdrawing Federal court jurisdiction. Where rights embodied in the Constitution are concerned, however, the discretion of Congress is limited. When Congress deprives a Federal court of the authority to hear a litigant's constitutional claims or defenses, it must provide that litigant with another Federal forum in which to seek an adequate remedy. The distinguished legal scholar Henry Hart once decried the use of the statutes withdrawing lower court jurisdiction to undermine constitutional rights: "Why, what monstrous illogic! To build up a mere power to regulate jurisdiction into a power to affect rights having nothing to do with jurisdiction! And into a power to do it in contradiction to all the other terms of the very document which confers the power to regulate jurisdiction!"

Applying these lessons to the divestiture bills now before Congress, there can be no doubt that all of them trench upon established constitutional rights. The Supreme Court has determined that busing may be a constitutionally required remedy in an appropriate case for violations of schoolchildren's equal-protection rights to an education in a desegregated public school. Chief Justice Burger has written for the Court: "Bus transportation has long been an integral part of all public educational systems, and it is unlikely that a truly effective remedy could be devised without continued reliance upon it." In the landmark case of *Roe v. Wade,* the Court firmly established a woman's constitutional right to an abortion. And for nearly two decades, the Court has found mandatory prayer in the public schools to violate the constitutional principle of separation of church and state.

One may disagree with these decisions; they may even transgress one's deepest moral convictions. But one cannot doubt that they were based upon informed interpretation of the Constitution — and not on the basis of political or ideological expediency. It is worth recalling the pungent words of Chief Justice Charles Evans Hughes: "We are under a Constitution, but the Constitution is what the judges say it is, and the judiciary is the safeguard of our liberty and of our property under the Constitution." Depriving the Federal courts of the power to adjudicate cases relating to such issues as desegregation, abortion and school prayer effectively precludes Federal protection — the constitutionally envisaged and most reliable form of protection — of our cherished constitutional rights.

The result of the proposed legislation would be to deny citizens the protection of constitutional rights that the Supreme Court has declared they possess. It would be strange indeed if Congress could accomplish through a jurisdictional bill what it clearly may not accomplish directly: a reversal of constitutional principle by an act of Congress. The law is clear, for example, that Congress has no power to declare racial discrimination in Federal Government employment legal. The "logic" of the arguments raised by the proponents of the divestiture bills would, however, permit Congress to remove from the Federal courts all jurisdiction to hear cases involving racial discrimination against Government employees. The motive, discrimination, would be equally patent in

129

7. SHOULD WE CURB THE POWER OF THE FEDERAL COURTS?

either instance.

If one needs to find language in the Constitution as a source for these restrictions on the power of Congress to control the jurisdiction of the lower Federal courts, it is in the due-process clause of the Fifth Amendment. The overarching guarantee of due process is the sacred assurance that the Federal Government will govern fairly, impartially and compassionately. All the powers of Congress — to tax, to make war, to regulate commerce — are constrained by its constitutional inability to deprive us of our rights to life, liberty and property without due process of law. As a power of Congress, the authority to control jurisdiction is therefore restricted by the right of due process.That is the wonder of the American Constitution as it lives and breathes.

Should Congress insist upon restricting the judiciary in ways that the Supreme Court may view as unconstitutional, the Supreme Court might well strike down the withdrawal-of-jurisdiction legislation, leaving Congress and the judiciary in conflict. This institutional dissension would continue, until Congress either accepted the Court's determination or passed a constitutional amendment restructuring the basic relationship between the judicial and legislative branches of government.

It is understandable that politically vulnerable legislators would react adversely to judicial nullification of their enactments. Yet those who criticize the courts for their unresponsiveness to the present national mood tend to forget that the judicial branch was not designed as just another barometer of current public opinion. Congress is superbly adequate for that function, and we ought not to presume that the framers intended the judiciary as an institutional redundancy. In exercising their power of judicial review, the courts have represented the long-term, slowly evolving values of the American people, as enshrined in the Constitution. And when the people have recognized Congressional court-curbing efforts for what they are — assaults on the Constitution itself — they have in every instance rejected them.

It is of no small interest that even some of the supporters of the divestiture bills have begun to question the constitutionality of these proposals. And, indeed, there is a glimmer of hope that these doubts will eventually permeate Congress. The long history of Congressional court-curbing measures reveals that the legislative branch has in every instance ultimately yielded to the judiciary's duty to interpret the Constitution and has not (at least since passing the statute involved in the *Klein* case more than a century ago) challenged the courts with a jurisdictional bill that would impinge upon the fulfillment of that duty. Robert McKay, former dean of the New York University Law School, wrote of bills to withdraw jurisdiction over apportionment cases: "Once again, as so often in the past, when the implications of the proposed legislation were made clear, the Congress would not quite cross the threshold of no return."

The political risks attending bills to withdraw Federal jurisdiction create another check on the legislative goal of certain Congressmen. Groups of all persuasions have attempted to achieve their political aims through attacks on the Court's authority to decide constitutional cases. While it is true that political conservatives are the strongest supporters of the current efforts to withdraw jurisdiction, liberal reformers have also utilized this strategy in the past. Employed successfully by today's political majority, it could easily be manipulated tomorrow by a different majority — and to other ends. . . .

POSTSCRIPT

SHOULD WE CURB THE POWER
OF THE FEDERAL COURTS?

The opposed positions on the scope of judicial power are customarily defined as judicial activism and judicial self-restraint, the former seeking to use judicial power to fulfill constitutional purposes, the latter yielding to the popularly elected branches of the government and to the people. Neither position should be pushed too far. None are so activist as to allow judicial initiative in areas where the courts have not been asked to render decisions, and few are so self-restraining as to withdraw entirely the power of the courts to declare unconstitutional the acts and actions of elected officials.

In THE PEOPLE AND THE COURT (Macmillan, 1960), Charles L. Black, Jr. carefully developed the argument that judicial review is compatible with, and the best safeguard of, constitutional government. Eugene V. Rostow, in THE SOVEREIGN IMPERATIVE (Yale, 1962), has gone further, maintaining that judicial review serves to keep the other branches democratic. The late Alexander Bickel was possibly the most influential and profound critic of judicial review in recent times. In THE LEAST DANGEROUS BRANCH (Bobbs-Merrill, 1962), and THE MORALITY OF CONSENT (Yale, 1975), Bickel has argued that relying too much on judicial power increases the risk of committing injustice in the name of moral duty. Archibald Cox, who was the original Watergate prosecutor, has written an account of THE ROLE OF THE SUPREME COURT IN AMERICAN GOVERNMENT (Oxford, 1976) that combines the virtues of thoughtfulness and brevity.

Debate on the scope of judicial power does not deter judges from continuing to render decisions in cases involving such controversial issues as compulsory busing, preferential treatment for minorities, the right of abortion and the power of the states to outlaw it, women's rights, unions' rights, and the President's right of executive privilege. Tocqueville's observation on judicial power in 1835 will not seem to be an overstatement today: "Scarcely any political question arises in the United States that is not resolved, sooner or later, into a judicial question." But a Supreme Court that boldly entertains bitterly divisive issues cannot escape becoming a subject of political controversy itself.

ISSUE 8

SHOULD GOVERNMENT REGULATE THE MASS MEDIA?

YES: Kevin Phillips, from "Controlling Media Output," *Society*, November/December 1977

NO: William Paley, from "Press Freedom: A Continuing Struggle," Address Before Associated Press Broadcasters, June 6, 1980

ISSUE SUMMARY

YES: Kevin Phillips, author and columnist, sees the increasing concentration of power in the hands of the mass media as cause for government action.
NO: Network executive, William Paley, fears any government interference with press freedoms.

In his book CLEARING THE AIR former CBS News correspondent Daniel Schorr recounted an incident in which a staff director of a Senate committee urged him to cover a hearing, assuring him that it would have great "visual appeal." When Schorr said that he would be unable to come that day, the staff director told him that the hearing would then have to be postponed because "it was not realistic to hold the hearing without cameras—most members of the committee would simply not turn up until informed by their aides that television was present." The incident is one example among many that could be cited of the mass media's power today—the power to command attention, to define issues, to shape the agenda of public discussion, and even, in this case, to influence the legislative calendar of Congress.

Along with the power of the contemporary press is a growth of concentration and uniformity within it. In 1910 the percentage of American cities and towns with competing daily newspapers was 57.1 percent. In 1930 it was 21.5 percent, and in 1970 it had dropped to 4.13 percent. Independent newspapers continue to die out or become consolidated into large newspaper chains; the remaining ones rely heavily on wire services for national news. Television, which is now more popular than newspapers as a news source, is largely monopolized by three networks, which also own newspapers, TV and radio stations, books, and record labels.

In short, the press in America has become a big business. It has also become a controversial business. Some religious and parents groups worry about the kinds of values that TV may be instilling, consumer groups often claim that the media advertise harmful products, political activists frequently accuse the media of distorting truth and pandering to the taste for sensationalism.

It is axiomatic in American society that whenever an industry becomes powerful, concentrated, and controversial, it becomes fair game for those who say that government should "do something about it"—either break it into smaller pieces (through anti-trust action), regulate it, or take it over. Can a case be made for undertaking some such course of action against the press? Anyone who would do so must take into account one important difference between the press and other businesses in America. The press is protected by the First Amendment of the Constitution, in language which is quite specific: "Congress shall make no law . . . abridging the freedom of speech, or of the press. . . ." Indeed, even aside from the language of the Constitution, the American political tradition puts freedom of the press on the same high level on which it places freedom of speech and religion. The question, then, is how much the press can be regulated without violating this heritage of freedom.

Should government do more to regulate the media, or to break up media conglomerates? Can it do so without violating the spirit of the First Amendment?

Columnist Kevin Phillips is one who thinks that it can and should. Phillips notes that when the First Amendment was written, "the press" meant a very large number of small publications; today the situation is almost exactly reversed, for what we have now is a small number of huge media conglomerates. He argues that it may be necessary for the government to protect the public against these new forms of monopoly. On the other side of the issue is William Paley, Chairman of the Columbia Broadcasting System (CBS), who in a speech to Associated Press Broadcasters argues that both the electronic and print media need to be free of government interference.

YES — 'Kevin Phillips

THE CASE FOR MORE REGULATION

There are a few people in the national media who will deny the great power they wield, but only a few. More argument comes over whether this so-called "new" role is indeed really new. After all, talk about the press being a fourth branch of government began in the French Revolutionary era. All of our great presidents—from Washington through Jefferson, Jackson, Lincoln, and Roosevelt—tangled with the press, and their supporters made frequent reference to its power and ability to set the agenda of the national debate. Which brings us to the central question: if today's argument about the media power is to be differentiated from those of the 1790s, 1860s, or 1930s, what new factors make it so?

COMMUNICATIONS REVOLUTIONS

America has undergone a postindustrial or communications revolution elevating the major media to an economic size, technological sophistication, and cultural (political socialization) importance totally unmatched in the day of Edmund Burke or even Robert A. Taft. Increasingly, we live in a polity and society that can be described as a "mediacracy"—where communications mechanisms and the "knowledge industry" elite play the dominant role that (1) land ownership, landed elites, and their values played in aristocratic societies and (2) manufacturing, capitalist elites, and the rising middle-class values played in the Western democracies of the industrial era.

If one accepts this notion of media power having reached a new critical mass because of postindustrialism, a lot of other things follow. So let us back up and look at some reasonably solid data.

In 1790, when Edmund Burke and others were talking about the press as a fourth branch of government, what was it—newspapers alone with a circulation of a couple of hundred thousand in countries with populations of five or

From, Kevin Phillips, "Controlling Media Output," *Society*, November/December 1977. Copyright 1977 by Transaction, Inc. Reprinted by permission.

ten million; no more than that. The communications industry—the production, consumption, and dissemination of knowledge—might have accounted for a few percentage points of the Gross National Product. Even a century later, when manufacturing had displaced agriculture as the mainstay of economic life in both Britain and the United States, the knowledge and communications industries were small potatoes, totaling no more than several percentage points of the GNP.

All of this began to change with the rise of electronic communications in the 1920s and 1930s. And the other economic segments of the knowledge industry grew, too—vast research, swelling bureaucracy, massive education, mushrooming skilled professional ranks, proliferating service workers. As a result, the percentage of the GNP accounted for by the production, consumption, and dissemination of knowledge soared. In 1920 it had been about 12 percent; by 1950 perhaps 20 percent; by 1960 about 25 percent. By the early 1970s Peter Drucker and others put it at between 30-40 percent of the GNP. The knowledge industry, broadly construed, had replaced manufacturing as the critical element of the U.S. economy.

THE "NEW CLASS"

Quite a few scholars have already painted this upheaval with a richness of statistics and theoretical amplification. Daniel Bell has called it the Postindustrial Revolution. John Kenneth Galbraith, in his book *The New Industrial State*, observed that "one should expect, from past experience, to find a new shift of power in the industrial enterprise, this one from capital to organized intelligence." Organized intelligence is a short description for the knowledge industry—an admittedly

overgeneralized but nevertheless useful term.

Irving Kristol has provided elaboration of another useful point —the notion of a "New Class." To Kristol the rising knowledge industry elite is anticapitalist, and anxious to flex its new muscle. In bygone days the press used to reflect competing segments of aristocratic or industrial society. Now—at least in the national media—that is less and less true. The major national media represent the interests of the emerging New Class—their *own* class. This is unique. It has not happened before. Until the postindustrial revolution, the New Class of the knowledge industry was too small to be a power elite in its own right.

Needless to say, the process is not complete. In New York, Boston, Washington, Chicago, and Los Angeles, the national media *do* strongly interact with the larger knowledge industry—with its scholars, bureaucrats, foundation executives, interest groups, and friendly politicians. Thus the major national media—the television networks, *Time, Newsweek,* the *New York Times,* the *Washington Post*—typically mirror New Class values. But not so the television affiliates or local newpapers in many, other, smaller cities. Irving Kristol, who believes that "the media *are* the New Class," and that educators *are* the New Class, ignores these regional differences. But it was equally true that in William Jennings Bryan's day, small town Nebraska bankers did not share the politics of culture of the Wall Street titans.

For our purposes, though, the major national media set the pace. Thus their articulation of New Class attitudes is enormously influential. And this new role is a far cry from the old one (which still prevails in many small towns and cities) of being a spokesman for local agricultural or industrial interests. The national media are the linchpin of knowledge industry interests and values, and this new role has lured many of the most talented members of the New Class.

None of this would be possible except for the new technological impact of the media. But the same postindustrial revolution that has elevated the knowledge industry to 35 percent of the GNP has given the media—especially the electronic media, but they all interact—an unprecedented ability to reach people and mold national opinion. As the *Columbia Journalism Review* proclaims, new heroes and villains can be introduced to the American people overnight.

POLITICAL IMPACT

At this point, it is useful to switch focus and consider just how the new political impact of the media is different from the old. Let us begin by setting aside superficial remarks about bias and loaded coverage of liberals versus conservatives. The real problem is a good bit more complex.

First, if we are going to think about the idea of a mediacracy, it is necessary to think in terms that go beyond CBS, *Time*, and the *Washington Post*. Use of computerized voter registration lists is reliance upon a communications medium. So is use of direct mail for fundraising. So are telephone banks. So is a presidential press conference or a presidental nationwide hook-up. And it would be foolish to forget the increasing importance of rock concerts. This, too, is media politics: music is a medium. Most of what is important in U.S. politics is now media based—using this larger view of the words "media" and "medium."

Has this changed politics? Sure it has. The old politics used to depend on local machines, on individuals with a lot of money, on powerful industrial era institutions. Today's politics is changing styles. For example, most of the 1976 Democratic presidential candidates came out for marijuana decriminalization. Otherwise, few rock stars would have helped their campaigns raise money.

Televison, of course, has also changed the style of politics. It puts a premium on mediagenic candidates rather than on the machine loyalists of yesterday—and the national media in general put a premium on people who embrace the general progressivism and value structure of the New Class. (An example of this can be found in the derogations by Lyndon Johnson of media politicians in David Halberstam's *CBS: The Power and the Profits*.) Celebrityhood is shifting. The old type of celebrity was a general, a local landholder, a big businessman. Now the celebrities increasingly come from the world of knowledge, artistic performance, and media (broadly construed). The difference is quite real.

The media are also increasingly the source of new fortunes. Agriculture and land yielded to manufacturing in this capacity a century ago, and now the knowledge industry and media are taking over. To paraphrase Marshall McLuhan, the medium is also the money. Books and movies have become a major source of wealth. And even in the field of business and industry, many of the new fortunes come from the knowledge industry—computer technology (both hardware and software), communications, various processes and patents. A growing percentage of America's rich have made their money in—and are interested in—the flow of change, ideas, information, systems. A media-based politics resting on this kind of establishment simply cannot be conservative in the traditional sense.

Moreover, a number of scholars have begun to argue that the rise of the media is directly related to the emerging alienation and instability of U.S. society. A media culture wallows in the exciting, weird, negative, and different. That is the nature of the beast. Think of the institutions that have suffered: business, the military, the neighborhood, and the family. As precommunications revolution institutions, these are arguably less important to the New Class than to the average citizen. Considering all of these issues together, the impact of the major media arguably has been to increase instability and alienation.

This level of media analysis—looking at the impact of the communications revolution on the parties, the political process, ideology, society, and political socialization—is more productive than elaborate computations of minutes (or lineage) devoted to different candidates in different elections. On the national level, the real, critical power of the media does not lie in the hypothetical ability to tip an election to presidential candidate X rather than candidate Y. Instead, it lies in the ability to trumpet an issue, cripple a power center, fan a mood, create a villain (topple two presidents?), or scuttle a war.

POWER CENTER

Which brings us to the question of the media as a power center ranking with the executive, legislative, and judicial branches. This is the key. Back in 1974, when the Watergate fire storm was raging most fiercely, a survey of national opinion leaders by *U.S. News & World Report* found that television was ranked ahead of the White House as the country's number one power center. By 1975, with Richard

Nixon out of office, the presidency was ahead again, and television was in second place.

By way of background, the big loser in the postindustrial power struggle of the last fifteen years has been Congress. During the 1960s the power centers gaining were clearly the executive, the judiciary, and the media. The legislative branch was losing ground. Superficially, to be sure, the toppling of Richard Nixon changed all of that. The presidency lost ground, the Congress gained. But in many ways the seeming rise of Congress has been a mirror image of the real rise of media power. Putting things another way, could it be the new visibility—and "power"—of Congress comes from the fact that the legislative branch is the branch increasingly willing to voice what the media want voiced?

Congress now reflects the will and interest of the press, and the American people are supposed to think and act accordingly. The major media exercise a form of censorship. To gain a place in the media sun, senators and congressmen must stay out of the shade of liberal establishment disapproval. Part of the power shift also flows from media monitoring increasingly technical political decision making and selection processes. Whatever the dynamics, a growing band of conservative theorists see the power of the media as having dwarfed, displaced, and even captured that of Congress. Thus the national media—linchpin of the New Class—are seen as *the* principal foe. The media are a bigger obstacle to conservatives than the Democratic party; only a powerful presidency can turn the tide.

I substantially agree with these analyses. However, if it is difficult to see any "conservative" politics succeeding unless it challenges the media, it is also difficult to see any politics that succeeds in challenging the media as being very "conservative." In this postindustrial era of ours, the national media and knowledge industry are too central a part of the U.S. power structure. Any politics that challenges that position will have to face up to its very real neopopulist nature. Any such challenge will profoundly divide those who presently wear the conservative label.

It is becoming very difficult for the national media and their New Class allies to deny power elite status. They dislike my "mediacracy" thesis and its implications. Yet American history suggests that major emerging socioeconomic elites have generated strong political oppositions, and this one is no exception. Indeed, partly as a result of post-1960 negative reaction to the liberal politics of the New Class, "conservatism" finds itself strongest in areas like the South and West that were the strongholds of previous *populist* movements. Elite areas are the *least* conservative.

This is not the digression it might appear. We are talking about power centers. To do this, one has to think in terms of classic issues, tactics, and constituencies—less traditionally "conservative" than the populist. The arguments to which the major media are vulnerable are not piddling analyses of bias but the age-old themes of privilege, concentrated power, secrecy, oligopoly, wealth, and arrogance toward the values and institutions of ordinary Americans.

INTELLECTUAL MARKETPLACE

Raising these issues is not easy. At the first sound of tough criticism, many in the media pull the First Amendment out of their pockets and charge us with trying to extinguish freedom of the press. And anyone who is cowed by this simply becomes an easier target. The best argument is the most direct and legitimate: that the rise of major communications interests in the last fifty years has inflated the First Amendment into a protective device in much the same way that the Fourteenth Amendment was perverted in the late nineteenth century to serve as a bulwark for emerging corporations asserting the amendment's "due process" clause to block public economic regulation.

Wait a minute, you will say. Does not the First Amendment and all it implies go back to the 1790s? Yes and no. There was very little interpretation of the First Amendment until after World War I. Only in the years since the rise of the communications industry has the First Amendment become what it now so clearly is—a legal umbrella of industrial protection. Publishing stolen classified documents, listing the names of CIA agents (who can then be assassinated), printing the names of rape victims, merchandising prejudicial pretrial publicity, showing pornography, or staging bottomless dances and nude ballets are or may be protected forms of communication. Fifty years ago they would not have been—or had yet to become—key questions. Law follows power, and the expansion of the First Amendment is no exception: it has followed the expanding power of the communications industry.

Critical mass will come when the major media are perceived as enormously powerful commercial operations—indeed, as among the newest and most highly developed forms of U.S. economic activity—that bear no socioeconomic relationship to the struggling backroom press of the 1790s. Gone are the days when anyone could start up the only existing communications vehicle—a newspaper or periodical—with a minimal outlay. Today it is still possible to start up a local newspaper or a specialized periodical, but who can start up a television network, a *Newsweek,* or a *Washington Post?* Nobody can. We are dealing with economic mass and concentration that would have been beyond the imagination of a Thomas Jefferson or James Madison. To hear their names invoked on behalf of, say, CBS, is tawdry and specious.

Perhaps increasing realization of this commercial magnitude and concentration will lead to more acceptance of the ideas of Ronald Coase, who argues that the normal treatment of governmental regulation of markets makes a unique distinction between the market for goods and services and the market for First Amendment-related commodities like speech and writing. Regulation of the goods market is applauded, regulation of the other condemned. As Coase notes, the ideas market is the only one where laissez faire is still respectable.

Conservatives may applaud, but more careful analysis is likely to be discouraging. Bear in mind that as manufacturing and industry had its laissez-faire period one hundred years ago, its elite used that freedom to triumph over agriculture and aristocracy. Laissez faire policies were a tool and expression of that triumph; a hundred years later, with business on the run, there is no more chance of restoring laissez faire in industry than there is of selling Manhattan back to the Indians. What is more, today's laissez faire license for the media oligopolies and their New Class viewpoints identified by Irving Kristol can generally be said to further threaten American manufacturing, agriculture, and natural resource producers. Indeed, laissez faire for the media under the banner of the First Amendment represents a threat to non-knowledge industry-favored public sector, just as laissez faire for mid-nineteenth century industry was a force for

aggrandizement of the industrial segment of the economy at the expense of the agricultural sector.

To be sure, the emergence of the knowledge sector is a force that will not be denied. But it seems just as certain historically that more and more regulation will be imposed. Coase suggests that although intellectuals "exalt the market for ideas and deprecate the market for goods," the market for ideas is equally commercial—the place where the intellectual does his trading—and worthy of regulation in the public interest. As the media gain importance, this will happen. Would it not be a fair turnabout if media products advocating busing, forgiveness for criminals, and the like could be removed from circulation by an Intellectual Product Safety Commission?

REGULATING THE MEDIA

If, as I have argued, the media have emerged as a massive national power center, and if the answer is (as I believe it to be) active and innovative regulation, the last question is "What kind of active and innovative regulation?"

In the case of the television networks, it seems high time to more fully assert public control of and authority over the airwaves. Increased competition from cable has by and large proven to be a pipe dream; that uncertain hope should no longer distract us from strong measures. If a reformer could work in a political vacuum, the following would seem desirable: (1) strengthening the fairness doctrine; (2) applying tough antitrust measures to break the three networks into eight or nine, and forcing all networks to divest themselves of their owned-and-operated stations in opinion-molding national markets like New York, Washington, and Los Angeles; and

(3) establishing a national commission (like Ontario's much applauded Royal Commission on Violence and the Communications Industry) to consider the impact of television in promoting crime, violence, social disintegration, and alienation, and then propose the necessary legislation and controls.

As for the print media, the leading cartels and concentrations deserve careful attention. We should begin by thinking of companies and marketplaces and narrowing the expanded industrywide First Amendment protections of the last forty or fifty years. For example, the *Washington Post* has a dominant or substantial share of the market on four levels—newspaper, newsweekly, television, and AM-FM radio—in Washington, D.C., a market which differs from others in the country in that it serves as a national news dissemination center. Concentration in this market—or in New York—should be treated differently regarding a national information product than a similar concentration in Boise. New antitrust legislation ought to differentiate media products and markets.

There is another aspect to considering media conglomerates as commercial entities rather than sacred First Amendment cows: should an editorial or other favorable media accolade be considered as a corporate contribution? Take the example of two corporations in the drug business: one also owns a newspaper, one does not. The one without a newspaper may not be able to use corporate funds to run advertisements in support of industry political goals. But the one with a newspaper can (1) run all the editorials it wants in support of drug industry political goals; (2) endorse any candidate it wants without giving space to an opponent; and (3) run all the editorials (or advertisements) it wants in support of the First Amendment and other items of political and commercial importance to the media industry. In the future this paradox will become clear, with more attention being paid to the public or shareholder interest in restraining the self-serving acts of media as well as other corporations.

PUBLIC'S "RIGHT TO KNOW"

At this point it may be appropriate to discuss that other great protest cry of the major media—"the public's right to know." Whenever a media corporation is seeking a privilege, like the right to boost its sales and peer group reputation by printing stolen classified information or other secrets, we hear about "the public's right to know." What they are doing is not really for themselves, but for the *people*. However, in the privacy of court or legislative deliberation, there is none of that. The major media, when other privileges are involved, dismiss any public "right to know."

The major media have become so important that they exercise some quasi-public functions in which the public clearly has a regulatory interest. This could prove to be a critical tool and approach. Using the Fourteenth Amendment, which prohibits states from denying anyone equal protection or due process, courts have held that this prohibition on state action can be extended to private corporations where corporations are working for the government or performing a public function. In this connection, bear in mind that thirty-odd years ago, the then whites-only primaries of the Democratic party in the South were deemed to be private affairs beyond the reach of federal law. But in 1944 the U.S. Supreme Court found that the Texas Democratic primary was, in essence, serving so critical a political function that it amounted to governmental action, and (Fifteenth Amendment) regulatory jurisdiction was thus established.

If the whites-only Democratic primary of Texas in 1944 represented so much of the political process that it could no longer be called "private," how long will it be until the major media fall afoul of a kindred standard? Richard Reeves, Edward Hunter, Jeffrey Hart, Pat Buchanan, and others have all bluntly described the relentless flow of political and quasi-governmental power in these private hands. And even *New York Times* reporter Les Brown, urging greater TV coverage, has characterized the networks as a "government of leisure" because of the average 6 - 7 hours the average American family views TV each day.

Which brings us back to the question of "the media"as "a power center." Speaking of the national media, of course, they are—one that will get bigger and bigger and bigger without effective countermeasures. And the politics of the next few decades will in no small measure be determined by what people are courageous enough to do about it.

● ● ●

NO   William Paley

WE MUST FIGHT
GOVERNMENT INCURSION

This is a lively and impressive gathering. Your agenda is timely. The subjects are vital. All of it bodes well for the profession of journalism.

To be in this setting would be stimulating to me in any case. But to be here to receive this singular award from you has its own special impact. I am very proud of this honor. And I also appreciate this opportunity to speak on a subject which has been close to my heart for the major portion of my adult life.

As historians have often observed, history is replete with ironies. To take an example very much on our own doorstep, the growing adversary relationship in America between two of our most important institutions, the courts and the press, is an irony of the choicest kind. We have a constitution which guarantees freedom of the press in a way unique among nations. Yet the Supreme Court, which has long been considered among the staunchest defenders of press freedoms, has in recent years, handed down a series of decisions which seriously weaken press rights which many of us believe the Constitution clearly intended to confer. The time has come when we need to ask ourselves what this new trend may mean to our future as a democracy.

My purpose today is not only to discuss what I see as the gradual erosion of press freedoms in general; I also want to focus on a new and rapidly developing situation—namely, that communications technology is creating for the print media some potential new First Amendment problems which are similar to those that we have faced in broadcasting for many years.

I don't believe anyone would argue seriously against the proposition that if a democracy is to function efficiently the public must be informed of the actions of all its governing institutions—including those of the judicial system. Jefferson's familiar words on this subject are even *more* valid today. He said:

> "The basis of our government being the opinion of the people, the very first object should be to keep that right; and were it left to me to decide whether we should

From, address before Associated Press Broadcasters Convention, Denver, Colorado, June 6, 1980, by William Paley. Reprinted by permission.

have a government without newspapers, or newspapers without a government, I should not hesitate a moment to prefer the latter."

Modern technology has made not only newspapers, but magazines and books available to everyone, while radio and television have brought the world into the homes of nearly all Americans.

In the midst of this abundance, however, there have been a number of recent Supreme Court decisions which have limited the First Amendment rights of the press. We've been complacent in the belief that no matter what the shifting ideological complexion of the Court might be, the First Amendment's meaning would, on balance, be preserved. But the trend of recent decisions gives us ample reason to believe that our complacency may not have been justified.

These decisions are remarkable for the range of their implications and deserve our thoughtful examination. In *Zurcher v. Stanford Daily,* the Court, in 1978, held that government agents could obtain a warrant to search a newsroom for photographs, notes and research files if they were seeking criminal evidence. It has since been argued that the press over-reacted to this decision, and that no newsrooms have yet been searched. Nevertheless, the power to do so exists. And that fact represents an ever-potential danger and inhibits press freedoms. As this case reflects, a majority of the Supreme Court has refused to recognize the need of the press for protection of its right to gather news.

In another series of cases the Court ruled that the press had no special right of access to a prison to report on prison conditions, despite the strong public interest in access to that information. The effect of that decision, quite simply, is to prevent the public from learning first-hand of the conditions of their own public institutions—and this may come as a result of decisions by public officials who may have their own strong interest in preventing disclosure of such conditions.

In 1979, the Supreme Court stunned the press with its decision in *Gannett Co. v. DePasquale.* There the Court ruled that a criminal court judge had the right to exclude the press and the public entirely from pretrial proceedings. As a result, pre-trial proceedings have been closed with alarming frequency. Indeed, some courts have used this decision as the basis for conducting actual trials behind closed doors. It was only four decades ago that the Supreme Court said that the business of the courts is public business. I suggest that in a democracy it is intolerable for the judicial process to be put beyond public scrutiny.

In the last few years, other decisions have further amplified these negative First Amendment trends. What it comes down to is this: Our longstanding concept that the media represent the public interest—that they are the buffer state between the governors and the governed—is now threatened by judicial decisions as never before in modern times.

As we reflect on this growing threat to our ability to inform the public fully, it is just as important to remind ourselves of our own primary obligation. We must report the news fairly and accurately. Objectivity may be an impossible ideal. But it is an ideal toward which we must strive constantly, maintaining standards so high that the public will be convinced of what we are trying to do. If we make errors—as inevitably we will—it is our duty to correct them and without delay. We must regard objectivity and accuracy as basic to our responsibility as custodians of a free press.

8. SHOULD GOVERNMENT REGULATE THE MASS MEDIA?

It is worth remembering that the First Amendment was enacted at a time when there was no concept of responsibility in the press and no inclination to create one. The ideals of objectivity and responsibility, voluntarily assumed by the press, are a product of *this* century, and it is an odd paradox that now, when the press has attained by far the greatest degree of responsibility and objectivity in its long history, is precisely the time when press freedoms have been given such adverse treatment by the Supreme Court and others.

Too many of us in print and broadcasting have imagined that we had separate destinies and separate problems, but the destinies and the problems of each are becoming the same.

The print media have a long tradition of freedom in this country, dating from the time in the early eighteenth century when they broke away at last from the control of British press licensing, then later from restrictions by provincial legislators.

The history of the broadcast media is quite different. In the early Twenties, the sudden, uncontrolled proliferation of radio stations filled the air with confusion. As a result, the broadcasters themselves appealed for government control to bring about technical order. But the government did more than that. It acted on the theory that the government, on behalf of the people, had a right to control the airwaves—which meant controlling the means of transmission. And so the Congress produced the Radio Act of 1927, with a Federal Radio Commission to enforce its terms, and then the Communications Act of 1934, enforced by a Federal Communications Commission.

It is certainly true that the framers of the First Amendment did not foresee the technology of broadcasting. But neither did the legislators who drew up the various communications acts foresee the pervasiveness of that technology: that very soon news broadcasting would become a most important part of the press especially in terms of numbers of people reached. Whatever the merits of the competing media may be, it is a fact that more people watch television news than read newspapers, and the polls show that more people believe what they see and hear on television and radio than what they read. It's strange, to say the least, that the medium on which the public places most reliance for news is the medium with the least First Amendment protection. Yet the Congress has resolutely refused to confront that fact, never seriously considering that broadcast journalism should have the same First Amendment protections enjoyed by the print media.

The fact is that today the print and electronic media are still running on separate legal and regulatory tracks. On the one hand, the print media are increasingly restrained by the actions of the courts; on the other, broadcast journalism is restrained not only by the same courts, but even more by such obsolete legislative and regulatory restrictions as the "equal time" and fairness doctrine provisions, the inhibiting effects of which are clearly inconsistent with the spirit of the First Amendment.

I believe broadcasting has, in fact, earned its claim to freedom. It has generally adhered to the principles of fairness in dealing with news and public affairs, and has followed its own voluntary guidelines to assure responsibility. Under the First Amendment, it seems to me, there can be no doubt that broadcasters—and not the government—must have the responsibility to define and resolve problems of fairness. They are answerable to their audiences. They are vulnerable to their competitors. They are exposed to constant public criticism. And they are conscientious, profes-sional journalists. Is any government agency better qualified, even assuming it had the right?

Yet the FCC chose to enunciate the policy known as the fairness doctrine. The doctrine so contradicts the basic premise of the First Amendment that the FCC has often exhibited moderation (and at times confusion) in implementing it, but the doctrine unquestionably gave a govern-ment agency the right to judge a news organization's performance. If it had been applied to newspapers instead, it is hard to believe that any court would have been able to construe it any other way than as a violation of the First Amendment.

Critics of broadcasting have long charged that the basic reason for regulating the medium through such measures as the fairness doctrine is that there is only room for a certain number of stations on the broadcast spectrum, but that there is no technical limitation on the number of newspapers that could be printed.

To anyone still arguing that this "scarcity principle" has any meaning as a grounds for enforced fairness, I can only point to the fact that a scarcity of broadcast outlets, as compared with daily newspapers, simply no longer exists. Indeed, it's the other way around. In 1927, there were 677 broad-casting stations in the United States and 1,949 daily newspapers. Today there are 1,756 daily newspapers and 9,774 broad-casting stations. The number of voices these stations produce far exceeds that provided by any other mass medium at any time in our history. It is also important to be aware that for every half hour spent with network news, viewers spend more than twice as much time with locally pro-duced newscasts.

I believe we must remove the "equal time" and fairness doctrine provisions from the books. They were wrong when promulgated, and they are wholly unreal today.

There is another First Amendment de-velopment we should focus on, a relatively new phenomenon involving print and broadcasting. Broadcasters and print people have been so busy improving and defending their own turf that it has es-caped some of us how much we are being drawn together by the vast revolution in "electronification" that is changing the face of the media today, and thereby bringing the issue of government control for both of us into even sharper focus.

What we've done is to create a vast complex of information machines, which are being fed by a storehouse of knowl-edge and entertainment of every conceiv-able kind. This endless mass of material is fed from diverse sources into the process, and it comes out the other end in a variety of ways. Technology is greatly increasing that variety every day. Even now, sitting at home, the consumer is able to tap not only the conventional radio and television broadcasts, comprehensive as they are—the phonograph records which stock his shelves—but a vast and growing array of audio and video cassettes, tape and film. What isn't packaged can come into the house by cable. With the aid of new computerized equipment, people will be able to select a remarkable range of what they want to see and hear, and have it brought to them aurally and visually, whether by pictures or printout. It is al-ready technically possible to bring news-papers and magazines into the home, both on the television screen and by printout. Before long all this will be delivered as easily as the television pictures which now come to you. And all of this refers to technology which already exists. Just think of the next wave of revolutionary communications technology which is in planning or will soon be off the drawing boards. The possibilities border on the incredible.

This new era of information plenty, with its convergence of delivery mechanisms for news and information, raises anew some critical First Amendment questions about our freedom which merit comprehensive rethinking. Once the print media comes into the home through the television set, or an attachment, with an impact and basic content similar to that which the broadcasters now deliver, then the question of government regulation becomes paramount for print as well.

Already the FCC has the same "equal time" and fairness doctrine powers over cable originators as it does over conventional broadcasts. And print may well find its way into the home through cable. It would be foolish indeed for the print media not be concerned that their output in this form may be drawn into the regulatory web whether through cable or other technology.

Before such a foothold is established, the print and broadcast media will have to unite and fight against the imposition of governmental controls on them, beginning with the removal of the present regulatory restraints on broadcasting. Let us recognize that our interests no longer run on separate tracks. It is imperative, in my view, that print and broadcasting people understand they have a common cause, and that cause is the removal of governmental intrusion in the editorial process. We must make our case not only to the courts and to the legislators, but most important, to the public itself.

Alexander Hamilton well understood that point. In 1788, Jefferson had argued that the press could be kept free merely by placing guarantees to that effect in the Constitution. But Hamilton was more prophetic. He observed that no matter what guarantee was inserted in any constitution, press freedom would never be secure without the support of public opinion. It depended, as he put it, "on the general spirit of the people and of the government."

I am fully convinced that one of our most urgent goals must be to help create that general spirit in the people and in the government—a spirit that will preserve the freedom of the press that is so essential to our democratic society.

Gaining freedom never comes easily. Remaining free calls for a matching measure of conviction and diligence.

● ● ●

POSTSCRIPT

SHOULD GOVERNMENT REGULATE
THE MASS MEDIA?

A former head of the General Motors Corporation once said, "what is good for the country is good for General Motors and vice-versa." The implication was that the General Motors Corporation represented the real interests of the American people. Those who would hesitate before affirming that proposition might also want to think hard about Paley's assertion that the American mass media "represent the public interest," and should therefore serve as "buffer state" in America.

Ronald Reagan has called it an "incestuous relationship." Timothy Crouse, in THE BOYS ON THE BUS (Random House, 1973) calls it "pack journalism." Both are referring to the tendency of reporters to build on each other's stories, repeating over and over the catch-phrases of a campaign season. Herbert J. Gans's DECIDING WHAT'S NEWS (Pantheon, 1979) lends some weight to the "incestuous" thesis by its finding that *Time, Newsweek,* and the three TV networks are strongly influenced by *The New York Times* when it comes to deciding what stories to cover. Edward Jay Epstein's NEWS FROM NOWHERE (Random House, 1973), though critical of television news, takes issue with the view that it is distorted because of ideological bias.

In the Introduction to this book we identified a "New Deal liberal" as one who supports government intervention in the economic sphere. By classifying the press as another irresponsible "big business," Phillips argues that it is as much a candidate for government regulation as any other big business which abuses its power. Since Phillips has allied himself with the right wing of the Republican party (see his THE EMERGING REPUBLICAN MAJORITY, Arlington House, 1969), it is hard to see how far Phillips would push his argument for government regulation. Would he support more regulation of oil companies, or an anti-trust suit against General Motors? If "the emerging Republican majority" follows the logic of Phillips's position, it could be the ultimate tribute to Franklin D. Roosevelt.

ISSUE 9

WILL TOUGHER SENTENCING CURB CRIME?

YES: J.Q. Wilson, from THINKING ABOUT CRIME (New York, 1975)
NO: David Bazelon, from *The Center Magazine,* Santa Barbara, California

---

ISSUE SUMMARY

YES: Political scientist Wilson contends that stricter sentencing practices would have dramatic impact on the crime rate in the U.S.
NO: Federal Judge Bazelon defends his position that meaningful crime control must focus on the social conditions which breed it in the first place.

Crime is a major social problem in America, and most Americans suspect that it is growing worse. There is little disagreement on objectives; everyone, except perhaps the criminals themselves, wants to eliminate crime. The question is: how?

The problem is serious and complex. The fact is that even the federal crime index does not give a precise idea of the incidence of major crime. (Major crimes are identified by the Federal Bureau of Investigation as criminal homicide, forcible rape, robbery, aggravated assault, burglary, larceny over $50, and auto theft.) We cannot even be certain whether the incidence of major crimes has increased strikingly in recent decades or whether more crimes are being reported by victims (the increase in personal, automobile, and home insurance has probably led to an increase in reported crimes) and better recorded by police.

There are, however, some aspects of crime in the United States that are indisputable. Crime is widespread but more concentrated in urban areas. It is disproportionately committed by the young, the poor, and members of minority groups. The commission of some crimes (those that require public knowledge of the activity, such as prostitution, drug selling, and gambling) will involve the corruption of law-enforcement officials. The rates for some crimes, particularly violent crimes, are much higher in the United States than in many other countries. For example, there are more criminal homicides in New York City (whose *rate* of homicide is lower than that of a number of other American cities) than in all of Great Britain or Japan, which have respectively nine and fifteen times the population of New York.

One more aspect of crime about which there is little dispute is the increased public awareness of the problem, and the widespread fear which people, particularly parents and older people, feel in high-crime areas. Something needs to be done, but what? Reform society? Reform criminals? There are those who would deal with what they describe as root causes, but our knowledge of aberrant behavior is too slight to give us confident belief that we know what the root causes of crime are. Others think that the solution lies in the severity of punishment. One often hears the slogan, "Lock them up and throw away the keys!" Short of such constitutionally (and morally?) questionable action, imprisonment raises questions even as it resolves others. Imprisonment for whom, for how long, and for what crimes? Most of the Watergate criminals, whose offenses endangered the American electoral process, were sent to country-club prisons for a matter of months. Lower-class criminals usually serve their longer terms in much bleaker surroundings. Is our system of justice biased in favor of white-collar and well-connected criminals? Even if it is not, or even if the bias is corrected, are most prisons serving the purposes they are supposed to serve? Do they really deter crime, or do they serve as schools for criminals, making them more hardened? Are there perhaps more "enlightened" ways of dealing with crime in America?

These are some of the questions touched upon by U.S. Court of Appeals judge David Bazelon and political scientist James Q. Wilson in the selections following. It will be seen that their answers are quite different from one another.

YES

James Q. Wilson

THINKING ABOUT CRIME

I argue for a sober view of man and his institutions that would permit reasonable things to be accomplished, foolish things abandoned, and utopian things forgotten. A sober view of man requires a modest definition of progress. A 20 per cent reduction in robbery would still leave us with the highest robbery rate of almost any Western nation but would prevent about sixty thousand robberies. A small gain for society, a large one for the would-be victims. Yet a 20 percent reduction is unlikely if we concentrate on improving police efficiency. Were we to devote those resources to a strategy that is well within our abilities—namely, to incapacitating a larger fraction of the convicted serious robbers—then not only is a 20 percent reduction possible, but even larger ones are conceivable.

Most serious crime is committed by repeaters. What we do with first offenders is probably far les. important than what we do with habitual offenders. A genuine first offender (and not merely a habitual offender caught for the first time) is in all likelihood a young person who, in the majority of cases, will stop stealing when he gets older. This is not to say we should forgive first offenses, for that would be to license the offense and erode the moral judgments that must underlie any society's attitude toward crime. The gravity of the offense must be appropriately impressed on the first offender, but the effort to devise ways of reeducating or uplifting him in order to insure that he does not steal again is likely to be wasted—both because we do not know how to reeducate or uplift and because most young delinquents seem to reeducate themselves no matter what society does.

After tracing the history of nearly ten thousand Philadelphia boys born in 1945, Marvin Wolfgang and his colleagues at the University of Pennslyvania found that over one-third were picked up by the police for something more serious than a traffic offense, but that 46 percent of these delinquents had no further police contact after their first offense. Though a third started on crime,

From THINKING ABOUT CRIME, ©1975, Basic Books Inc. Reprinted by permission.

nearly half seemed to stop spon-
taneously—a good thing, because the
criminal justice system in that city, already
sorely taxed, would in all likelihood have
collapsed. Out of the ten thousand boys,
however, there were six hundred twenty-
seven—only 6 percent —who committed
five or more offenses before they were
eighteen. Yet these few chronic offenders
accounted for *over half* of all the
recorded delinquencies and about *two-
thirds* of all the violent crimes committed
by the entire cohort.

Only a tiny fraction of all serious crimes
lead immediately to an arrest, and only a
slightly larger fraction are ultimately
"cleared" by an arrest, but this does not
mean that the police function is meaningless. Because most serious crime is committed by repeaters, most criminals
eventually get arrested. The Wolfgang
findings and other studies suggest that
the chances of a persistent burglar or
robber living out his life, or even going a
year, with no arrest are quite small. Yet a
large proportion of repeat offenders. . .
suffer little or no loss of freedom. Whether
or not one believes that such penalties, if
inflicted, would act as a deterrent, it is
obvious that they could serve to incapacitate these offenders and thus, for the
period of the incapacitation, prevent
them from committing additional crimes.

We have a limited (and declining) supply of detention facilities, and many of
those that exist are decrepit, unsafe, and
overcrowded. But as important as expanding the supply and improving the
decency of the facilities is the need to
think seriously about how we wish to
allocate those spaces that exist. At
present, that allocation is hit or miss. A
1966 survey of over fifteen juvenile cor-
rectional institutions revealed that about
30 percent of the inmates were young

persons who had been committed for
conduct that would not have been judged
criminal were it committed by adults.
They were runaways, "stubborn children," or chronic truants—problem
children, to be sure, but scarcely major
threats to society. Using scarce detention
space for them when in Los Angeles over
90 percent of burglars with a major prior
record receive no state prison sentence
seems, to put it mildly, anomalous.

Shlomo and Reuel Shinnar have
estimated that the effect on crime rates in
New York State of a judicial policy other
than that followed during the last decade
or so. Given the present level of police
efficiency and making some assumptions
about how many crimes each offender
commits per year, they conclude that the
rate of serious crime would be only *one-
third* what it is today if every person
convicted of a serious offense were imprisoned for three years. This reduction
would be less if it turned out (as seems
unlikely) that most serious crime is committed by first-time offenders, and it
would be much greater if the proportion
of crimes resulting in an arrest and conviction were increased (as also seems
unlikely). The reduction, it should be
noted, would be solely the result of incapacitation, making no allowance for
such additional reductions as might result
from enhanced deterrence or rehabilitation.

The Shinnar estimates are based on
uncertain data and involve assumptions
that can be challenged. But even assuming they are overly optimistic by a
factor of two, a sizable reduction in crime
would still ensue. In other countries such
a policy of greater incapacitation is in fact
followed. A robber arrested in England,
for example, is more than three times as
likely as one arrested in New York to go to

9. WILL TOUGHER SENTENCING CURB CRIME?

prison. That difference in sentencing does not account for all the difference between England and American crime rates, but it may well account for a substantial fraction of it.

That these gains are possible does not mean that society should adopt such a policy. One would first want to know the costs, in additional prison space and judicial resources, of greater use of incapacitation. One would want to debate the propriety and humanity of a mandatory three-year term; perhaps, in order to accommodate differences in the character of criminals and their crimes, one would want to have a range of sentences from, say, one to five years. One would want to know what is likely to happen to the process of charging and pleading if every person arrested for a serious crime faced a mandatory minimum sentence, however mild. These and other difficult and important questions must first be confronted. But the central fact is that *these are reasonable questions* around which facts can be gathered and intelligent arguments mustered. To discuss them requires us to make few optimistic assumptions about the malleability of human nature, the skills of officials who operate complex institutions, or the capacity of society to improve the fundamental aspects of familial and communal life.

Persons who criticize an emphasis on changing the police and courts to cope with crime are fond of saying that such measures cannot work so long as unemployment and poverty exist. We must acknowledge that we have not done very well at inducting young persons, especially but not only blacks, into the work force. Teenage unemployment rates continue to exceed 20 percent; though the rate of growth in the youthful component of the population has slowed, their unemployment shows little sign of abating. To a degree, anticrime policies may be frustrated by the failure of employment policies, but it would be equally correct to say that so long as the criminal justice system does not impede crime, efforts to reduce unemployment will not work. If legitimate opportunities for work are unavailable, many young persons will turn to crime; but if criminal opportunities are profitable, many young persons will not take those legitimate jobs that exist. The benefits of work and the costs of crime must be increased simultaneously; to increase one but not the other makes sense only if one assumes that young people are irrational.

One rejoinder to this view is the argument that if legitimate jobs are made absolutely more attractive than stealing, stealing will decline even without any increase in penalties for it. That may be true provided there is no practical limit on the amount that can be paid in wages. Since the average "take" from a burglary or mugging is quite small, it would seem easy to make the income from a job exceed the income from crime. But this neglects the advantages of a criminal income. One works at crime at one's convenience, enjoys the esteem of colleagues who think a "straight" job is stupid and skill at stealing is commendable, looks forward to the occasional "big score" that may make further work unnecessary for weeks, and relishes the risk and adventure associated with theft. The money value of all these benefits—that is, what one who is not shocked by crime would want in cash to forego crime—is hard to estimate, but is almost certainly far larger than what either public or private employers could offer to unskilled or semiskilled young workers. The only alternative for society is to so increase the risks of theft that its value is depreciated below what society can afford to pay in legal wages, and then take whatever steps are necessary to insure that those legal wages are available.

Another rejoinder to the "attack poverty" approach to crime is this: The desire to reduce crime is the worst possible reason for reducing poverty. Most poor persons are not criminals; many are either retired or have regular jobs and lead conventional family lives. The elderly, the working poor, and the willing-to-work poor could benefit greatly from economic conditions and government programs that enhance their incomes without there being the slightest reduction in crime—indeed, if the experience of the 1960s is any guide, there might well be, through no fault of most beneficiaries, an increase in crime. Reducing poverty and breaking up the ghettoes are desirable policies in their own right, whatever their effects on crime. It is the duty of government to devise other measures to cope with crime, not only to permit antipoverty programs to succeed without unfair competition from criminal opportunities, but also to insure that such programs do not inadvertently shift the costs of progress, in terms of higher crime rates, onto innocent parties, not the least of whom are the poor themselves.

One cannot press this economic reasoning too far. Some persons will commit crimes whatever the risks; indeed, for some, the greater the risk greater the thrill, while others—the alcoholic wife beater, for example—are only dimly aware that there are any risks, But more important than the insensitivity of certain criminal activities to changes in risks and benefits is the impropriety of casting the crime problem wholly in terms of a utilitarian calculus. The most serious offenses are crimes not simply because society finds them inconvenient, but because it regards them with moral horror. To steal, to rape, to rob, to assault—these acts are destructive of the very possibility of society and affronts to the humanity of their victims. It is my experience that parents do not instruct their children to be law abiding merely by pointing to the risks of being caught, but by explaining these these acts are wrong whether or not one is caught. I conjecture that those parents who simply warn their offspring about the risks of crime produce a disproportionate number of young persons willing to take those risks.

Even the deterrent capacity of the criminal justice system depends in no small part on its ability to evoke sentiments of shame in the accused. If all it evoked were a sense of being unlucky, crime rates would be even higher. James Fitzjames Stephens makes the point by analogy. To what extent, he asks, would a man be deterred from theft by the knowledge that by committing it he was exposing himself to one chance in fifty of catching a serious but not fatal illness— say, a bad fever? Rather little, we would imagine—indeed, all of us regularly take risks as great or greater than that when we drive after drinking, when we smoke cigarettes, when we go hunting in the woods. The criminal sanction, Stephens, concludes, "operates not only on the fears of criminals, but upon the habitual sentiments of those who are not criminals. A great part of the general detestation of crime. . . arises from the fact that the commission of offenses is associated . . . with the solemn and deliberate infliction of punishment wherever crime is proved."

Much is made today of the fact that the

criminal justice system "stigmatizes" those caught up in it, and thus unfairly marks such persons and perhaps even furthers their criminal careers by having "labeled" them as criminals. Whether the labeling process operates in this way is as yet unproved, but it would indeed be unfortunate if society treated a convicted offender in such a way that he had no reasonable alternative but to make crime a career. To prevent this, society ought to insure that one can "pay one's debt" without suffering permanent loss of civil rights, the continuing and pointless indignity of parole supervision, and frustration in being unable to find a job. But doing these things is very different from eliminating the "stigma" from crime. To destigmatize crime would be to lift from it the weight of moral judgment and to make crime simply a particular occupation or avocation which society has chosen to reward less (or perhaps more!) than other pursuits. If there is not stigma attached to an activity, then society has no business making it a crime. Indeed, before the invention of the prison in the late eighteenth and early nineteenth centuries, the stigma attached to criminals was the major deterrent to and principal form of protection from criminal activity. The purpose of the criminal justice system is not to expose would-be criminals to a lottery in which they either win or lose, but to expose them in addition and more importantly to the solemn condemnation of the community should they yield to temptation.

Anyone familiar with the police stations, jails, and courts of some of our larger cities is keenly aware that accused persons caught up in the system are exposed to very little that involves either judgment or solemnity. They are instead processed through a bureaucratic maze in which a bargain is offered and a haggle ensues at every turn—over amount of bail, degree of the charged offense, and the nature of the plea. Much of what observers find objectionable about this process could be alleviated by devoting many more resources to it, so that an ample supply of prosecutors, defense attorneys, and judges were available. That we do not devote those additional resources in a country obsessed with the crime problem is one of the most interesting illustrations of the maxim, familiar to all political scientists, that one cannot predict public policy simply from knowing popular attitudes. Whatever the cause, it remains the case that in New York County (Manhattan) there were in 1973, 31,098 felony arrests to be handled by only 125 prosecutors, 119 public defenders, and 59 criminal court judges. The result was predictable: of those arrested, only 4130 pleaded guilty to or were convicted on a felony charge.

One wonders whether the stigma properly associated with crime retains much deterrent or educative value. My strong inclination is to resist explanations for rising crime that are based on the alleged moral breakdown of society. I resist in part because most of the families and communities I know have not broken down, and in part because, had they broken down, I cannot imagine any collective action we could take consistent with our civil liberties that would restore a moral consensus, and yet the facts are hard to ignore. Take the family: Over one-third of all black children and one in fourteen of all white children live in single-parent families. Over two million children live in single-parent (usually father absent) households, almost *double* the number of ten years ago. In 1950, 18 percent of black families were female-headed; in 1969 the proportion had risen to 27 percent; by 1973 it exceeded 35 percent. The average income for a single-parent family with children under six years of age was, in 1970, only $3100, well below the official "poverty line."

Studies done in the late 1950s and the early 1960s showed that children from broken homes were more likely than others to become delinquent. In New York State, 58 percent of the variation in pupil achievement in three hundred schools could be predicted by but three variables—broken homes, overcrowded housing, and parental educational level. Family disorganization, writes Urie Bronfenbrenner, has been shown in thousands of studies to be an "omnipresent overriding factor" in behavior disorders and social pathology. And that disorganization is increasing.

These facts may explain some elements of the rising crime rate that cannot be attributed to the increased number of young persons, high teenage unemployment, or changed judicial policies. The age of persons arrested has been declining for more than fifteen years and the median age of convicted defendants (in jurisdictions for which data are available) has been declining for the last six years. Apparently, the age at which persons begin to commit serious crime has been falling. For some young people, thus, whatever forces weaken their resistance to criminal activity have been increasing in magnitude, and these forces may well include the continued disorganization of the family and the continued deterioration of the social structure of inner city communities.

One wants to be objective, if not optimistic. Perhaps single-parent families today are less disorganized or have a different significance than such families in the past. Perhaps the relationship between family structure and social pathology will change. After all, there now seem to be good grounds for believing that, at least on the East Coast, the heroin epidemic of the 1960s has run its course; though there are still thousands of addicts, the rate of formation of new addicts has slowed and the rate of heroin use by older addicts has dropped. Perhaps other aspects of the relationship among family, personality, and crime will change. Perhaps.

No one can say how much of crime results from its increased profitability and how much from its decreased shamefulness. But one or both factors must be at work, for population changes alone simply cannot account for the increases. Crime in our cities has increased far faster than the number of young people, or poor people, or black people, or just plain people who live in those cities. In short, objective conditions alone, whether demographic or economic, cannot account for the crime increase, though they no doubt contributed to it. Subjective forces—ideas, attitudes, values—played a great part, though in ways hard to define and impossible to measure. An assessment of the effect of these changes on crime would provide a partial understanding of changes in the moral structure of our society.

But to understand is not to change. If few of the demographic factors contributing to crime are subject to planned change, virtually none of the subjective ones are. Though intellectually rewarding, from a practical point of view it is a mistake to think about crime in terms of its "causes" and then to search for ways to alleviate those causes. We must think instead of what it is feasible for a government or a community to do, and then try

155

to discover, by experimentation and observation, which of those things will produce, at acceptable costs, desirable changes in the level of criminal victimization.

There are, we now know, certain things we can change in accordance with our intentions, and certain ones we cannot. We cannot alter the number of juveniles who first experiment with minor crimes. We cannot lower the recidivism rate, though within reason we should keep trying. We are not yet certain whether we can increase significantly the police apprehension rate. We may be able to change the teenage unemployment rate, though we have learned by painful trial and error that doing this is much more difficult than once supposed. We can probably reduce the time it takes to bring an arrested person to trial, even though we have as yet made few serious efforts to do so. We can certainly reduce the arbitrary and socially irrational exercise of prosecutorial discretion over whom to charge and whom to release, and we can most definitely stop pretending that judges know, any better than the rest of us, how to provide "individualized justice." We can confine a larger proportion of the serious and repeat offenders and fewer of the common drunks and truant children. We know that confining criminals prevents them from harming society, and we have grounds for suspecting that some would-be criminals can be deterred by the confinement of others.

Above all, we can try to learn more about what works, and in the process abandon our ideological preconceptions about what *ought* to work. Nearly ten years ago I wrote that the billions of dollars the federal government was then preparing to spend on crime control would be wasted, and indeed might even make matters worse if they were merely pumped into the existing criminal justice system. They were, and they have. In the next ten years I hope we can learn to experiment rather than simply spend, to test our theories rather than fund our fears. This is advice, not simply or even primarily to government—for governments are run by men and women who are under irresistible pressures to pretend they know more than they do—but to my colleagues: academics, theoreticians, writers, advisers. We may feel ourselves under pressure to pretend we know things, but we are also under a positive obligation to admit what we do not know and to avoid cant and sloganizing. The government agency, the Law Enforcement Assistance Administration, that has futilely spent those billions was created in consequence of an act passed by Congress on the advice of a presidential commission staffed by academics, myself included.

It is easy and popular to criticize yesterday's empty hopes and mistaken beliefs, especially if they seemed supportive of law enforcement. It is harder, and certainly most unpopular, to criticize today's pieties and pretensions, especially if they are uttered in the name of progress and humanity. But if we were wrong in thinking that more money spent on the police would bring down crime rates, we are equally wrong in supposing that closing our prisons, emptying our jails, and supporting "community-based" programs will do any better. Indeed, there is some evidence that these steps will make matters worse, and we ignore it at our peril.

Since the days of the crime commission we have learned a great deal, more than we are prepared to admit. Perhaps we fear to admit it because of a newfound modesty about the foundations of our knowledge, but perhaps also because the implications of that knowledge suggest an unflattering view of man. Intellectuals, although they often dislike the common person as an individual, do not wish to be caught saying uncomplimentary things about humankind. Nevertheless, some persons will shun crime even if we do nothing to deter them, while others will seek it out even if we do everything to reform them. Wicked people exist. Nothing avails except to set them apart from innocent people. And many people, neither wicked nor innocent, but watchful, dissembling, and calculating of their opportunities, ponder our reaction to wickedness as a cue to what they might profitably do. We have trifled with the wicked, made sport of the innocent, and encouraged the calculators. Justice suffers, and so do we all.

●   ●   ●

NO

David L. Bazelon

OUR FAILING SOCIAL JUSTICE SYSTEM

There has been a good deal of inflamed, get-tough rhetoric about crime from politicians seeking votes. This rhetoric is echoed by some academicians, who are asked—and funded—to advise us what we must do to keep the lid on. The public and the press are demanding that we hired hands in the criminal justice system—police, prosecutors, courts, and corrections—sweep away this disturbing problem. But can we—without dealing with the social injustice that breeds this behavior?

For many years, it was widely believed that the solution to crime was to rehabilitate the offender. Now we are told by those who have studied recidivism rates that this expectation is beyond our abilities. The guiding faith of corrections—rehabilitation—has been declared a false god.

Of course, not everyone concedes that rehabilitation cannot work. Many corrections officials have argued that we have never really supported it enough to judge its possibilities and limitations. But I do not wish to rehash this debate with you here. For now, let us assume that a man's soul cannot be reformed by coercion or by the enticement of early release from prison. And let us assume that no one has the professional expertise to "cure" the people from the bottom of the socio-economic ladder who commit street crimes.

Conceding all this, should we strip our prisons of all nonessential services and settle for mere warehousing? If we cannot show that a particular program has lowered recidivism rates, should we toss it on the garbage heap?

The answer, I submit, is emphatically no. Rehabilitation—by which I mean educational, counseling, and social service—should never have been sold on the promise that it would reduce crime. Recidivism rates cannot be the only measure of what is valuable in corrections. Simple decency must count too. It is amoral, if not immoral, to make cost-benefit equations our lodestar in corrections. Neither the costs nor the benefits of providing or withholding vital human services can be objectified. Whether in prison or out, every person is entitled to physical necessities, medical and mental health services, and a

Reprinted by permission of *The Center Magazine*, Santa Barbara California.

measure of privacy. Beyond these requisites of decent custodial care, prisoners should be given the opportunity to make their time in prison something other than dead time, time without hope. They need programs to provide relief from boredom and idleness, which are surely among the greatest cruelties and causes of violence in our prisons as they are in our streets. For those who are willing, there should be tools available for self-improvement — libraries, classes, physical and mental activities.

Community-based programs are probably our most humane hope in dealing with people who have already turned to crime. Yet, I believe we delude society if we bill any of these programs as more than after-the-fact treatments that never prevent, and only occasionally cure, criminal behavior. If our goal is to reduce street violence, more is needed than additional probation officers. Even one-on-one supervision will not suffice. We must look to the conditions that bred the crime in the first place, or else expect the offender to break the law again when we send him back to those conditions.

Also, as much as I long for the day when we can dynamite the bastilles of this nation, I fear that we will always need prisons to isolate dangerous offenders. The day Adam stepped from the garden, we had to begin worrying about protecting the sheep from the wolves. Some offenders simply must be locked up to protect society; otherwise, we face the prospect of escalating street violence, including lynchings, to avenge the victims. Everyone would probably agree that the dangerous offender must be imprisoned. The problem—the terrible problem—is to define "dangerous" and then find the tools to measure it. As it now stands, we are being pushed to lock up ten

suspected of being dangerous in an effort not to miss one who actually is. I only note the questions. I could not begin to answer them here, even if I were able.

Where there is no alternative to incarceraton, we should consider new approaches. The most basic change that can be made is to reduce the size of our prisons. Experience has shown that our super-fortresses housing thousands of inmates carry a built-in brutality. Control over these huge prison populations tends to come by harsh disciplinary measures, or not at all.

On the other end of the spectrum from the abolitionists there are growing numbers of criminologists and politicians who are promising society great victories in the war on crime by changing our sentencing policies. They speak of flat sentences, uniform sentences, mandatory sentences, presumptive sentences. Under one proposal, a new sentencing commission would set standards,and appellate courts would review sentencing decisions to insure that those standards are implemented.

Some of these proposals come from those who have given up on rehabilitation and indeterminate sentencing, which uses the unfixed release date to induce prisoners to reform themselves. Since prisons now seem to serve no purpose but punishment and isolation, they say, there is no reason that like crimes should not receive like sentences. These people rest their case for uniform sentences on fairness for prisoners themselves, who are too often kept ignorant of their release date or subjected to unequal treatment.

Perhaps it is true that "we have not achieved either the individual love and understanding or the social distribution of power and property that is essential if

9. WILL TOUGHER SENTENCING CURB CRIME?

discretion is to serve justice." Yet, I ·still cling to the ideal of individualized justice. As others have recognized, in abandoning individualism here, we make it progressively easier to abandon it elsewhere. I fear that if we shift from concern for the individual to mechanical principles of fairness, we may cease trying to learn as much as possible about the circumstances of life that may have brought the particular offender to the bar of justice.

At present, sentencing discretion is shared by prosecutors, judges, parole boards, and others. Uniform and mandatory sentencing would merely transfer most of this discretion to prosecutors, who would in effect set sentences by their decisions about whom to charge with what crime and whether to plea bargain. Since prosecutors need not reveal their reasons, their exercise of discretion is not reviewable.

Of course, keeping discretion in judges' hands is preferable only if judges explain their decisions and make themselves accountable to the public. Sentencing discretion cannot appear fair or serve justice or teach anyone anything unless its exercise is fully explained. Unfortunately, most judges now give only boiler-plate reasons, if that, for their sentencing. I would guess that some judges—those who are moved by retribution and vengeance—would be ashamed to say so forthrightly. Others suppose there must be right and wrong sentences, so they are embarrassed to reveal their understandable dilemma in not knowing one from the other. And finally, there are those who can't be troubled; if they bothered to probe their own minds, who knows what useful insights or disturbing biases they would find?

All the proposals for sentencing reform are worthless unless trial judges clearly and honestly reveal in writing the reasons for the sentence imposed. Without such reasons, no review—judicial or otherwise—would have any basis for determining whether the judge abused his sentencing discretion. And without reasons, we would be denied the experience which would be essential for fixing sentencing standards and guidelines by any court, commission, or legislature.

I am also disturbed by the movement for mandatory and uniform sentencing because some people advertise it as a way of reducing crime. Led by Harvard University's James Wilson and New York University's Ernest van den Haag, this group argues that increasing the certainty of a prison sentence will decrease the crime rate, either by removing the more prolific criminals from the streets or by deterring others from yielding to temptation. Some politicians have told me that they are highly impressed with the theory, which they attribute to Wilson, that the current surge in crime is caused by the postwar baby boom. Apparently, the idea is that as this generation enters its crime-prone years, all that is required is essentially a holding action—put these people away until the population bulge passes, and eventually the problem of unacceptable crime statistics will largely solve itself.

What can society really expect from these proposals? Of course, all these proposals are almost certain to increase the number of prisoners, even if sentences are shortened. Most state systems are already overcrowded; many are operating at 130 percent or more of capacity. In one state, the Department of Corrections has stopped issuing a capacity figure "because we keep passing it." New prison construction, totalling billions of dollars, is scheduled for the next few years; yet at a cost of thirty-five to fifty thousand dollars per cell, we can safely assume that overcrowding will get worse before it gets better.

Can society expect harsher sentences to deter crime? The white-collar offender may weigh the risks of punishment, but the street offender—the one who is the cause of our alarm—most probably does not. With no job, no opportunity, no close family ties, he may well believe he has more to gain than he has to lose. More than three percent of this nation's non-white male population between the ages of eighteen and thirty-four was imprisoned in 1970. This is six times the percentage for whites. Can anyone doubt the connection between these out-of-proportion figures and the out-of-proportion unemployment rates and lack of opportunity facing this country's non-white slum dwellers?

Also, even *if* it is true that we can reduce crime simply by locking up enough lawbreakers, we must ask, for how long and at what cost to them and to ourselves? Is the plan to keep them behind bars for life? Even if it succeeds, will this approach make our society more just, or merely more repressive?

Most disturbing, all these proposals fail to consider the social injustices that breed crime. Can it be true that this nation would rather build a new prison cell for every slum dweller who turns to crime than try to alleviate the causes of his lawlessness? I do not understand how politicians can have a clear conscience preaching repression as the solution to crime, unless, of course, they believe that despite the accident of birth everyone in this country is equally endowed, mentally and physically, and has the same opportunities they have had to get ahead.

If the present debates in corrections are aimed at making prisons less brutal and sentencing more fair, then the effort is worthwhile. But if they are aimed at reducing crime, they are dangerously off-target. They are dangerous because they risk repression and greater suffering. They are off-target because they encourage society to expect magic cures rather than facing the real causes of crime.

One of the few clues that we do have about the sources of street crimes is that a viable family structure is crucial for social integration. A child needs a family because that is where his roots and his education are. Mothers and fathers who spend time with their child are better at it than are most organized group-care arrangements. We are learning that the child-rearing practices of the poor do not differ markedly from the most affluent. Statistics show that with a rising income, the same mother spends more time with her child.

But many poverty-level parents have less time and energy for their families. They are easily overwhelmed simply by the struggle for survival. A frantic and harassed mother is not a real mother. A father filled with failure and exasperation is not a real father, and he may not even stay around long enough to try. A parent who cannot put food on the table cannot convey to a child a sense of order, purpose, or self-esteem. The poor are confronted by the same problems which confront the rich, and more of them. The difference is simply that they do not have the resources or the time to cope. And when they slip, they find it all the harder to come back.

I am not saying poverty equals crime. That would be silly. I am merely stating the obvious: that poverty—and the

9. WILL TOUGHER SENTENCING CURB CRIME?

deprivation and discrimination that so often go with it—creates the conditions that make street crime more likely.

It doesn't take an expert to guess that too many children reared in the slums, where acknowledgment of one's own identity or worth is impossible, will develop at best a hard insensitivity to other humans. My own experience with delinquents and criminals is that they feel cut off from and hated by society, and they in turn feel nothing but hatred toward their victims. Presentencing reports call these youths "streetwise"— which means merely that they have the mental armor to survive in the streets. Almost every one of the thousands of criminal defendants that have come before me has had a long record reaching back to age ten, nine, or even younger. As the child is the father of the man, so is the juvenile delinquent the father of the hardened criminal.

None of our providers of treatment services—psychiatrists, psychologists, or social workers—have the know-how to implant our middle-class sensibilities into youngsters who have been actively neglected twenty-four hours a day, every day. There is no magic humanizing pill for these youths.

One step we can take is to guarantee to every family an income sufficient to enable parents to provide the kind of home environment their children need. Of course, we cannot be sure that more money given directly to the family will prevent delinquency, but there is no chance of preventing delinquency without it. Most important, it is right for its own sake. . . .

Society should be as alarmed by the silent misery of those who accept their plight as it is by the violence of those who do not. I see no hope for reducing violent street crime in this country until our society reaches this level of concern and humanity.

Prison reform and tougher sentencing seem like hollow promises when we realize that it is *this* kind of crime with *these* causes that we are really talking about. At worst, the present attacks on crime are repressive. At best, they are mere nibbling.

Of the more humane reforms that I call "nibbling," Norval Morris argues that "it is a serious mistake to oppose any reform until all can be reformed." Of course I agree. Making sentences more fair and relieving overcrowding in prisons need not wait for the elimination of poverty in this country. Surely review of the sentencing judge's discretion—accompanied by a requirement that he give his reasons—could eliminate *wide* disparities in sentencing without ignoring differences in individual offenders that justify different treatment.

But what I reject is the notion we should strive to achieve *only* these changes in the criminal justice system. Instead, we must try to hold in mind the full picture. We must not forget that the people I have been speaking about in the criminal justice system are merely the end products of our failing social justice system.

● ● ●

POSTSCRIPT

WILL TOUGHER SENTENCING
CURB CRIME?

It may be said of crime, as Mark Twain said of the weather, that everyone talks about it, but no one does anything about it. Perhaps this is because the easy solutions only sound easy. We could lock up the criminals, but where would we put them? And would society be prepared to pay the staggering cost? We could remedy the poverty, inequality, and discrimination that purportedly lead to crime, but where and how do we begin? And, again, is society willing to foot the bill?

If we separate out the superficial and hysterical accounts of crime on the one hand and the technical and statistical studies by criminologists on the other, there is a paucity of thoughtful reading. Former U.S. Attorney General Ramsey Clark takes a position strongly opposed to James Wilson's in CRIME IN AMERICA (Simon and Schuster, 1970). Clark urges not only sweeping social reform, but the reform of human character. Two recent studies have sought to deal thoroughly with the causes of prevention of major categories of crime. Yong Hyo Cho, PUBLIC POLICY AND URBAN CRIME (Ballinger Publishing Co., Cambridge, 1974) and Stuart Palmer, THE PREVENTION OF CRIME (Behavioral Publications, New York, 1973) both contain a wealth of factual information as well as assessments of the proposed solutions. The most far-reaching governmental study is that of the President's Commission on Law Enforcement and Administration of Justice, THE CHALLENGE OF CRIME IN A FREE SOCIETY (U.S. Government Printing Office, 1967).

It is unlikely that objective analysis will have much influence on most people's thinking about crime. Fear, compassion, religious teaching, and generalized morality are not easily altered by statistics. The man or woman in the street suspects that "facts" on the incidence of crime are not altogether reliable, and "facts" on the causes of crime are almost entirely lacking. Yet, reasoning need not be abandoned. Judge Bazelon and Professor Wilson provide powerful reasons to support opposed approaches. Where Bazelon is convinced that we must do what is necessary, Wilson insists that it is futile to attempt to do more than is possible. Both criticize prevailing practices toward crime and punishment as unjust, and both urge reform, but they differ in their assessment of the injustice as they do in their prescriptions for reform. Society may never definitively resolve these issues, but it cannot escape them.

ISSUE 10

IS CAPITAL PUNISHMENT JUSTIFIED?

YES: Walter Berns, from FOR CAPITAL PUNISHMENT: CRIME AND THE MORALITY OF THE DEATH PENALTY (New York, 1979)

NO: Donal E.J. MacNamara, from *Social Action,* April 1961

ISSUE SUMMARY

YES: Professor Berns is convinced that the death penalty has a place in modem society, and that it serves a need now as it did when the Constitution was framed.
NO: Criminologist MacNamara presents a 10 point argument against capital punishment, raising ethical and practical questions concerning the death penalty.

Although capital punishment (the death penalty) is ancient, both the definition of capital crimes and the legal methods of putting convicted persons to death have changed. In eighteenth-century Massachusetts, there were fifteen capital crimes, including blasphemy and the worship of false gods. Slave states often imposed the death sentence upon blacks for crimes that, when committed by whites, were punished by two or three years' imprisonment. It has been estimated that in this century approximately ten percent of all legal executions have been for the crime of rape, one percent for all other crimes (robbery, burglary, attempted murder, etc), and nearly 90 percent for the commission of murder.

Although the number of murders has increased, the number of executions has declined in recent decades, from 1667 in the 1930s to 717 in the 1950s. Seven persons were executed in 1965, one in 1966, and two in 1967, when the last legal executions took place before the execution of Gary Gilmore in 1977. Put another way, in the 1930s and 1940s, there was one execution for every sixty or seventy homicides committed in states which had the death penalty; in the first half of the 1960s, there was an execution for every 200 homicides; and by 1966 and 1967, there were only three executions for approximately 20,000 homicides.

Despite the sharp decline in the administration of the death penalty, many hundreds of convicted persons were sentenced to death, and "death rows" swelled in numbers during the years after the U.S. Supreme Court suspended the carrying out of the death penalty in 1972. The constitutional issue was and remains whether the death penalty is cruel and unusual punishment, which is prohibited to the federal government by the Eighth Amendment to the Constitution, and prohibited to the states by interpretation of the Fourteenth Amendment. Two Justices, in separate opinions, concluded that the death penalty is too severe, although both alluded to the arbitrary and discriminatory manner of its exercise. Three other Justices, each in a separate opinion, stressed the rarity of the death penalty, its arbitrariness, and the fact that executed persons were disproportionately likely to be black, poor, uneducated and young. The four dissenters together and separately deplored the use of the death penalty but defended the right of the states to impose it.

Some Americans prematurely concluded that the Supreme Court had abolished capital punishment, but what the Court had done was forbid its unfair exercise without resolving the basic constitutional issue. When the Court returned to examine new state laws involving capital punishment in 1976, seven Justices concluded that it was within the power of a state to take the life of a convicted murderer. (Internal analysis of the 1972 and 1976 opinions suggests that capital punishment will not be upheld for crimes other than murder.) On the other hand, states are forbidden to exercise this power in an arbitrary or discriminatory manner. One of the ways in which many states hoped to overcome the Supreme Court's 1972 objections to the rarity and capriciousness of the exercise of the death penalty was to mandate death sentences for first-degree murder and certain other categories. This, the Court said in 1976 and again in 1977, was unduly harsh.

When an issue such as the death penalty involves considerations of justice, morality, and public safety, it is unlikely that debate will be rational. Although many nations have abolished the death penalty, its abandonment in the United States seems unlikely in the foreseeable future, given the nation's high homicide rate and the power of the fifty states individually to decide upon penalties. Legislatures will continue to alter their laws to meet what they conceive to be the prevailing judicial standards, and those standards will be set by the U.S. Supreme Court.

In the readings which follow, Donal E. J. MacNamara sums up virtually every widely used argument against the death penalty, while Walter Berns focuses his defense upon the moral right of retribution and its compatibility with the American Constitution.

YES

CRIME AND THE MORALITY
OF THE DEATH PENALTY

It must be one of the oldest jokes in circulation. In the dark of a wild night a ship strikes a rock and sinks, but one of its sailors clings desperately to a piece of wreckage and is eventually cast up exhausted on an unknown and deserted beach. In the morning, he struggles to his feet and, rubbing his salt-encrusted eyes, looks around to learn where he is. The only human thing he sees is a gallows. "Thank God," he exclaims, "civilization." There cannot be many of us who have not heard this story or, when we first heard it, laughed at it. The sailor's reaction was, we think, absurd. Yet, however old the story, the fact is that the gallows has not been abolished in the United States even yet, and we count ourselves among the civilized peoples of the world. Moreover, the attempt to have it abolished by the U.S. Supreme Court may only have succeeded in strengthening its structure . . . .

Perhaps the Court began to doubt its premise that a "maturing society" is an ever more gentle society; the evidence on this is surely not reassuring. The steady moderating of the criminal law has not been accompanied by a parallel moderating of the ways of criminals or by a steadily evolving decency in the conditions under which men around the world must live their lives. . . .

An institution that lacks strength or purpose will readily be what its most committed constituents want it to be. Those who maintain our criminal justice institutions do not speak of deferring to public opinion but of the need to "rehabilitate criminals"—another pious sentiment. The effect, however, is the same. They impose punishments only as a last resort and with the greatest reluctance, as if they were embarrassed or ashamed, and they avoid executing even our Charles Mansons. It would appear that Albert Camus was right when he said that "our civilization has lost the only values that, in a certain way, can justify [the death] penalty." It is beyond doubt that our intellectuals are of this opinion. The idea that the presence of a gallows could indicate the presence of a civilized people is, as I indicated at the outset, a joke. I certainly thought so the first time I heard the story; it was only a few years ago that I began to

From Walter Berns, FOR CAPITAL PUNISHMENT: CRIME AND THE MORALITY OF THE DEATH PENALTY (New York; Basic Books, 1979). c Walter Berns. Pp. 3, 5, 7, 8-9, 31-40, 153-155, 188-189.

suspect that that sailor may have been right. What led me to change my mind was the phenomenon of Simon Wiesenthal.

Like most Americans, my business did not require me to think about criminals or, more precisely, the punishment of criminals. In a vague way, I was aware that there was some disagreement concerning the purpose of punishment—deterrence, rehabilitation, or retribution—but I had no reason then to decide which was right or to what extent they may all have been right. I did know that retribution was held in ill repute among criminologists. Then I began to reflect on the work of Simon Wiesenthal, who, from a tiny, one-man office in Vienna, has devoted himself since 1945 exclusively to the task of hunting down the Nazis who survived the war and escaped into the world. Why did he hunt them, and what did he hope to accomplish by finding them? And why did I respect him for devoting his life to this singular task? He says that his conscience forces him "to bring the guilty ones to trial." And if they are convicted, then what? Punish them, of course. But why? To rehabilitate them? The very idea is absurd. To incapacitate them? But they represent no present danger. To deter others from doing what they did? That is a hope too extravagant to be indulged. The answer—to me and, I suspect, everyone else who agrees that they should be punished—was clear: *to pay them back.* And how do you pay back SS Obersturm-führer Franz Stangl, SS Untersturm-führer Wilhelm Rosenbaum, SS Ober-sturmbannführer Adolf Eichmann, or someday—who knows?—Reichsleiter Martin Bormann? As the world knows, Eichmann was executed, and I suspect that most of the decent, *civilized* world

agrees that this was the only way he could be paid back. . . .

The argument . . . does not turn on the answer to the utilitarian question of whether the death penalty is a deter-rent. . . . The evidence on this is unclear and, besides, as it is usually understood, deterrence is irrelevant. The real issue is whether justice permits or even requires the death penalty. I am aware that it is a terrible punishment, but there are terrible crimes and terrible criminals. . . .

Anger is expressed or manifested on those occasions when someone has acted in a manner that is thought to be unjust, and one of its bases is the opinion that men are responsible, and should be held responsible, for what they do. Thus, anger is accompanied not only by the pain caused by him who is the object of anger, but by the pleasure arising from the expectation of exacting revenge on someone who is thought to deserve it. We can become very angry with an inanimate object (the door we run into and then kick in return) only foolishly attributing re-sponsibility to it, and we cannot do that for long, which is why we do not think of returning later to revenge ourselves on the door. For the same reason, we cannot be more than momentarily angry with an animate creature other than man; only a fool or worse would dream of taking revenge on a dog. And, finally, we tend to pity rather than to be angry with men who—because they are insane, for example—are not responsible for their acts. Anger, then, is a very human passion not only because only a human being can be angry, but also because it acknowl-edges the humanity of its objects: it holds them accountable for what they do. It is an expression of that element of the soul that is connected with the view that there

167

is responsibility in the world; and in holding particular men responsible, it pays them that respect which is due them as men. Anger recognizes that only men have the capacity to be moral beings and, in so doing, acknowledges the dignity of human beings. Anger is somehow connected with justice, and it is this that modern penology has not understood; it tends, on the whole, to regard anger as merely a selfish passion. . . .

Criminals are properly the objects of anger, and the perpetrators of terrible crimes—for example, Lee Harvey Oswald and James Earl Ray—are properly the objects of great anger. They have done more than inflict an injury on an isolated individual; they have violated the foundations of trust and friendship, the necessary elements of a moral community, the only community worth living in. A moral community, unlike a hive of bees or a hill of ants, is one whose members are expected freely to obey the laws and, unlike a tyranny, are trusted to obey the laws. The criminal has violated that trust, and in so doing has injured not merely his immediate victim but the community as such. He has called into question the very possibility of that community by suggesting that men cannot be trusted freely to respect the property, the person, and the dignity of those with whom they are associated. If, then, men are not angry when someone else is robbed, raped, or murdered, the implication is that there is no moral community because those men do not care for anyone other than themselves. Anger is an expression of that caring, and society needs men who care for each other, who share their pleasures and their pains, and do so for the sake of the others. It is the passion that can cause us to act for reasons having nothing to do with selfish or mean calculation; indeed, when educated, it can become a generous passion, the passion that protects the community or country by demanding punishment for its enemies. It is the stuff from which heroes are made. . . .

THE CONSTITUTIONAL ARGUMENT

We Americans have debated the morality and necessity of the death penalty throughout almost the entire period of our experience as a nation, and, until 1976 when the Supreme Court ruled in favor of its constitutionality, it had been debated among us in constitutional terms, which is not true elsewhere. The Eighth Amendment clearly and expressly forbids the imposition of "cruel and unusual punishments," a prohibition that applies now to the states as well as to the national government; it was argued that the death penalty was such a punishment.

It is, of course, incontestable that the death penalty was not regarded as cruel and unusual by the men who wrote and ratified the amendment. They may have forbidden cruel and unusual punishments but they acknowledged the legitimacy of capital punishment when, in the Fifth Amendment, they provided that no person "shall be held to answer for a capital . . . crime, unless on a presentment or indictment of a Grand Jury," and when in the same amendment they provided that no one shall, for the same offense, "be twice put in jeopardy of life or limb," and when, in the Fifth as well as in the Fourteenth Amendment, they forbade, not the taking of life, but the taking of life "without due process of law." We also know that the same Congress which proposed the Eighth Amendment also provided for the death penalty for murder and treason, and George Washington, despite powerful entreaties, could not be persuaded to commute the death sentence imposed on Major John Andre, the British officer and spy involved in Benedict Arnold's treachery. So the death penalty can be held to be cruel and unusual in the constitutional sense only if it has somehow become so in the passage of time. . . .

In 1958 the Supreme Court . . . said that the meaning of cruel and unusual depends on "the evolving standards of decency that mark the progress of a maturing society." Surely, it is argued, hanging or electrocution or gassing is, in our day, regarded as equally cruel as expatriation, if not more cruel. Is it not relevant that the American people have insisted that executions be carried out by more humane methods, that they not be carried out in public, and that the penalty be imposed for fewer and fewer crimes; and is it not significant that juries have shown a tendency to refuse to convict for capital crimes? In these ways the people are merely demonstrating what has been true for centuries, namely, that when given the opportunity to act, the average man (as opposed to judges and vindictive politicians) will refuse to be a party to legal murder. . . . The fact of the matter, or so it is alleged, is that American juries have shown an increasing tendency to avoid imposing the death penalty except on certain offenders who are distinguished not by their criminality but by their race or class. Justice Douglas emphasized this in his opinion in the 1972 capital punishment cases. "One searches our chronicles in vain for the execution of any members of the affluent strata of this society," he said. "The Leopolds and Loebs are given prison terms, not sentenced to death.". . . Death sentences are imposed not out of a hatred of the crimes committed, it is said, but out of a hatred of blacks. Of the 3,859 persons executed in the United States in the period 1930-1967, 2,066, or 54 percent, were black. More than half of the prisoners now under sentence of death are black. In short, the death penalty, we have been told, "may have served" to keep blacks, especially southern blacks, "in a position of subjugation and subservience." That in itself is unconstitutional.

In the 1972 cases only two of the nine justices of the Supreme Court argued that the death penalty as such is a violation of the Eighth Amendment, regardless of the manner of its imposition. Justice Brennan was persuaded by what he saw as the public's growing reluctance to impose it that the rejection of the death penalty "could hardly be more complete without becoming absolute." Yet, on the basis of his own evidence it is clear that the American people have not been persuaded by the arguments against the death penalty and that they continue to support it for *some* criminals—so long as it is carried out privately and as painlessly as possible. At the very time he was writing there were more than 600 persons on whom Americans had imposed the sentence of death. He drew the conclusion that the American people had decided that capital punishment does not comport with human dignity, and is therefore unconstitutional, but the facts do not support this conclusion. This may explain why his colleague, Justice Marshall, felt obliged to take up the argument.

Marshall acknowledged that the public opinion polls show that, on the whole, capital punishment is supported by a majority of the American people, but he

10. IS CAPITAL PUNISHMENT JUSTIFIED?

denied the validity—or the "utility"—of ascertaining opinion on this subject by simply polling the people. The polls ask the wrong question. It is not a question of whether the public accepts the death penalty, but whether the public when "fully informed as to the purposes of the penalty and its liabilities would find [it] shocking, unjust, and unacceptable."

> In other words, the question with which we must deal is not whether a substantial proportion of American citizens would today, if polled, opine that capital punishment is barbarously cruel, but whether they would find it to be so in the light of all information presently available.

This information, he said, "would almost surely convince the average citizen that the death penalty was unwise." He conceded that this citizen might nevertheless support it as a way of exacting retribution, but, in his view, the Eighth Amendment forbids "punishment for the sake of retribution"; besides, he said, no one has ever seriously defended capital punishment on retributive grounds. It has been defended only with "deterrent or similar theories." From here he reached his conclusion that "the great mass of citizens" would decide that the death penalty is not merely unwise but also "immoral and therefore unconstitutional." They would do so if they knew what he knew, and what he knew was that retribution is illegitimate and unconstitutional and that the death penalty is excessive and unnecessary, being no more capable than life imprisonment of deterring the crimes for which it is imposed. He conceded that the evidence on the deterrence issue is not "convincing beyond all doubt, but it is persuasive."

Thus, the death penalty *is* cruel and unusual punishment because the American people *ought* to think so. Shortly after this decision thirty-five states enacted new statutes authorizing the death penalty for certain crimes.

This public support for capital punishment is a puzzling fact, especially in our time. It is a policy that has almost no articulate supporters in the intellectual community. The subject has been vigorously debated and intensively investigated by state after state and country after country—California and Connecticut, Texas and Wisconsin; Britain and Canada, Ceylon and "Europe"; even the United Nations; and, of course, various committees of the U.S. Congress. Among those willing to testify and publish their views, the abolitionists outweigh the "retentionists" both in number and, with significant exceptions, in the kind of authority that is recognized in the worlds of science and letters. Yet the Harris poll reports 59 percent of the general population to be in favor of capital punishment, and that proportion is increasing—at this time, at least. . . .

It is sometimes argued that the opinion polls are deceptive insofar as the question is posed abstractly—and can only be posed abstractly—and that the responses of these publics would be different if they had to decide whether particular persons should be executed. This is entirely possible, or even probable; nevertheless, there is no gainsaying the fact that juries, for whom the issue is very concrete indeed, continue to impose death sentences on a significant number of criminals. Ordinary men and women seem to be unpersuaded by the social science argument against deterrence, or they regard it as irrelevant; they seem to be oblivious to the possibility that innocent people might be executed; they know nothing about the natural public law disagreement between Beccaria and Kant; they surely do not share the opinion that executions are contrary to God's commands; indeed, they seem to display the passions of many a biblical character in their insistence that, quite apart from all these considerations, murderers should be paid back. In fact, the essential difference between the public and the abolitionists is almost never discussed in our time; it has to do with retribution: the public insists on it without using the word and the abolitionists condemn it whenever they mention it.

The abolitionists condemn it because it springs from revenge, they say, and revenge is the ugliest passion in the human soul. They condemn it because it justifies punishment for the sake of punishment alone, and they are opposed to punishment that serves no purpose beyond inflicting pain on its victims. Strictly speaking, they are opposed to punishment. They may, like Beccaria, sometimes speak of life imprisonment as the alternative to executions, but they are not in fact advocates of life imprisonment and will not accept it. . . .

They condemn retribution because they see it, rightly or wrongly, as the only basis on which the death penalty can be supported. To kill an offender is not only unnecessary but precludes the possibility of reforming him, and reformation, they say, is the only civilized response to the criminal. Even murderers—indeed, especially murderers—are capable of being redeemed or of repenting their crimes. . . .

The goal of the abolitionists is not merely the elimination of capital punishment but the reform or rehabilitation of the criminal, *even*, if he is a murderer. The public that favors capital punishment is of the opinion that the murderer deserves to be punished, and does not deserve to be treated, even if by treatment he *could* be rehabilitated. . . .

When abolitionists speak of the barbarity of capital punishment and when Supreme Court justices denounce expatriation in almost identical language, they ought to be reminded that men whose moral sensitivity they would not question have supported both punishments. Lincoln, for example, albeit with a befitting reluctance, authorized the execution of 267 persons during his presidency, and ordered the "Copperhead" Clement L. Vallandigham banished; and it was Shakespeare's sensitivity to the moral issue that required him to have Macbeth killed. They should also be given some pause by the knowledge that the man who originated the opposition to both capital and exilic punishment, Cesare Beccaria, was a man who argued that there is no morality outside the positive law and that it is reasonable to love one's property more than one's country. There is nothing exalted in these opinions, and there is nothing exalted in the versions of them that appear in today's judicial opinions. Capital punishment was said by Justice Brennan to be a denial of human dignity, but in order to reach this conclusion he had to reduce human dignity to the point where it became something possessed by "the vilest criminal." Expatriation is said by the Court to be unconstitutional because it deprives a man of his right to have rights, which *is* his citizenship, and no one, no matter what he does, can be dispossessed of the right to have rights.

(Why not a right to the right to have rights?) Any notion of what Justice Frankfurter in dissent referred to as "the communion of our citizens," of a community that can be violated by murderers or traitors, is wholly absent from these opinions; so too is any notion that it is one function of the law to protect that community.

But, contrary to abolitionist hopes and expectations, the Court did not invalidate the death penalty. It upheld it. It upheld it on retributive grounds. In doing so, it recognized, at least implicity, that the American people are entitled *as a people* to demand that criminals be paid back, and that the worst of them be made to pay back with their lives. In doing this, it gave them the means by which they might strengthen the law that makes them a people, and not a mere aggregation of selfish individuals.

● ● ●

NO

Donal E.J. MacNamara

THE CASE AGAINST CAPITAL PUNISHMENT

The infliction of the death penalty is becoming less frequent and the actual execution of the sentence of death even more rare, both in the United States and in foreign countries. Not only is this trend apparent in those nations and states which have formally repudiated the *lex talionis* and have eliminated capital punishment from their penal codes but it is almost equally clear in many of the jurisdictions which still retain the ultimate sanction for from one to fourteen crimes. This diminished frequency is a reflection of the popular distaste for executions and of the recognition by many criminologically and psychiatrically oriented judges, juries, prosecutors, and commuting and pardoning authorities that capital punishment is as ineffective as a special capital crimes deterrent as it is ethically and morally undesirable.

The case against the death penalty is supported by many arguments—with the order of their importance or precedence dependent upon the orientation of the proponent or the composition of the audience to whom the argument is being addressed. The late Harold Laski, in opening his series of lectures to one of my graduate seminars in political theory, suggested that a lecturer or writer was under obligation to his audience to define both the articulate and inarticulate basic premises upon which his theoretical structure, and its practical application to the matters under discussion, rested. This writer, then, is a practicing criminologist with both administrative and operational experience in police and prison work over a period of more than two decades; he was brought up in a Catholic household, went to parochial schools for twelve years, and then took degrees from two non-sectarian institutions. He is a "convert" to abolition, for during his active police and prison career he not only accepted the death penalty pragmatically as existent, necessary, and therefore desirable but participated in one or another formal capacity in a number of executions.

The case against capital punishment is ten-fold:

Reprinted by permission of The Office for Church in Society, United Church of Christ. **173**

10. IS CAPITAL PUNISHMENT JUSTIFIED?

1. *Capital punishment is criminologically unsound.* The death penalty is the antithesis of the rehabilitative, non-punitive, non-vindictive orientation of twentieth century penology. It brutalizes the entire administration of criminal justice. No criminologist of stature in America or abroad gives it support. And those "arm-chair" and so-called "utilitarian" criminologists who plead its necessity (never its desirability or morality) do so in terms of Darwinian natural selection and/or as a eugenics-oriented, castration-sterilization race purification technique, an economical and efficient method of disposing of society's jetsam. Those who advance these arguments are probably not aware that they are rationalizing a residual lust for punishment or propagating an immoral, virtually paganistic, philosophy.

2. *Capital punishment is morally and ethically unacceptable.* The law of God is "Thou shalt not kill," and every system of ethics and code of morals echoes this injunction. It is well recognized that this Commandment (and the laws of man based upon it) permit the killing of another human being "in the lawful defense of the slayer, or of his or her husband, wife, parent, child, brother, sister, master or servant, or of any other person in his presence or company" when there is "imminent danger" and in "actual resistance" to an assault or other criminal act. It is equally well recognized that society, organized as a sovereign state, has the right to take human life in defending itself in a just war against either internal or external unjust aggression. But the individual citizen has no right in law or morals to slay as punishment for an act, no matter how vile, already committed; nor has he legal or moral justification to kill when—his resistance to an attempted criminal act having proved successful short of fatal force—the imminent danger is eliminated and the criminal attack or attempt discontinued.

Individuals in groups or societies are subject to the same moral and ethical codes which govern their conduct as individuals. The state, through its police agents, may take human life when such ultimate measure of force is necessary to protect its citizenry from the imminent danger of criminal action and in actual resistance to felonious attempts (including attempts forcibly to avoid arrest or escape custody). Once, however, the prisoner has been apprehended and either voluntarily submits to custody, or is effectively safeguarded against escape (maximum security confinement), the right of the state to take his life as punishment, retribution, revenge, or retaliation for previously committed offenses (no matter how numerous or heinous) or as an "example" to deter others, or as an economical expedient, does not exist in moral law.

I argue this despite the fact that it is a position which is contrary to that expounded by a number of eminent theologians, notably Thomas Aquinas. Writing in times long past and quite different and expressing themselves in terms of conditions, logic and experiences of those times, such theologians have defended the right of the state to take human life as a punishment "when the common good requires it." Moreover they have held that, under certain conditions, the state is morally bound to take human life and that not to take it would be sinful. Although I am philosophically opposed to war whether as an extension of diplomacy or an instrument of national policy, I recognize the right of a nation through its armed forces and in accor-

174

with the rules of civilized warfare, to take human life in defense of its sovereignty, its national territory, and its citizens. Such recognition is in no way inconsistent with my views [against] the death penalty, for the Geneva Convention makes it clear that the killing of one's enemy (no matter how many of one's troops he has slaughtered in battle) after he has laid down his arms, surrendered, or been taken prisoner, will not be countenanced by civilized nations.

3. Capital punishment has demonstrably failed to accomplish its stated objectives. The proponents of the death penalty base their support largely on two basic propositions: (1) that the death penalty has a uniquely deterrent effect on those who contemplate committing capital crimes; and (2) that the provision of the death penalty as the mandatory or alternative penalty for stated offenses in the statute books removes for all time the danger of future similar offenses by those whose criminal acts have made them subject to its rigors.

Neither of these propositions will stand logical or statistical analysis. Proposition 1 is dependent upon acceptance of the repudiated "pleasure-pain" principle of past-century penology. This theory presupposes a "rational man" weighing the prospective profit or pleasure to be derived from the commission of some future crime against the almost certain pain or loss he will suffer in retribution should he be apprehended and convicted. That many persons who commit crimes are not "rational" at the time the crime is committed is beyond dispute. Avoiding the area of psychiatric controversy for the moment, let it be sufficient to report that Dr. Shaw Grigsby of the University of Florida in his recent studies at the Raiford (Florida) State Penitentiary found that

more than seventy-five percent of the males and more than ninety per cent of the females then in confinement were under the influence of alcohol at the time they committed the offenses for which they were serving sentence; and that Dr. Marvin Wolfgang's studies of the patterns in criminal homicide in Philadelphia in large measure lend support to Dr Grigsby's findings.

While perhaps the theological doctrine of "sufficient reflection and full consent of the will" as necessary prerequisites to mortal sin is somewhat mitigated by the mandate to "avoid the occasions of sin" in the determination of moral responsibility, we are here discussing rationality in terms of weighing alternatives of possible prospective deterrence rather than adjudicated post-mortem responsibility. Proposition 1 further presupposes knowledge by the prospective offender of the penalty provided in the penal code for the offense he is about to commit—a knowledge not always found even among lawyers. It further assumes a non-self-destructive orientation of the offender and, most importantly, a certainty in his mind that he will be identified, apprehended, indicted, convicted, sentenced to the maximum penalty, and that the ultimate sanction will indeed be executed. When one notes that of 125 persons indicted for first degree murder in the District of Columbia during the period 1953–1959, only one (a Negro) was executed despite the mandatory provision of the law; and further that, despite the fact that more than three million major felonies were known to the police in 1960, the total prison population (federal and state) at the 1961 prison census (including substantially all the convicted felons of 1960 and many from prior years) stood at a miniscule 190,000, the rational criminal might very well elect to "play the odds."

The second part of the proposition assumes that all or a high proportion of those who commit crimes for which the death penalty is prescribed will in fact be executed—an assumption, rebutted above, which was false even in the heyday of capital punishment when more than two hundred offenses were punishable on the gallows. It shows no awareness that the mere existence of the death penalty may in itself contribute to the commission of the very crimes it is designed to deter, or to the difficulty of securing convictions in capital cases. The murderer who has killed once (or committed one of the more than thirty other capital crimes) and whose life is already forfeit if he is caught would find little deterrent weight in the prospect of execution for a second or third capital crime— particularly if his victim were to be a police officer attempting to take him into custody for the original capital offense. The suicidal, guilt-haunted psychotic might well kill (or confess falsely to a killing) to provoke the state into imposing upon him the punishment which in his tortured mind he merits but is unable to inflict upon himself.

Prosecutors and criminal trial lawyers have frequently testified as to the difficulty of impa. elling juries in capital cases and the even greater difficulty of securing convictions on evidence which in non-capital cases would leave little room for reasonable doubt. Appeals courts scan with more analytical eye the transcripts in capital cases, and error is located and deemed prejudicial which in non-capital cases would be overlooked. The Chessman case is, from this viewpoint, a monument to the determination on the part of American justice that no man shall

be executed while there is the slightest doubt either as to his guilt or as to the legality of the process by which his guilt was determined. Criminologists have pointed out repeatedly that the execution of the small number of convicts (fewer than fifty each year in the United States) has a disproportionately brutalizing effect on those of us who survive. Respect for the sanctity and inviolability of human life decreases each time human life is taken. When taken formally in the circus-like atmosphere which unfortunately characterizes twentieth century trials and executions (both here and abroad), emotions, passions, impulses and hostilities are activated which may lead to the threshold of murder many who might never have incurred the mark of Cain.

4. *Capital punishment in the United States has been and is prejudicially and inconsistently applied.* The logic of the retentionist position would be strengthened if the proponents of capital punishment could demonstrate that an "even-handed justice" exacted the supreme penalty without regard to race or nationality, age or sex, social or economic condition; that all or nearly all who committed capital crimes were indeed executed; or, at least, that those pitiful few upon whom the sentence of death is carried out each year are in fact the most dangerous, the most vicious, the most incorrigible of all who could have been executed. But the record shows otherwise.

Accurate death penalty statistics for the United States are available for the thirty-year period, 1930-1959. Analysis of the more than three thousand cases in which the death penalty was exacted discloses that more than half were Negroes, that a very significant proportion / were defended by court-appointed lawyers, and that few of them were professional killers. Whether a man died for his offense depended, not on the gravity of his crime, not on the number of such crimes or the number of his victims, not on his present or prospective danger to society, but on such adventitious factors as the jurisdiction in which the crime was committed, the color of his skin, his financial position, whether he was male or female (we seldom execute females), and indeed oftentimes on what were the character and characteristics of his victim (apart from the justifiability of the instant homicidal act.)

It may be exceedingly difficult for a rich man to enter the Kingdom of Heaven but case after case bears witness that it is virtually impossible for him to enter the execution chamber. And it is equally impossible in several states to execute a white man for a capital crime against a Negro. Professional murderers (and the directors of the criminal syndicates which employ them) are seldom caught. When they are arrested either they are defended successfully by eminent and expensive trial counsel; or they eliminate or intimidate witnesses against them. Failing such advantages, they wisely bargain for a plea of guilty to some lesser degree of homicide and escape the death chamber. The homicidal maniac, who has massacred perhaps a dozen, even under our archaic M'Naghten Rule, is safely outside the pale of criminal responsibility and escapes not only the death penalty but often even its alternatives.

5. *The innocent have been executed.* There is no system of criminal jurisprudence which has on the whole provided as many safeguards against the conviction and possible execution of an innocent man as the Anglo-American. Those of us who oppose the death penalty do not raise this argument to condemn our courts or our judiciary, but only to underline the fallibility of human judgment and human procedures. We oppose capital punishment for the guilty; no one save a monster or deluded rationalist (e.g., the Captain in Herman Melville's *Billy Budd*) would justify the execution of the innocent. We cannot however close our minds or our hearts to the greater tragedy, the more monstrous injustice, the ineradicable shame involved when the legal processes of the state, knowingly or unknowingly, have been used to take the life of an innocent man.

The American Bar Foundation, or some similar research-oriented legal society, might well address itself to an objective analysis of the factors which led to the convictions of the many men whose sentences for capital crimes have in the past few decades been set aside by the appellate courts (or by the executive authority after the courts had exhausted their processes), and who later were exonerated either by trial courts or by the consensus of informed opinion. Especial attention should be directed to the fortunately much smaller number of cases (e.g., the Evans-Christie case in England and the Brandon case in New Jersey) in which innocent men were actually executed. Perhaps, too, a reanalysis would be profitable of the sixty-five cases cited by Professor Edwin Borchard in his CONVICTING THE INNOCENT, the thirty-six cases mentioned by U.S. Circuit Court of Appeals Judge, Jerome Frank in *COURTS ON TRIAL*, and the smaller number of miscarriages of justice outlined by Erle Stanley Gardner in COURT OF LAST RESORT.

6. *There are effective alternative penalties.* One gets the impression all too frequently, both from retentionist spokesmen and, occasionally, from the

10. IS CAPITAL PUNISHMENT JUSTIFIED?

statements of enthusiastic but ill-informed abolitionists, that the only alternative to capital punishment is no punishment; that, if the death penalty does not deter, then surely no lesser societal response to the violation of its laws and injury to its citizens will prove effective.

The record in abolition jurisdictions, some without the death penalty, both in the United States and abroad, in which imprisonment for indeterminate or stated terms has been substituted for the penalty of death, is a clear demonstration that alternative penalties are of equal or greater protective value to society than is capital punishment.

In every instance in which a valid statistical comparison is possible between jurisdictions scientifically equated as to population and economic and social conditions, the nations and states that have abolished capital punishment have a smaller capital crimes rate than the comparable jurisdictions that have retained the death penalty. Further, the capital crimes rate in those jurisdictions which, while retaining the death penalty, use it seldom or not at all is in most instances lower than the capital crimes rates in the retentionist jurisdictions which execute most frequently.

And, finally, comparing the before, during, and after capital crimes rates in those jurisdictions (nine in the United States) which abolished capital punishment and then restored it to their penal codes, we find a consistently downward trend in capital crimes unaffected by either abolition or restoration. Startling comparisons are available. The United State Navy has executed no one in more than 120 years; yet it has maintained a level of discipline, effectiveness, and morale certainly in no sense inferior to

that of the United States Army which has inflicted the death penalty on more than 150 soldiers in just the last three decades.

Delaware, most recent state to abolish the death penalty, experienced a remarkable drop in its capital crimes rate during the first full year of abolition. No criminologist would argue that abolition will necessarily reduce capital crimes; nor will he attempt to demonstrate a causal connection between absence of the death penalty and low capital crime rates. In point of fact, homicide is the one major felony which shows a consistent downward trend in both capital punishment and abolition jurisdictions—indicating to the student of human behavior that the crime of murder, particularly, is largely an irrational reaction to a concrescence of circumstances, adventitiously related, wholly independent of and neither positively nor negatively correlatable with the legal sanction provided in the jurisdiction in which the crime actually took place. Dr. Marvin Wolfgang has pointed out with some logic that our decreasing murder rate is probably in no small part due to improved communictions (ambulance gets to the scene faster), improved first aid to the victim, and the antibiotics, blood banks, and similar advances in medicine which save many an assault victim from becoming a corpse—and of course his assailant from being tagged a murderer. The consistent upward trend in assaultive crimes gives support to Dr. Wolfgang's thesis.

7. *Police and prison officers are safer in non-death penalty states.* The studies of Donald Campion, S.J., associate editor of AMERICA, and others indicate (albeit with restricted samplings) that the life of a police officer or a prison guard is slightly safer in the non-death penalty states, although the difference is so slight as to

be statistically insignificant. Prison wardens overwhelmingly support abolition but large segments of the police profession support the retention of the death penalty both as a general crime deterrent (which it demonstrably is not) and as a specific safeguard to members of their own profession. Significantly, few of the police officers who serve in non-death penalty states are active in the fight to restore capital punishment and most of those who oppose abolition in their own jurisdictions have never performed police duties in an abolition state. It is a criminological axiom that it is the certainty, not the severity, of punishment that deters. Improvements in the selection, training, discipline, supervision, and operating techniques of our police will insure a higher percentage of apprehensions and convictions of criminals and, even without the death penalty, will provide a greater general crime deterrent and far more safety both for the general public and for police officers than either enjoys at present.

8. *Paroled and pardoned murderers are no threat to the public.* Studies in New Jersey and California, and less extensive studies of paroled and pardoned murderers in other jurisdictions, indicate that those whose death sentences have been commuted, or who have been paroled from life or long-term sentences, or who have received executive pardons after conviction of capital crimes are by far the least likely to recidivate. Not only do they not again commit homicide, but they commit other crimes or violate their parole contracts to a much lesser extent than do paroled burglars, robbers, and the generality of the non-capital crimes convicts on parole. My own study of nearly 150 murderers showed that not a single one had killed again and only two

had committed any other crime subsequent to release. Ohio's Governor Michael DiSalle has pointed out (as Warden Lewis Lawes and other penologists have in the past) that murderers are by and large the best and safest prisoners; and he has demonstrated his confidence by employing eight convicted murderers from the Ohio State Penitentiary in and about the Executive Mansion in Columbus in daily contact with members of his family.

9. *The death penalty is more costly than its alternatives.* It seems somewhat immoral to discuss the taking of even a murderer's life in terms of dollars and cents; but often the argument is raised that capital punishment is the cheapest way of "handling" society's outcasts and that the "good" members of the community should not be taxed to support killers for life (often coupled with the euthanasian argument that "they are better off dead"). The application of elementary cost accounting procedures to the determination of the differential in costs peculiar to capital cases will effectively demonstrate that not only is it not "cheaper to hang them"; but that, on the contrary, it would be cheaper for the taxpayers to maintain our prospective executees in the comparative luxury of first-rate hotels, with all the perquisites of non-criminal guests, than to pay for having them executed. The tangible costs of the death penalty in terms of long-drawn-out jury selection, extended trials and retrials, appeals, extra security, maintenance of expensive, seldom-used death-houses, support of the felon's family, etc., are heavy.

10. *Capital punishment stands in the way of penal reform.* Man has used the death penalty and other forms of retributive punishment throughout the centuries

to control and govern the conduct of his fellows and to force conformity and compliance to laws and codes, taboos and customs. The record of every civilization makes abundantly clear that punishment, no matter how severe or sadistic, has had little effect on crime rates. No new approach to the criminal is possible so long as the death penalty, and the discredited penology it represents, pervades our criminal justice system. Until it is stricken from the statute books, a truly rehabilitative approach to the small percentage of our fellowmen who cannot or will not adjust to society's dictates is impossible of attainment. That there is a strong positive correlation between advocacy of the death penalty and a generally punitive orientation cannot be gainsaid. Analysis of the votes for corporal punishment bills, votes against substitution of alternatives for mandatory features in the few mandatory death penalty jurisdictions, votes against study commissions and against limited period moratoria, and comparison with votes for bills increasing the penalties for rape, narcotics offenses, and other felonies discloses a pattern of simple retributive punitiveness, characterizing many of our legislators and the retentionist witnesses before legislative committees.

Many church assemblies of America and individual churchmen of every denomination have underscored the moral and ethical nonacceptability of capital punishment. Church members have the responsibility to support the campaign to erase this stain on American society. Capital punishment is brutal, sordid, and savage. It violates the law of God and is contrary to the humane and liberal respect for human life characteristic of modern democratic states. It is unsound criminologically and unnecessary for the protection of the state or its citizens. It makes miscarriages of justice irredeemable; it makes the barbaric *lex talionis* the watchword and inhibits the reform of our prison systems. It encourages disrespect for our laws, our courts, our institutions; and, in the words of Sheldon Glueck, "bedevils the administration of justice and is the stumbling block in the path of general reform in the treatment of crime and criminals."

● ● ●

POSTSCRIPT

IS CAPITAL PUNISHMENT JUSTIFIED?

Opinion in the United States has always been sharply divided on the death penalty. While Massachusetts in 1785 defined nine capital crimes (that is, crimes punishable by death), and North Carolina as late as 1837 had more than twenty, other states early rejected the death sentence entirely. American sentiment has been so divided that at least eleven of the states have abolished the death penalty only to restore it some years later.

In the readings in this chapter, MacNamara acknowledges a variety of assertions made in defense of the penalty as well as his need to rebut each of them. By contrast, Berns emphasizes the emotional appeal to our desire for retribution.Neither of these closely reasoned examinations should obscure the fact that most consideration of capital punishment is not as rational. Deep emotional and moral convictions are not likely to be much influenced by statistics on murder and executions, the relationship between murder rates and frequency of executions, and the constitutional issue of whether or when the death sentence constitutes "cruel and unusual punishment."

The student who prefers evidence to emotion will find a wealth of historical and statistical material in William J. Bowers, EXECUTIONS IN AMERICA (Lexington Books, 1974). The movement that led to the abolition of the death penalty in Great Britain prompted the publication of several books, the most stimulating of which is Arthur Koestler and C.H. Rolph, HANGED BY THE NECK (Penguin, 1961). Probably the most reflective, and almost certainly the most engrossing, literature on the subject in the United States is to be found in the many books dealing with the executions of Sacco and Vanzetti (plays and films have also dealt with their case), the Rosenbergs, and Caryl Chessman. In each of these cases, deep feelings favoring and opposing their execution were aroused by political issues and questions regarding their guilt, as well as by divided sentiments on the exercise of capital punishment. Almost certainly, popular attitudes toward the death sentence in these cases were never entirely separable from other circumstances.

Apart from the constitutional issues, the debate is more narrowly drawn than in earlier times. Although the death penalty is sometimes urged as punishment for such acts as treason or skyjacking, it is principally considered in connection with the crime of murder. There is little dispute with the proposition that the manner of execution should be the least painful—no one is drawn and quartered in modern civilized society—although there is no unanimity of opinion as to whether death by electrocution, gas, or hanging best meets that test. However, it is neither the question of how or how often to impose capital punishment, but whether to take a life for a life that society is obliged to examine.

ISSUE 11

DO WE NEED MORE GUN CONTROL?

YES: Sam Fields, from "Handgun Prohibition and Social Necessity," HANDGUNS (Foundation for Handgun Education, Washington, DC)

NO: Barry Bruce-Briggs, from "The Great American Gun War," *The Public Interest,* Fall 1976

ISSUE SUMMARY

YES: Sam Fields, Field Director of the National Coalition to Ban Handguns, points out that handguns are ineffective for self defense and are useful only as weapons in the commission of crimes.
NO: Author and historian, Barry Bruce-Briggs, cites evidence to suggest that handguns are useful for self protection and that laws to restrict their manufacture and sale are ill-advised.

The recent handgun murders of famous people has dramatically called public attention to the issue of the relationship between handguns and crime. Grim statistics are usually cited by the advocates of more strict gun control. Ten thousand people are killed in the United States each year (two-thirds of all murder victims) by handguns. In fact, during the period of the Vietnam war, more people were killed at home by handguns than died in battle. The handgun murder rate in this country is one hundred times higher than that in England, where these weapons cannot be easily obtained, and two hundred times higher than in Japan, where handguns are virtually unobtainable.

Opponents of gun control reply that the lower murder rates in countries which have stronger gun control laws are actually the result of different cultures and criminal justice systems. They note that most households in Switzerland and Israel possess firearms, yet the murder rate in both countries is very low. Moreover, the opponents of gun controls have their own statistics to cite. Fewer than one-tenth of one percent of all handguns are used for any illegal purpose. Comparative studies do not support any significant correlation between gun control and the reduction of crime.

Existing federal law, the Gun Control Act of 1968, has been attacked by both sides. Those who would impose greater controls on gun ownership point out that, although gun dealers are barred from selling handguns to drug addicts, ex-mental patients and fugitives from justice, in practice the prospective purchaser answers these questions without facing any further investigation. Advocates of gun control also criticize existing law because it permits the sale of cheap handguns (so-called Saturday Night Specials) which seem to have no purpose other than inflicting bodily injury. Gun regulation is virtually non-existent when the number of gun dealers (170,000) exceeds the number of gasoline stations. In recent years, the most important legislation in Congress is the Kennedy-Rodino bill. This bill is designed to check prospective buyers (through a 21 day waiting period for an eligibility check), outlaw Saturday Night Specials, and reduce the number of gun dealers through the imposition of stricter requirements.

Equally unhappy with existing law are the opponents of gun control. The McClure-Volkmer bill would ease the legal movement of firearms, restrict the regulatory powers of the federal government, and impose harsher penalties on criminals who use guns. The opponents of gun control insist that current controls are useless when they are not harmful. The potential harm comes from the possibility that licensing and registration of all firearms can lead to confiscation and the usurpation of power.

Gun control is not simply an issue of public policy; it is also an issue of constitutional law. The Second Amendment to the United States Constitution reads:

A well regulated Militia being necessary to the security of a free state, the right of the people to keep and bear Arms, shall not be infringed.

At the time it was written, a clear right to bear arms existed in England. Alexander Hamilton referred to the people as the "unorganized militia." Against the claim of an unconditional constitutional right, the U.S. Supreme Court asserted in 1939, and confirmed in 1980, that:

The Second Amendment guarantees no right to keep and bear a firearm that does not have 'some reasonable relationship to the preservation or efficiency of a well-regulated militia.'

Pro-gun groups believe that regulating handguns is only a first step to banning them, and then to banning other firearms as well. Handgun control groups respond that other guns serve social or recreational purposes, such as hunting or target-shooting. Those opposed to handgun control rebut this distinction by pointing out that handguns are also used for these purposes. Moreover, to protect one's life with a handgun is also a legitimate social purpose. The National Rifle Association has gone so far as to argue that any law which impairs the right to have guns "would strip a citizen of his or her most basic right—the right to live."

Both sides cite public opinion in their favor. On the one hand, most Americans favor some handgun regulation and a ban on Saturday Night Specials. On the other hand, most Americans oppose an outright ban on handguns and doubt that regulations will keep criminals from getting guns. The opposed positions are represented in the following selections by Sam Fields and B. Bruce Briggs.

YES

Sam Fields

THE HANDGUN HAS BECOME A MENACE TO OUR SOCIETY

The proposition is simple: for technological reasons a certain type of firearm, the handgun, has become a menace to our society. Measured by any yardstick—law and order, human tragedy, financial—the cost-benefit ratio is overhwelmingly against a system that allows easy access to handguns. A sampling of the tangible and intangible tragedies interwoven in the handgun menace indicates that $500 million is spent annually in hospital care for handgun wounds, that annually, handguns take the lives of over twenty thousand individuals with potential lifetime earnings of $116,000 and that thousands of families are reduced to welfare for want of a breadwinner. . . .

The modern handgun began its career of death and destruction in the 1870s with the creation of the Colt .45 Peacemaker. In the hundred and one years since the introduction of the double action, hard cased cartridge revolver there has been little change in American handgun technology. Such technology brought convenient, ultimate violence within everyone's reach by supplying a dependable, easy-to-carry, ever-ready destructive device. The sidearms race was on. If you did not have one your neighbor might, so you better get one yourself. The development of the handgun changed the character of American life as much as any other single technical advance.

Initially, the Peacemaker and its competitors supplied a valuble service to law enforcement, but whatever value the handgun had in the late 1800's, it is now a major social polluter. Like the industries that first created jobs and later caused environmental damage, it was not long before the handgun became the number one murder weapon in the country.

Although early figures are sketchy, in the century since the introduction of the double action handgun, it may be fairly estimated that handguns have been used in over half a million murders, almost twice that number of suicides and another 200,000 accidental deaths. Furthermore, over the past ten to fifteen years, handgun misuse of all kinds has not only increased in absolute numbers, it has dramatically increased in relation to the overall crime picture. Between 1966 and 1973, handgun homicide as a percentage of overall homicide increased from thirty-seven precent to fifty-two percent. In serious assaults it rose from nineteen percent to twenty-nine percent.

It is no coincidence that the handgun's greater percentage of the growing crime picture came at a time when handgun sales reached all-time record levels. It is also not a coincidence that the highest regions of misuse are the areas of highest ownership and weakest gun control laws. In spite of all the urban poverty and deterioration in the Northeast, the number of handguns and, overall, the number of homicides and aggravated assaults remain lowest in this troubled region. The South and the West, with the weakest laws, show the highest levels of handgun ownership along with the highest levels of misuse.

Estimates are that today in the United States there are 210-220 million firearms. Of this population, approximately forty-five to fifty million are handguns. The rest, 165-175 million, are long guns consisting of shotguns and rifles, with the former being the more popular of the two. The figures surprise most people, because as one listens to the radio, watches the nightly news or reads the paper it appears that handguns are the weapons invariably used in crime or involved in accidents. The mistaken, but understandable conclusion is that the handgun must be the most common firearm. In fact, handguns represent no more than twenty to twenty-five percent of the firearms population and yet they account for ninety percent of criminal and accidental firearms misuse. . . .

[T]he self-defense value provided by handguns is negligible. The accuracy and stopping power of handguns is almost zero when compared to long guns, whether rifles or shotguns. If one were under attack from a mob, . . . handguns, and particularly short barrel concealable handguns, would be the least dependable firearms.

The severe technological limitations intrinsic to handguns can be easily demonstrated. Within one hour and one hundred rounds of ammunition an *average* person can learn to fire a rifle as accurately as the world's *best* handgun shooter, in the same way as an average ten year old can learn, in a shorter time, to throw a baseball farther than the world's *best* shotputter can put the official sixteen pound shot. Such a demonstration says little of the student or teacher, *only* of the different capabilities of the instruments.

It is obvious, because of technological limitations, that the handgun is a poor choice as a defensive weapon in situations of group attack. Those depending on such weapons are needlessly risking tragic consequences. But what about the more typical situations of assault, robbery, burglary or attempted rape? . . .

According to a study by the U.S. Conference of Mayors, ninety percent of all burglaries are completed when no one is home, so that a handgun kept on the premises for property protection is almost worthless. And, in any case, as Mr. Bruce-Briggs indicates, "it is far more likely that a gun will be stolen than . . . used against a burglar . . ." As one burglar explained it, "If I wanted to meet people, I would have been a mugger.". . .

There are numerous studies that have analyzed the self-protection value of firearms and all agree that any self-protection benefits offered by handguns are far outweighed by the liabilities they create for the owner, the family and the community.

A study done in Boston showed that of 220 victims of residential burglary, seventeen percent had firearms in their house-

11.   DO WE NEED MORE GUN CONTROL?

holds versus ten percent of a random sample of 682 non-victims. The U.S. Conference of Mayors cites an unpublished study in Toronto, Canada that produced similar results.

Occasionally, burglar-resident confrontations do occur. What do the studies say of the value of firearms? The School of Medicine at Case Western Reserve University studied Cleveland area accidental deaths and concluded that over a fifteen year period, from 1958-1973, "only twenty-three burglars, robbers or intruders . . . were killed by guns of any kind in the hands of persons who were protecting their homes. During the same interval, six times as many fatal accidents occurred in the home."

This does not include the number of handgun homicides committed in familial disputes. Their inclusion would raise the six to one ratio fifty fold. In addition, what is the fate of the tens of thousands of Cleveland self-defense handguns stolen from homes in this fifteen year period and channeled into the criminal market? These, of course, fuel the felony murder aspect of homicide.

The uselessness of a handgun for civilian self-protection is inversely proportional to its value as a tool for crime, especially among high crime age groups (fifteen to twenty-five year olds) where the presence of a weapon encourages impulse crime. According to a 1977 study of gun crime inmates in a Florida prison, only 8.8 percent acquired a handgun for crime purposes. Eighty-seven percent acquired it for self-defense, hunting or target practice, etc. Only 22.8 percent of the gun murderers said they still would have committed the crime without a handgun. Altogether only 13.2 percent of the assaults and murders were planned in advance. Typically, the handgun was acquired from a

friend and carried for self-protection and machismo reasons. It stretches the imagination that all of these people would have carried a five pound, ten inch sawed off shotgun or semi-automatic rifle in the same way they carried their keys, wallet, or handgun.

Are rifles and shotguns ever more useful than handguns for criminals? For political assassins or psychopaths sitting up on the top of the Texas Bell Tower, the answer is yes. But for ninety-nine percent of all criminals, for knocking off the local Seven-Eleven or the local Exxon Station, or for pushing into the ribs of a victim walking down a lonely street, handguns are made to order. That is why nine out of ten criminals use them and seventy-one percent use them with barrels under three inches.

Thus, we now have floating around a relatively small group of firearms that regularly grease the skids of firearms misuse. Moments of anger are exacerbated so that simple assaults become aggravated assaults and aggravated assaults become homicides.

But, even in planned crimes of gain, study after study show that, like poverty, handguns are an ingredient that encourage, embolden and elevate criminal activity, particularly among the inner city fifteen to twenty-five year old population, the number one source of violent criminal behavior.

Why is the handgun the criminal choice nine [of] ten times? . . . [L]et's consider the criminal's viewpoint.

What does he need to facilitate robbery? First and foremost he wants to convince his victim of the futility of resistance while protecting himself if the need arises. The solution is, of course, a firearm. Unmistakable lethality is found in all of them. That, however, is as far as the similarity goes. Beyond lethality, the criminal has some rather specific requirements for his fire-arms to assure success and safety. To this end he requires from his weapon: conceal-ability, multiple rapid fire, portability and easy reload. . . .

Is the handgun more of a threat to life than other concealable weapons? Vis-a-vis other firearms, it is obviously more of a threat because its compactness guarantees that it is more likely to be around in volatile situations than rifles or shotguns. . . .

On a practical level, although both knife and handgun can probably be drawn at equal speed, the range of the knife (unless thrown, leaving the perpetrator without a weapon) has no effect beyond arm's length and moves no quicker than the arm. The revolver offers six shots, and, inside a ten foot radius, almost perfect accuracy, as well as an instantaneous velocity of 1000 feet per second. That is why handgun assaults end in homicide five times more often than knife assaults. . . .

All of this discussion about the inef-fectiveness of handguns as self-defense weapons might prompt a "so what?" from the reader. Even if it is an ineffective or stupid method of self-protection there is no moral or criminal law against self-inflicted stupidity. Unfortunately, it is not so simple. Leaving aside the potential danger created for family members, often as not children, we come to an additional problem touched upon by Mr. Bruce-Briggs—handgun theft.

In terms of exact numbers, how many and what kinds of guns are stolen is a matter of dispute. But by any standard, the number is great. What is more important is the long-range effect of stolen firearms, particularly stolen handguns. More than any other item commonly found in the home, *nothing* has the cash value of a handgun. The retail value of a [1978] nineteen inch Sony Trinitron television is approximately $500. On the other hand the retail price of an S&W .38 caliber snub nose revolver varies from $110 to $140. Which will convert to greater cash? Not the Trinitron. It will probably be fenced for fifty to seventy-five dollars. The S&W .38 is not generally a consumer item. It is a tool of the trade for muggers, youth gangs, drug deal-ers and the like. Knowing this, the burglar can, with little effort, sell the .38 for a price close to retail.

Does it work out in practice? Most as-suredly, though figures vary because of the lack of required record keeping, and even weaker reporting requirements. However, in 1975, the Bureau of Alcohol, Tobacco and Firearms Director offered the fol-lowing statistics: 153,812 firearms were entered into the National Crime Infor-mation Center computer as stolen. Of this number seventy percent or 107,668, were handguns. When stealing, criminals are specifically choosing the least numerous type of firearm—the handgun. Like its high incidence in misuse, its extraordinary theft rate is a result of purposeful action.

The figure 107,668, of course, repre-sents only the handguns reported stolen. It may prove to be just the tip of the iceberg; studies by the Law Enforcement Assist-ance Administration show that as much as *forty-eight percent* of burglaries and *sev-enty-seven percent* of larcenies go un-reported. It is not, therefore, out of line to assume, as Steven Brill does in *Firearm Abuse: A Research and Policy Report*, that a truer figure is closer to 200,000 hand-guns stolen per year. Thus, along with cash and jewelry, the handgun is the nation's most stolen item.

But, unlike cash and jewelry, the hand-gun is the ghost that comes back to haunt us again and again. The so-called self-defense handgun stolen in one neigh-

187

borhood becomes the street punk's murder weapon in the next.

What then is the balance sheet on handguns acquired for self-protection? On the plus side, the NRA (National Rifle Association) [has] been able to assemble a series of anecdotes of which, in any given year a mere handful (well under thirty) show possible need for a handgun and a handgun *alone*. On the negative side, so called "self-defense" handguns are involved annually in thousands of murders and accidental deaths, over 150,000 gunshot wounds, and ultimately in resupplying the criminal element with 200,000 weapons tailored to crime. The cost-benefit ratio is so absurdly one-sided in favor of controlling handguns that it would make equal sense to deny the value of penicillin in the name of the dozen or so individuals who annually suffer adverse reaction to what is otherwise a lifesaving antibiotic. . . .

Criticism of the effectiveness of a law ought to be based on the practical capabilities of the law and not on strawmen set up by the opponents of the law. The case in point is the Sullivan Law in New York City. It is one of the nation's oldest and toughest handgun laws. It is also the number one whipping boy of handgun control opponents . . . [who] readily point to the high gun crime rates in New York City.

Briefly, the Sullivan Law requires handgun registration and establishes a strict permit system to possess and/or carry. Unlike states such as North Carolina, the New York permit is hard to come by. The background check is extensive and the applicant must establish a definitive need to own a handgun.

Practically speaking, the Sullivan Law gives authorities the power to regulate handguns that are commerced in New York. It has no authority to reach into neighboring states, nor can, nor should the New York police be expected to set up permanent firearms checkpoints at every New York state border entry.

The result is that as far as handguns commerced in New York are concerned, the Sullivan Law maintains the toughest controls and drastically limits their criminal use. A Bureau of Alcohol, Tobacco and Firearms (BATF) Project Identification analysis showed that, based on a 1973 sample of 2546 New York City crime guns, only four percent came from New York State. The rest came from states with little or no regulations.

New York's dilemma can be compared to a state law prohibiting pollution discharges in a river. The net value of a Missouri law prohibiting waste dumpage in the Mississippi is going to be greatly reduced if any or all of the first four states that the Mississippi flows through treat it like an open sewer. The [incorrect] conclusion would be that anti-pollution laws do not work. However, the evidence indicates that pollution is a problem that can be solved with appropriate interstate compacts or federal legislation. So it goes with handgun laws. Unless a tough minimum federal standard is enacted, the weak link states will continue to undermine, although not totally destroy, the intent and effect of state and local laws. . . .

Pollsters have asked the question in a dozen different ways and more than a dozen different times. Forty years of polling reveal that Americans overwhelmingly and consistently support stiff regulation of handguns *and* the banning of cheap handguns. . . .

Even among gun owners, poll after poll shows strong support for handgun control. Six Gallup and Harris polls between 1959 and 1975 showed that gun owners, by almost a two to one margin favored "gun control" (Harris and Gallup terminology) in the form of registration.

Why doesn't Congress act? Congress, like most of government, is crisis oriented. In government spending and tax reform it responds to California's Proposition 13 and in handgun control it responds to assassination. While all assassinations do not necessarily result in legislation, it is hardly a coincidence that the last federal legislation was passed in 1968, only months after the murders of Martin Luther King and Robert F. Kennedy. Ironically, handgun control would probably have little deterrence on planned political assassination. But politics moves on symbols. When there is an underlying current for change, it takes a Rosa Parks on a Montgomery, Alabama bus or a Robert Kennedy dying before millions of television viewers to spark that change. Lacking that mandate, Congress will opt for inaction. In the immediate case inaction on handgun

control is fueled by millions spent by handgun manufacturers and the National Rifle Association in lobbying and campaign contributions. Only in the last three years have organizations like the National Coalition to Ban Handguns been formed to oppose the NRA.

Will effective federal handgun control come about? Those who believe otherwise are fighting the future and misreading the forces of history. Thus, did George Wallace discover after his 1962 declaration of "segregation forever" that "forever" meant until June 1963.

And, like the racist demagogues, the handgun demagogues could, unfortunately, cause an unexpected and overwhelming reaction that will hurt the rights of all legitimate gun owners. In fact, Smith & Wesson, the gun manufacturers, fully comprehend this dilemma by supporting "handgun licensing".

The United States *needs* handgun contol, the only question is when and how.

• • •

NO

B. Bruce-Briggs

THE GREAT AMERICAN GUN WAR

For over a decade there has been a powerful and vocal push for stricter government regulation of the private possession and use of firearms in the United States—for "gun control." The reader cannot help being aware of the vigorous, often vociferous debate on this issue. Indeed, judging from the amount of energy devoted to the gun issue—Congress has spent more time on the subject than on all other crime-related measures combined—one might conclude that gun control is the key to the crime problem. Yet it is startling to note that no policy research worthy of the name has been done on the issue of gun control. The few attempts at serious work are of marginal competence at best, and tainted by obvious bias. Indeed, the gun control debate has been conducted at a level of propaganda more appropriate to social warfare than to democratic discourse.

No one disagrees that there is a real problem: Firearms are too often used for nefarious purposes in America. In 1974, according to the FBI's Uniform Crime Reports, 10,000 people were illegally put to death with guns, and firearms were reportedly used in 200,000 robberies and 120,000 assaults, as well as in a small number of rapes, prison escapes, and other crimes. There is universal agreement that it would be desirable, to say the least, that these numbers be substantially reduced. So everybody favors gun control. But there is wide disagreement about how it can be achieved. Two principal strategies are promoted. To use the military terminology now creeping into criminology, they can be called "interdiction" and "deterrence."

Advocates of deterrence recommend the establishment of stricter penalties to discourage individuals from using firearms in crimes. But "gun control" is usually identified with interdiction—that is, the reduction of the criminal use of firearms by controlling the access of all citizens to firearms. The interdictionist position is promoted by a growing lobby, supported by an impressive alliance of reputable organizations, and sympathetically publicized by most of the national media. Every commission or major study of crime and violence has advocated much stricter gun-control laws. The only reason that this pressure has failed to produce much tighter controls of firearms is a powerful and well-organized lobby of gun owners, most notably the National Rifle Association (NRA), which has maintained that improved interdiction will have no effect on crime, but will merely strip away the rights and privileges of Americans—and perhaps even irreparably damage the Republic. The organized gun owners advocate reliance on deterrence.

The debate between the "gun controllers" (as the interdictionists are generally identified) and the "gun lobby" (as the organized gun owners have been labeled by a hostile media) has been incredibly virulent. In addition to the usual political charges of self-interest and stupidity, participants in the gun-control struggle have resorted to implications or downright accusations of mental illness, moral turpitude, and sedition. The level of debate has been so debased that even the most elementary methods of cost-benefit analysis have not been employed. One expects advocates to disregard the costs of their programs, but in this case they have even failed to calculate the benefits.

THE PREVALENCE OF FIREARMS

While estimates vary widely, it can be credibly argued that there are at least 140 million firearms in private hands in the United States today. This number has been expanding rapidly in recent years.[1] Since 1968, 40 million firearms have been produced and sold. And these counts do not include the millions of guns brought back from the wars and/or stolen from military stocks. These figures are usually cited by advocates of interdiction as demonstrative of the enormity of the problem and as implying the dire necessity for swift and postive action. But they also demonstrate the incredible difficulty of dealing with the problem.

In the gun-control debate, the most outlandishly paranoid theories of gun ownership have appeared. Some people seem to believe that private arsenals exist primarily for political purposes—to kill blacks, whites, or liberals. But of course, the majority of firearms in this country are rifles and shotguns used primarily for hunting. A secondary purpose of these "long guns" is target and skeet shooting. Millions of gun owners are also collectors, in the broad sense of gaining satisfaction from the mere possession of firearms, but even the serious collectors who hold them as historical or aesthetic artifacts number in the hundreds of thousands.

The above uses account for the majority of firearms owned by Americans. Weapons for those purposes are not intended for use against people. But there is another purpose of firearms—self-defense. In poll data, some 35 per cent of gun owners, especially handgun owners, indicated that at least one reason they had for possessing their weapons was self-defense. A Harris poll found two-thirds of these people willing to grant that they would, under certain circumstances, kill someone with their weapon. This sounds very ominous, but it is such a widespread phenomenon that interdictionists have felt obliged to conduct studies demonstrating that the chance of being hurt with one's own weapon is greater than the chance of inflicting harm upon an assailant. The studies making this point are so ingeniously specious that they are worth expanding upon.

For example, the calculation is made that within a given jurisdiction more people are killed by family and friends, accidents, and sometimes suicide, than burglars are killed by homeowners. In a Midwestern county it was found that dead gun owners outnumbered dead burglars by six to one. Both sides of that ratio are fallacious. People do not have "house guns" to kill burglars but to prevent burglaries. The measure of the effectiveness of self-defense is not in the number of bodies piled up on doorsteps, but in the property that is protected. We have no idea how many burglars are challenged and frightened off by armed householders. And, of course, there is no way to measure the deterrent effect on burglars who know that homeowners may be armed. Though the statistics by themselves are not particularly meaningful, it is true that the burglary rate is very low in Southern and Southwestern cities with high rates of gun ownership. Burglary in Texas would seem a risky business.

The calculation of family homicides and accidents as costs of gun ownership is equally false. The great majority of these killings are among poor, restless, alcoholic, troubled people, usually with long criminal records. Applying the domestic homicide rate of these people to the presumably upstanding citizens whom they prey upon is seriously misleading.

Other studies claim to indicate that there is little chance of defending oneself with a weapon against street crime or other assaults. But almost without exception, such studies have been held in cities with strict gun-control laws. My favorite study was the one purporting to show that it was very dangerous to attempt to defend yourself with a gun because the likelihood of suffering harm in a mugging was considerably higher if you resisted. But the data indicated only that you got hurt if you yelled, kicked, or screamed—but not if you used a gun. . . .

EXISTING GUN CONTROL

There are reportedly some 20,000 gun-control ordinances in the various jurisdictions of the United States. Most are prohibitions against discharging a weapon in urban areas or against children carrying weapons, and are trivial, reasonable, and uncontroversial. Most states and large cities have laws against carrying concealed weapons, the rationale being that no person has a legitimate reason to do so. In a few large cities and states, particularly in the Northeast, a license is required to buy or possess a handgun, and in a very few but growing number of Northeastern cities and states a permit or license is required to possess any sort of firearm.

At first sight, licensing seems eminently reasonable. Dangerous criminals should not have weapons, nor should the mentally disturbed. But the administrative "details" of licensing become incredibly difficult. It is fairly easy to check out an applicant for a criminal record, which can be a legitimate reason for denying a license. But many criminals, judging from the comparison between reported crime and conviction rates, are not convicted of crimes, especially violent crimes, so the difficulty exists of whether to deny people the privilege of purchasing weapons if they have merely been arrested, but then set free or acquitted. Civil libertarians should be taken aback by this prospect. The question of mental competence is even nastier to handle. Is someone to be denied a firearm because he sought psychiatric help when his wife died?

From the point of view of the organized gun owners, licensing is intolerable because of the way that it has been enforced in the past. One of the peculiarities of most local licensing is the lack of reciprocity; unlike marriage licensing. what is recognized in one jurisdiction is not in another. In the Eastern states it is nearly impossible to travel with a firearm without committing a felony (not, of course, that this troubles many people).

This sort of anecdotal evidence can be continued almost indefinitely. It suggests to the organized gun owners that licensing systems are a screen not against criminals but against honest citizens, and that licensing authorities are not to be trusted with any sort of discretionary power. It is certainly an inefficient system that dribbles out gun permits and refuses to recognize self-defense as a legitimate reason for owning a gun, while muggers operate with impunity, illicit pistols are exchanged openly on the streets, and penalties for gun-law violations—even by people with criminal records—are very rarely imposed.[2] . . .

THE LIMITS TO INTERDICTION

So the utility of interdiction has not and perhaps cannot be demonstrated. While the lack of evidence that a policy can be effective should make prudent men wary of promoting it, that does not mean the policy is necessarily without merit. Nevertheless, in the case of gun control it is possible to identify some weaknesses in the principles behind the policy.

To begin with, gun control as a general anti-crime strategy is flawed because most

crimes, including many of the crimes most feared, are not committed with guns. Firearms are rarely employed for rape, home burglary, or street muggings. On the other hand, a good portion of the most heinous crime, murder, is not a serious source of social fear. The majority of murders are the result of passionate argument, and although personal tragedies, are not a social concern—ditto for crimes committed by criminals against one another. Furthermore, the worst crimes, involving the most dangerous and vicious criminals, will not be affected by gun control. No serious person believes that an interdiction program will be effective enough to keep guns out of the hands of organized crime, professional criminals, or well connected terrorists and assassins. And almost all the widely publicized mass murderers were eligible for licensed guns.

Gun-control advocates grant this, and emphasize the need to limit spontaneous murders among "family and friends" that are made possible by the availability of firearms. But the commonly used phrase "family and friends" is misleading. The FBI's Uniform Crime Reports classify relationships between murderers and victims as "relative killings," "lovers' quarrels," and "other arguments." The last can be among criminal associates, as can the others. Nor can we necessarily conclude that such murders are spontaneous. The legal distinction between premeditated and nonpremeditated murder prompts killers (and their lawyers) to present murders as unplanned.

The very nature of interdiction suggests other weakness. It is a military term used to describe attempts, usually by aerial bombing, to impede, not halt, the flow of enemy supplies to the battlefield. Interdiction has been the principal strategy used in drug control; it works only when pressure is being applied at the street level at the same time that imports and production are being squeezed. If there are 140 million privately owned firearms in the United States and guns can last centuries with minimum maintenance, merely cutting off the supply will have little or no effect for generations, and if the supply is not cut off entirely (which no serious person believes it can be), an interdiction policy is hardly likely to have a major effect even over the very long run. To my knowledge, no interdiction advocate has given a plausible answer to the very simple question of how to get 140 million firearms out of the hands of the American people.

Even more to the point, is it cost-effective to try to deal with 140 million weapons when you are presumably concerned with a maximum at the outside of 350,000 weapons used in violent crimes? The odds of any gun being criminally used are roughly on the order of one in 400. For handguns the rate is considerably higher; for rifles and shotguns considerably lower. I estimate that in 1974, roughly one of every 4,000 handguns was employed in a homicide, compared with one in 30,000 shotguns and one in 40,000 rifles. There are probably more privately owned guns in America than there are privately owned cars, and with the obvious exception of murder, the rate of criminal use of firearms is almost certainly less than the rate of criminal use of automobiles. How are we to control the 400 guns to prevent the one being used for crime? And if we decide the only way is to reduce the 400, to what must we reduce it? It must be assumed that the one gun used for crime will be the 400th.

Moreover, interdiction is a countermeasure against crime. Countermeasures provoke counter-countermeasures. Substitution is the most obvious strategy. If guns cannot be bought legally, they can be obtained illegally—organized crime is ready to cater to any illicit demand. If cheap handguns are unobtainable, expensive handguns will be used. If snub-nosed pistols and revolvers are banned, long-barreled weapons will be cut down. If the 40-million-odd handguns disappear, sawed-off rifles and shotguns are excellent substitutes. If all domestic production is halted, we will fall back on our tradition of smuggling. If all manufactured weapons vanish, anyone with a lathe and a hacksaw can make a serviceable firearm. In the 1950's, city punks produced zip guns from automobile aerials. A shotgun is easily made from a piece of pipe, a block of wood, several rubber bands, and a nail. . . .

INTERNATIONAL EXPERIENCE

Many peripheral arguments used in the gun control debate have little relevance to the issue, but must be addressed. Both sides will deploy the testimony of police chiefs on the desirability or futility of gun-control laws. Liberal interdictionists often cite the testimony of those gentlemen who have most illiberal views on most other law-enforcement matters. Most, but not all, big-city chiefs favor interdiction, while small-town chiefs generally oppose it, both nicely reflecting the views of their political superiors. But, for what it is worth, one can cite the Sheriff of Los Angeles County staunchly demanding stricter gun control laws and the Chief of Police of Los Angeles City saying that public order has broken down so far that only a fool would not arm himself. The gun owners gained strong reinforcement when the Superintendent of Scotland Yard recently pointed out that the number of guns available in America makes an interdiction strategy impossible.

A surprising amount of attention has been paid in the gun-control debate to international experience. In the world of gun control there seem to be only three foreign countries: Great Britain, Japan, and Switzerland. British gun control is taken by the interdictionists as the model of a desirable system. Guns are tightly regulated in the United Kingdom, violent crime is trivial by United States standards, and even the police are unarmed. But, as James Q. Wilson recently pointed out in this journal, the English situation is slowly eroding. The key to the low rates of personal violence in England is not in rigorous gun-control laws (which only date from 1920), but in the generally deferential and docile character of the populace. Perhaps it is significant that interdictionists point to "Great Britain" as their model; gun-control laws are even stricter in the other part of the United Kingdom, Northern Ireland.

Japan is an even more gun-free country. Not only does it restrict the ownership of weapons, but it has prohibited the ownership of handguns altogether, and the rates of violent crime are so low as to be hardly credible to Americans. To which the organized gun owners reply that Japanese-Americans have even lower rates of violence than Japanese in Japan. . . .

[U]nderlying the gun control struggle is a fundamental division in our nation. The intensity of passion on this issue suggests to me that we are experiencing a sort of low-grade war going on between two alternative views of what America is and ought to be. On the one side are those who take bourgeois Europe as a model of a civilized society: a society just, equitable, and democratic; but well ordered, with the lines of responsibility and authority clearly drawn, and with decisions made rationally and correctly by intelligent men for the entire nation. To such people, hunting is atavistic, personal violence is shameful, and uncontrolled gun ownership is a blot upon civilization.

On the other side is a group of people who do not tend to be especially articulate or literate, and whose world view is rarely expressed in print. Their model is that of the independent frontiersman who takes care of himself and his family with no interference from the state. They are "conservative" in the sense that they cling to America's unique pre-modern tradition—a non-feudal society with a sort of medieval liberty writ large for everyman. To these people, "sociological" is an epithet. Life is tough and competitive. Manhood means responsibility and caring for your own.

This hard-core group is probably very small, not more than a few million people, but it is a dangerous group to cross. From the point of view of a right-wing threat to internal security, these are perhaps the people who should be disarmed first, but in practice they will be the last. As they say, to a man, "I'll bury my guns in the wall first." They ask because they do not understand the other side, "Why do these people want to disarm us?" They consider themselves no threat to anyone; they are not criminals, not revolutionaries. But slowly, as they become politicized, they find an analysis that fits the phenomenon they experience: Someone fears their having guns, someone is afraid of their defending their families, property, and liberty. Nasty things may happen if these people begin to feel that they are cornered.

It would be useful, therefore, if some of the mindless passion, on both sides, could be drained out of the gun-control issue. Gun control is no solution to the crime problem, to the assassination problem, to the terrorist problem. Reasonable licensing laws, reasonably applied, might be marginally useful in preventing some individuals, on some occasions, from doing violent harm to others and to themselves.

195

But so long as the issue is kept at white heat, with everyone having some ground to suspect everyone else's ultimate intentions, the rule of reasonableness has little chance to assert itself.

1   One obvious reason for the growing gun sales is that the prices of firearms, like most mass-produced goods, have not risen as fast as incomes. The classic deer rifle, the Winchester 94, in production since 1894, cost 250 per cent of an average worker's weekly take-home salary in 1900, 91 per cent in 1960, and 75 per cent in 1970. The relationship to annual median family income has been even more favorable—from 2.8 per cent in 1900 to 1.4 per cent in 1960 and 1.0 per cent in 1970. More important, increased competition during the past decade has lowered the absolute price of handguns.

2   The Police Foundation is currently engaged in a study of the details of local handgun-law enforcement. Unfortunately, because its head is known as a vocal interdictionist, the credibility of its results will necessarily be somewhat compromised.

●   ●   ●

POSTSCRIPT

DO WE NEED MORE GUN CONTROL?

Neither Fields nor Bruce-Briggs adopts as extreme a position on gun control as do some commentators on this issue. Neither thinks he is privy to the thoughts of the authors of the Second Amendment. Both attempt to analyze the evidence where some others engage in veiled allusions to sinister forces which are, from one perspective, trying to render us helpless by disarming law-abiding Americans, and, from another perspective, storing arms to take over the government and establish a totalitarian state.

Nevertheless both authors adopt clear and strong positions in opposition to one another. Bruce-Briggs asserts that "no policy research worthy of the name has been done on the issue of gun control." Do the studies and statistics cited by Field rebut that contention? Note how they read the same evidence and arrive at different conclusions. In part the disagreement has to do with the proportion of crimes committed with handguns, in part with the practical consequences of licensing and other regulations to limit their possession.

"Guns don't kill people; people do," proclaims the leading lobby opposed to increased gun control, the National Rifle Association. GUNS DON'T DIE—PEOPLE DO, responded Nelson T. Shields, chairman of Handgun Control, Inc., in the title of his book. These interest groups are excellent sources for periodical and pamphlet literature on the issue as well as a comprehensive Report of a subcommittee of the Senate Committee on the Judiciary, *The Right to Keep and Bear Arms* (U.S. Government Printing Office, 1982). A point-by-point rebuttal of Shields can be found in the essays collected in Don B. Kates, Jr., RESTRICTING HANDGUNS: THE LIBERAL SKEPTICS SPEAK OUT (North River Press, 1979).

Despite the efforts of Fields and Bruce-Briggs to examine the studies and statistics, most public and congressional consideration of handgun crime and handgun control gives the impression that the advocates begin with their conclusions and proceed to choose and interpret the facts to support their position.

197

ISSUE 12

IS AFFIRMATIVE ACTION REVERSE DISCRIMINATION?

YES: Carl Cohen, from "The Defunis Case, Race and the Constitution, *The Nation,* February 8, 1975

NO: Justice Thurgood Marshall, from *Dissenting Opinion, Regents of the University of California vs Allan Bakke,* 1978

ISSUE SUMMARY

YES: Professor Cohen presents his argument that racial distinctions are contrary to the spirit and the letter of the Constitution, regardless of the intent.

NO: Associate Supreme Court Justice, Thurgood Marshall, contends that some remedy must be found for years of inequality and oppression.

Equality is as basic a political principle in America as liberty. "All men are created equal" is the most famous phrase in the Declaration of Independence. More than half a century later, Alexis de Tocqueville examined DEMOCRACY IN AMERICA and concluded that its most essential ingredient was the equality of condition. We know it was not true, not for women, not for blacks, not for Indians and other racial minorities, and not for other disadvantaged social classes. Nevertheless the ideal persisted. When slavery was abolished after the Civil War, the Constitution's then-new Fourteenth Amendment proclaimed: "No State shall . . . deny to any person within its jurisdiction the equal protection of the laws."

Equality has been a long time coming. For nearly a century after the freeing of the slaves, American blacks were denied equal protection by law in some states and by social practice nearly everywhere. One-third of the states and the national capital either permitted or compelled racially segregated schools, and a similar result was achieved elsewhere through housing policy and social behavior. In 1954 the Supreme Court reversed a 58-year-old standard which had found "separate but equal" schools compatible with equal protection of the law. A unanimous Court in *Brown v. Board of Education* held that, separate is not equal for the members of the discriminated-against group when the segregation "generates a feeling of inferiority as to their status in the community that may affect their hearts and minds in a way unlikely ever to be undone." The 1954 ruling on public elementary education has been extended to other areas of both governmental and private conduct, including housing and employment.

Even if judicial decisions and congressional statutes could end all segregation and racial discrimination, would we have achieved equality—or simply perpetuated the *status quo*? Black unemployment today is about twice that of whites. Disproportionately large numbers of blacks experience poverty, brutality, broken homes, physical and mental illness, and early death, while disproportionately low numbers of them have reached positions of affluence and prestige. It seems likely that much of this *de facto* inequality results from three hundred years of slavery and segregation. If we do no more than to cease this ill-treatment, have we done enough to end the injustices? No, say the proponents of "affirmative action."

In various cases the Supreme Court has considered the merits of affirmative action. In *Regents of the University of California v. Bakke* (1978) a five-to-four majority agreed that Bakke, a white applicant to the medical school, had been wrongly excluded due to the school's affirmative action policy, but the majority did not agree that admission policies must be completely "color-blind." Indeed, Justice Lewis Powell, whose opinion seemed to hold the balance in the case, specifically affirmed that race may be taken into account in considering a candidate's qualifications. In *United Steelworkers of America v. Weber* (1979) a five-to-two majority upheld an agreement between an aluminum plant and a union to establish a quota for blacks in admitting applicants to a special training program. In *Fullilove v. Klutznick* (1980) a six-to-three majority upheld the constitutionality of a Federal public works program requiring that ten percent of spending be reserved for minority contractors. Here, again, as in *Bakke,* the Court was broken into a variety of positions on affirmative action. Three justices upheld the program on the ground of congressional power, three wrote a separate opinion upholding it on broader grounds, two joined in a dissent based upon the doctrine of "color-blindness," and one dissented on narrower grounds. It appears that the court has not yet reached a clear-cut consensus on the highly sensitive issue of affirmative action.

In the following selections Supreme Court Justice Thurgood Marshall and author Carl Cohen debate its merits. The Marshall selection, from his opinion in *Bakke,* emphasizes the need to remedy past injustices, while Cohen's essay turns upon his contention that even well-informed forms of racial discrimination are unconstitutional and immoral.

YES   Carl Cohen

RACE AND THE CONSTITUTION

Are classifications on the basis of race, for purposes of law school admission and the like, *per se* unconstitutional? The correct answer is yes.
Indeed, the Fourteenth Amendment was deliberately formulated to prohibit
precisely such classifications. The Constitution is and always must be, in that
sense, color blind. It cannot be, from time to time and at the discretion of
certain agencies or administrators, color conscious in order to become color
blind at some future date. The principle that a person's race is simply not
relevant in the application of the laws is a treasured one. If we are prepared to
sacrifice that principle now and then, in an attempt to achieve some very
pressing and very honorable objective, we will have given up its force as
constitutional principle. No doubt intentions here are of the best, but so often,
are the intentions of those who would from time to time sacrifice other
constitutional principles for the attainment of other very worthy ends. The
enforcement of justice, the redistribution of wealth, the very protection of the
nation, might all be more conveniently, more efficiently, even more effectively
accomplished if, from time to time, we winked at the Constitution and did
what, as we will be told with honest fervor, is of absolutely overriding
importance. In this way is the Congressional authority to declare war
conveniently ignored; in this way is the constitutional protection of our
persons, houses, papers and effects from unreasonable search and seizure
effectively (of course only temporarily) by-passed. In this way, in sum,
constitutional government, fragile network of principles that it is, comes apart.

But, some will reply, those other objectives—national security, protection
against crime, etc.—are only claimed to be compelling; racial justice, so long
deliberately denied, really is so. Of course. And every person and every group
has, at some time, objectives that are, to its complete and profound conviction,
so utterly compelling that nothing must be allowed to stand in the way of their
accomplishment. But every such party must yield in turn to the restrictions of

From, "The Defunis Case, Race and the Constitution," *The Nation,* February 8, 1975 ®*The Nation,* 1975.
Reprinted by permission.

constitutional government; if those in authority do not enforce these restrictions, the Constitution is but paper. A constitution, ideally, is not an expression of particular social ends; rather, it identifies very general common purposes and lays down principles according to which the many specific ends of the body politic may be decided upon and pursued. Its most critical provisions will be those which absolutely preclude certain means. Thus to say that a protection afforded citizens is "constitutional" is at least to affirm that it will be respected, come what may. The specific constitutional provision that each citizen is entitled to equal protection of the laws is assurance that, no matter how vital the government alleges its interest to be, or how laudable the objective of those who would temporarily suspend that principle, it will stand. The highest obligation to respect it is owed by public institutions and government agencies.*

Preferential admission systems present instances of this sometimes agonizing tension between important ends and impermissible means. Hence the persuasiveness of the argument on both sides. In facing dilemmas of this kind long experience has taught the supremacy of the procedural principle. With societies, as with individuals, the use of means in themselves corrupt tends to corrupt the user, and to infect the result. So it is with wiretapping, with censorship, with torture. So it is with discriminatory preference by racial grouping for racial balance.

But this is racial classification, the Court insisted, not racial discrimination. The latter is indeed ruled out, said they, but the former is not; *Brown* and other powerful precedents forbid invidious racial classification, not all racial classification. This argument misses the central point—the sharpest bite of *Brown* and like cases—that in the distribution of benefits under the laws *all* racial classifications are invidious. Invidious distinctions are those tending to excite ill will, or envy, those likely to be viewed as unfair—and that is what racial classifications are likely to do and be when used as instrument for the apportionment of goods or opportunities.

Perhaps the Court would respond: Some such invidiousness is difficult to deny, but our main point is that the racial classifications condemned by *Brown* and succeeding cases are those that stigmatize one of the groups distinguished, stamping it with inferiority. But the change of phrase provides no rescue. To stigmatize is to brand, or label, generally with disgrace—and that is exactly what is done by racial classification in this context. Indeed, put to the service of preferential admissions such classification is doubly stigmatizing. It marks one racial group as formally to be handicapped, its members burdened specifically by virtue of race; for the majority applicant (as formerly the minority) earned personal qualifications will not be enough. Persons in the other racial category are to be officially treated as though unable to

*The only previous suspension of this constitutional protection was a national moral disaster. To meet the alleged danger of sabotage and espionage during the Second World War, American citizens of Japanese descent were peremptorily rounded up, moved, and excluded from large sections of our West Coast. The Supreme Court was pained, but found this roundup and detention justified by "pressing public necessity." (*Korematsu v. United States*, 323 U.S. 216, 1944) Never before or since has the use of race in applying constitutional protection been expressly approved by our highest Court.

compete for the good in question on an equal basis; by physical characteristic the minority applicant is marked as in need of special help. On both sides morale is subverted, accomplishments clouded. On the one side all carry the handicap, regardless of their past deeds or capacity to bear it; on the other, all are received with the supposition of inferiority, regardless of their personal attainments or hatred of condescension. For all, the stigmata are visually prominent and permanent.

I conclude that the first and fundamental step of the Court's argument in defense of preferential admissions cannot be justly taken. Racial classifications, in the application of the laws, or in the distribution of benefits under the laws, are always invidious, always stigmatizing. That is why they are, *per se*, unconstitutional. . . .

Those who say, with the first Justice Harlan, "Our Constitution is color blind, and neither knows nor tolerates classes among citizens" do not suppose that the courts may not attend to the special character of past wrongs done. Rather, the principle they are emphasizing is cautionary: in all circumstances courts must scrupulously avoid and prohibit the use of a person's race as, in itself, a qualification (or a disqualification) for anything that persons of another race are, for that racial reason disqualified (or qualified) for. . . .

Furthermore, even in the school desegregation cases in which a deliberate racial injustice is identified for which specific remedy is sought, the attention to racial mix in providing that remedy is very delicately supervised by the courts. There is all the difference in the world between a specific remedy thus controlled (as in the *Swann* case) and a general license to

professional schools, or universities, or other institutions to ignore the constitutional prohibition of racial discrimination, and to engage in "reasonable" discriminatory activity to correct the effects of past social injustice as they consider such measures needful or convenient. To permit such practice is to abandon constitutional principle entirely.

Preferential admission procedures certainly do result in the discriminatory apportionment of benefits on the basis of race or ethnicity. When any resource is in short supply, and some by virtue of their race are given more of it, others by virtue of their race get less. If that resource be seats in a law school, procedures that assure preference to certain racial groups in allotting those seats necessarily produce a correlative denial of access to those not in the preferred categories. This plain consequence should not be overlooked. Whether the numbers be fixed or flexible; whether "quotas" be established and called "benign", whether they be measured by percentages or absolute quantities; whether the objective be "reasonable proportionality" or "appropriate representation"—the setting of benefit floors for some groups in this context inescapably entails benefit ceilings for other groups. . . .

If racial classifications are ever to be used, I conclude, they must pass a far more protective test than that invoked by the Court. The user of any racial classification must show that consideration of race is necessary to the accomplishment of a compelling state interest, *and* that such consideration does not result in adverse consequence to any person simply because of that person's race or ethnic membership. Now it has been demonstrated that one result of preferential policies is to deny to some persons, simply because of their race, what they in every other respect deserve and would receive, were they of the preferred skin color. It is therefore manifest that on this more protective standard no policy of preferential admission by race is acceptable. . . .

Racial integration is indeed a deep and powerful interest. It is not, however, an interest compelling in the sense that, to serve it, any steps are justified. Integration does not, as an objective, justify racial discrimination believed useful in its achievement. Lawyers, judges and prosecutors of all colors and ethnic identities we do need; but we cannot afford to pay for improvement on that front by basing professional qualifications partly on skin color. A community is not justified in advancing its own general health by denying to some of its members constitutional protections that apply to all. It is because the classification of persons by irrelevant, physical properties is so generally odious that the courts are explicit in demanding that the interests served by such classification be literally compelling, overriding. Grave though the need for integration is, overriding in the sense required by the judicial test proposed it is not.

A second general interest urged by the advocates of preferential admissions policies is the achievement of numerical proportionality among the races in the legal (and other) professions. Much different from integration, this is a conception of racial balance which not only measures justice by counting numbers of minority group members in the professions or professional schools, but also finds any result unsatisfactory that does not manifest "reasonable proportionality" or "appropriate representation."

Much that needs to be said on this aspect of compensatory justice cannot be said here. On two levels, however, it quickly becomes clear that racial proportionality is not a compelling need. Numerical proportionality of races in the professions is most commonly defended on the ground that without it the interests of minority groups cannot be properly served. Surely this belief is mistaken if it incorporates the conviction that only black lawyers can serve black clients adequately, that Indians, when sick, are treated properly only by Indian physicians, or that white defendants cannot be fairly tried before black judges. The insistence that proper and conscientious fulfillment of professional function is dependent upon harmony of race or heritage between client and practitioner is not only destructive but incorrect. The record of professional services completely transcending differences of race, religion and national origin is long and honorable.

We agree (the rejoinder might begin) that much professional service crosses racial lines; but as a practical matter it cannot be denied that, without racial balance in the professional corps, it has proved impossible for racial minorities to obtain professional services in the quantity and quality needed. There is a confusion here. It is true that legal and health needs of minority groups have not been fairly or adequately met, but it is far from clear that the remedy for that lies in racial proportionality. Differences in professional services are most closely tied to economic considerations, within as well as between races; proportionality does not even speak to that fundamental problem. Moreover, to defend forced proportionality on the basis of the professional needs of the minority is to assume, tacitly, that minority group lawyers will, in fact, devote themselves to ethnically exclusive practice. No doubt this will be true for many, but to expect that black professionals will practice only in the black community, or Mexican-Americans only in the Mexican-American community, is quite wrong. The parochialism implicit in the expectation exerts heavy and unfair pressure upon minority professionals.

Well then (the rejoinder might continue) is there not a residual need felt by minority group members for lawyers (and doctors, et al.) of the same race or cultural heritage who are sensitive to their special attitudes and circumstances, share their ethnic spirit, and who alone can make them comfortable? See where this argument takes us. If comfort, in this sense, really is good ground for official preference on the basis of race, it would be entirely appropriate for firms with chiefly minority clientele to discriminate openly against applicants from the ethnic majority in their hiring practices. "Our clients cannot be comfortable with white attorneys," they may say, "and good professional service to our clients requires their psychological confidence. That confidence is possible only with community of heritage." But racism is a two-way street. Depend upon it, that argument, so long used to justify racial discrimination against minority professionals, will be accepted with satisfaction by bigots on all sides. . . .

There is [another] general interest that the advocates of racially preferential policies aim to advance: *compensation*. That wrongful injuries earlier done be compensated for now, to the extent possible, is part of the demands of justice. How they should be compensated for no general principles can determine. Much depends upon the nature and gravity of the injury, upon the wants of the injured, and upon the circumstances at the time compensation is undertaken. To say that compensation for a past injury is required now is to call for an immediate process of tangible redress, suitable in form and substance. But that cannot tell us what precisely is to be done. Compensation is not a particular, describable end, like integration; it is at once more pressing and less measurable, an aim of justice having no certain form.

This compensatory interest is compelling, but no scheme of racial or ethnic preference can be necessary to serve it. Compensation being a form of redress, it is justifiable only as a response to specific wrongs done to specific persons. Preferential admissions policies, by giving favor to all members of certain racial or ethnic groups, cannot be appropriate remedies for the wrongs in question.

Specific past injuries may justify specific present efforts to make up for what was wrongly done. In that spirit it is fair that those who have suffered wrongful economic disadvantage, or wrongful denial of opportunity, now be assisted with affirmative action to help redress those wrongs. Thus in deciding upon admissions to professional schools it may be quite reasonable to take into consideration some past injuries—e.g., whether schooling appropriate to ability had been denied a particular applicant, whether the economic need to work while in school had resulted in another applicant's lessened performance there, etc. Concrete assistance to those so disadvantaged, special efforts to recruit such applicants for professional courses and to retain such students by supplying special needs having root in that earlier maltreatment, offend no reasonable sense of justice.

Responses in this compensatory spirit, however, cannot be tied to race or ethnicity; their being compensatory supposes that they will be devised with a view to the injuries suffered by particular applicants, whatever their surname or color. Of each individually it may be asked: Is there, in this case, a history of wrongfully imposed disadvantage so grave as to justify special treatment now?

At this point advocates of preferential systems may contend that I have missed the point. For the injury suffered by many (say they) is inextricably bound up with race, and hence the remedy must be so as well. That point, powerful in some contexts, is misapplied here. In the public schools of North Carolina, where the task was that of desegregating large numbers of equally qualified students, already enrolled in the system, who had long been sorted by race, a racially attentive remedy was in order. But this consideration cannot justify a remedy that is, intrinsically prejudicial. However ugly past uses of race have been, constitutional rights are now enjoyed by citizens entirely without regard to race. Hence no deprivation of such individual rights, based on race alone, may be tolerated. The equal protection clause is a safeguard not for categories of persons but for every citizen singly.

On this point the language of the U.S. Supreme Court is definitive: "The rights created by the first section of the Fourteenth Amendment are, by its terms, guaranteed to the individual. The rights established are personal rights. It is, therefore, no answer to these petitioners to say that the Court may also be induced to deny white persons rights of ownership and occupancy on grounds of race or color. Equal protection of the laws is not achieved through indiscriminate imposition of inequalities." [Shelly v. Kraemer, 344 U.S. 22.]

The tacit supposition that rights are possessed by racial groups has caused much confusion here. But the formulation of the Fourteenth Amendment, recognizing rights as pertaining only to individuals, is exact on this matter. No state shall "deny to any person within its jurisdiction the equal protection of the laws." Any single individual, denied some benefit to which he is otherwise entitled, on the ground of his classification by race or ethnic origin, will have had his rights under that clause infringed. The social interest in compensating other persons who are members of other groups which have, in general, been very cruelly treated in the past, gives no justification for deliberate discrimination against this individual now.

Many among our ethnic minorities have suffered grievous disadvantage simply because they were black or brown or yellow. But the degree of disadvantage suffered, and even the fact of it, varies from case to case. Some have suffered no more than many non-minority persons who have unjustly experienced severe economic hardship or family catastrophe. Since every early adversity cannot be weighed in the school admissions process, it is usually thought right to consider the great majority of applicants on an equal footing, without analysis of past disadvantage, when reviewing admission qualifications.

Some past injuries may be thought so cruel and damaging as to justify special consideration for professional school admission. But whether a particular person has been so injured is a question of fact, to be answered in each case separately. If special consideration is in order for those whose early lives were cramped by extreme poverty, the penurious Appalachian white, the oppressed Oriental-American from a Western state, the impoverished Finn from upper Michigan—these and all others who similarly qualify are entitled to that consideration. . . .

What we may not do, constitutionally or morally, is announce: "You are black, you get plus points; you are yellow, you don't." An admissions committee must not classify by race or ethnicity and assume, for special consideration, cultural and/or economic deprivation for all of one category and for none of another. Nor may it do what amounts to the same thing—attend to the deprivations and injuries experienced by members of one ethnic group, but not to those experienced by members of others. Many small, foreign-language subgroups in our country have been humiliated, ostracized, oppressed; some religious groups have been scandalously treated; many in the white, Christian majority have suffered the terrible blight of family disorder and penury. Compensatory affirmative action, if undertaken at all, must be undertaken for every person who qualifies on some reasonably objective standard, a standard free of social orientation. . . .

Some final notes on the counter-productivity of racial preference:

(1) Systems of preferential admission do not integrate, they *dis*integrate the races. However much the advocates of such systems may hope for ultimate integration (though some may not share the integrationist ideal), the consequence of such systems in practice is ever greater attention to race, agitation about race. The invidious consideration of ethnicity in inappropriate contexts results in rewards and penalties generally thought to be unfair, undeserved. And all with focus on race. No prescription for long-term disharmony among races could be surer of success.

(2) Achieving racial proportionality in the professions through the consideration of race in professional school admissions, even where intellectual and other pertinent considerations are counterindicative, must result in the tendency, at least statistical, to yield minority group professionals less well qualified, less respected, less trusted than their counterparts in the majority. That is a great disservice to minority groups, stigmatizing their members in a most unfortunate way. "I wouldn't hit a dog with some of the minority students I've seen," says Dr. Charles DeLeon, a black psychiatrist at Case Western Reserve University Hospital, "and I have an idea that you honkies are taking in these dummies so that eight years from now you'll be able to turn around and say, 'Look how bad they all turned out.' " [*The New York Times*, April 7, 1974.]

Results on bar examinations have been painful. In Michigan, for example, in the summer of 1971, results showed a passing rate of 71 per cent for white candidates, 17 per cent for black candidates. Some contend that such discrepancies, also encountered elsewhere, are due to the hidden racial bias of the bar exams. The measures may indeed be faulty; but it is unlikely that their flaws fully explain so large a discrepancy. Bar exams are given after three years of law school, the examination papers identified and graded by number, not name. It is probable that poorly prepared minority students, admitted preferentially to law schools, receive a sympathetic consideration in classes that is not possible in the grading of bar examination papers. The general suitability of bar examinations is now much discussed. . . . Whatever is necessary to evaluate candidates for the bar in a racially neutral way must be done, of course. But if, on such reasonable measures of performance as there are, preferential admission has distinctly invidious results, it is likely to do much damage to the minority it aims to assist.

(3) One consequence of preferential admissions programs is certain: fully qualified minority group professionals come to be viewed by many, of all races, as having gained their professional positions through favor by virtue of their race. No matter their excellence; it will be suspected that their credentials were received on a double, lower standard. It is a cruel result.

The cruelty comes clear in this statement by Prof. Thomas Sowell, educated in Harlem, now associate professor of economics at UCLA:

> . . . the actual harm done by quotas is far greater than having a few incompetent people here and there—and the harm that will actually be done will be harm primarily to the *black* population.

What all the arguments and campaigns for quotas are really saying, loud and clear, is that *black people just don't have it*, and that they will have to be *given* something in order to have something. The devastating impact of this message on black people—particularly black young people—will outweigh any few extra jobs that may result from this strategy. Those black people who are already competent, and who could be instrumental in producing more competence among the rising generation, will be completely undermined, as black becomes synonymous—in the minds of black and white alike—with incompetence, and black achievement becomes synonymous with charity or payoffs.
Black Education, Myths and Tragedies

The counterproductivity of racial preference should not be surprising. The health of the body politic depends upon a widely shared confidence by its members that public process will be governed by a few very basic principles—among them, that the laws, however imperfect, will apply to all persons equally. Any device that seeks to remedy a sickness in that body by tinkering with its basal metabolism may be expected to do damage that far outweighs its good effects.

● ● ●

NO   Thurgood Marshall

REMEDIES FOR PAST
DISCRIMINATION

Three hundred and fifty years ago, the Negro was dragged to this country in chains to be sold into slavery. Uprooted from his homeland and thrust into bondage for forced labor, the slave was deprived of all legal rights. It was unlawful to teach him to read; he could be sold away from his family and friends at the whim of his master; and killing or maiming him was not a crime. The system of slavery brutalized and dehumanized both master and slave.

The denial of human rights was etched into the American colonies' first attempts at establishing self-government. When the colonists determined to seek their independence from England, they drafted a unique document cataloguing their grievances against the King and proclaiming as "self-evident" that "all men are created equal" and are endowed "with certain unalienable Rights," including those to "Life, Liberty and the pursuit of Happiness." The self-evident truths and the unalienable rights were intended, however, to apply only to white men. An earlier draft of the Declaration of Independence, submitted by Thomas Jefferson to the Continental Congress, had included among the charges against the King that

> "[h]e has waged cruel war against human nature itself, violating its most sacred rights of life and liberty in the persons of a distant people who never offended him, captivating and carrying them into slavery in another hemisphere, or to incur miserable death in their transportation thither." Franklin 88.

The Southern delegation insisted that the charge be deleted; the colonists themselves were implicated in the slave trade, and inclusion of this claim might have made it more difficult to justify the continuation of slavery once the ties to England were severed. Thus, even as the colonists embarked on a course to secure their own freedom and equality, they ensured perpetuation of the system that deprived a whole race of those rights.

From, Dissenting Opinion, *Regents of the University of California vs. Allan Bakke*, 1978.

The implicit protection of slavery embodied in the Declaration of Independence was made explicit in the Constitution, which treated a slave as being equivalent to three-fifths of a person for purposes of apportioning representatives and taxes among the States. Art. I. Sec. 2. The Constitution also contained a clause ensuring that the "migration or importation" of slaves into the existing States would be legal until at least 1808, Art. I, Sec. 9, and a fugitive slave clause requiring that when a slave escaped to another State, he must be returned on the claim of the master, Art. IV, Sec. 2. In their declaration of the principles that were to provide the cornerstone of the new Nation, therefore, the Farmers made it plain that "we the people," for whose protection the Constitution was designed, did not include those whose skins were the wrong color. As Professor John Hope Franklin has observed, Americans "proudly accepted the challenge and responsibility of their new political freedom by establishing the machinery and safeguards that insured the continued enslavement of blacks." Franklin 100. . . .

The status of the Negro as property was officially erased by his emancipation at the end of the Civil War. But the long awaited emancipation, while freeing the Negro from slavery, did not bring him citizenship or equality in any meaningful way. Slavery was replaced by a system of "laws which imposed upon the colored race onerous disabilities and burdens, and curtailed their rights in the pursuit of life, liberty, and property to such an extent that their freedom was of little value." *Slaughter-House Cases*, 16 Wall. 36, 70 (1873). Despite the passage of the Thirteenth, Fourteenth, and Fifteenth Amendments, the Negro was systematically denied the rights those amendments were supposed to secure. The combined actions and inactions of the State and Federal Government maintained Negroes in a position of legal inferiority for another century after the Civil War.

The Southern States took first steps to re-enslave the Negroes. Immediately following the end of the Civil War, many of the provisional legislatures passed Black Codes, similar to the Slave Codes, which, among other things, limited the rights of Negroes to own or rent property and permitted imprisonment for breach of employment contracts. Over the next several decades, the South managed to disenfranchise the Negroes in spite of the Fifteenth Amendment by various techniques, including poll taxes, deliberately complicated balloting processes, property and literacy qualifications, and finally the white primary.

Congress responded to the legal disabilities being imposed in the Southern States by passing the Reconstruction Acts and the Civil Rights Acts. Congress also responded to the needs of the Negroes at the end of the Civil War by establishing the Bureau of Refugees, Freedmen, and Abandoned Lands better known as the Freedmen's Bureau, to supply food, hospitals, land and education to the newly freed slaves. Thus for a time it seemed as if the Negro might be protected from the continued denial of his civil rights and might be relieved of the disabilities that prevented him from taking his place as a free and equal citizen.

That time, however, was short-lived. Reconstruction came to a close, and, with the assistance of this Court, the Negro was rapidly stripped of his new civil rights. In the words of C. Vann Woodward: "By narrow and ingenious interpretation [the Supreme Court's] decisions over a period of years had whittled away a great part of the authority presumably given the government for protection of civil rights." Woodward 139.

The Court began by interpreting the Civil War Amendments in a manner that sharply curtailed their substantive protections. *See e.g., Slaughter-House Cases, supre; United States v. Reese,* 92 U.S. 214 (1874); *United States v. Cruikshank,* 92 U.S. 542 (1876). Then in the notorious *Civil Rights Cases,* 109 U.S. 3 (1883), the Court strangled Congress' efforts to use its power to promote racial equality. In those cases the Court invalidated sections of the Civil Rights Act of 1875 that made it a crime to deny equal access to "inns, public conveyances. . . , theatres, and other places of public amusement." According to the Court, the Fourteenth Amendment gave Congress the power to proscribe only discriminatory action by the State. The Court ruled that the Negroes who were excluded from public places suffered only an invasion of their social rights at the hands of private individuals, and Congress had no power to remedy that *Id.,* at 24-25. "When a man has emerged from slavery, and by the aid of beneficient legislation has shaken off the inseparable concomitants of that state," the Court concluded, "there must be some stage in the progress of his elevation when he takes the rank of a mere citizen, and ceases to be the special favorite of the laws. . . ." *Id.,* at 25. As Justice Harlan noted in dissent, however, the Civil War Amendments and Civil Rights Acts did not make the Negroes the "special favorite" of the laws but instead "sought to accomplish in reference to that race. . . —what had already been done in every State of the Union for the White race—to secure and protect rights belonging to them as freemen and citizens; nothing more." *Id.,* at 61.

The Court's ultimate blow to the Civil

War Amendments and to the equality of Negroes came in *Plessy v. Ferguson,* 163 U.S. 537 (1896). In upholding a Louisiana law that required railway companies to provide "equal but separate" accommodations for whites and Negroes, the Court held that the Fourteenth Amendment was not intended "to abolish distinctions based on color, or to enforce social, as distinguished from political equality, or a commingling of the two races upon terms unsatisfactory to either." *Id.,* at 544. Ignoring totally the realities of the positions of the two races, the Court remarked:

> "We consider the underlying fallacy of the plaintiff's argument to consist in the assumption that the enforced separation of the two races stamps the colored race with a badge of inferiority. If this be so, it is not by reason of anything found in the act, but solely because the colored race chooses to put that construction upon it." *Id.,* at 551.

Mr. Justice Harlan's dissenting opinion recognized the bankruptcy of the Court's reasoning. He noted that the "real meaning" of the legislation was "that colored citizens are so inferior and degraded that they cannot be allowed to sit in public coaches occupied by white citizens." *Id.,* at 560. He expressed his fear that if like laws were enacted in other States, "the effect would be in the highest degree mischevous." *Id.,* at 563. Although slavery would have disappeared, the States would retain the power "to interfere with the full enjoyment of the blessings of freedom; to regulate civil rights, common to all citizens, upon the basis of race; and to place in a condition of legal inferiority a large body of American citizens. . . ." *Id.,* at 563. . . .

The enforced segregation of the races continued into the middle of the 20th century. In both World Wars, Negroes were for the most part confined to separate military units; it was not until 1948 that an end to segregation in the military was ordered by President Truman. And the history of the exclusion of Negro children from white public schools is too well known and recent to require repeating here. That Negroes were deliberately excluded from public graduate and professional schools— thereby denied the opportunity to become doctors, lawyers, engineers, and the like— is also well established. It is of course true that some of the Jim Crow laws (which the decisions of this Court had helped to foster) were struck down by this Court in a series of decisions leading up to *Brown v. Board of Education of Topeka,* 347 U.S. 483 (1954). *See e.g. Morgan v. Virginia,* 328 U.S. 373 (1946); *Sweatt v. Painter,* 339 U.S. 629 (1950); *McLaurin v. Oklahoma State Regents,* 339 U.S. 637 (1950). Those decisions, however, did not automatically end segregation, nor did they move Negroes from a position of legal inferiority to one of equality. The legacy of years of slavery and of years of second-class citizenship in the wake of emancipation could not be so easily eliminated.

The position of the Negro today in America is the tragic but inevitable consequence of centuries of unequal treatment. Measured by any benchmark of comfort or achievement, meaningful equality remains a distant dream for the Negro.

A Negro child today has a life expectancy which is shorter by more than five years than that of a white child. The Negro child's mother is over three times more likely to die of complications in childbirth, and the infant mortality rate for Negroes is nearly twice that for whites. The median income of the Negro family is only 60% that of the median of a white family, and the percentage of Negroes who live in families with incomes below the poverty line is nearly four times greater than that of whites.

When the Negro child reaches working age, he finds that America offers him significantly less than it offers his white counterpart. For Negro adults, the unemployment rate is twice that of whites, and the unemployment rate for Negro teenagers is nearly three times that of white teenagers. A Negro male who completes four years of college can expect a median annual income of merely $110 more than a white male who has only a high school diploma. Although Negroes represent 11.5% of the population, they are only 1.2% of the lawyers and judges, 2% of the physicians, 2.3% of the dentists, 1.1% of the engineers and 2.6% of the college and university professors.

The relationship between those figures and the history of unequal treatment afforded to the Negro cannot be denied. At every point from birth to death the impact of the past is reflected in the still disfavored position of the Negro.

In light of the sorry history of discrimination and its devastating impact on the lives of Negroes, bringing the Negro into the mainstream of American life should be a state interest of the highest order. To fail to do so is to ensure that America will forever remain a divided society.

I do not believe that the Fourteenth Amendment requires us to accept that fate. Neither its history nor our past cases lend any support to the conclusion that a University may not remedy the cumulative effects of society's discrimination by giving consideration to race in an effort to increase the number and percentage of Negro doctors.

211

12. IS AFFIRMATIVE ACTION REVERSE DISCRIMINATION?

This Court long ago remarked that

"in any fair and just construction of any section or phrase of these [Civil War] amendments, it is necessary to look at the purpose which we have said was the pervading spirit of them all, the evil which they were designed to remedy. . . ." *Slaughter-House Cases,* 16 Wall., at 72.

It is plain that the Fourteenth Amendment was not intended to prohibit measures designed to remedy the effects of the Nation's past treatment of Negroes. The Congress that passed the Fourteenth Amendment is the same Congress that passed the 1866 Freedmen's Bureau Act, an act that provided many of its benefits only to Negroes. Act of July 16, 1866, ch. 200, 14 Stat. 173; see p. 4 *supra.* Although the Freedmen's Bureau legislation provided aid for refugees, thereby including white persons within some of the relief measures, 14 Stat., at 174; see also Act of Mar. 3, 1865, ch. 90, 13 Stat. 507, the bill was regarded to the dismay of many Congressmen, as "solely and entirely for the freedmen, and to the exclusion of all other persons. . . ." Cong. Globe, 39th Cong., 1st Sess., 544 (1866) (remarks of Rep. Taylor). See also *id.,* at 634-635 (remarks of Rep. Ritter); *id.,* at App. 78, 80-81 (remarks of Rep. Chanler). Indeed, the bill was bitterly opposed on the ground that it "undertakes to make the negro in some respects . . . superior . . . and gives them favors that the poor white boy in the North cannot get." *Id.,* at 401, (remarks of Sen. McDougall). See also *id.,* at 319 (remarks of Sen. Hendricks); *id.,* at 362 (remarks of Sen. Saulsbury); *id.,* at 397 (remarks of Sen. Willey); *id.,* at 544 (remarks of Rep. Taylor). The bill's supporters defended it—not by rebutting the claim of special treat-

ment—but by pointing to the need for such treatment:

"The very discrimination it makes between 'destitute and suffering' negroes and destitute and suffering white paupers, proceeds upon the distinction that, in the omitted case, civil rights and immunities are already sufficiently protected by the possession of political power, the absence of which in the case provided for necessitates governmental protection." *Id.,* at 75 (remarks of Rep. Phelps).

Despite the objection to the special treatment the bill would provide for Negroes, it was passed by Congress. *Id.,* at 421, 688. President Johnson vetoed this bill and also a subsequent bill that contained some modifications; one of his principal objections to both bills was that they gave special benefits to Negroes. VIII Messages and Papers of the Presidents 3596, 3599, 3620, 3623 (1866). Rejecting the concerns of the President and the bill's opponents, Congress overrode the President's second veto. Cong. Globe, at 3842, 3850.

Since the Congress that considered and rejected the objections to the 1866 Freedmen's Bureau Act concerning special relief to Negroes also proposed the Fourteenth Amendment, it is inconceivable that the Fourteenth Amendment was intended to prohibit all race-conscious relief measures. It "would be a distortion of the policy manifested in that amendment, which was adopted to prevent state legislation designed to perpetuate discrimination on the basis of race or color," *Railway Mail Association v. Corsi,* 326 U.S. 88, 94 (1945), to hold that it barred state action to remedy the effects of that discrimination. Such a result would pervert the intent of the framers by substituting abstract equality for the genuine equality the amendment was intended to achieve.

As has been demonstrated in our joint opinion, this Court's past cases establish the constitutionality of race-conscious remedial measures. Beginning with the school desegregation cases, we recognized that even absent a judicial or legislative finding of constitutional violation, a school board constitutionally could consider the race of students in making school assignment decisions. See Swann v. Charlotte-Mecklenberg Board of Education, 402 U.S. 1, 16 (1971). McDaniel v. Barresi, 402 U.S. 39, 41 (1971). We noted, moreover, that a

> "flat prohibition against assignment of students for the purpose of creating a racial balance must inevitably conflict with the duty of school authorities to disestablish dual school systems. As we have held in Swann, the Constitution does not compel any particular degree of racial balance or mixing, but when past and continuing constitutional violations are found, some ratios are likely to be useful as starting points in shaping a remedy. An absolute prohibition against use of such a device—even as a starting point—contravenes the implicit command of Green v. County School Board, 391 U.S. 430 (1968), that all reasonable methods be available to formulate an effective remedy." Board of Education v. Swann, 402 U.S. 43, 46 (1971).

As we have observed, "[a]ny other approach would freeze the status quo that is the very target of all desegregation processes." McDaniel v. Barresi, supra, at 41.

Only last Term, in United Jewish Organizations v. Carey, 430 U.S. 144 (1977), we upheld a New York reapportionment plan that was deliberately drawn on the basis of race to enhance the electoral power of Negroes and Puerto Ricans; the plan had the effect of diluting the electoral strength of the Hasidic Jewish Community. We were willing in UJO to sanction the remedial use of a racial classification even though it disadvantaged otherwise "innocent" individuals. In another case last Term, Califano v. Webster, 430 U.S. 313 (1977), the Court upheld a provision in the Social Security laws that discriminated against men because its purpose was "the permissible one of redressing our society's long standing disparate treatment of women'." Id., at 317, quoting Califano v. Goldfarb, 430 U.S. 199, 209 n. 8 (1977) (plurality opinion). We thus recognized the permissibility of remedying past societal discrimination through the use of otherwise disfavored classifications. . . .

It is more than a little ironic that, after several hundred years of class-based discrimination against Negroes, the Court is willing to hold that a class-based remedy for that discrimination is permissible. In declining to so hold, today's judgment ignores the fact that for several hundred years Negroes have been discriminated against, not as individuals, but rather solely because of the color of their skins. It is unnecessary in 20th century America to have individual Negroes demonstrate that they have been victims of racial discrimination; the racism of our society has been so pervasive that none, regardless of wealth or position, has managed to escape its impact. The experience of Negroes in America has been different in kind, not just in degree, from that of other ethnic groups. It is not merely the history of slavery alone but also that a whole people were marked as inferior by the law. And that mark has endured. The dream of America as the great melting pot has not been realized for the Negro; because of his skin color he never even made it into the pot.

12. IS AFFIRMATIVE ACTION REVERSE DISCRIMINATION?

These differences in the experience of the Negro make it difficult for me to accept that Negroes cannot be afforded greater protection under the Fourteenth Amendment where it is necessary to remedy the effects of past discrimination. In the *Civil Rights Cases, supra,* the Court wrote that the Negro emerging from slavery must cease "to be the special favorite of the laws." 109 U.S., at 25; see p. 5, *supra.* We cannot in light of the history of the last century yield to that view. Had the Court in that case and others been willing to "do for human liberty and the fundamental rights of American citizenship, what it did . . . for the protection of slavery and the rights of the masters of fugitive slaves," *id.,* at 53 (Harlan, J., dissenting), we would not need now to permit the recognition of any "special awards."

Most importantly, had the Court been willing in 1896 in *Plessy v. Ferguson,* to hold that the Equal Protection Clause forbids differences in treatment based on race, we would not be faced with this dilemma in 1978. We must remember, however, that the principle that the "Constitution is colorblind" appeared only in the opinion of the lone dissenter. 163 U.S., at 559. The majority of the Court rejected the principle of color blindness, and for the next 60 years, from *Plessy* to *Brown v. Board of Education,* ours was a Nation where, *by law,* an individual could be given "special" treatment based on the color of his skin.

It is because of a legacy of unequal treatment that we now must permit the institutions of this society to give consideration to race in making decisions about who will hold the positions of influence, affluence and prestige in America. For far too long, the doors to those positions have been shut to Negroes. If we are ever to become a fully integrated society, one in which the color of a person's skin will not determine the opportunities available to him or her, we must be willing to take steps to open those doors. I do not believe that anyone can truly look into America's past and still find that a remedy for the effects of that past is impermissible.

● ● ●

POSTSCRIPT

IS AFFIRMATIVE ACTION
REVERSE DISCRIMINATION?

Critics of affirmative action might consider it ironic that Justice Marshall quotes approvingly from the opinions of Justice Harlan in the late 1800s, for it was Harlan who insisted that the law must always be "color-blind." Marshall's response seems to be that if the Court had been willing to enforce "color-blindness" then, it wouldn't be necessary today for reformers to take color into account. One question—for which we have no ready answer—is whether this remedial color-consciousness could lead us back to the degrading color-consciousness of the past.

Robert M. O'Neil, in DISCRIMINATING AGAINST DISCRIMINATION (Indiana, 1975), studied preferential admissions to universities, and supported preferential treatment without racial quotas. Those critical of this distinction hold that preferential treatment necessarily implies racial quotas, or at least race-consciousness. Another area that requires officials to focus upon race is that of busing, a policy of which Lino A. Graglia's DISASTER BY DECREE (Cornell, 1976) is highly critical. The focus of Allan P. Sindler's BAKKE, DeFUNIS, AND MINORITY ADMISSIONS (Longman, 1978) is on affirmative action in higher education.

Whatever the Supreme Court says today or in the future, it will not be easy to lay to rest the issue of affirmative action. There are few issues on which opposing sides are more intransigent. It appears as if there is no satisfactory "solution," and, at the moment, no compromise that can satisfy the passionate convictions on both sides. Those who are sick of the whole controversy may be tempted to fall back on the cliche that "time will heal all wounds" and the corresponding hope that the controversy will someday be resolved to everyone's satisfaction. They should be reminded of Martin Luther King's stoical observation: "Actually time is neutral. It can be used either destructively or constructively."

ISSUE 13

SHOULD WELFARE BE TRIMMED?

YES: Robert B. Carleson and Kevin R. Hopkins, from "The Reagan Rationale," *Public Welfare,* Fall 1981

NO: George McGovern, from "An Opposing View," *Public Welfare,* Fall 1981

ISSUE SUMMARY

YES: Robert Carleson and Robert Hopkins, Special Assistants to President Reagan, argue that except for cases of physical survival, income should belong to those who earn it.
NO: Former Senator, George McGovern, responds that society, through government, has a responsibility to those at the lower end of the economic scale.

In 1982 a polling organization asked a representative sample of Americans which item in the government's budget ought to be cut first if cuts had to be made. Included among the choices was "aid to the needy." Only seven to nine percent would have cut from that area. The rest would rather see the money come out of parks, streets and colleges. Then the pollsters tried a semantic switch. They subsituted the word "welfare" for "aid to the needy." Now it ranked first among all the items the majority of the respondents would cut.

Ronald Reagan may have sensed this ambivalence when he ran for President in 1980. He promised to trim "welfare," but he also promised to maintain adequate financial support to the "truly needy." By his second year in office his commitment to the first promise was beyond dispute. In 1981 he pushed through Congress cuts in the growth of domestic spending totalling $35 billion. He then proposed spending cuts for subsequent years which would not only reduce the rate of growth but cut the absolute level of federal spending on such key welfare programs as food stamps and Aid to the Families of Dependent Children (AFDC). It was the second of Reagan's promises, to maintain a "safety net" of adequate support payments to the truly needy, which his critics claimed he had violated. Stories in the mass media about needy families hurt by the cuts were seized upon by his Democratic opponents as evidence of the administration's callousness. Administration officials challenged the accuracy of the stories, just as their critics had disputed the accuracy of Reagan's own stories about "welfare queens" ripping off the taxpayers. Both sides, it seemed, resorted to melodrama, when the real story of welfare and welfare dependency is closer to tragedy.

When the first programs of mass public assistance at the federal level were inaugurated in the 1930s, it was assumed that they were serving families normally supported by a "breadwinner." Public assistance was something to be considered for the most part as marginal and temporary in nature. By the 1970s, however, welfare was no longer a marginal phenomenon. As a percentage of our Gross National Product it had grown from 4.5 percent in 1945 to 20 percent in 1975. One of the fastest-growing programs was Aid to the Families of Dependent Children (AFDC), and the greatest increase in AFDC rolls occurred during the prosperous 1960s. The reason for this increase even during good times for the economy seems to be connected with what was once called "family breakups"—in more neutral language, the growth of single-parent, female-headed households. A disproportionate number of these families live below the poverty line, and their percentage in the population increased from 9.3 in 1960 to 14.6 in 1980. (Over a similar period black families headed by single female parents increased from 20.9 percent of total black families to 40.3 percent.) Such families, lacking the example and support of a breadwinner with earning skills, tend to become mired in welfare dependency, creating what sociologist Gunnar Myrdahl calls a perennial economic "underclass" of the unemployed.

The existence of the "underclass" is a challenge to all sides in the current welfare debate. Instead of relying upon welfare, President Reagan would reduce poverty by stimulating business activity; the idea is that this economic vitality will filter down to the poor in the form of job opportunities. "A rising tide will lift all boats." The problem, as Bernard Anderson has pointed out, is that a rising tide will not raise shipwrecks at the bottom of the sea; men and women lacking even rudimentary work skills. Reagan's Democratic opponents must also confront the reality of the "underclass." Democratic programs during the 1960s for motivating and training the hardcore unemployed were not notably successful in reducing dependency, and cash handouts may even increase it. Experiments conducted in Seattle and Denver during the 1970s showed that poor families receiving guaranteed annual incomes experienced a higher rate of family breakups.

Both liberal and conservative nostrums for the related problems of poverty and dependence thus seem to have their own peculiar blind spots. Perhaps the long-run solution may come from a synthesis of liberal and conservative programs, or from some approach that defies ideological labeling. In the meantime, it is important to grasp some of the basic positions in the current welfare controversy. Toward that end we present a defense of Reagan's policies by two Administration officials, Robert B. Carleson and Kevin R. Hopkins, and a criticism of the policies by former Senator George McGovern.

YES

Robert B. Carleson
and Kevin R. Hopkins

THE REAGAN RATIONALE

Few domestic policy issues evoke as intense emotions as welfare reform. On one hand, numerous spectacular reports of welfare fraud have convinced some Americans that most welfare recipients are undeserving; on the other, recurring feature stories about welfare-dependent poor families imply that any reduction of welfare benefits to the poor is cruel because it condemns helpless people to starvation or worse.

Rational analysis must reject both these impressions as inaccurate caricatures of America's public support system. The great majority of welfare recipients are not cheats. They are honest people who rely on federal transfer programs simply because the benefits help them meet burdensome living expenses. Moreover, not all welfare recipients are destitute; for a large number of families, the combination of benefits available provides appreciably more than a minimal standard of living. The current welfare system is thus neither wholly irresponsible nor wholly inviolable. While it is a useful mechanism for implementing income support policies, its nature and scope is a valid subject for political delimitation based on substance rather than emotional argumentation.

The debate over the nature of welfare intrinsically occurs on two levels: one, what should be the basis of the commitment to transfer income (*Who* should receive welfare?), and two, what should be the dollar amount of the commitment (*How much* should they receive?). Despite the emphasis on how much welfare recipients should get, as a purely budgetary matter, it is only consideration of who should receive welfare that makes possible fundamental reform of the welfare system. For once the basis for support is established, the determination of the associated dollar level of support will generally follow.

Deciding who deserves welfare is, however, not an easy task. It means choosing between two apparently conflicting American beliefs: that poor people should be helped (i.e., they should have higher incomes than they do

From, "The Reagan Rationale," by Robert Carleson and Kevin Hopkins, *Public Welfare*, Fall 1981. Copyright 1981. Reprinted by permission of *Public Welfare*.

now), and that people should be able to spend their earnings as they see fit. Resolution of this dilemma cannot be achieved *in vacuo,* but requires that we denote an underlying value system.

INCOME BELONGS TO THOSE WHO EARN IT

One of the primary tenets of American economic and political relationships is that income earned belongs individually to the people who earn it. It does not belong to the state, nor does it belong by right to any other segment of the population. The income produced belongs, by natural right, to the person who produced it. This is no meaningless manifestation of ideological purity. Possession of title to the fruits of one's labor is an essential part of American freedoms, for its antithesis is economic servitude.

Yet inasmuch as governments are instituted among people, those governments must be funded. Governments receive their revenues largely by way of taxes assessed with the consent of the taxed. In other words, people partially relinquish the right to spend their incomes as they individually wish when they direct the government to perform certain collective functions for them. But even then, they do not fully abandon control over their incomes: they can still hold the government accountable for spending their money according to the principles and functions for which they agreed to be taxed.

One of the important functions of government is to provide a means for Americans to help their truly needy fellow citizens—unfortunate persons who, through no fault of their own, have nothing but public funds to turn to in order to secure a minimal standard of living. The Reagan administration strongly supports this notion.

It is no accident that the first-stated principle in the president's *Budget Reform Plan* was the preservation of the social safety net. The budget document noted that "these essential commitments transcend differences of ideology, partisanship, and fiscal priorities." During the past few decades, Americans have agreed to devote a significant portion of their earnings to ensuring that truly needy Americans are able to survive. The government has been designated as the mechanism through which this assurance is provided.

This governmental function involves a transfer of income from certain citizens to others for a specified purpose: namely, to assist those persons who basically are unable to help themselves. Unfortunately, this commitment has been construed far differently—qualitatively differently—by many who oppose reductions of virtually any kind of burgeoning social programs. The prevailing notion—implicit or explicit—seems to be that those who economically "have more" should be required to assist, i.e., give tax dollars to, those who "have less," regardless of the recipient individuals' true need. Those who are relatively poor—precisely because they are relatively poor—are said to have a legitimate entitlement to part of the incomes of those who are relatively better off.

But in any functioning society, there are bound to be "relatively poor" individuals; that is, not everyone will have the same level of income. Skills, opportunities, and luck differ among all people—radically so at times—meaning the marketplace will inevitably value some peoples' talents more than others. Consequently, their incomes will be higher. Likewise, there will be those whose talents are valued less than the norm, and their incomes will be less.

The response to this situation varies with one's value system. To those who believe

13. SHOULD WELFARE BE TRIMMED?

individuals have a right to their own income and that no one in the society should have so little income that he or she cannot survive, the principal concern will be whether the very poor are able to meet their basic needs. Inequality of incomes in itself becomes something to be corrected only to the extent that the poorest do not have sufficient resources to provide for their needs. On the other hand, those who believe in greater equality of incomes as an end in itself will tend to argue that those who are relatively poor should receive more income from the relatively nonpoor, purely for the sake of increasing their income, and with little regard for their true need.

In isolation, of course, there is no question that poor people are better off with higher incomes. However, federal transfer payments do not take place in isolation but amidst a complex set of economic variables and on the basis of many individual decisions. Thus, the direct and intended effect—making the poor better off—does not in the long run necessarily occur as a result of direct federal transfers of income to the not truly needy poor.

But there is an even more basic consideration. The idea that the federal government should help all relatively poor people just because they are relatively poor—that is, should help equalize incomes—may be noble in spirit, but it ignores fundamental reality. First, it implicitly assumes the government has the money to help the relatively poor. It does not. The money must be extracted by taxation from the citizenry for this purpose.

Moreover, the idea presumes that this tax base (the sum of all incomes generated by individuals in a society) is a collective endowment of the society, and politicians are charged with preserving a "fair share" of that endowment for its relatively poor

citizens. This is not the case. As previously argued, incomes do not by right belong to the state or to groups of other individuals, but to those who earn them. Any transfer of income from these people to others must take place as a result of citizens confering that function on the government.

Historically and experientially, the American people have considered it both compassionate and legitimate to help those who cannot help themselves and have implicitly bestowed this function on their government. This sanction, however, has not extended to transferring money to others just because they are relatively poor. Merely having less income than another person does not by itself entitle the first person to a share of the second person's income.

Emotional arguments aside, the sum of "working people's" incomes is not a political well of funds to be divided among others purely at the discretion of politicians. Yet subsidies to the not truly needy poor have become so extensive that many relatively poor people are taxed on what little income they earn to help provide benefits to other relatively poor people who are little or no worse off than those who are taxed. This surely confounds the principle of government assistance to those in true need.

Moreover, such extensive federal redistribution has wreaked substantial economic harm, particularly among the not truly needy poor. As the Denver and Seattle Income Maintenance Experiments have demonstrated, guaranteeing a level of income higher than necessary to meet basic needs substantially reduces a person's incentive to work. This tends to make welfare recipients dependent on federal payments and thus locks them into an intergenerational welfare cycle. The result is that many youth are born into families in which the ethic of work has been replaced by an ethic of dependence.

Perhaps even worse, the redistribution of income has dramatically reduced incentives to work, produce, save, and invest. The high marginal tax rates, large budget deficits, and low productivity that result have greatly slowed economic growth and accelerated inflation. The effect has been devastating for all Americans, particularly the poor.

As a consequence of such policies, average weekly earnings—after taxes and inflation—have dropped by more than 14 percent since 1972. The cost of necessities has risen to 74 percent of an average family's budget and much higher for a poor family's. As a result, the escape from destitution proceeded far more slowly in the 1970s, when the economy was growing with little vigor, than in the high growth 1960s. And black Americans, who realized a net real income gain of 5 percent per year in the 1960s, actually lost real income in the 1970s.

Thus, the restructuring of the welfare system so that the benefit payments are directed to the truly needy is not only right but economically salutary. Those who contend that these steps cannot be taken without harm to the poorest Americans simply refuse to recognize that current entitlement programs provide many billions of dollars of payments to persons who are not in true need.

For instance, at the time the Reagan budget reforms were announced—

● AFDC payments were going to families whose full resources were not being computed in order to determine their eligibility for the payments;

● food stamps were being provided to families whose incomes far exceeded not only the state standard of need, but also the so-called poverty level;

● school lunch subsidies were going to middle- and upper-income families;

● social security student benefits were being given to students regardless of need and at a time when other needs-tested, educational benefits were available;

● unemployment insurance payments were being provided to persons who had been offered jobs but turned them down; and

● residents of subsidized public housing units were permitted to pay a far smaller share of their income for housing than people with equivalent incomes who lived in private housing and paid their own rent.

The essential first step in eliminating these unintended beneficiaries is to ensure that the analysis of and eligibility for welfare-type payments are based on an accurate measure of recipients' incomes. Two common errors are frequently made in this regard.

First is overreliance on the "poverty level," a popular index which is no more than arbitrary artifice that often has little accurate relationship to an individual's true need. By this measure, devised by the Social Security Administration in 1964, the number of people in poverty has decreased only slightly despite the billions of dollars that have been spent on social programs since the mid-sixties. This proves either that the programs have been extremely ineffective in lifting poor people from destitution, or the effect of the periodic upward adjustments in the poverty level has been so great as to define the poverty problem into permanence regardless of the socioeconomic changes that have taken place. Particularly in the latter case, the true dimensions of individual need are hopelessly obscured. Much more reliable indicators are the state standards of need, which define need according to the specific income level necessary to meet a minimal standard of living in the various states in order to accommodate divergent economic conditions throughout the nation.

Even more disingenuous is the failure of many eligibility standards to include the value of in-kind benefits in a family's income. Many households receive food stamps, Medicaid, free or subsidized school breakfasts and lunches, and housing subsidies. All these benefits increase a family's standard of living and are used for purchases that would otherwise have to be made out of pocket. Excluding these in-kind benefits when measuring a family's eligibility thus not only serves to artificially magnify the extent of the poverty problem, but also discriminates against nonrecipient families with equivalent total incomes.

WHO SHOULD RECEIVE WHAT KIND OF HELP?

Having established an accurate measure of income to direct the distribution of welfare benefits—the empirical part of the welfare problem—the next step is to set forth the guiding principles that help determine the mechanics of distribution. These principles should include the following:

Those who are not physically able to support themselves should receive adequate benefits at all times. Those who, because of advanced age or permanent and total disability, are unable to support themselves should receive adequate benefits, particularly during inflationary times when their fixed incomes, if any, cannot keep pace with higher living costs.

Those who are not physically able to support themselves should be encouraged and assisted to take treatment or training that may lead to partial or complete self-sufficiency. Many who are disabled can be retrained or rehabilitated so that they can become productive members of society. Others, through treatment, training, or with supportive services, can become self-sufficient and free of the need for institutional care. Successes in this area bring dignity and self-respect to the individual and benefit all by avoiding the high costs of institutional care.

Those who have children should support them whether they are a mother or father, married or single. In our society the freedom to conceive or bear children should carry with it a responsibility to provide support. Today, more than half of all mothers with children are working to support themselves and their children or to contribute to their family income. A mother on welfare has as great an obligation to support her children as a father. The success of the Child Support Enforcement Program with absent parents has strengthened this principle as it relates to the absent parent. We must do more to see that able-bodied single parents support themselves and their children. For instance, many mothers with several children can provide child care for one or two more in order to free other mothers for work. Once working, a mother can move toward total self-support and, it is to be hoped, break the welfare cycle for her family.

Able-bodied welfare recipients should be required to work in useful public employment for their benefits until they are able to find work in the private sector. If able-bodied persons do not do all they can to support themselves and their families and instead take assistance from those citizens who are working to support themselves and their families, not only are they debased and demeaned, but an unfair burden is placed on the taxpaying workers as well. Moreover, as Martin Anderson so ably documented in his seminal study or welfare, no mix of benefits and incentives will provide for basic human needs at an affordable cost and not discourage gainful employment. The higher the benefit rate, the more people will find it economically preferable to take welfare instead of a job.

Despite their long record of generosity to the truly needy, the American people do not expect their welfare system to provide benefits to those who will not help themselves. The message of the recent welfare work requirement in Bordentown, New Jersey, is that able-bodied welfare recipients will find jobs when it is made clear that they are expected to earn their benefits. In Bordentown, confronted with the work requirement, twenty-three of the twenty-six people who had been on welfare dropped from the rolls. The others found jobs in the private sector, found other ways to earn money, or moved from the town.

Local and state governments should be given greater freedom in administering welfare programs through the replacement of federal categorical grants by block grants. Eventually, welfare should be transferred wholly back to the states and localities, along with the tax resources to pay for it. Local and state governments are uniquely suited for implementing social welfare programs. Because they are closer to the people, the decisions they make will more perfectly reflect the popular will. This is to be preferred to decisions made in Washington for a number of reasons, but chief among them is the ratification of popular beliefs about the way tax dollars should be spent. As long as the decisions made by citizens through their local and state elected officials are within the law, they are presumably appropriate. To the extent they differ from those made by unelected federal officials in the welfare bureaucracy, it is likely the state and local

decisions will more closely parallel the desires of the state's residents. Therefore, any indictment should in general be of federal decisions, rather than state and local ones.

In particular, whether someone is able-bodied, working, or absent cannot be determined from a central office in Washington. Work, child care, or supportive services can be provided only in the state or community where the people live. Benefits or work availability should start when and where need starts, and benefits should end when need ends. Benefit levels should be adequate to meet basic needs at all times but should not compete with an area's prevailing wages for those who are able-bodied. Therefore, instead of moving toward more federal control, the welfare system should move toward less federal and more state control.

The present open-ended matching structure of financing the AFDC program, however, tends to minimize the incentive for states to make their programs more efficient. The federal government assumes a large portion—50 to 80 percent—of state costs on a completely open-ended basis. The more states spend or waste, the more money comes to them. On the other hand, when states reduce spending by eliminating waste or moving people from welfare to employment, they lose federal matching funds. The whole system rewards waste and penalizes frugal economical management. Proposals to provide fiscal relief to states by way of increased matching funds would only worsen this situation.

With block grant funding instead of a matching approach, the incentive can be reversed. The amount of the grant can be established at the level required to replace present federal funding with whatever adjustments considered necessary or de-

13. SHOULD WELFARE BE TRIMMED?

sirable. That grant level, once set for a state and indexed for some measure of inflation, population changes, and unusually high unemployment, would remain in place without regard to increases or decreases in the state's caseload. This would give each state the strongest possible incentive to improve the operation and structure of its program. If an ineligible person were kept off the rolls or an eligible person given a job, the full amount saved would be available to the state to use for increasing the grants to eligible persons or for whatever purpose the state finds appropriate.

Another advantage of the block grant approach is that it permits a reduction in overhead because there are fewer federal personnel involved in processing paper and fewer burdensome requirements on state and local governments. Moreover, block grants permit state and local officials to allocate funds to the most urgent areas of need. Thus, a block grant program funded at a lower level can provide as many or more benefits for the truly needy recipients in a state as a higher level of funding for a multiplicity of narrow categorical grant programs.

Indeed, when states have been given the authority in the past to make such adjustments in their welfare programs, they have demonstrated their ability and determination to focus benefits on those in true need. For example, in California, benefits were *increased* to AFDC recipients by an initial 26 percent—after thirteen years of no increases—while millions of dollars were being saved in the overall welfare program and total welfare rolls were being reduced, between 1971 and 1974, by more than 300,000 persons. Similarly, Mississippi, historically the nation's lowest benefit state, has doubled its AFDC benefit in recent years to ensure that the neediest receive more support.

Those who oppose these reasonable reforms in the welfare system have been inclined to raise any number of red flags in order to prevent a diminution of federal officials' authority over tax dollars and welfare recipients' lives. Charges are made that a reduction in welfare payments will cripple the poor, that it is not fair to "take money away" from those who have less than others, that government is helping the rich at the expense of the poor when it permits people greater freedom to spend the money they earn as they wish, and that letting states instead of the federal government make decisions on welfare will lead to deprivation and discrimination. All these statements have been dealt with in this article. But one charge merits special refutation: that reducing the sum of money the federal government spends on welfare and related programs—by directing benefits to the intended recipients—will lead to massive waves of unrest and crime.

Such a prediction ignores the fact that most unrest is not precipitated by indigence. The riots of the 1960s were racial conflicts, as was the Liberty City riot in Miami. In addition, participants in the New York City riot during the 1977 blackout were not jobless. Unpleasant home lives, societal maladjustment, poor law enforcement, and the like are still more important factors and must be addressed individually. To the extent indigence is a contributor to unrest, it serves no one's interests to mask such problems with social programs whose net effect, due to the depressive impact on the economy's growth, is to produce economic stagnation and lower long-term levels of prosperity. As long as the truly needy are cared for, the best way to permanently diminish the indigence component of unrest is to promote the creation of more wealth in society, thereby opening new opportunities for the indigent to improve their economic condition.

But to argue that because removing unintended beneficiaries from welfare rolls will produce unrest and riots—a dire exaggeration at best—those people must be kept on the rolls, is to confound both economic sense and political rightness. If people are receiving welfare who should not be, then they should be removed from the recipient lists. Period. No threat of unrest, whether idle or not, should be permitted to cow a government into transferring income from one group of people to another when that transfer is not justified by accepted social norms. Yielding to this argument would merely perpetuate the conditions that allowed it to be raised in the first place, while the conditions could be permanently corrected by appropriate economic policies.

As Ronald Reagan stated in 1972 in testimony before the Senate Finance Committee, "Welfare needs a purpose—to provide for the needy, of course—but more than that, to salvage these our fellow citizens, to make them self-sustaining, and, as quickly as possible, independent of welfare. There has been something terribly wrong with a program that grows ever larger even when prosperity for everyone else is increasing. We should measure welfare's success by how many people leave welfare, not by how many more are added."

This approach to welfare, then, offers the greatest hope for the greatest number of Americans, most particularly the poor: a welfare system consonant with a growing economy, providing rich new opportunities for employment and advancement. Those who are truly needy will always find support in any reasonable welfare system. But a truly responsive system will reduce the need for welfare and at the same time leave individuals the greatest possible control over their own incomes. This is the type of system the Reagan administration advocates because it is most consistent, we believe, with America's concepts of freedom and compassion.

● ● ●

NO
George McGovern

UNENLIGHTENED SELF INTEREST

When Congress adopted a budget resolution accepting many of the cutbacks in social welfare programs proposed by the Reagan administration, black journalist William Raspberry wrote:

> If it were the work of racists, it might be possible to rally decent-minded Americans to fight. But the dismantling of America's social programs, its sense of social justice, and its commitment to do what it can for disadvantaged citizens is the work of people whose stated motivation is not racism but the restoration of the American economy.

It was not the work of racists. It was the end product of a confluence of biases and fantasies about welfare and the economy that took office with the Reagan administration.

That "stated motivation" of concern for the economy was persuasive enough to break down any effective opposition to reversing a national social policy that Republican as well as Democratic administrations have implemented for the past forty-five years.

Concern for the economy should not, however, be considered the administration's only motivation. The determination to slash social welfare programs is wholly in keeping with the philosophy of a long-rejected brand of conservatism that has only now become politically transcendent.

Regrettably, it is a philosophy rooted in the Horatio Alger fiction that achievement is but a matter of will; it is scornful of all that science tells us about the physical, psychological, environmental, economic, and social factors that can inhibit the realization of human potential.

It is a philosophy that, for all its extravagant piety, ignores the admonition in Micah to "do justice and to love mercy" and the message in Corinthians that tells us charity is the highest of virtues.

From, "An Opposing View," by George McGovern, *Public Welfare*, Fall 1981. Copyright 1981. Reprinted by permission of *Public Welfare*.

It is a philosophy of unenlightened self-interest that puts a higher value on property rights than on human rights. When newsman Bill Moyers once asked Ronald Reagan if he thought materialism was the source of our country's greatness, Mr. Reagan confidently answered, "Sure."

It is, thus, a philosophy that easily lends itself to attacking social welfare programs while countenancing government subsidies to business—and finding food stamp cheating more reprehensible than white-collar crime, corporate bribery, price gouging, collusion, and antitrust violations. Who can forget Ronald Reagan's denunciation of the "Chicago welfare queen" before an endless succession of prosperous audiences?

The administration's reliance on supply-side economics suggests, then, that by directing governmental benefits to the wealthy and corporate taxpayer, those with additional funds will invest in job-producing activities—thus taking the place of government in providing for those who presently are at or below the poverty line.

This presupposes a compassion on the part of the corporate citizen that thus far has not been evident. I find it hard to believe a corporation would embark on extensive job-creating enterprises if the economic and regulatory burden of government were lessened or eliminated altogether. I suspect the beneficiaries of such a policy would more likely be stockholders than the unemployed individuals at the plant gates.

But all this raises the very basic question of whether government has a responsibility for those of its citizens who are at the lower end of the economic scale. It is popular in these times of retrenchment to fault the New Deal and Great Society programs for the current ills of governmental budget deficits as having failed in their public service missions.

The fact remains that while each of the several programs involved could have been better administered and more closely monitored, malnutrition and poverty have diminished, and job programs have worked to train and employ millions of previously unemployed Americans.

ENOUGH FOR THOSE WITH TOO LITTLE?

So if, as a society, we decide through our political leaders that the government has no responsibility to make life better for those at the lower end of the economic scale, we consign upwards of some 30 million people to the welfare/poverty cycle from which there is little possibility of escape. And without escape, the gap between the "haves" and the "have nots" will widen; and frustration will result in disorder and violence. History is clear in its documentation of poverty, frustration, and violence; and by removing the government from any intercession—except perhaps the law-and-order aspect—we insure the continuation of the cycle.

One need only look into South America to see what happens when society and government are controlled by a landed elite, leaving a large percentage of the population to scramble for their daily bread. The instability of those governments is due as much to the economic disenfranchisement of the poor as to a desire for a change in the form of government. History again teaches us that the totalitarianism of both the left and right find fertile breeding grounds among those who have lost hope in the existing government.

It was in part to meet this problem that the New Deal was begun and, to a lesser

13. SHOULD WELFARE BE TRIMMED?

extent, that the Great Society programs were initiated. A compassionate government has little to fear, but a government that turns its back on the underprivileged is a government at risk.

It is also a fact that these programs, initially earmarked for the poor, have had an economically beneficial effect on the middle class. For example, the food stamp recipient's expenditures benefit the retail grocer, the wholesaler, the food processer, and ultimately the farmer. There is a similar chain of economic benefit for most other government programs as well. So, while the poor are first to be hit by program reductions and eliminations, the pocketbooks of the middle class soon feel the loss as well.

The fact remains that millions of low-income Americans eat better, have improved housing, adequate medical care, and job training—and at least have the hope of a better life than they had in the past.

To now suggest, as some religious and political groups have done, that the churches must shoulder social service responsibilities with assistance from corporations is to ignore the historical and economic realities of the American experience. Even if all of the available resources of every religious denomination were earmarked for these programs and entitlements, they would amount to only a fraction of the present expenditure level.

The programs that have incurred the administration's wrath are the ones that have provided housing for the low-income and the elderly, helped to eliminate hunger, and increased the nutritional balance for millions. They are the programs that have improved the quality of life through the development of electric power in rural areas, by the construction of water systems and sewers, and by increased support for

small businesses and communities through the construction of airports, highways, schools, hospitals—and hundreds of other projects that touch lives and welfare.

But as frustrating and potentially dangerous as the philosophy of curtailing social services is, this is the philosophy behind an administration that will be in power for another three years.

From a time when Franklin Roosevelt said, "The test of our progress is not whether we add more to the abundance of those who have more; it is whether we provide enough for those who have too little," we have regressed to a time when Budget Director David Stockman can call the federal budget a "coast-to-coast soup line" without arousing a storm of protest. And he can add,

> I don't believe that there is any entitlement, any basic right to legal services or any other kind of services, and the idea that's been established over the last ten years that almost every service that someone might need in life ought to be provided, financed by the government as a matter of basic right, is wrong.

The Reagan administration argues that too many people who are not in genuine need have come to depend upon federal help. No responsible person would argue that abuses do not exist in the present welfare system. But defining "genuine need" is as difficult as making blanket judgments of where individual responsibility ends and government's obligation begins.

Need varies as circumstances vary, as the state of the economy varies, as the individual's makeup varies. Failure to recognize these variances is a failure to recognize the realities of the human condition.

The children of a jobless teacher who

has exhausted his savings and his unemployment benefits can get just as hungry as the children of a ghetto parent. Moreover, the bootstrap philosophy of the Reagan administration only applies if one has boots. Abandoning a human being whose determination to be self-sufficient has been stultified by deprivation and discrimination is as morally arrogant as it is callous.

Since the time of the New Deal, this country's social policy has been directed toward meeting human need—however, whenever, and wherever it exists. It has not always succeeded. At times it has been counterproductive. But the intent at least has been noble and humane.

In contrast, the policy advanced by the Reagan administration could cut programs for the poor to finance tax cuts for those in the highest income brackets. For example, the administration's economic plan would cut off unemployment benefits to those out of work more than three months unless they take jobs below the level of their job skills and employment history, but it would provide a $52,000-a-year tax cut to a family of four earning $200,000 a year in property income. It would reduce by a third to a half the funding of nutrition programs for poor mothers, their unborn, or their very young children, but it would give over $8 billion in tax deductions to families earning between $80,000 and $100,000 a year. It would eliminate 400,000 poor families from food stamp benefits, while giving 546,000 more affluent families tax reductions averaging $27,000 per family. Those losing food stamps would be the working poor and the elderly living on social security. Those who would receive the highest tax reductions would be families earning $100,000 a year.

THE ADMINISTRATION'S STUBBORN BIAS

Behind the administration's social counterrevolution apparently lies a mistaken assumption that there has been a great shift of resources from the rich to the poor in the last forty years. There has been no shift in resources from the rich to the poor. Forty years ago, families in the lowest 20 percent income bracket had the same share of total resources as they have today.

Moreover, this administration acts as though it believes most Americans are looking for a free ride at government expense, that even the ignominies of welfare are preferable to the pride of honest labor. No study that I have seen confirms that view.

The Reagan administration's stubborn bias in such matters underscores former Health, Education, and Welfare Secretary Joseph Califano's observation that the welfare issue has long been "encrusted with myth, demagoguery, regional politics, and racial prejudice."

The many myths and prejudices about the food stamp program, for example, have been refuted again and again by facts published here and elsewhere; but facts fail to impress either the administration or some of its key supporters on Capitol Hill.

To wit:

● Almost 87 percent of the households receiving food stamps gross less than poverty-level income. Six million Americans with incomes below that level do not get food stamps.

● Sixty percent of the food stamp households have no liquid assets. Two-thirds do not own cars.

● Only about 15 percent of all food stamp household heads are employable and subject to work requirements.

● Students, whom Treasury Secretary

229

13. SHOULD WELFARE BE TRIMMED?

Regan says rip off the stamp program to buy "booze and beer," make up only two-tenths of 1 percent of all food stamp users. Strikers, another frequent target of the program critics, make up less than 1 percent of the total, and they have to meet strict income and assets tests to qualify.

Nor is the program a runaway giveaway. In the last two years, Congress has eliminated a million-and-a-half people from the food stamp rolls and added both new penalties for violations and significant new financial incentives for states to tighten administrative practices. The available evidence, contrary to what critics claim, indicates that the level of fraud is statistically low and that food stamp families buy more nutrients per dollar than other shoppers.

Too often lost in the debate over food stamps is the ultimate question of its worth to the nation. A dozen years ago, medical researchers from the Field Foundation uncovered widespread hunger and malnutrition in this most affluent of nations. About the same time, television viewers were shocked by a CBS documentary titled "Hunger in America." But several years ago, Field Foundation researchers retraced their original steps. They returned to report that while poverty remained a serious problem, hunger and malnutrition no longer were.

And to what did these researchers attribute this remarkable turnabout in human well-being? In large part, they said, credit goes to the food stamp program, the school lunch and breakfast program, and the supplemental feeding program for women, infants, and children (WIC)—programs the Reagan administration now wants to slash.

But set aside the callousness of motivation and the insensitivity of approach. What of the administration's argument that the end justifies the means, that the economy is so endangered that only heavy tax cuts and radical surgery on domestic programs can save it?

Ironically, the administration's insistence that the sickness of the economy is worsening has trapped it in a political quandary. Economic indicators continue to defy the doomsayers. The economy not only refuses to slip into recession, it appears to be making modest gains. One might reasonably expect the administration to take credit for this welcome development, but to do so would undermine its case.

But suppose the economy does begin to worsen again. Would that justify the severity of the cuts the administration proposes in social welfare?

"If there was real hope that the sacrifices they (the disadvantaged Americans) are being forced to endure would fix the economy," wrote Raspberry, "we could put them in the category of harsh but effective medicine—temporarily distressing but in the long term good. My own fear—shared by some of the President's own conservative supporters—is that the Reagan economic plan won't work and that, therefore, the pain it is imposing upon the most helpless among us will be economically useless, socially devastating and permanent."

Raspberry's fears are well founded. The administration maintains it can reduce inflation, increase production, and lower unemployment by blending monetarist theory with supply-sided tax reductions. It also claims that it can increase military spending and balance the budget at the same time it cuts taxes. Yet it is clearly evident now that few, if any, reputable economists or Wall Street analysts find this scenario credible.

A BLEAK OUTLOOK

Most appeared taken aback when an administration—ostensibly committed to a hardheaded, analytical, businesslike, and traditionally conservative approach to economic matters—chose instead to follow the obscurantist social philosophy of George Gilder and the mystical economics of Arthur Laffer. In sum, the administration has embraced a plan that is as short on proof as it is long on faith.

Nor do the incongruities end here. The paring of social programs makes mockery of the administration's oft-expressed commitment to the work ethic and the preservation of families. An analysis by the Center for the Study of Welfare Policy at the University of Chicago found that the cuts in human services called for by the Reagan administration would push poor people without jobs into poverty but would hurt the working poor even more. Whatever economic edge the working poor now hold over the jobless poor, the study concluded, would be so narrowed by the cuts as to "reduce or entirely eliminate the financial incentive to work for welfare recipients."

Other analyses of the impact of the cuts show that the administration's commitment to what it calls the foundation of our social order seems limited to such concerns as abortion, sex education, and prayer in the schools, ignoring the terrible strains that joblessness, deprivation, and poor housing exert on the family structure.

As an analysis by the Democratic Study Group in April 1981, pointed out:

A single family could be hit by not one, but by several cuts. There could be a sudden loss of income due to loss of a CETA job or AFDC eligibility, loss of health care assistance for both children and adults, loss of food assistance through cuts in food stamps and the school lunch program, and loss of housing and home heating assistance. Loss of support in any one of these areas could pose a serious problem for a low-income family, but a chain of reduced assistance to a single family could be devastating.

To all the protests about the severity of the proposed cuts in welfare programs, to all the warnings about the potential consequences, the administration and its supporters turn a smug and sanguine face. Private giving, they blandly assure us, will have to make up the difference.

The point at issue, however, is whether private giving can fill the vacuum. Brian O'Connell, president of Independent Sector, an organization that encourages giving and not-for-profit intiatives, is skeptical. He points out that even before double-digit inflation, giving had been declining as a proportion of both personal income and the gross national product. "Now, in the face of continued inflation and unemployment," he says, "it is just not realistic to expect individuals to pick up the sudden slack."

The bleakness of the outlook was aptly summed up in this passage from an article by James Tobin published earlier this year in the *New Republic*, titled "Sleight of Mind":

Marginal tax rates are to be lowered for the rich to provide incentives. The disincentives implicit in needs tests for food stamps and other programs for the poor and working poor are to be raised. Increased autonomy for the states in the administration of welfare and Medicaid is a step backwards. Regional differences in benefits, eligibility standards, and humaneness of administration will become an even greater source of privation, inequity, and migration. Cuts in federal aid

13. SHOULD WELFARE BE TRIMMED?

will create serious fiscal crises for state and local governments, which will have to raise taxes, issue more debt and curtail services. . . . The new president clearly has capacities for political leadership that we have not seen in the 'bully pulpit' of the White House for many years. It is too bad the rare opportunity is being wasted, far worse that it is being exploited to engineer a social counter-revolution.

And if the counterrevolution fails, if the hardship resulting from the cuts is not eased by private giving, if the Reagan administration's economic policies fail, if the present victims are not rewarded with a better future—what then?

Then, conjectures William Raspberry, "the tendency will be for each of us to look to his own best interest, and to hell with the well-being of the nation. Such an attitude, if it becomes widespread, could rip the nation apart."

And so it could.

• • •

POSTSCRIPT

SHOULD WELFARE BE TRIMMED?

The analyses of McGovern and Carleson-Hopkins clash, but in doing so they also complement one another. When Carleson and Hopkins premise their argument on the proposition that income belongs to those who "earn" it, they do not mention that the "earner" may have benefited, directly or indirectly, from tax write-offs, protective tariffs, government subsidies to industry, or other government benefits not usually called "welfare." Mc-Govern fills in the missing facts. Yet, when McGovern defends a social policy "directed toward meeting human need—however, whenever, and wherever it exists"—on the ground that the *intent* behind such an ambitious policy is "noble and humane," Carleson and Hopkins remind us that good intentions sometimes produce disastrous effects.

A book much valued and quoted by Reagan Administration officials is Martin Anderson's WELFARE (Hoover Institute Press, 1978), which analyzes the problem of work "disincentives" resulting from welfare. On the other side, as the title makes abundantly clear, Robert Lekachman's GREED IS NOT ENOUGH: REAGANOMICS (Pantheon, 1982) is a critical study of Reagan's alternatives to welfare. A book which provides factual ammunition for both sides of the dispute, but refreshingly little of the simplistic "left" and "right" ideology in which the dispute seems entangled, is Ken Auletta's THE UNDERCLASS (Random House, 1982).

One of the tough questions which Americans may eventually have to ask themselves is whether there may not have grown up in America a permanent class of dependent people, people who may lack both the skills and the aspiration to support themselves in today's society. Some recent studies (reported in Auletta's book) suggests that while many welfare mothers respond well to skills training courses, young high school dropouts and ex-offenders suffer a very high dropout rate even from programs especially designed to help them. It may be premature, however, to ask about the incorrigibly unemployed in this present period of recession, in which so many who are eager to work cannot find jobs.

ISSUE 14

SHOULD OBSCENITY BE PROTECTED AS FREE SPEECH?

YES: Judge Jerome Frank, from concurring opinion, *United States vs Roth,* 1956

NO: Harry M. Clor, from CENSORSHIP AND FREEDOM OF EXPRESSION (Gambier, Ohio, 1971)

ISSUE SUMMARY

YES: Judge Frank submits his contention that the potential evil effects of obscenity cannot justify its suppression by society.

NO: Writer Clor argues that the basic values which make civilized society possible, are threatened by pornography and that we cannot afford not to control it.

"Congress shall make no law . . . abridging the freedom of speech, or of the press." The language is clear—or is it? The Supreme Court has often acknowledged that certain categories of speech or expression simply are not included within that constitutional protection, including lewd and obscene, libelous, or seditious speech, and "fighting" words which incite a breach of the peace.

Remarkably, the Supreme Court did not establish a constitutional rule for obscenity until 1957, although it has never since been entirely free of the issue. The 1957 decision (*Roth v. U.S.*) excluded obscenity from the constitutional protection accorded freedom of expression. Justice William J. Brennan, author of the *Roth* opinion, carefully distinguished obscenity from sex: "Obscene material is material which deals with sex in a manner appealing to prurient interests." As for "prurient interests," Brennan adopted a dictionary definition: "itching, longing; . . . lewd." For some people, the Bible or Shakespeare might cause itching or longing, so Brennan added that the "dominant theme of the material taken as a whole" must seem prurient to "the average person, applying contemporary community standards."

The Court was seriously divided in deciding *Roth.* Two Justices would not accept the argument that obscenity, or for that matter any other expression, should be excluded from First Amendment protection. Another Justice would have distinguished between the standards applied to the federal government and those applied to the states. (He would have given the states greater latitude to define obscenity according to their standards.) Still another Justice held that the crucial element was not the content of the allegedly obscene material but the way it was distributed and advertised, that is, its commerical exploitation.

Four new Nixon appointees reflected or responded to that criticism. In five obscenity cases decided in 1973, a new majority (the Nixon appointees plus Justice Byron White) made successful prosecution of obscenity easier, and therefore more likely. It is no longer necessary to demonstrate that the allegedly obscene material is "utterly without redeeming social value," only that it lacks "serious value." Furthermore, for the first time the Court made clear that the community standards to be applied were those of the local community. The increase in prosecutions since 1973 has been prompted not only by the change in judicial attitude but also by change in the postal law, allowing prosecution of obscene material in the place of delivery or receipt as well as the place of mailing. One consequence is that if a prosecution fails in one place, another can be attempted elsewhere. The pornographic film *Deep Throat* was tried and its producers and actors acquitted in Sioux Falls, Jacksonville, and Boston. With no verdicts, trials ended in hung juries in Austin, Houston, and Beverly Hills, before conviction was secured in Memphis. The publishers of a weekly sex news paper, *Screw*, were convicted in Wichita, Kansas where the publication was unavailable on the newsstands and fewer than twenty people in the state (including four postal inspectors!) had mail subscriptions. In 1977, Larry Flynt, publisher of *Hustler* magazine, with editorial offices in Columbus, Ohio, was convicted under Ohio law of pandering obscenity. All of these remain subject to further prosecution in other jurisdictions.

The issues are unlikely to be resolved by the Supreme Court or any other. "Does obscenity hurt?" is an empirical question, and psychologists, criminologists, and sociologists have long studied the question without reaching any consensus, and often without reaching any conclusion. The most that can be said is that the evidence isn't all in and, given the difficulties in conducting research in this area, it probably never will be. "Is obscenity immoral?," "Does it run counter to social values?," and "Is it offensive?" are all questions involving value judgments, and it is obvious that values differ. There are still other questions, questions of "pandering" (how the obscene material is advertised and marketed) and privacy (what are the rights of persons who would shun exposure to obscenity?).

In the following selections, Judge Jerome Frank offers a classic defense of the broadest latitude for free expression, including obscenity, while Harry Clor argues that liberty is not license and society's most fundamental values require that limits be set.

YES

Jerome Frank

THE DANGEROUSLY INFECTIOUS
NATURE OF CENSORSHIP

Freedom to speak publicly and to publish has, as its inevitable and important correlative, the private rights to hear, to read, and to think and to feel about what one hears and reads. The First Amendment protects those private rights of hearers and readers. . . .

Some of those who in the twentieth century endorse legislation suppressing "obscene" literature have an attitude toward freedom of expression which does not match that of the framers of the First Amendment (adopted at the end of the eighteenth century) but does stem from an attitude toward writings dealing with sex which arose decades later, in the mid-nineteenth century, and is therefore labeled—doubtless too sweepingly—"Victorian." It was a dogma of "Victorian morality" that sexual misbehavior would be encouraged if one were to "acknowledge its existence or at any rate to present it vividly enough to form a lifelike image of it in the reader's mind"; this morality rested on a "faith that you could best conquer evil by shutting your eyes to its existence," and on a kind of word magic. The demands at that time for "decency" in published words did not comport with the actual sexual conduct of many of those who made those demands: "The Victorians, as a general rule, managed to conceal the 'coarser' side of their lives so thoroughly under a mask of respectability that we often fail to realize how 'coarse' it really was. . . ." Could we have recourse to the vast unwritten literature of bawdry we should be able to form a more veracious notion of life as it (then) really was. The respectables of those days often, "with unblushing license," held "high revels" in "night houses." Thanks to them, Mrs. Warren's profession flourished, but it was considered sinful to talk about it in books. Such a prudish and purely verbal moral code, at odds (more or less hypocritically) with the actual conduct of its adherents was (as we have seen) not the moral code of those who framed the First Amendment. One would suppose, then, that the courts should interpret and enforce that Amendment according to the views of those framers, not according to the later "Victorian" code. . . .

Judge Jerome Frank Concurring In U.S. vs.Roth, 237 F, 2nd 796 (2nd Cir. 1956.)

THE STATUTE AS JUDICIALLY INTERPRETED, AUTHORIZES PUNISHMENT FOR INDUCING MERE THOUGHTS, AND FEELINGS, OR DESIRES

For a time, American courts adopted the test of obscenity contrived in 1868 by L.J. Cockburn, in *Queen V. Hicklin*, L.R. 3 Q.B. 360: "I think the test of obscenity is this, whether the tendency of the matter charged as obscenity is to deprave and corrupt those whose minds are open to such immoral influences, and into whose hands a publication of this sort might fall." He added that the book there in question "would suggest . . . thoughts of a most impure and libidinous character."

The test in most federal courts has changed: They do not now speak of the thoughts of "Those whose minds are open to . . . immoral influences" but, instead, of the thoughts of average adult normal men and women, determining what these thoughts are, not by proof at the trial, but by the standard of "the average conscience of the time," the current "social sense of what is right."

Yet the courts still define obscenity in terms of the assumed average normal adult reader's sexual thoughts or desires or impulses, without reference to any relation between those "subjective" reactions and his subsequent conduct. The judical opinions use such key phrases as this: "suggesting lewd thoughts and exciting sensual desires," "arouse the salacity of the reader," "allowing or implanting . . . obscene, lewd, or lascivious thoughts or desires," "arouse sexual desires." The judge's charge in the instant case reads accordingly: "It must tend to stir sexual impulses and lead to sexually impure thoughts." Thus the statute, as the

courts construe it, appears to provide criminal punishment for inducing no more than thoughts, feelings, desires.

NO ADEQUATE KNOWLEDGE IS AVAILABLE CONCERNING THE EFFECTS ON THE CONDUCT OF NORMAL ADULTS OF READING OR SEEING THE "OBSCENE"

Suppose we assume, *arguendo*, that sexual thoughts or feelings, stirred by the "obscene," probably will often issue into overt conduct. Still it does not at all follow that that conduct will be antisocial. For no sane person can believe it socially harmful if sexual desires lead to normal, and not antisocial, sexual behavior since, without such behavior, the human race would soon disappear.

Doubtless, Congress could validly provide punishment for mailing any publications if there were some moderately substantial reliable data showing that reading or seeing those publications probably conduces to seriously harmful sexual conduct on the part of normal adult human beings. But we have no such data.

Suppose it argued that whatever excites sexual longings might *possibly* produce sexual misconduct. That cannot suffice: Notoriously, perfumes sometimes act as aphrodisiacs, yet no one will suggest that therefore Congress may constitutionally legislate punishment for mailing perfumes. It may be that among the stimuli to irregular sexual conduct, by normal men and women, may be almost anything—the odor of carnations or cheese, the sight of a cane or a candle or a shoe, the touch of silk or a gunnysack. For all anyone now knows, stimuli of that sort may be far more provocative of such misconduct than reading obscene books

237

or seeing obscene pictures. Said John Milton, "Evil manners are as perfectly learnt, without books, a thousand other ways that cannot be stopped."

EFFECT OF "OBSCENITY" ON ADULT CONDUCT

To date there exist, I think no thoroughgoing studies by competent persons which justify the conclusion that normal adults' reading or seeing of the "obscene" probably induces antisocial conduct. Such competent studies as have been made do conclude that so complex and numerous are the causes of sexual vice that it is impossible to assert with any assurance that "obscenity" represents a ponderable causal factor in sexually deviant adult behavior. "Although the whole subject of obscenity censorship hinges upon the unproved assumption that "obscene" literature is a significant factor in causing sexual deviation from the community standard, no report can be found of a single effort at genuine research to test this assumption by singling out as a factor for study the effect of sex literature upon sexual behavior." What little competent research has been done points definitely in a direction precisely opposite to that assumption.

Alpert reports that, when, in the 1920s, 409 women college graduates were asked to state in writing what things stimulated them sexually, they answered thus: 218 said men; 95 said books; 40 said drama; 29 said dancing; 18 said pictures; 9 said music. Of those who replied "that the source of their sex information came from books, not one specified a 'dirty' book as the source. Instead, the books listed were: The Bible, the dictionary, the encyclopedia, novels from Dickens to Henry James, circulars about venereal diseases, medical books, and Motley's *Rise of the Dutch Republic.*" Macaulay, replying to advocates of the suppression of obscene books, said: "We find it difficult to believe that in a world so full of temptations as this, any gentleman whose life would have been virtuous if he had not read Aristophanes or Juvenal, will be vicious by reading them." Echoing Macaulay, Jimmy Walker, former mayor of New York City, remarked that he had never heard of a woman seduced by a book. New Mexico has never had an obscenity statute; there is no evidence that, in that state, sexual misconduct is proportionately greater than elsewhere.

EFFECT ON CONDUCT OF YOUNG PEOPLE

. . . Judge Clark speaks of "the strongly held views of those with competence in the premises as to the very direct connection" of obscenity "with the development of juvenile delinquency." . . . One of the cited writings is a report, by Dr. [Marie] Jahoda and associates, entitled "The Impact of Literature: A Psychological Discussion of Some Assumptions in the Censorship Debate" (1954). I have read this report (which is a careful survey of all available studies and psychological theories). I think it expresses an attitude quite contrary to that indicated by Judge Clark. In order to avoid any possible bias in my interpretation of that report, I thought it well to ask Dr. Jahoda to write her own summary of it, which, with her permission, I shall quote. . . .

Dr. Jahoda's summary reads as follows:

Persons who argue for increased censorship of printed matter often operate on the assumption that reading about sexual matters or about violence and brutality leads to antisocial actions, particularly to juvenile delinquency. An examination of the pertinent psychological literature has led to the following conclusions:

1. There exists no research evidence either to prove or to disprove this assumption definitively.

2. In the absence of scientific proof two lines of psychological approach to the examination of the assumption are possible: (a) a review of what is known on the causes of juvenile delinquency; and (b) a review of what is known about the effect of literature on the mind of the reader.

3. In the vast research literature on the causes of juvenile delinquency there is no evidence to justify the assumption that reading about sexual matters or about violence leads to delinquent acts. Experts on juvenile delinquency agree that it has no single cause. Most of them regard early childhood events, which precede the reading age, as a necessary condition for later delinquency. At a later age, the nature of personal relations is assumed to have much greater power in determining a delinquent career than the vicarious experiences provided by reading matter. Juvenile delinquents as a group read less, and less easily, than nondelinquents. Individual instances are reported in which so-called "good" books allegedly influenced a delinquent in the manner in which "bad" books are assumed to influence him.

Where childhood experiences and subsequent events have combined to make delinquency psychologically likely, reading could have one of two effects: it could serve a trigger function releasing the criminal act or it could provide for a substitute outlet of aggression in fantasy, dispensing with the need for criminal action. There is no empirical evidence in either direction.

4. With regard to the impact of literature on the mind of the reader, it must be pointed out that there is a vast overlap in content between all media of mass communication. The daily press, television, radio, movies, books and comics all present their share of so-called "bad" material, some with great realism as reports of actual events, some in clearly fictionalized form. It is virtually impossible to isolate the impact of one of these media on a population exposed to all of them. Some evidence suggests that the particular communications which arrest the attention of an individual are in good part a matter of choice. As a rule, people do not expose themselves to everything that is offered, but only to what agrees with their inclinations.

Children, who have often not yet crystallized their preferences and have more unspecific curiosity than many adults, are therefore perhaps more open to accidental influences from literature. This may present a danger to youngsters who are insecure or maladjusted who find in reading (of "bad" books as well as of "good" books) an escape from reality which they do not dare to face. Needs which are not met in the real world are gratified in a fantasy world. It is likely, though not fully demonstrated, that excessive reading of comic books will intensify in children those qualities which drove them to the comic book world to begin with: an inability to face the world, apathy, a belief that the individual is hopelessly impotent and driven by uncontrollable forces and, hence, an acceptance of violence and brutality in the real world.

It should be noted that insofar as causal sequence is implied, insecurity and maladjustment in a child must precede this exposure to the written word in order to lead to these potential effects. Unfortunately, perhaps, the reading of Shakespeare's tragedies or of Anderson's and Grimm's fairy tales might do much the same. . . .

Maybe someday we will have enough reliable data to show that obscene books and pictures do tend to influence children's sexual conduct adversely. Then a federal statute could be enacted which would avoid constitutional defects by authorizing punishment for using the mails or interstate shipments in the sale of such books and pictures to children.

It is, however, not at all clear that children would be ignorant, in any considerable measure, of obscenity, if no obscene publications ever came into their hands. Youngsters get a vast deal of education in sexual smut from companions of their own age. A verbatim report of conversations among young teen-age boys (from average respectable homes) will disclose their amazing proficiency in obscene language, learned from other boys. Replying to the argument of the need for censorship to protect the young, Milton said: "Who shall regulate all the . . . conversation of our youth . . . appoint what shall be discussed . . . ?" Most judges who reject that view are long past their youth and have probably forgotten the conversational ways of that period of life: "I remember when I was a little boy," said Mr. Dooley, "but I don't remember how I was a little boy."

THE OBSCENITY STATUTE AND THE REPUTABLE PRESS

Let it be assumed, for the sake of the argument, that contemplation of published matter dealing with sex has a significant impact on children's conduct. On that assumption, we cannot overlook the fact that our most reputable newspapers and periodicals carry advertisements and photographs displaying women in what decidedly are sexually alluring postures, and at times emphasizing the importance of "sex appeal." That women are there shown scantily clad increases "the mystery and allure of the bodies that are hidden," writes an eminent psychiatrist. "A leg covered by a silk stocking is much more attractive than a naked one: a bosom pushed into a shape by a brassiere is more alluring than the pendant realities." Either, then, the statute must be sternly applied to prevent the mailing of many reputable newspapers and periodicals containing such ads and photographs, or else we must acknowledge that they have created a cultural atmosphere for children in which, at a maximum, only the most trifling additional effect can be imputed to children's perusal of the kind of matter mailed by the defendant. . . .

IF THE OBSCENITY STATUTE IS VALID, WHY MAY CONGRESS NOT VALIDLY PROVIDE PUNISHMENT FOR MAILING BOOKS WHICH WILL PROVOKE THOUGHTS IT CONSIDERS UNDESIRABLE ABOUT RELIGION OR POLITICS?

If the statute is valid, then, considering the foregoing, it would seem that its validity must rest on this ground: Congress, by statute, may constitutionally provide punishment for the mailing of books evoking mere thoughts or feelings about sex, if Congress considers them socially dangerous, even in the absence of any satisfactory evidence that those thoughts or feelings will tend to bring about socially harmful deeds. If that be correct, it is hard to understand why, similarly, Congress may not constitutionally provide punishment for such distribution of books evoking mere thoughts or feelings about religion or politics which Congress considers socially dangerous, even in the absence of any satisfactory evidence that those thoughts or feelings will tend to bring about socially dangerous deeds.

THE JUDICIAL EXCEPTION OF THE "CLASSICS"

As I have said, I have no doubt the jury could reasonably find, beyond a reasonable doubt, that many of the publications mailed by defendant were obscene within the current judicial definition of the term as explained by the trial judge in his charge to the jury. But so, too, are a multitude of recognized works of art found in public libraries. Compare, for instance, the books which are exhibits in this case with Montaigne's ESSAY ON SOME LINES OF VIRGIL or with Chaucer. Or consider the many nude pictures which the defendant transmitted through the mails, and then turn to the reproductions in the articles on paintings and sculptures in the ENCYCLOPEDIA BRITANNICA (14th edition). Some of the latter are no less "obscene" than those which led to the defendant's conviction. Yet these Encyclopedia volumes are readily accessible to everyone, young or old, and, without let or hindrance, are frequently mailed to all parts of the country. Catalogues of famous art museums, almost equally accessible and also often mailed, contain reproductions of paintings and sculpture, by great masters, no less "obscene."

To the argument that such books (and such reproductions of famous paintings and works of sculpture) fall within the statutory ban, the courts have answered that they are "classics,"—books of "literary distinction" or works which have "an accepted place in the arts," including, so this court has held, Ovid's ART OF LOVE and Boccacio's DECAMERON. There is a "curious dilemma" involved in this answer that the statute condemns "only books which are dull and without merit," that in no event will the statute be applied to the "classics," that is, books "of literary distinction." The courts have not explained how they escape that dilemma, but instead seem to have gone to sleep (although rather uncomfortably) on its horns.

. . . No one can rationally justify the judge-made exception. The contention would scarcely pass as rational that the "classics" will be read or seen solely by an intellectual or artistic elite, for, even ignoring the snobbish, undemocratic nature of this contention, there is no evidence that that elite has a moral fortitude (an immunity from moral corruption) superior to that of the "masses." And if the exception, to make it rational, were taken as meaning that a contemporary book is exempt if it equates in "literary distinction" with the "classics," the result would be amazing: Judges would have to serve as literary critics; jurisprudence would merge with aesthetics; authors and publishers would consult the legal digests for legal-artistic precedents; we would some day have a Legal Restatement of the Canons of Literary Taste. . . .

HOW CENSORSHIP UNDER THE STATUTE ACTUALLY OPERATES

Prosecutors, as censors, actually exercise prior restraint. Fear of punishment serves as a powerful restraint on publication, and fear of punishment often means, practically, fear of prosecution. For most men dread indictment and prosecution; the publicity alone terrifies, and to defend a criminal action is expensive. If the definition of obscenity had a limited and fairly well-known scope, that fear might deter restricted sorts of publications only. But on account of the extremely vague judicial definition of the obscene, a person threatened with prosecution if he mails (or otherwise sends in interstate commerce) almost any book which deals in an unconventional, unorthodox manner with sex, may well apprehend that, should the threat be carried out, he will be punished. As a result, each prosecutor becomes a literary censor (dictator) with immense unbridled power, a virtually uncontrolled discretion. A statute would be invalid which gave the Postmaster General the power, without reference to any standard, to close the mails to any publication he happened to dislike. Yet, a federal prosecutor, under the federal obscenity statute, approximates that position: Within wide limits, he can (on the advice of the Postmaster General or on no one's advice) exercise such a censorship by threat without a trial, without any judicial supervision, capriciously and arbitrarily. Having no special qualifications for that task, nevertheless, he can, in large measure, determine at his will what those within his district may not read on sexual subjects. In that way, the statute brings about an actual prior restraint of free speech and free press which strikingly flouts the First Amendment. . . .

THE DANGEROUSLY INFECTIOUS NATURE OF GOVERNMENTAL CENSORSHIP OF BOOKS

Governmental control of ideas or personal preferences is alien to a democracy. And the yearning to use governmental censorship of any kind is infectious. It may spread insidiously. Commencing with suppression of books as obscene, it is not unlikely to develop into official lust for the power of thought-control in the areas of religion, politics and elsewhere. Milton observed that "licensing of books . . . necessarily pulls along with it so many other kinds of licensing." Mill noted that the "bounds of what may be called moral police" may easily extend "until it encroaches on the most unquestionably legitimate liberty of the individual." We should beware of a recrudescence of the undemocratic doctrine uttered in the seventeenth century by Berkeley, Governor of Virginia: "Thank God there are no free schools of preaching, for learning has brought disobedience into the world, and printing has divulged them. God keep us from both."

THE PEOPLE AS SELF-GUARDIANS: CENSORSHIP BY PUBLIC OPINION, NOT BY GOVERNMENT

Plato, who detested democracy, proposed to banish all poets; and his rulers were to serve as guardians of the people, telling lies for the people's good, vigorously suppressing writings these guardians thought dangerous. Governmental guardianship is repugnant to the basic tenet of our democracy: According to our ideals, our adult citizens are self-guardians, to act as their own fathers, and thus become self-dependent. When our governmental officials act towards our citizens on the thesis that "Papa knows best what's good for you," they enervate the spirit of the citizens: To treat grown men like infants is to make them infantile, dependent, immature. . . .

So, we come back, once more, to Jefferson's advice: The only completely democratic way to control publications which arouse mere thoughts or feelings is through non-governmental censorship by public opinion.

THE SEEMING PARADOX OF THE FIRST AMENDMENT

Here we encounter an apparent paradox: The First Amendment, judicially enforced, curbs public opinion when translated into a statute which restricts freedom of expression (except that which will probably induce undesirable conduct). The paradox is unreal: The Amendment ensures that public opinion—the "common conscience of the time"—shall not commit suicide through legislation which chokes off today the free expression of minority views which may become the majority public opinion of tomorrow.

PRIVATE PERSONS OR GROUPS MAY VALIDLY TRY TO INFLUENCE PUBLIC OPINION

The First Amendment obviously has nothing to do with the way persons or groups, not a part of government, influence public opinion as to what constitutes "decency" or "obscenity." The Catholic Church, for example, has a constitutional right to persuade or instruct its adherents not to read designated books or kinds of books. . . .

In our industrial era when, perforce, economic pursuits must be, increasingly, governmentally regulated, it is especially important that the realm of art—the non-economic realm—should remain free, unregimented, the domain of free enterprise, of unhampered competition at its maximum. An individual's taste is his own private concern. *De gustibus non disputandum* represents a valued democratic maxim. . . .

To vest a few fallible men—prosecutors, judges, jurors—with vast powers of literary or artistic censorship, to convert them into what Mill called a "moral police," is to make them despotic arbiters of literary products. If one day they ban mediocre books as obscene, another day they may do likewise to a work of genius. Originality, not too plentiful, should be cherished, not stifled. An author's imagination may be cramped if he must write with one eye on prosecutors or juries; authors must cope with publishers who, fearful about the judgments of governmental censors, may refuse to accept the manuscripts of contemporary Shelleys or Mark Twains or Whitmans.

Some few men stubbornly fight for the right to write or publish or distribute books which the great majority at the time consider loathsome. If we jail those few, the community may appear to have suffered nothing. The appearance is deceptive. For the conviction and punishment of these few will terrify writers who are more sensitive, less eager for a fight. What, as a result, they do not write might have been major literary contributions. "Suppression," Spinoza said, "is paring down the state till it is too small to harbor men of talent."

• • •

NO   Harry M. Clor

CENSORSHIP AND FREEDOM
OF EXPRESSION

A new consideration has been introduced into the long-standing controversy over moral censorship and freedom of expression. Most people who
write and debate about these matters have now come to agree that we are
living through moral changes of such a magnitude as to warrant the
designation "sexual revolution." There is, of course, little agreement about the
value of this "revolution"—its potentialities for good or evil in our lives. Such
ethical questions, questions about what is good for us and what is bad for us as
human beings, are difficult to resolve with any certitude. Yet we cannot avoid
grappling with the ethical issues if we are to arrive at reasoned judgments
about the controversy over obscenity and about the sexual revolution which is
now inextricably involved in that controversy.

The sexual revolution, or "the moral and sexual revolution," as it is
sometimes called, may be said to have two distinguishing features—one in the
realm of expression and the other in the realm of conduct. In recent years we
have been witnessing a rapidly accelerating trend toward increasingly candid,
or blatant, presentations of sexual and related subjects in literature and the
arts, in public displays and advertising, and in public discourse generally. And,
in the realm of conduct, we have been witnessing a similar trend toward sexual
freedom, or promiscuity, among the young and in large sections of adult
society as well.

Yet, in spite of this apparent moral and sexual revolution, the law continues
to be concerned with the restraint of certain kinds of literature, motion
pictures, and public performances as "obscene." The Supreme Court . . .
has steadily and sharply confined the operation of obscenity laws. But the law
may still act to prevent the commercial distribution of materials which, among
other things, predominantly "appeal to prurient interests." It is an interesting
question why legislative majorities (backed, according to most available
evidence, by substantial popular majorities) continue to pass and support

From, CENSORSHIP AND FREEDOM OF EXPRESSION, ©1971, The Public Affairs Conference Center,
Kenyon College, Gambier Ohio. Reprinted by permission.

such laws. It is highly probable that the expanding market and multitudes of willing customers for erotic literature are provided, in part, from among the popular majorities that regularly indicate their support for censorship. The advocate of the sexual revolution and his frequent ally, the ideological libertarian, are inclined to explain this paradox as a result of sheer hypocrisy. Large sections of the American public are unwilling to acknowledge in public the sexual passions they indulge in private. But a somewhat different explanation is possible. As a private individual, the average American may be quite susceptible to the allure of prurient appeals. But in his capacity as a citizen and member of the public, and when called upon to render a judgment in that capacity, he still clings to the belief that there is something wrong with blatant appeals to prurient interest.

But what could be the matter with a prurient appeal? If "prurience" means, as courts have said, an arousal of "lust," and lust means sexual desire, what could possibly be wrong with that? We have it not only from the moral revolutionaries but also from the highest medical authorities that sexual desire is quite normal and healthy, and that it is the repression thereof which is unhealthy and productive of troubles. Why, then, should we disapprove of literature that stimulates a desire without which, as Judge Jerome Frank has seen fit to remind us, the human race would not survive? And should we not positively rejoice at the open and candid treatment of a subject so long shrouded in morbid secrecy?

Academic discussions of this issue frequently suffer from overabstraction: overabstraction in deference, perhaps, to what remains of nonrevolutionary morality. The following are some more-or-less (but not wholly) concrete examples of the literature now prevalent as a result of the new candor and the new freedom of expression.

The "adult book shops" now flourishing in many of our larger cities feature what is called "spreader" pictorial magazines. These involve total nudity, very explicit portrayal of the female sexual organs (usually with the legs spread wide apart), and naked men and women posed together in provocative postures that stop just short of actual intercourse. Some of the magazines specialize in homosexual or lesbian portrayals. Often a large number of the "adult" shops are clustered in a central section of the city, with window displays advertising quite openly what is to be found inside.

One of the many New York "exploitation film" theaters just off Times Square recently featured a movie called *The Morbid Snatch*. Two men conceive and execute a plan to capture a young girl, imprison her, and compel her to submit to sexual acts of various sorts. The girl is drugged, confined in a basement, stripped naked, and subjected to sexual intercourse, first with one of the men, then with both the man and the lesbian simultaneously. Periodically, the camera focuses very closely upon the sexual organs of all participants. Periodically also the girl (whose age is, perhaps by intention, difficult to determine; she could be as young as sixteen or as old as twenty-five) is represented as responding erotically to these acts. The sexual scenes, and preparation for them, constitute practically the sole content and surely the sole interest of this film. A companion film about twenty minutes long consists of nothing but close-up shots of a nude woman masturbating. The "coming attractions" promise films devoted to rape, violence, mass orgies, and the intercourse of women with apes.

Finally, consider the now standard theme of a whole *genre* of contemporary paperback novelettes—the systematic violation, humiliation, and domination of women. There are several variations on this theme. A recent novel, THE ORGIASTS, features the gradual introduction of a respectable woman to the practices of a "sex club," and her eventual complete subjection to the will and desires of its members. The plot is typical: by a combination of seduction and compulsion, the woman is induced to desire her own subjection. This is how it is done. Stage one: seduction. Stage two: she begs to be violated. Stage three: she is drawn irresistibly into deviant practices with multi-participation. Stage four: she has lost all will of her own and has become a tool at the disposal of the group. In conjunction with vivid description of the verbal side of this process, there is a detailed portrayal of its physical side—the woman's sexual organs and contortions while under the domination of passion.

Another variation on this theme involves heavy emphasis upon violence in connection with the sexual act—the explicit interweaving of brutality and sensuality. In this kind of scenario, the woman is literally beaten into submission and is vividly portrayed as desiring and inviting this treatment. A recent novelette carries this principle to its utmost logical conclusion: the hero seduces women, tortures them, and then kills them.

Let us return to the original question. What is wrong with appealing to prurient interests? What, if anything, is the matter with the literature described above? If

there is nothing the matter with it, then reasonable men are not entitled to be shocked by its relatively sudden liberation from social and moral restraints. Now, the moralist is inclined to answer our question with terms such as "smut," "filth," and "moral pollution," and many citizens are inclined to simply leave it at that. But revulsion and outrage do not constitute arguments. Common decency might suggest an obvious answer, but we can no longer take the claims of common decency for granted. This is a profoundly skeptical age in which, with regard to moral matters at least, little can be taken for granted. The rising generation of youth and many of their teachers do not accept the traditional ethical assumptions. Today's intellectual climate imposes a heavy burden of argument upon anyone who would defend any aspect of traditional morality.

Our question has two dimensions and can be broken down into two distinct inquiries. First, one must explore the nature of a "prurient appeal" and the intrinsic qualities of materials describable as prurient. And then, one must consider what social harms, if any, can result from the widespread circulation of such materials. If it can be reasonably concluded that legitimate community interests are endangered by obscenity, then there is a further question to be asked. What may organized society do to protect these interests?

The reader will note that I have presented my examples of obscene literature in a certain order and progressive sequence. They constitute a continuum of prurient appeals, beginning with those that arouse "lust" but do not portray violence, and concluding with those clearly recognizable as outright sadism. The intermediate forms portray sexu-

acts involving some degree of compulsion or constraint, but they do not portray torture or murder, and the infliction of physical pain does not constitute their explicit erotic appeal.

Now some of my readers may wish to argue as follows. There is nothing wrong with the "adult" pictorial magazines or with any other erotic material that simply appeals to normal sexual desire, but sadism is justly condemned. If moral judgment is to be rendered upon literature, it should be rendered at that point in our continuum where violence enters and is made sensually alluring. This argument relies on the distinction between erotic literature which portrays and, hence, stimulates some perverted, distorted, or ugly form of sexuality.

This distinction has some merits but it is inadequate. It is inadequate for description and evaluation of our literary examples, and it is inadquate as a psychological analysis of what is going on between the reader and viewer and the prurient materials. Whatever is the perversion, distortion, or ugliness of outright sado-masochistic pornography, that perversion, distortion, or ugliness is also present in the "adult" pictorials, in a film or highly specific description of people copulating, however normally, and in the seduction scenes of THE ORGIASTS. The last literary items in our spectrum represent only the most extreme and flagrant form of an appeal that was present in all the items and which is present in all literature properly called "obscene."

We are on the way to understanding the nature of that appeal when we consider how the woman in the "spreader" pictorial is presented to the viewer. First of all, and most obviously, she is presented naked. What is normally concealed, and exposed only in private situations, is wholly exposed and placed conspicuously on public display. Secondly, she is presented as nothing more than an object for the gratification of the viewer's passions. She is not a woman but a plaything. All the indicators of human personality have been removed from the picture. What the observer sees is a person who has been stripped down to a mere body at his disposal. It can even be said that the body itself has been stripped down to a sexual organ; it is not the human body but an organ upon which the eye of the viewer is focused.

Essentially the same kind of voyeurism is solicited by the typical exploitation film and pornographic novel. The viewer of THE MORBID SNATCH is invited to enjoy the spectacle of a young woman reduced, as it were, to her parts and to a helpless object of manipulation. In THE ORGIASTS this appeal is made more explicit. The woman is represented as desiring her denigration to a passive tool, and the reader is thus made more consciously aware of what it is that he is invited to enjoy. By the time we arrive at that kind of pornography which specializes in cruel violence or brutishness, we should not be at all surprised. For there is a certain violence and brutishness in all the forms of obscenity examined here. Aspects of life believed to be intimately private are intrusively invaded, and the dignity of human personality has been violated.

In the most general terms, obscenity is that kind of representation which makes a gross public display of the private physical intimacies of life, and which degrades human beings by presenting them as mere objects of impersonal desire or violence. There are various

14. SHOULD OBSCENITY BE PROTECTED AS FREE SPEECH?

forms of obscene portrayals, but they all have one thing in common—graphically and in detail they reduce human life to a subhuman or merely animal level.

In the usual pornographic novel, love is reduced to sex and sex is vividly reduced to the interaction of organs and parts of organs. The "characters" are not presented as persons: they are (or in the process of the plot they become) little more than sexual instruments, stimulating in a reader the desire for sexual instruments. This kind of literature is predominantly calculated to arouse depersonalized desire. This is what is really meant by "stimulating lust": the systematic arousal of passions that are radically detached from love, affection, personal concern, or from any of those social, moral, and aesthetic considerations that make human relations human. Persons then become *things* to be manipulated for the gratification of the manipulator. What is sometimes termed "the obscenity of violence" is only the logical conclusion of this way of viewing and representing human beings.

The foregoing description and judgment of obscenity has presupposed certain moral concepts. Expressions such as "the dignity of human personality" are in frequent use today, but we seldom explore with real care the meaning and implications of these concepts. More specifically, there is need for exploration of the relation between personal dignity and privacy, and between those feelings we call love or affection and privacy.

Imagine, hypothetically, a man who is required to perform every act of his life in public and in the nude. Would those observing his acts be able to respect him, and would he be able to form a concept of his own dignity? We may well speculate on why it is difficult to answer with a confident "yes." Our dignity, or sense of self-respect, appears to depend heavily upon there being some aspects of our lives that we do not share indiscriminately with others. A sense of self-respect requires that there be some things that are protected, shielded from the world at large, belonging to the individual alone or to his very special relationships. And it would seem that the body and some of its acts belong in this category, demanding a shield of privacy.

Our human dignity is often said to derive from the fact that we possess higher and rational faculties having primacy, or potential primacy, over the lower and merely animal appetites. It is the very essence of pornography that, in it, the lower appetites are rendered supreme. The more specifically human part of us is represented, to the extent that it is represented at all, as the slave of the passions. These passions are indeed powerful. In ordinary life we are assisted in controlling them by social conventions, such as clothing and various moral and aesthetic proprieties, including verbal proprieties. Without any of these conventions we would be constantly confronted with the animal side of our existence and reminded of its demands. The conventions, by partially concealing that side of our existence, serve to subordinate it; to put it in its proper place. Our hypothetical wholly-public man would be, like the characters in a pornographic novel, utterly without any of the protection which this concealment affords. . . .

Public concern about obscenity is sometimes justified on the grounds that salacious literature directly promotes "antisocial conduct." With regard to the direct effects of salacious literature upon the conduct of adults such evidence as we have is problematic and informed opinion is divided. While evidence does not preclude a reasoned judgment that exposure to obscenity is sometimes a factor in the causation of violent or indecent acts, the case for public concern about it cannot rest solidly on this consideration alone. The ultimate evils of unrestrained obscenity are more subtle and far-reaching. The ultimate evils include influences upon the cultural and moral environment of a people and, hence, upon mind and character. The fact that influences of this kind are always too subtle for exact measurement does not relieve us of either the responsibility or the opportunity for reasoning about them. . . .

The censorship of obscenity rests upon two presuppositions: (1) that its unrestrained circulation endangers values and qualities of character that are indispensable for responsible citizenship and decent social relations; (2) that in society's effort to preserve values and qualities that are important to it, there is a legitimate role for the law. . . .

Laws against obscenity constitute some of the community's rules of civility. They affirm that the society has a standard of decency and indecency—a public morality. The majority of us usually require some guidance from communal standards. And it would seem that no community of men can do without a public morality. By means of laws against the more extreme forms of obscenity, we are reminded, and we remind ourselves, that "We, the People" have an ethical order and moral limits. The individual is made aware that the community in which he lives regards some things as beyond the pale of civility. This educative function of obscenity laws is ultimately more

significant than their coercive function. . . .

We might well consider whether, in the total absence of a public morality, it would be possible to protect children from obscenity. In an obscenity-saturated cultural environment, what good would it do to make laws forbidding the sale of prurient literature to children?. . .

Elsewhere I have suggested a legal formula for weighing and balancing the literary or intellectual qualities of a work against its prurient appeals. This "balancing" approach would have to include special provisions for protection of serious literature. It should be provided that in borderline cases the consideration of redeeming social importance shall always predominate. And it might be a further condition that works clearly acknowledged by the literary community as possessing *a high degree* of aesthetic worth are absolutely protected, regardless of their prurient effect on the average man. . . .

An ethic of self-expression need not result in unlimited sexual freedom and the wholesale dissolution of civility in self-indulgence. But when this result is avoided it is probably because the ethic of self-expression has been resisted and modified by a countervailing ethic. And the countervailing ethic cannot be expected to maintain itself without any attention from educational and other social institutions.

The most thoughtful proponents of the sexual revolution do not advocate or welcome unlimited sexual freedom. They seek a proper balance between individual spontaneity and restraint in the sexual relation, and they believe that this can be promoted by the new permissiveness. But a proper balance requires that there be guidelines and standards that sometimes take the form of rules, customs, and conventions. Guidelines and standards can also take the form of models of excellence—models of the better and the worse, the noble and the base, in sexual, moral, and aesthetic matters. But neither rules nor models of excellence can long survive in those places where nothing is taught and preached but liberation.

The total triumph of an ethic of self-expression would constitute a national catastrophe, endangering not just morality but freedom itself. The freedom to express ourselves is rendered meaningless when it becomes its own end and the only end. For, then, we lose the capacity to distinguish between a free exchange of ideas and an outburst of passion, between a genuine search for truth and an appeal to sensuality, between the art that ennobles and the pornography that debases. In such a climate of moral and aesthetic indifference, freedom of expression loses its justification. And the consequences of its abuse may then become too great for the community to bear.

These larger ethical and cultural issues are beyond the reach of the law. They are questions of education in the broadest sense. We need a countervailing ethic.

● ● ●

POSTSCRIPT

SHOULD OBSCENITY BE PROTECTED
AS FREE SPEECH?

Not all opponents of obscenity will concede, as Clor does, that the available evidence does not warrant a causal connection between obscenity and antisocial conduct. However, Clor's appeal is to society's right to preserve basic values, such as the privacy and dignity of human beings. What are basic "values" for Clor are matters of "taste" for Frank. Frank's most cherished value, which he believed was enshrined in the Constitution's First Amendment, is the right to advocate dissenting values.

Professor Clor has himself provided elsewhere the fullest philosophical analysis of the issue in the context of American practice. in OBSCENITY AND PUBLIC MORALITY (University of Chicago, 1969), Clor developed at length a position similar to that expressed in this essay. From the perspective of a public prosecutor of pornography, Richard H. Kuh has written a non-technical defense of legal censorship in FOOLISH FIGLEAVES (Macmillan, 1967). Charles Rembar, who was attorney for the defense in several leading obscenity cases, has written a lively defense of the right of obscenity in THE END OF OBSCENITY (Random House, 1968).

But there is no "end of obscenity" or of debate about it. Every age redefines it, and in the United States at the present time, we may suspect that every court defines it differently. The 1973 decisions are by no means the last word from the Supreme Court. Changing morals and changing issues, changing perceptions of the social consequences of obscenity and pornography, and (not least) changing membership of the Supreme Court will result in still more refinements of what legal standards are compatible with constitutional guarantees. Scholars will also contribute to clarification—and confusion—of the issue. The ten volumes of the presidential Commission on Obscenity and Pornography, published in 1970, have been followed by a number of technical studies on the relationship between obscenity and social behavior. Where evidence is likely to remain less than conclusive, advocates of opposed positions are likely to find confirmation of their biases.

ISSUE 15

NATIONAL SECURITY VERSUS CIVIL LIBERTY: SHOULD IT BE A CRIME TO IDENTIFY C.I.A. AGENTS?

YES: Senator John Chafee, from *Hearings on the Intelligence Identities Protection Act of 1981*, 97th Congress

NO: Jerry Berman and Morton Halperin, from *Hearings on the Intelligence Identities Protection Act of 1981*, 97th Congress

---

ISSUE SUMMARY

YES: Senator John Chafee outlines his view that the publication of the names of C.I.A. agents is a threat to the lives of the agents as well as to the national security and should be prohibited.

NO: Former Defense Department official Halperin and legislative council Berman, contend that the names of many agents are available from the government's own sources and that to prohibit the publication of these names would violate the principles of free speech.

Even before the Constitution was drafted there were worries about the security of the nation against rebels and renegades. The Constitutional Convention of 1787 was haunted by the specter of "Shays' Rebellion," an agrarian uprising in western Massachusetts. Writing from France, Thomas Jefferson scoffed at the alarums: "I hold it that a little rebellion now and then is a good thing. . . ." Jefferson may have been right, but slightly more than seventy years later the nation faced not a "little rebellion" but a cataclysm, and Abraham Lincoln took a sterner view. He jailed newspaper editors, allowed civilians to be tried in summary military courts, and defied an order by the Chief Justice of the Supreme Court to release a rebel suspect. Replying to the charge that he was violating the Constitution, Lincoln said that, on the contrary, he was defending it. "Are all the laws *but one* to go unexecuted, and the government itself to go to pieces lest that one be violated?" Much the same reasoning was used by government officials during World War I to justify their prosecution of antiwar activists, and the Supreme Court later backed them up in a famous case. In *Schenck v. United States* (1919) the Supreme Court held that during the war emergency certain speeches that would otherwise be protected by the First Amendment could be punished by the government. "The character of every act depends upon the circumstances in which it is done."

In the present period of American history the danger is less easy to define. Since shortly after World War II the United States and the Soviet Union have not been involved in a shooting war with each other, but they can hardly be said to be living in peace. Thomas Hobbes, a philosopher of the seventeenth century, put it shrewdly enough to sum up the present situation: "For WAR consisteth not in battle only, or the act of fighting; but in a tract of time, wherein the will to contend by battle is sufficiently known. . . ." This "will to contend" is demonstrated in countless ways, from the soldiers on both sides practicing missile launches to the struggle going on in the back alleys of the world between the Soviet and American secret services, each with its shadowy army of informers, turncoats, and double agents.

What is troubling about the present period of tension is its length. The Cold War has occupied a Hobbesian "tract of time" which approaches forty years, and there is no end in sight. What freedoms must be sacrificed so that our "will to contend"—or our means—can remain strong? A dramatic case study of how this issue applies today is the controversy growing out of the activities of Philip Agee, an ex-C.I.A. agent.

In the early 1970s Philip Agee not only left the C.I.A. but turned against it with a vengeance. In 1974 he published *Inside the Company: C.I.A. Diary*, which purported to describe the secret operations of the Agency and included names of persons Agee claimed were covert agents. Around the same time he became associated with a magazine called *Counterspy*, which also listed alleged agents. Shortly after being named in *Counterspy* the C.I.A. Station Chief in Athens, Richard Welch, was assasinated. Agee later became affiliated with a newletter, *Covert Action Information Bulletin*, which continued the practice of naming individuals which it identified as C.I.A. operatives. In 1980 the *Bulletin's* chief editor, Louis Wolf, held a press conference in Jamaica at which he identified fifteen Americans living there as C.I.A. officers. Wolf listed their names, home addresses, license plate numbers, and descriptions of their cars. The homes of two of those named were later attacked by men armed with machine guns and grenades.

To protect American intelligence agents against the kind of exposure to which Agee and others have dedicated themselves, Congress in 1980 began work on the Intelligence Identities Act, which was signed into law two years later by President Reagan. The most controversial section of the statute is one which makes it a serious crime for anyone with "reason to believe" that such revelations would harm our intelligence service to engage in a "pattern of activities" designed to expose American secret agents. This section may be broad enough to allow prosecution of someone who names agents after consulting material already published and in the public domain, and it does not require direct proof of malicious intent. These are among the reasons why Jerry Berman and Morton Halperin of the American Civil Liberties Union testified against the bill when it was being debated before a Senate subcommittee in 1981. During those same hearings, Senator John H. Chafee of Rhode Island, the bill's chief Senate sponsor, argued the need and propriety of such legislation. Their testimony follows.

YES

John Chafee

THE DANGERS OF NAMING NAMES

Thank you, Mr. Chairman, and members of the committee.

First I want to say that I appreciate a great deal, Mr. Chairman and members that you have moved expeditiously with this piece of legislation that I consider of great importance. . . .

The purpose of the Intelligence Identities Protection Act is to strengthen the intelligence capabilities of the United States by prohibiting the unauthorized disclosure of information identifying certain American intelligence officers, agents, and sources of information. In short, the bill places criminal penalties on those enemies of the American intelligence community engaged in the pernicious activity of naming names.

In my judgment, the governmental protection of the identities of American intelligence officers is an idea whose time has come and indeed it is long overdue. As has been mentioned in previous remarks, others have made efforts in this field. My colleague, Senator Bentsen, introduced bills which would accomplish this purpose in 1976 and 1977, following the tragic murder of Richard Welch in Athens in December 1975. . . .

The Republican Party platform in 1980 contained a plank supporting legislation "to invoke criminal sanctions against anyone who discloses the identities of U.S. intelligence officers." Mr. William Casey and Admiral Turner have both publicly expressed their support for intelligence identities protection, and of course I am delighted that Mr. Casey will be testifying this morning.

Our bill, this one we are considering today, is the only one to receive the endorsement of both the Reagan and the Carter administrations' Justice Departments. Support for this legislation also comes from a broad, bipartisan base of Senators with extensive knowledge and experience in intelligence and national security affairs. . . .

Mr. Chairman, the expeditious passage of this legislation in my judgement is vital to the lives and safety of those Americans who serve this Congress and

From, *Hearings on the Intelligence Identities Protection Act of 1981,* 97th Congress.

this Nation on difficult and dangerous missions abroad.

Now, Mr. Chairman, opponents of this legislation prevented its coming to the floor of the Senate last year in the closing hours. As a result, the 96th Congress completed its business without offering us the opportunity for free debate and vote. Since that time, I am told that the Covert Action Information Bulletin has published additional names of alleged covert agents, and their editors have traveled abroad to pursue this pernicious activity. As a consequence, six Americans were expelled from Mozambique recently following charges of engaging in espionage there.

A great deal of debate has centered on the constitutional issues of intelligence identities legislation. The American Civil Liberties Union, for example, recently referred to this sort of legislation as "a violation of the first amendment."

The section of the first amendment to the Constitution that pertains to our discussion states that: "Congress shall make no law . . . abridging the freedom of speech, or of the press. . . ." The first point that I wish to make with regard to this amendment is the provisions of the Bill of Rights cannot be applied with absolute literalness; but are subject to exceptions.

It has long been recognized that the free speech clause of the Constitution cannot wipe out common law regarding obscenity, profanity, and the defamation of individuals. This point was reiterated by Justice Oliver Wendell Holmes in the classic Espionage Act decisions in 1919 when he stated:

> The first amendment . . . obviously was not intended to give immunity for every possible use of language. . . . The most stringent protection of free speech would not protect a man in falsely shouting fire in a theater and causing a panic.

A second and equally important part is that if unlimited speech interferes with the legitimate purposes of Government, there must be some point at which the Government can step in. My uncle, Zechariah Chafee, who was the leading defender of free speech during his 37 years at the Harvard Law School, wrote in his book entitled "FREE SPEECH IN THE UNITED STATES" as follows:

> The true meaning of freedom of speech seems to be this. One of the most important purposes of society and government is the discovery and spread of truth on subjects of general concern. This is possible only through absolutely unlimited discussion. . . . Nevertheless, there are other purposes of government, such as order, the training of the young, protection against external aggression. Unlimited discussion sometimes interferes with these purposes, which must be balanced against freedom of speech.
>
> Or to put the matter another way, it is useless to define free speech by talk about rights. . . . Your right to swing your arms ends just where the other man's nose begins.
>
> The true boundary line on the first amendment can be fixed only when Congress and the courts realize that the principle on which speech is classified as lawful or unlawful involves the balancing against each other of two very important social interests, in public safety and in the search for truth.
>
> Thus, our problem of locating the boundary line of free speech is solved. It is fixed close to the point where words will give rise to unlawful acts.

It is evident, Mr. Chairman, that the activity of naming names has given rise to unlawful acts, and that it has endangered the lives and safety of American citizens abroad. I have already mentioned the

255

15. SHOULD IT BE A CRIME TO IDENTIFY C.I.A. AGENTS?

murder of Richard Welch in Greece. I am sure you also know of the series of assassination attempts in Kingston, Jamaica, following the Covert Action Information Bulletin's publication of the names of 15 alleged CIA officers there last year. What you may not know—and I think this is very important, Mr. Chairman and members of the committee—is how terribly those events have affected the lives of the American officials involved, their wives, and their children.

Mrs. Richard Kinsman, who wrote to me last year on this issue and whose letter I would like to insert into the record, has since stated that her life has been "terribly disrupted" by the assassination attempt on her husband and her family. Her children, one of whose bedrooms was riddled by machinegun bullets, "did not understand why anyone would want to hurt them."

The family has been forced to move several times for reasons of their own personal safety, required to give up jobs, sever friendships, withdraw from and re-enter schools, and suffer long periods of separation. They also wonder whether they will ever travel abroad again for any purpose.

I understand that another wife whose home was also the target of an assassination attempt in Jamaica last year was hospitalized for stress disorders following the incident. They have also left Jamaica. It is clear, then, that the personal safety and missions of those named have been placed in jeopardy by naming names.

In the balancing of two important social interests, public safety, and the search for truth, it is clear that the protection of the lives of our agents overseas far outweighs a pattern of activities which identifies and discloses the names of those agents. And I use the term "pattern of activity," Mr.

Chairman, because that is the language in section 601(c) of the act.

In this regard, Mr. Chairman, I think it is essential, and it is important to stress, that this bill would not prevent Mr. Philip Agee from publishing the articles contained in his publications, obnoxious though they might be. This bill would only restrain his publication of the names of persons he claims are covert agents.

By the same token, there is nothing in this bill which would prevent Louis Wolf from continuing to publish his Covert Action Information Bulletin which does contain articles purporting to be based on research into U.S. intelligence operations at home and abroad. I wish to stress this: This bulletin can continue to be published. The only impact of this legislation would be on the section of the bulletin entitled "Naming Names." And here, Mr. Chairman [indicating], is an example of "Naming Names." It sets forth the names of alleged agents serving this Nation and this Congress abroad.

I hope that this brief review of the constitutional questions will show that the first amendment does not provide absolute protection for all speech; and that the Government can in certain circumstances intervene in the exercise of free speech in the interest of public safety without jeopardizing the search for truth.

As the Attorney General stated last year on this subject:

> Our proper concern for individual liberties must be balanced with a concern for the safety of those who serve the Nation in difficult times and under dangerous conditions.

It goes without saying that these important constitutional considerations were very much in our minds when my colleagues and I worked up the final draft of the Intelligence Identities Protection Act. We are not challenging the Constitution. We are working with it. In my judgement, we have worked well within its limits. We have successfully followed what my uncle called the boundary line of free speech.

Mr. Chairman, I will not take the time this morning to discuss the specific provisions of S. 391, or to point out in detail how this formulation reflects our proper concern for first amendment rights. This has been the subject of previous testimony, and others will testify this morning, and it is part of the extensive record on this issue. I recommend the Intelligence Committee's Report on this subject, as well as the published hearing record of both the Intelligence and the Judiciary Committees.

However, there is one additional issue which I believe must be addressed before I conclude my remarks, because there has been so much confusion surrounding it. During the long debate on this issue, and in the hearings before the Senate Intelligence Committee, I have heard it suggested or implied that it should be acceptable for people to disclose the names of covert agents if this information derives from unclassified sources.

The implication of this view is that there exists somewhere in this Government an official but unclassified list of covert agents; and that those who have found this list should be free to publish the names thereon.

Mr. Chairman, I have studied the matter of covert agents within the Senate Intelligence Committee, and have even held a series of detailed hearings on the subject. Without going into specifics in this session, I can assure you that there is no such list. What we have found are unclassified official or semiofficial documents which contain the names of covert agents in among the names of other officials of the U.S.

Government. The covert agents are not identified. The very purpose of these documents is to cover or to hide the true identity of the covert agents named thereon, and in no case is an identification explicitly made.

However, to say that the Government has never published an unclassified list of covert agents as such does not mean that certain persons, employing basic principles of counterespionage, and after considerable effort, cannot determine identities of covert agents with some degree of accuracy. It is possible.

It is the purpose of S. 391 to punish the publication of names acquired through these techniques, regardless of whether the identification was made with reference to classified or unclassified material. It is not the mechanism of identification which places people's lives in jeopardy or threatens our intelligence capabilities; it is the actual publication of the names as covert agents that does so. It is the pattern of activity involved in the pernicious business of naming names that we want primarily to prevent.

In closing, Mr. Chairman, I would like to make a special appeal to you and to my colleagues on your committee to report S. 391 intact so that the interminable delays which seem to follow any change to a bill might be avoided. You have my assurance, in turn, that I will do whatever I can to see that this vital bill is moved with the deliberate speed it deserves.

Over the past 5 years, more than 2,000 names of alleged CIA officers have been identified and published by a small group of individuals whose stated purpose is to expose U.S. intelligence operations. I think it is time we legislated an end to this pernicious vendetta against the American intelligence community.

Mr. Chairman, we send fellow Americans, we in the U.S. Congress, members of the U.S. Government, abroad on dangerous missions. We owe it to them to do our utmost to protect their lives as we go about our business.

Finally, Mr. Chairman, it has been my privilege as a member of the Intelligence Committee to have traveled somewhat in different sections of the world. In doing so, I make an attempt to meet with our intelligence agent station chiefs and converse with them, discuss with them their problems, what we might do in the U.S. Senate as Members of the Senate, as members of the Intelligence Committee, to be more helpful to them in discharging their duties.

I can say, Mr. Chairman, that everywhere I go, without question, unanimously the question is raised that the most disconcerting activity that takes place, the most demoralizing activity, is the publication of names in [bulletins]. Our officers find it difficult to understand why nothing can be done about this.

Mr. Chairman, I have a deep personal interest in seeing—and I know this concern is shared by Members of the Committee here and Members of the Senate throughout—to do the best we can to protect the lives of our agents and their families abroad.

Thank you, Mr. Chairman. I would be glad to answer any questions that you might have. . . .

Senator Leahy. I wonder if I just might, Mr. Chairman, with your indulgence, ask a couple of questions. . . .

There is no question that we want to put an end to the pernicious practice of naming names of our cover intelligence personnel, especially in the case of the Covert Action Information Bulletin where it is being done purposely to impede foreign intelligence activities in the United States.

We all agree absolutely that that has to stop. What I am concerned about is how

we do it. The issues of the constitutionality of section 601(c) have been raised. Philip Heymann has suggested different language, and so on.

Maybe it is a philosophical question, John, that I have more than anything else. Do we run a great risk—even a greater risk in some ways—if we passed the bill, and if section 601(c) were to be found unconstitutionally broad? In some ways, is that not a greater risk? If that is the result of this effort, haven't we opened the floodgates, wouldn't it take years to restore any sense of security not only to our own personnel but to those that may act against them?

A number of constitutional scholars have said it would not be constitutional unless it contained an element of malicious intent or had purpose. Do you think we should adopt that approach?

Senator Chafee. First, Mr. Chairman and Senator Leahy, I want to pay tribute to the work you have done on the Senate Intelligence Committee, a very valuable member and you have as great concern in this area as any one member of the committee. I know that you have worked extremely hard to devise an approach in which we might solve this problem which bedevils all of us.

This section 601(c) has had support from the Justice Department. The version that is in the House is somewhat different in that it has an "intent" standard—what the Justice Department calls a "subjective standard of intent," whereas you will notice on line 4 in the bill where it uses the word "intended" in connection with the "pattern of activities," that is described as an "objective standard of intent," one that is not in the mind but can be weighed objectively.

So in answer to your question, it seems to me that what we have done here is to replace the subjective standard of intent with a more objective standard which re quires that the disclosure must be "in the course of a pattern of activities intended to identify and to expose covert agents and with reason to believe that such activities would impair and impede the foreign intelligence activities of the United States."

I do not think it has to be done with any malicious intent, because we have described the action. It is like—I suppose analogies are always dangerous—shooting somebody. You shoot them, and whether you do it with "intent" or not to murder them, it is a "killing" and it is punishable.

Senator Leahy. But you do recognize philosophically the problem that we would face? That if we were to pass one part of the statute and have it held unconstitutional, that it would almost encourage these activities?

Senator Chafee. Well, I do not think so, because I do not think that if this were found unconstitutional—I am not accepting the assumption—but if it were found unconstitutional, I just do not think responsible American citizens are going to go out and say: Three cheers! We can now publish all the names of all the agents we can discover, and we will do it freely.

I mean, I do not believe that the mass majority of Americans are going to do this. There is a limited group that is doing it now. But it is enough to cause damage.

● ● ●

NO

Jerry Berman
and Morton Halperin

CHILLING PUBLIC DEBATE

Mr. Chairman,

We want to thank you for extending the American Civil Liberties Union this opportunity to testify on S. 391, the "Intelligence Identities Protection Act of 1981." The American Civil Liberties Union is a non-profit, and non-partisan organization of over 200,000 members dedicated to defending the Bill of Rights.

The driving force behind S. 391 is, of course, the desire of the Administration and the Congress to provide protection for Americans serving their country abroad under cover and to prevent their intelligence relationships from becoming known to foreigners who may seek to harm them or neutralize their work. We do not condone the practice of naming names and we fully understand Congress' desire to do what it can to provide meaningful protection to those intelligence agents serving abroad, often in situations of danger.

At the same time, we believe the Congress must be mindful—and we believe it is—that this legislation, particularly section 601(c) will operate in an area, as one Committee Report puts it, "fraught with first amendment concerns. As such, it deserves the most careful scrutiny both to determine (1) whether its prohibitions will provide meaningful protection to our agents serving abroad so as to justify its limitation on freedom of speech, and (2) whether the legislation is drawn in such a way as to pass constitutional muster.

In testifying on last year's identical version of this bill, S. 2216 as reported by the Senate Intelligence Committee, we stressed before this Committee our view, one shared by over 60 law professors and constitutional experts, that section 601(c) (formerly section 501(c)) is unconstitutional on its face. While reiterating our position that the section is unconstitutional we want to focus our comments today on whether this bill will accomplish the purpose it is

From, *Hearings on the Intelligence Identities Protection Act of 1981*, 97th Congress.

designed to serve. In particular, will section 601(c)'s prohibitions make it difficult or impossible for foreign intelligence services, terrorist organizations, or others opposed to our interests to identify our intelligence officers serving under cover abroad? We believe the answer is no. If we are correct, then the legislation before you is merely symbolic in its protection for agents but does violence to the principles of the First Amendment. Certainly, Congress should not enact such legislation.

At the outset, we want to make it clear that we do not view sections 601(a) and (b) as symbolic or constitutionally defective. These sections would make it a crime for a present or former government official who learned the identity of CIA or FBI agents or sources through access to classified information to knowingly reveal those identities to an unauthorized person. Since such officials have obtained access to the identities of sources through their employment, we do not think the imposition of a criminal penalty on the disclosure of such information by these officials to be unreasonable. Moreover, these officials are in a position to reveal the identities of agents and sources under deep cover and whose identities cannot be gleaned from public sources.

Section 601(c), on the other hand, would seek to punish any person who "discloses any information that identifies an individual as a covert agent," even if the information is in the public domain or readily available to any person or group who takes the trouble to ferret it out. The information which is needed to identify most of those whose names are published is available, the CIA admits, from the *Biographic Register* and the diplomatic lists. According to the CIA, the group that is targeted for prosecution under this section, the Covert Action Information Bulletin, prints lists of CIA agents that are

> a regurgitation from some compendium ... others could be taken from reports or other kinds of documents that may have been in a classified context ... In short what they are taking it from is a garden variety biographical compendium. They are saying this is past history, but presently he is the CIA station chief in country X.

The *Biographic Register* is, of course, a United States government publication whose back issues are available in libraries around the world. Although the issues for the past few years have not been released, the State Department has not classified them, and the government may be forced to release them as a result of a pending Freedom of Information Act lawsuit brought on behalf of diplomatic historians. *Simpson v. Vance*, No. 79-1889 (D.C. Cir., Sept. 25, 1980). Indeed, the State Department considered decision not to classify the *Biographic Register* casts considerable doubt on the need for and wisdom of congressional enactment of section 601(c).

The techniques for determining the identities of CIA employees under light diplomatic cover from these publically available sources have been explained in several widely published articles. The root of the problem, according to the CIA, is that

> because of the disclosure of sensitive information based on privileged access and made by faithless government employees with the purpose of damaging U.S. intelligence efforts ... the public has become aware of indicators in these documents that can sometimes be used to distinguish CIA officers.

If the CIA were completely candid, it would admit that without regard to faithless employees, it has been widely known for many years that the *Biographic Register* could be used to determine which persons listed there are likely to be CIA officials, and journalists and academics have routinely used this technique to determine who the CIA officers in any given capital are.

The issue, Mr. Chairman, is not disclosures made by the press or public but the failure to provide adequate cover for our intelligence officers abroad. And we are not alone in making this observation. As the Heritage Foundation states in its report and recommendations on the Intelligence Community:

> Unfortunately, the 'official cover' provided to officers of the Central Intelligence Agency, usually by the Department of State, is routinely inadequate to withstand all but the most cursory of inspections.

The main import of this is that Congress cannot, by virtue of this legislation, prevent any group in a foreign country which seeks to disrupt American intelligence activities or to harm CIA employees from learning the identities of the CIA employees stationed under diplomatic cover in its capital. Certainly, the bill will not protect against the counterintelligence activities of hostile intelligence services or others who use the surveillance techniques these groups are said to use.

THE FIRST AMENDMENT ISSUE

While section 601(c) will not stop foreigners from learning the identities of CIA employees under diplomatic cover and may even encourage them to use the above mentioned techniques by underscoring their effectiveness, section 601(c) will clearly succeed in chilling public debate about intelligence matters in violation of the First Amendment. The legislation before you could make criminal the publication of identities in circumstances fully protected by the First Amendment and in many circumstances where the publication of intelligence identities is essential for understanding or debating important issues.

To understand the potential impact of this bill on public debate, it is first of all necessary to separate rhetoric from reality as to the breadth of the intelligence identities protected by this legislation. Because the protection of Americans serving abroad in a covert capacity is the principal concern of the bill's drafters, they have often described the reach of the legislation in terms which would lead the public to believe that only the identities of Americans serving abroad would be off limits to the press or public. As Senator Chaffee put it last year:

> We send fellow Americans abroad on dangerous missions which are supported by us as Senators. We owe it to them to do our utmost to protect their lives as they go about our business.

Or as Frank Carlucci, former Deputy Director of Central Intelligence, stated before this Committee in September of 1980

> (O)ur officers willingly have accepted the risks necessarily inherent in their taxing and dangerous occupation. They have not accepted the risk of being stabbed in the back by their fellow countrymen and of being left unprotected by their Nation's government.

In fact, S. 391's definition of "cover agent" (sec. 606(4)) is far broader. While it covers United States intelligence officers or employees who are serving abroad or who have served abroad in the last five years and United States citizens who are residing abroad and acting outside the United States as agents, informants, or sources of operational assistance to our intelligence agencies, it also includes all foreigners in the United States and abroad who at any time have served as agents, informants, or sources of operational assistance to our intelligence agencies. By amendment last year, covert agent also includes FBI agents and informants with the foreign counterintelligence and counterterrorism components of the FBI in the United States or abroad.

Because of the breadth of the definition of "covert agent," witnesses before this and other committees have fairly argued that, unless narrowed in some other way, section 601(c) could have applied to a number of past press stories, academic studies, and other research had it been on the books. For example,

—the *New York Times* story that Francis Gary Powers was pilot of the U-2 spy plane;
—the *Washington Post* story that King Hussein of Jordan was an agent or source of operational assistance to the CIA;
—press stories about Cubans involved in the Bay of Pigs operation;
—FBI agents involved in illegal breakins targeted against persons associated with the Weather Underground (a counterintelligence, counterterrorism investigation);
—a *Wall Street Journal* article detailing covert ties between the CIA and Boeing's Japanese agent.

In all of these stories, the press or an author made the decision that the name was essential to tell the story or to give it credibility. All of the stories involve "covert agents" as defined in S. 391, even though in none of these cases is it arguable that the narrow purpose of the bill is being served— the protection of Americans serving abroad

in circumstances which place their lives in jeopardy.

According to the bill's drafters and supporters, it is not their intent to reach cases such as this, but only those who are in the business of "naming names." To avoid this result, they added the requirement that a person must be shown to be engaged in

a pattern of activities intended to identify and expose covert agents . . .

However, we believe this describes the activities of the press, researchers, and scholars. The very act of investigative reporting to uncover CIA involvement in foreign assassination plots or illegal FBI COINTELPRO activities is a "pattern of activities intended to identify and expose covert agents . . ." And the Justice Department testified that "a single act of disclosure" meets the disclosure element of the bill.

Although the Senate Intelligence Committee Report of last year is replete with language that suggests that the bill distinguishes between public communication and information essential to informed discussion and the indiscriminate naming of names, the committee made a change in the bill during mark-up at the suggestion of Justice Department officials who wanted to avoid such distinction. It included an objective "reason to believe" standard rather than a subjective, bad purpose test. This "objective" standard would clearly cover members of the press and those contributing to public debate and not simply those in the business of naming names.

Given the definition of covert agent, the absence of bad purpose, and the fact that investigative reporters may engage in a "pattern of activities intended to identify and expose covert agents," S. 391 as

15. SHOULD IT BE A CRIME TO IDENTIFY C.I.A. AGENTS?

introduced could reach the following scenarios,

—A reporter suspects that the Administration in its eagerness to give aid and assistance to the Savimbi led effort in Angola has interpreted the Clark Amendment to permit aid which is used for other than military purposes. He investigates, discovers, and exposes the fact that the CIA is giving such aid to Savimbi. He reports also that the intelligence committees were not notified of the aid, in apparent violation of the oversight provisions of the National Security Act as amended last year.

—A reporter suspects that a terrorist group made up of Cuban exiles in Florida is controlled by persons who were former sources of operational assistance to the CIA. She investigates, uncovers the past CIA relationships, and publishes the story, giving their identities.

These scenarios and a number of others make it clear that the scope of the bill would cover legitimate newsgathering activity and public debate on important intelligence and foreign policy issues. We understand the drafters to be saying they have no intention of covering such situations, but the plain language of the bill remains very broad and would clearly chill public debate.

THE CONSTITUTIONAL ISSUE

We believe that section 601(c) is facially unconstitutional in punishing the publication of information which has come into the possession of private citizens, the public, and the press. We believe this is so even if the information were classified, see *New York Times v. United States*, 403 U.S. 713 (1971) but particularly because it includes information—however sensitive— which has come into the public domain. The government has the right to restrict sensitive information, but it cannot attempt to punish its publication once it has become public or comes into the possession of the press. A line of Supreme Court cases supports this position. *Landmark Communications, Inc. v. Virginia*, 435 U.S. 829 (1978) (statute prohibiting publication of confidential proceeding into judicial misconduct); *Cox Broadcasting v. Cohn*, 420 U.S. 469 (1975) (statute prohibiting publication of the identity of a juvenile offender which [the] press obtained from court records). As Justice Burger has stated

> The government cannot restrain publication of whatever information the media acquires—and which they elect to reveal.

... Perhaps the case most directly on point is the widely quoted opinion of Judge Learned Hand in *United States v. Heine*, 151 F. 2d 813 (1945). Heine engaged in an activity very similar to that which appears to have given rise to section 601(c) of S. 391. In overturning this conviction for espionage, Judge Hand stated

> The information which Heine collected was from various sources: ordinary magazines, books and newspapers: technical catalogues, handbooks and journals; . . . This material he condensed and arranged in his reports . . . All this information came from sources that were lawfully accessible to anyone who was willing to take the pains to find, sift, and collate it.

Although it can be argued that *Heine* simply involves statutory interpretation, it can also be read as a judicial interpretation which saved the constitutionality of the espionage statute by excluding analysis of published information even if undertaken to aid a hostile foreign nation. In this regard, it should be pointed out that the Justice Department last year cited *Heine* in testifying that section 501(c) of S. 2216 and H.R. 5615 was constitutionally dubious. Stating that no one can be convicted of espionage or of compromising information relating to the national defense "if the information was made available to the public, or if the government did not attempt to restrict its dissemination or if the information was available to everyone from lawfully accessible sources," Deputy Assistant Attorney General Robert L. Keuch expressed critical doubts about section 501(c):

> In proposing a section of such breadth, S. 2216 marches overbodly, we think, into a difficult area of political, as opposed to scientific, 'born classified' information, in a context that will often border on areas of important public policy debate . . . A speaker's statements about covert activities could be punished even though they are not based on access to classified information, do not use inside methodology acquired by the speaker in government service, and are unimbued with any special authority from former government service. . . .

Unaccountably, the Justice Department retracted its constitutional concerns when the Senate Intelligence Committee amended section 501(c) (now 601 (c)) to add a "pattern of activities" element and changed the specific intent requirement (intent to impair or impede intelligence activities) to an objective intent (reason to believe that such activities would impair or impede the foreign intelligence activities of the United States). To be sure, the Justice Department expressed the concern that the subjective intent element could have a "chilling effect" on critics of intelligence activities:

> A mainstream journalist who occasionally writes stories based on public information concerning which foreign leaders are thought to have intelligence relationships with the United States may fear that any other stories by him critical of the CIA will be taken as evidence of an intent to impede foreign intelligence activities.

However, the "reason to believe" standard does not cure the "chilling effect" since critic and non critic must guess as to whether or not he or she is covered by the statute and certainly does not resolve the "political born classified" problem.

Significantly, while the ACLU and a number of constitutional experts such as Lawrence Tribe of Harvard and Floyd Abrams believe that the section cannot be made constitutional, the weight of opinion is that if section 601(c) has any chance of passing constitutional muster, it must include a specific intent, or bad purpose requirement. Not, we might add, a general "intent to impair or impede intelligence activities" as set forth in H.R. 4—which every citizen has a right to go through speech and communication under the First Amendment—but a bad purpose such as giving advantage to a foreign power or neutralizing the activities of an agent by the fact of disclosure itself. In this regard, see *Gorin v. United States*, 312 U.S. 19 (1941) interpreting the espionage statute's "intent or reason to believe that (information) will be used to the injury of the United States or to the advantage of a foreign nation" to require bad faith on the part of the defendant. . . .

CONCLUSION

Mr. Chairman, S. 391 is unprecedented legislation. Only twice in our history has

15. SHOULD IT BE A CRIME TO IDENTIFY C.I.A. AGENTS?

Congress legislated a prohibition on the right of the press to publish classified information, a narrow prohibition on publishing codes, 18 U.S.C. S. 798 and highly sensitive atomic energy information, 42 U.S.C. S. 2274. Both involve highly technical information which minimally restrict the flow of news. When broader categories of information have been involved, such as when Congress considered and enacted the current espionage laws, the press and publication were excluded from the reach of the statutes. . . .

As we and others have shown, S. 391's section 601(c) can seriously impact on speech and communication concerning important intelligence and foreign policy matters. It is opposed on policy and constitutional grounds by almost every major press organization, by leading newspapers including the *New York Times,* the *Washington Post* and, *Chicago Tribune,* and by over 60 law professors and constitutional experts. Even most constitutional experts who favor this legislation, oppose the Senate version.

Moreover, the bill may have a serious impact on First Amendment principles without solving the problem of protecting our agents and intelligence activities overseas. Because of light cover, the bill may amount to no more than a symbolic gesture if passed.

We urge you not to pass S. 391's section 601(c). However, if you are going to proceed, we ask you to explore ways to narrow the reach of the bill. For example, the definition of covert agent should be narrowed to include only those U.S. officers or employees serving overseas. Foreign leaders and FBI agents at home should be excluded from the definition. At the same time, the bill should substitute a bad purpose, perhaps along the lines of the espionage statutes, in place of the objective "reason to believe" standard. (We submit that both intent and reason to believe present similar prosecution proof and graymail problems and should not be the basis for choosing one or the other formulation). Finally, we believe that a "justification" defense, which professor Robert Bork implies, should be spelled out in the bill, so that it will not apply if the disclosure involves illegal or unauthorized intelligence activities.

We again thank you for the opportunity to testify today on S. 391.

• • •

POSTSCRIPT

SHOULD IT BE A CRIME TO
IDENTIFY C.I.A. AGENTS?

Note that Berman and Halperin, far from holding any brief for Philip Agee, apparently would not object to legislation punishing actions such as his; we can infer this from their stated support of those sections of the Intelligence Identities Protection Act which would punish any former government official who revealed to unauthorized persons classified names of C.I.A. officials. The mainstream media generally take a similar view, and even liberal newspapers like the *New York Times* and the *Washington Post* have harshly condemned Agee's exposures. All of this raises an interesting question. If even liberal spokesmen see nothing unconstitutional in punishing an ex-C.I.A. agent who reveals classified names, then what about punishing a newspaper reporter who obtains the names from the ex-agent and then publishes them? Are the cases logically separable? The second case may not be purely hypothetical. In a 1981 article in *The Nation,* Agee said that one *New York Times* reporter spoke to him on the phone between New York and Amsterdam for four hours, taking down "name after name." Agee added, sarcastically: "For the *Times* to publish those names and others was, of course, 'legitimate' reporting. . . ."

It may be a sign of the changing times that Halperin and Berman strike a more cautious and conservative note in their 1981 testimony than that in a book Halperin co-authored with Daniel Hoffman in 1977. In that book, TOP SECRET (New Republic Books), the press was criticized for being too timid, too willing "to accept official interpretations of the needs of national security." The authors were prepared to concede that their proposals for "a substantially more open system" might well "interfere with certain aspects of national security policy as presently conceived." Halperin's commitment to "openness" may be in part a reaction to his own experience of being secretly wiretapped while serving on the staff of Henry Kissinger during the Nixon Administration—apparently at Kissinger's own directive. This and other intrusions into privacy in the name of "national security" are detailed in David Wise's THE AMERICAN POLICE STATE (Random House, 1976). For a more general and long-term historical treatment of the issue of liberty versus security in America, see the classic work by Senator Chafee's late uncle Zechariah, THE BLESSINGS OF LIBERTY (Greenwood, 1973), a reprint of the 1956 edition.

ISSUE 16

SHOULD ABORTION BE OUTLAWED?

YES: John Noonan, from A PRIVATE CHOICE: ABORTION IN AMERICA IN THE SEVENTIES (The Free Press, 1979)

NO: Riane Eisler, from "The Human Life Amendment and the Future of Human Life," *Humanist,* September/October 1981

ISSUE SUMMARY

YES: Professor of Law, John Noonan, holds that the right to abortion on demand is divisive, dangerous and destructive of liberty.

NO: Attorney, Riane Eisler, voices her concern that the proposed Constitutional amendment to ban abortion will rob women of their most basic right—to exercise control over their own bodies.

At one time, laws forbade even the publication of information regarding contraception and abortion, and it was not until 1965 that the Supreme Court declared that the law could not prohibit the dispensing of contraceptive devices to married men and women. In 1973 the Supreme Court made its landmark rulings on abortion which have shaped the subsequent political debates. The Court ruled that during the first trimester of pregnancy women have a constitutionally protected right to secure an abortion, and during the second trimester of pregnancy (that is, the fourth through sixth months), only restrictions reasonably related to a woman's health could be imposed upon her right to secure an abortion. Only during the final three months of pregnancy, the Supreme Court ruled, may the state prohibit abortion, but even then medical judgment can overrule the state where physicians believe an abortion is indicated to preserve the mother's life or health. This includes psychological as well as physical well-being.

The Court's rulings aroused a storm of controversy that has not abated, and it is not likely to die down within the foreseeable future. Although illegal abortions were widely performed before state laws forbidding abortions had been invalidated, the number of abortions increased rapidly in the years after the Court's 1973 decisions. It has been estimated that over one million abortions have been performed in each of the past several years. If current trends continue, four out of every ten girls will become pregnant between the ages of fourteen and twenty. Barring changes in the law, half of these pregnancies will be terminated by abortion.

Can a statute declare the existence of a scientific fact? For the opponents of abortion, the beginning of life at conception is a fact, and law may appropriately restate and enforce it. They argue that the human fetus is a live human being, and they note all the familiar signs of life displayed by the fetus: a beating heart, brain waves, thumb-sucking, and so on. For the defenders of abortion, human life does not begin before the development of specifically human characteristics and possibly not until the birth of a child. As Justice Blackmun put it in 1973: "There has always been strong support for the view that life does not begin until live birth."

Distinctions can be made regarding the right to abortion where pregnancy is caused by rape or results from incest, where the health of either the pregnant woman or the baby may be adversely affected, where the pregnant woman is unmarried and either unwilling or unable to marry the man with whom she was intimate, or where economic circumstances create pressures to limit family size, and where the pregnant woman makes a private choice not to have a child. Most of the people who feel most strongly about the right of abortion do not make most of these distinctions, and either favor or oppose the right without qualifications. While public opinion polls show majorities favoring the right of abortion where rape, incest or the life of the mother are involved, different polls reach contradictory conclusions regarding public sentiment as to the general right of abortion.

The opponents of abortion have launched a counterattack against the Supreme Court's decisions. Federal funding for Medicaid abortions has been cut off, and federal courts have affirmed the Congress's right not to pay for abortions. Critics of the law have charged that it simply discriminates against poor women, because it does not inhibit the ability to obtain an abortion for women who are able to pay for it. Broader efforts to outlaw abortion have taken the forms of a proposed Human Rights Amendment and a Human Rights Bill. The Amendment, as proposed by Utah Senator Orrin Hatch, would declare the right of the federal government or any of the states to outlaw abortions.

Can an act of Congress reverse a Supreme Court decision? If the Court had declared the existence of a constitutional right, opponents of the proposal believe that an act of Congress cannot change the fundamental law. On the other side, those who advocate adoption of a law believe that it would demonstrate the intent of the nation's lawmakers, prod the Court to reconsider the issue, and perhaps lead to a constitutional amendment.

At bottom, for all the politics in the analyses of John T. Noonan urging the outlawing of abortion and of Riane Eisler defending the right of abortion, the controlling factors for most Americans are moral. On one side abortion is perceived, in the words of the American Life Lobby, as "the death of a new life." On the other side it is viewed, in Justice Brennan's opinion in the 1973 abortion cases, as "the right of the individual . . . to be free from unwarranted governmental intrusion."

YES   John T. Noonan, Jr.

A PRIVATE CHOICE

Once or twice in a century an issue arises so divisive in its nature, so far-reaching in its consequences, and so deep in its foundations that it calls every person to take a stand. Abortion, it once appeared, was an unlikely candidate to be such an issue. The nature of the act of abortion, for those who contemplated it steadily, and the unpleasantness of the procedures for anyone involved in them induced most persons to turn their attention elsewhere. Politically, the subject was untouchable before the 1960s. No one in a public forum sought to challenge the accepted limits. Later, when challengers did come forward, few politicians wanted to take sides: The issue cut across party lines, the parties had no pat partisan formulas for containing it, and each side was good at remembering its enemies. The politicians wished that the subject had never come up. Then they wished it would go away. In this respect abortion became what slavery had been: a plague for the parties and the party professionals.

Abortion has not gone away. Today it divides the country. Neutrality for a legislator is impossible. Each side believes with deep conviction that it is right. But both sides cannot be right, and conflict in theory means conflict in practice. Legalized as a private act, abortion has become a public issue. It has become the kind of public issue that compels almost everyone to take a stand.

Each act of abortion is, by declaration of the Supreme Court of the United States, a private decision. Yet each act of abortion bears on the structure of marriage and the family, the role and duties of parents, the limitations of the paternal part in procreation, and the virtues that characterize a mother. Each act of abortion bears on the orientation and responsibilities of the obstetrician, the nurse, the hospital administrator, and the hospital trustee. The acceptance of abortion affects the professor and student of medicine and the professor and student of law. In the United States, abortion on a large scale requires the participation of the federal and state governments.

Overarching the whole system of private choice is the command of the judiciary, whose will has brought abortion to public acceptability and whose power has intervened constantly to sustain the liberty of abortion against public repudiation. The duties of the judges vis-a-vis an elected legislature, the respect of federal judges for the states in a federal system, the constitutional authority of judges to appropriate money from the federal Treasury — all of these questions of judicial conduct have become entwined with the abortion controversy.

The "issue" of abortion is not a single dispute over a hairline distinction. It is many-faceted. It has turned into a multiplicity of issues. Response to one aspect or another of the controversy has affected the consciences of college students in San Diego, jurymen in Boston, physicians in Philadelphia, and Treasury officials in Washington. As abortion has acted on their consciences, their responses have shaped their sense of their social obligations. What is by decree of the Supreme Court the most private of choices has become in recent American experience the center of the most public of conflicts.

In DEMOCRACY IN AMERICA, Tocqueville describes the key role in American government of "the party" of lawyers. By that phrase he does not mean to indicate that the lawyers were organized like the Democrats or Whigs or that they acted by prearranged concert. He means that by education, interest, and values the lawyers shared certain goals and, without the necessity of consultation as to specific plans, worked together to achieve those goals.

To adapt Tocqueville's concept of party to the present, there is in the United States today a group of persons, connected by no organization or formal tie, whose common education, interest, and values are such that having worked together to create the liberty of abortion in America, they now work to maintain it. Their dynamism expands the conflict and makes its consensual resolution chimerical.

Part of the public controversy is intractable. It depends on assumptions and judgments about what human beings are and about what human beings should do for one another. These convictions and conclusions are not easily reached by argument. They rest on particular perspectives that are bound to the whole personality and can shift only with a reorientation of the person. But much of the controversy lies in a less personal domain and can be resolved by looking at evidence, the kind of evidence which is normally decisive in any battle over social policy, evidence of what a policy means for the society. In this case the evidence is how acceptance of abortion as a private choice affects American society.

Tocqueville long ago observed that we are a nation of lawyers and that every national issue is turned into a judicial question. Abortion as a public matter has been primarily a matter of what judges have decided the public must do. Without the courts the whole controversy would have had a very different, and much smaller, shape. The federal judiciary has created a new constitutional liberty, fed it, fostered it, and protected it. The Supreme Court in behalf of this liberty has revolutionized the legal structure of the family. Individual federal judges have not hesitated to set aside the oldest of laws — that on murder itself — and the most basic of constitutional distributions of power — that giving Congress the power of the purse — to make the new liberty effective in America. The impact of the acts of the judges on the Constitution, on federalism, and on the legal position of the family is evidence to be assessed by every participant in the

American political process as each participant decides whether the judge-made liberty of abortion should be fortified, expanded, or expunged.

Other evidence is of a more palpable
kind: One should be able to touch it with
one's finger or see it with one's eye. It
includes what happens in dilation and
curettage, in suction vacuuming, and in
saline or prostaglandin injection. It includes the nature of the object of these
operations. This evidence is physical, and
it is far more than physical, since the
response of a human being to phenomena
is more than a physical reaction. Such facts
can be read in the light of human experience and have a strength and significance beyond their gross physical dimensions. One can look at them and intuit how
the issue should be decided.

Walter Jackson Bate, in his memorable
life of that master moralist, Samuel Johnson, observes that the secret of Johnson's
power was his unblinking perception of
reality, Bate writes, to attend to "that rarest
of all things for confused and frightened
human nature — the obvious." The evidence to be examined is of that rare kind.

Yet the obvious is hard to see for a
physical reason: The living unborn child is
not normally accessible to perception, although ultrasound, television, and fetol-
ogy have been lifting this physical barrier.
The evidence is also hard to see because
the legends embroidered by partisans and
conveyed by the press have shielded
Americans from what has happened in
their courts and in their hospitals. The
evidence is hardest to see because we are
reluctant to see it. . . .

The difficulty for professionals of grasp-
ing that what they do for professional
reasons may be evil is extreme. It is even
difficult for them to understand that it is

their own conduct which is questioned.
The readers of Orwell do not suppose that
they are the ones making the linguistic
changes necessary for an Orwellian society.

Among the German researchers convicted at Nuremberg of experimenting on
human beings without their consent was
Gerhard Rose, described by the American
court that convicted him as "a physician of
large experience, for many years recognized as an expert in tropical diseases."
The research for which other German
physicians were punished by the American
tribunal included work to develop a vaccine for typhus, work on a vaccine for
malaria, work to test a vitamin compound
designed to make sea water usable in
emergencies. In each of these instances
the research design, which included experiments on human subjects, was not
framed in wanton cruelty but composed to
further highly humane purposes. The principal defendant, Karl Brandt, could exclaim, "Here I am, a subject of the most
frightful charges, as if I had been a man
without heart or conscience. . . . Every patient was to me like a brother." Gerhard
Rose could observe that all medical advance depended on experiment on human
beings and that in the majority of cases
there was no true consent but an "exploitation of ignorance, frivolity, or economic distress." He could say in good faith
that he had only done what other researchers did, "to serve the good of humanity." The defendant Wilhelm Beigl-
bock was able to invoke the words over the
entrance gate of the General Hospital in
Vienna, "*Saluti et solatio aegrorum* — To
the health and consolation of the sick."
These words, he could say, "demand the
highest accomplishments of a doctor's
duties" and are "the motive for the most
successful work in the large field of medical
work." It was with this motive, he would

tell his judges, that he had worked on the vitamins to transform sea water and had used human beings in his experiments. These were professional men carrying out professional tasks. They were unwilling to believe that what they had done was evil. . . .

If we look at "that rarest of all things for confused and frightened human nature — the obvious," the unborn child is the object of an abortion. If the masks are to be removed, we must ask what an abortion is. Three methods are usual:

In the first trimester, dilation and curettage (D and C) is most common. The cervix is dilated and the unborn child is the subject of the curettage. The curettage is either "sharp" or "suction." Sharp curettage is by a stainless steel scraper called a curet or curette, wielded by hand. Suction curettage is by a vacuum pump with a curet attached.

The method of operation in sharp curettage may be gleaned from this technical evaluation in a standard textbook, WILLIAMS' OBSTETRICS, edited by Louis Hellman, later the Deputy Assistant HEW Secretary for Population Affairs: "It is our opinion that a sharp curette is more efficacious and that its dangers are not greater than those of the dull instrument in the usual therapeutic abortion. Perforations of the uterus rarely occur on the downstroke of the curette, but may occur when any instrument is introduced into the uterus; since the knife edge of a sharp curette is directed downward, it can have no bearing on this hazard." A curettage, then, is a form of cutting. If improperly used, the knife will cut the mother. Properly used, the knife will cut the unborn child.

The curet used in suction is set in a hollow tube with a moderate-size opening near the top. A glass trap is interposed between the curet and a vacuum pump. Curets used in suction can be either stain-less steel or plastic. They are often sold under the name "Vacuettes." The pumps employed are specifically designed for this kind of vacuuming; a popular model is "the Berkeley aspirator." Curettage by suction is a relatively recent invention, having first been developed for use in Communist China.

Here is how the process is currently practiced at the Concord Medical Center, a private outpatient clinic in Chicago:

> After anesthetic and dilation of uterus, the uterus was evacuated with a rigid plastic suction curet attached to a Berkeley aspirator. After completion of the suction curettage the uterus cavity was gently explored with a sharp curet and suction was reapplied. All tissues were sent to the pathologist for examination.

Another standard medical work, TECHNIQUES OF ABORTION, may be used to supplement this description of an early abortion:

> The suction machine is turned on, and a finger is used to block the handle until a small amount of suction is obtained. . . . A vacuum is created in the uterus. [The curet is rotated.] At any point that material is felt flowing into the tube, motion is stopped until the flow stops. Then the slow up-and-down gradual rotation pattern is continued. Bloody fluid and bits of pink tissue will be seen flowing through the plastic tubing during the entire suction curettage. However, the procedure should be continued until the entire endometrial cavity is covered at least twice. . . . If no more tissue is obtained and the endometrial surface gives a consistently gritty resistance to the sharp edge of the curet, the procedure is finished.

This method has not been so common in the second trimester, but it is now being used with success as this description of current practice at Detroit Memorial Hospital indicates: "The cervix was then dilated with Pratt dilators to No. 39 or No. 43. A No. 12 or No. 14 section cannula was inserted to remove the amniotic fluid and a ring forceps was used to extract fetal parts. With a sharp curet, the placenta and any additional fetal parts were removed from the uterine cavity." The fetal parts referred to are the dismembered portions of the body of the unborn child, who has been cut up and vacuumed.

The most common method in the second trimester is what is known as intra-amniotic instillation. Water with a salt solution is injected by catheter into the amniotic fluid which surrounds the unborn child. The precise way in which death is then caused is not known, but two specialists in abortion offer this theory:

In all probability, 20% sodium chloride is a chemical poison. If by accident it is injected subcutaneously, intraperitoneally, or intramyometrially, it produces exquisite and severe pain. If it is injected into the amniotic cavity, and the membranes rupture at the end of the procedure, the abortion usually still occurs on schedule. In general, no fetal heart sounds are detectable one or two hours after the procedure. Some patients begin to experience painful uterine contractions at the end of the instillation, indicating the onset of labor. . . . Intra-amniotic hypertonic saline probably exercises its effect by chemically stopping fetal and placental function and thereby initiating labor.

In layman's language, the fetus is poisoned, dies within two hours, and is expelled.

Richard Selzer, a surgeon and medical writer at Yale Medical School, had never seen an abortion. He decided to observe and describe one performed through the injection of prostaglandins into the amniotic fluid surrounding an unborn child twenty-four weeks old. His account begins with the doctor reassuring the adult patient that there will only be "a little pinprick" without further pain. A needle has been inserted. The doctors and nurses are busy.

Then:

I see something! It is unexpected, utterly unexpected, like a disturbance in the earth, a tumultuous jarring. I see something other than what I expected here. I see a movement — a small one. But I have seen it.

And then I see it again. And now I see that it is the hub of the needle in the woman's belly that has jerked. First to one side. Then to the other side. Once more it wobbles, is tugged, like a fishing line nibbled by a sunfish.

Again! And I know! . . .

I close my eyes. I see the inside of the uterus. It is bathed in ruby gloom. I see the creature curled upon itself. Its knees are flexed. Its head is bent upon its chest. It is in fluid and gently rocks to the rhythm of the distant heartbeat.

It resembles . . . a sleeping infant . . .

What I saw I saw as that: a defense, a motion from, an effort away. And it has happened that you cannot reason with me now. For what can language do against the truth of what I saw?

The linguistic mask put aside, Selzer saw. The observations of a woman, Magda Denes, a psychologist who herself had had an abortion and later decided to study life in a New York City abortion clinic, are not dissimilar. She describes what she saw at the end of an abortion: "I look inside the bucket in front of me. There is a small naked person in there floating in a bloody liquid — plainly the tragic victim of a drowning accident. But then perhaps this was no accident, because the body is purple with bruises and the face has the agonized tautness of one forced to die too soon." She continues: "Death overtakes me in a rush of madness." She will not deny her consciousness that a life has been taken. She will not suppress her reflection that "the agony of an early death is the same anywhere," whether it is a "death factory" in Europe or an abortion clinic in New York City.

Bernard Nathanson, the director of an abortion clinic in New York City, came to the same conclusion as to what was occurring in the establishment he headed. Nathanson had been a founder of the National Association for the Repeal of Abortion Laws; he had welcomed the legalization of abortion in New York; and for a year and a half he was the director of the largest abortion clinic in the world. When he resigned, he reported the impact the work had had on him and on his staff. The constant immersion in the clinic's business, he observed, had been demoralizing for the people engaged in it: "I was seeing personality structures dissolve in front of me on a scale I had never seen before in a medical situation. Very few members of the staff seemed to remain fully intact through their experiences." As for himself, he declared, "[I] was deeply troubled by my own increasing certainty that I had in fact presided over 60,000 deaths," Those terminations of pregnancy, which he judged as deaths, came from 60,000 acts of killing. His responsibility, which he did not evade, was for presiding over the taking of 60,000 lives.

Twenty inquiries have explored the nature of the liberty of abortion and its boundaries, its jurisprudential and constitutional context, its political constituencies, its legends, and its dynamism. Its impact on the legal structure of the family, on the practice of medicine, on the political process itself have been observed. It is time to gather in one place the conclusions these inquiries support.

First. The liberty established by *The Abortion Cases* has no foundation in the Constitution of the United States. It was established by an act of raw judicial power. Its establishment was illegitimate and unprincipled, the imposition of the personal beliefs of seven justices on the women and men of fifty states. The continuation of the liberty is a continuing affront to constitutional government in this country.

No "discrete and insular minority" can feel secure when its constitutional existence may be affected by the exercise of such raw power. And we are all members of discrete and insular minorities, depending on the criterion employed to set up the categories. The population may be divided a thousand ways to suit the preferences of the judges, who have power to define who is a person, who have even power to declare who is alive. If it becomes settled that it is the Supreme Court's will that confers personhood and existence, no one is safe.

Second. The Abortion Cases rest on serious errors. They invoke history but mistakenly assert that the historical purpose of American abortion laws was the protection of the health of the gravida. They invoke medical standards but mistakenly treat abortion as a procedure medically acceptable after the fifth month. They appeal to Holmes's criterion of liberty and in fact apply the contrary criterion of *Lochner*. They invoke the freedom of women but ignore what American women believe and want. They claim not to decide when human life begins and in fact decide that human life begins at birth. Their multiple errors of history, medicine, constitutional law, political psychology, and biology require their erasure.

Third. The liberty established by *The Abortion Cases* is destructive of the structure of the family. It sets up the carrier as autonomous and isolated. It separates her from her partner in procreation. It separates her when she is a minor from her parents. It is destructive of the responsibility of parents for their daughters. It is destructive of a father's responsibility for his offspring. Its exercise is the reverse of a mother's care of her offspring. Its exercise is a betrayal of the most paradigmatic of trusts, that which entrusts to a mother the life of her helpless child.

Fourth. The liberty is oppressive to the poor. Its existence has led to depriving the pregnant poor of assistance for their dependent unborn children. Its existence has intensified the pressure on the poor to destroy their unborn children. The obligation of the government is to aid the disadvantaged by social assistance and economic improvement; the liberty transforms this responsibility to the poor into a responsibility to reduce poverty by reducing the children of the poor.

Fifth. The liberty violates the ethic of Western medicine from Hippocrates to the present. It narrows the service of the obstetrician from caring for two patients, mother and child, to caring for one. The doctor's duty to preserve every human life he touches is converted into a duty to take human lives. He is turned from a healer in all seasons to a bringer of death on occasion.

Sixth. The liberty divides the country. Never before has the nation been split on who shall live and who shall die. Only once before has it been split on who was to be respected as a person and who was not. The present division has not been brought about by the defenders of the lives of the unborn. They adhere to the law and traditions of our people as they were understood for almost two hundred years, until January 22, 1973. The division has been brought about by the abortion liberty and the aggressive actions on its behalf. It is the abortion liberty which has fanned religious animosity by setting Protestants against Catholics, secularists against believers. It is the abortion liberty which has assaulted the structure of the family, setting daughter against mother and father, wife against

husband, mother against unborn child. It is advocates of abortion who have made the liberty of abortion part of the ideology of the emancipation of women. It is expounders of the liberty who say men and women are not partners in procreation and make a woman a solo entity and the solo judge of whether jointly conceived offspring shall live or die.

Seventh. The liberty encourages the coercion of conscience. Already it has led college administrators to force students to pay for acts the students believe to be the killing of human beings. Already it has led judges to order communities to pay for actions the communities believe are evil. Already it has permitted governors to disregard the consciences of their citizens and force them to finance abortions repugnant to their consciences. In the view of a philosopher of the pro-abortion party, a conscientious opponent of abortion should be made to perform an abortion with his own hands. In the view of the American Civil Liberties Union, that custodian of the American conscience, the hospitals of those who abhor abortion should be commandeered for their performance. In the view of the counsel for Planned Parenthood, a doctor who fails to advise an abortion is open to the charge of practising sectarian medicine. In the view of the counsel for an ACLU affiliate, a mayor who enforces a law regulating an abortion clinic may be personally liable in damages. The dynamism of the liberty does not allow for neutrality. He or she who does not conform must be made to cooperate.

Eighth. Implementation of the liberty has subverted other parts of the Constitution in addition to the Ninth and Fourteenth Amendments, which were specifically distorted by *The Abortion Cases.* The organic distribution of powers made by Article I has been violated. A federal court has ordered the federal government to pay money not appropriated by Congress, in violation of the constitutional command that "no money shall be drawn from the Treasury, but in Consequence of Appropriations made by Law." The Treasury has complied, paying out large sums for elective abortions for which no congressional appropriation existed.

Ninth. The liberty has fostered a sinister and Orwellian reshaping of our language in which "child" no longer means child in the womb; the unborn dead have become fetal wastage; a dying infant has become a fetus *ex utero;* pregnancy has come to mean abortion; and new human life within a mother has been officially declared to be not alive.

Tenth. The liberty has led to the use of the unborn child and the dying infant for experiments. The experiments have not been for their benefit. Without their consent, the unborn child and the infant dying after an abortion have been utilized for the benefit of others. In disregard of the great codes of medical ethics, the Nuremberg Code, the Oath of Geneva, and the Declaration of Helsinki, they have been treated as disposable; and the liberty has permitted their classification and use as things.

Eleventh. The liberty has diminished the care due a child capable of life outside the womb if the child is marked for abortion. The acts of the physician affecting that child's life before birth have been shielded from inquiry. Whether such child had been born alive has been made a matter of cursory examination. The practice in our great teaching hospitals has been denounced by a leading pediatric surgeon as the practice of infanticide. A philosopher has argued for the complete acceptance of infanticide. Lawyers and judges have assaulted the laws protecting the infant outside the womb.

Twelfth. The liberty of abortion has caused a very high loss of human life. The liberty of abortion is acting as its proponents expected it to act: It is reducing the birthrate by increasing the number of abortion deaths. The loss of human life now annually attributable to the liberty in the United States is in the hundreds of thousands. More than one million have died through the exercise of the liberty. No plague, no war has so devastated the land.

There must be a limit to a liberty so mistaken in its foundations, so far-reaching in its malignant consequences, and so deadly in its exercise. There must be a surpassing of such liberty by love.

•   •   •

NO

Riane Eisler

THE HUMAN LIFE AMENDMENT
AND THE FUTURE OF HUMAN LIFE

An unprecedented battle is gathering momentum in this country. On the surface it is about the legality of abortion, declared a constitutionally protected right by the U.S. Supreme Court in the 1973 case of *Roe v. Wade*. But underneath the surface is an even more fundamental conflict, with the most far-reaching implications for the present and future lives of both women and men.

This battle is over the proposed amendment to the United States Constitution called the Human Life Amendment (HLA). To date, HLA backers have introduced almost two dozen resolutions to pass such an amendment in the ninety-seventh Congress. Some versions would constitutionally redefine persons to include "unborn offsprings at every stage of their biological development." Others assert that "actual human life exists from conception." And still other versions would read: "The paramount right to life is vested in each human being from the moment of fertilization without regard to age, health, or condition of dependency." . . .

In addition, HLA backers have also introduced several Human Life Bills in Congress. Being a law, as distinguished from a constitutional amendment, a Human Life Bill (HLB) would require only a simple congressional majority for passage. Most constitutional experts see such a law as clearly unconstitutional under the 1973 U.S. Supreme Court ruling. However, HLB backers hope that the Court will reverse itself, particularly since, by the time such a bill would be tested, the Court's composition might be sufficiently altered by retirements and subsequent replacements by a president avowedly pro-HLA to ensure that it would, despite *Roe v. Wade,* be upheld.

The leading edge of the opposition to the Human Life Amendment has come from women. They fear not only the proposed amendment's obvious implications for family planning and birth control— which are more severe than is generally believed, since the HLA would also outlaw the use of the intrauterine device (IUD) and the most medically safe, low-estrogen birth control pill. Women also fear that, for women, the Human Life Amendment, which political observers believe presently has a good chance of passage, presages a future of more, rather than less, subordination, inequality, and repression. They protest the HLA's definition of women as primarily containers or vehicles for the production of offspring rather than as persons possessed of the fundamental right of bodily integrity and self-determination.

The fear of repression also lies at the heart of the opposition to HLA based on traditions of religious freedom and the, until now, constitutionally guaranteed separation of church and state.

According to its proponents, the HLA's purpose is to prevent the taking of life. In their view, an abortion is a killing — a violation of God's commandment prohibiting the taking of human life. However, from a medical or scientific standpoint, a fertilized egg or fetus is not a human life: it has only the potential for human life, as do sperm and ova. The question of whether or not abortion is the taking of a human life is thus a question of theology. Moreover, the theological position that human life begins from the moment of fertilization, which would be adopted through the Human Life Amendment, actually represents a minority position.

The majority of religious groups — Protestant and Jewish — do not hold that the individual "soul" and the human being come into existence at the moment of conception. Their position is instead that both an individual's spiritual and physical person come into existence at the moment of birth; in other words, at the moment at which there is a separate individual, a live baby rather than an organism residing in and dependent for its existence on a woman's womb.

The incorporation into the highest law of the United States — our Constitution — of the theological position that human life begins at fertilization would constitute a radical departure from the First Amendment's guarantee of freedom of religion and separation of church and state. Many religious and secular leaders point out that the founders of this country included these principles in our Constitution to ensure that the combination of church and state, which in Europe led to terrible religious persecutions, could never come about here. They are particularly alarmed about passage of the HLA at a time when a tide of religious intolerance is gaining momentum and when, in the name of God, country, and morality, old and new hatreds and prejudices are being rekindled all over our land.

But there is yet another growing concern about the Human Life Amendment; one that, at first glance, sounds like something straight out of science fiction. This is a twofold concern. The first relates to the fact that, by enshrining in the United States Constitution the principle that the government may through its laws interfere with nothing less than an individual's right to determine what happens in one's own body, the Human Rights Amendment would set an unparalleled precedent regarding constitutionally permissible personal controls. The second relates to the fact that, by defining a fetus as a separate

16. SHOULD ABORTION BE OUTLAWED?

entity, the Human Life Amendment could eventually open the door to the danger to human liberty represented by a future of government-directed genetic engineering. . . .

To some, fears about a future of government-controlled programs aimed at the production of a "superior" or "pure" race and concerns about body and mind controls may sound like undue and indeed fantastic alarms, particularly here in the United States. But there are others who see the danger of a future of technocratic totalitarianism as a very real possibility, and, moreover, one that must be carefully guarded against in these times of mounting economic and social instability and violence, when Americans so desperately yearn for simple solutions in an ever more complex and bewildering world.

This is by no means to say that those who favor HLA, including President Reagan, intend such results. But that results are not intended, or even generally foreseen, does not mean they cannot happen. For example, the Fourteenth Amendment, adopted in 1868, was a response to the so-called "black codes" passed by Southern states after the Civil War in order to force freed blacks back to virtual slavery. It was certainly not intended, foreseen, and even, perhaps, foreseeable that this constitutional amendment would be used to protect American citizens' freedom of assembly and expression from unwarranted police interference, to prevent gerrymandering and assessment of poll taxes, or to require that poor people have court-appointed attorneys in criminal prosecutions.

While these results could not have been predicted at the time the Fourteenth Amendment was passed, it was predictable that, by protecting blacks from governmental repression, this amendment would

generally strengthen the principle of individual protection against governmental interference and control — the hallmark of American constitutional and political history. The Human Life Amendment would mark a sharp break with this tradition. To those committed to the protection of civil liberties, its gaining momentum is therefore a warning signal of a potentially very different new era in American constitutional history. . . .

National polls show that the majority of Americans do *not* favor constitutional interference with reproductive freedom of choice. In fact, according to an August 1980 Gallup poll, even the majority of people who consider themselves evangelical or born-again Christians — allegedly the constituency behind the Human Life Amendment — do *not* favor a ban on all abortions. Neither is the HLA backed by any of the major labor, professional, or women's groups or by the vast majority of American religious groups, including Catholics who have explicitly repudiated the Vatican's position on abortion and birth control.

While HLA is heavily backed by Catholic church money and has considered support from the Mormon church, as well as from such organizations as the Ku Klux Klan and neo-Nazi groups, its most massive political support has come from a powerful new political alliance. This is the alliance between fundamentalist religious groups such as the Moral Majority and the Christian Voice — largely supported by television ministers who each week preach their "pro-life" message to forty-seven million Americans — and both new and old right-wing political groups such as the Conservative Caucus, the John Birch Soci-

280

ety, and the Committee for the Survival of a Free Congress. . . .

Although it is becoming increasingly recognized that issues such as the Human Life Amendment are serving as power-politics vehicles for the American right, this strategy has clearly been one that works. For example, in the 1980 election, the rightest-fundamentalist alliance put together a hit-list of congressional incumbents. . . .

In the words of defeated Senator George McGovern, "The 'family' issue raised by the right wing was a code word for putting women back in the kitchen and stripping them of all decision on the question of abortion and forcing them back into the old orthodox roles. There was a counter-revolutionary aspect to this campaign, and women were the chief victims, along with the poor."

One paradox is that, while the leadership that supplies the big money in support of the HLA is predominantly male, the rank and file of the workers in the pro-life movement are women, many from lower socioeconomic groups. Moreover, while many of these women are Catholics and most are religiously motivated the underlying reason for their support of HLA (and opposition to ERA) is based on the same socioeconomic and ideological subordination of women that impels feminists to work for equality of opportunities and rights. For where feminists are inspired by the hope that this goal can be achieved, these women believe that, either for divinely ordained or other reasons, it cannot and that their only hope in a world dominated by men is to work for a social order of more marital economic security: one in which men's contact with "bad women" — those who engage in extramarital sex —

would be severely limited and in which "good women," such as themselves, could not so easily be abandoned.

Those who have attended pro-life conventions and had the opportunity for personal contact with these women report how, more than anything else, it is this fear of abandonment — stemming from the economic and psychological powerlessness of women in a society in which their extramarital economic opportunities are so vastly inferior to those of men — which compels them to work for a constitutional ban on abortions.

This sense of powerlessness and fear of abandonment — particularly in a time of worsening economic conditions — seems, in a large part, to account for something that has baffled so many observers of the pro-life movement: the obvious contradiction between these women's deeply felt and evidently genuine moral concern for, in their words, "the helpless unborn child" and their evident lack of concern for human beings who have already been born. It is out of their own desperate sense of helplessness that they seem to identify more with the symbolic conceptualization of human life, in the form of a fetus or fertilized egg, than with the well-documented suffering of women who are forced to seek illegal abortions or to give birth involuntarily to children who are born unwanted.

The contradiction between the pro-life movement's attitude toward "unborn children" and their attitude toward children who have been born has long puzzled observers. For example, not only the leadership but also the rank and file of pro-lifers are staunch opponents of government welfare programs to help support needy and dependent children. These people are also characteristically in favor of the death penalty and see killings in wars not only as inevitable but as noble and heroic.

A look at the voting records of pro-choice and anti-choice legislators dramatically illustrates this point. For example, a 1974 survey of voting patterns of abortion foes in the United States Senate showed that there was a highly significant statistical relationship between voting *against* abortion and voting *for* capital punishment and continued support of the Vietnam war. There was, in addition, a highly significant correlation of anti-abortion voting and voting against hand-gun control.

Senators who voted for the 1974 Bartlett Amendment (prohibiting Medicaid funds from being used to help poor women pay for abortions) also generally scored very low on the National Farmers' Union Family Nurturance Scale, which measures legislators' support for farm families, poverty-relief programs, food programs, and other welfare programs for children, the elderly, and other disadvantaged people. And when these relationships were again tested in connection with the 1977 Helms Amendment (another measure which, like the subsequently passed Hyde Amendment, was designed to cut off federal abortion aid to poor women), this same pattern was confirmed. Fifteen out of twenty-one senators (71 percent) who received the *lowest* family nurturance scores *opposed* abortion, while, in sharp contrast, nineteen out of twenty-one (90 percent) of the senators who had the *highest* family nurturance scores *supported* abortion.

These figures may not come as a surprise to those who have followed the pro-lifers rhetoric of violence as, for example,

the prayer at the 1980 Convention of the National Right to Life Committee at the Disneyland Hotel, which asked the Lord to "send the enemy to the pit of destruction," as well as their vandalism and arson at abortion clinics. However, even the knowledgeable observer may be surprised by the cross-cultural comparison reported by anthropologist R. B. Textor in his book, *A Cross-Cultural Summary* (1967), in which a striking correlation between severe punishments for abortion and a *lack* of respect for the value and dignity of human life was found.

Based on data from approximately four hundred preindustrial societies, Textor's book, a standard anthropological resource, reports that societies in which abortion is severely punished tend to be societies in which we find the killing, torturing, and mutilation of enemies captured in warfare, slavery, repressive sexuality, polygamy, and patrilineal descent. In contrast, societies in which penalties for abortion are either absent or mild tend to be those in which enemies captured in warfare are not killed, tortured, and mutilated; in which slavery, polygamy, and repressive sexuality are not found; and in which descent is matrilineal, that is, traced through the mother rather than through the father

These and other studies of both past and present societies show that the issue of reproductive freedom is fundamental to the total social, political, and economic organization of both women and men. This is not surprising, since the control of one-half of humanity by the other half — around which the battle over reproductive freedom of choice revolves — has now also been shown by a variety of studies to be central to an authoritarian and highly violent form of social organization. . . .

In light of these findings, even a "compromise" Human Life Amendment, exempting rape victims and cases in which a woman's life is at stake; can only be seen as a bellwether signaling a regression to a more authoritarian and violent way of life.

In these terms, the battle over the Human Life Amendment is indeed a battle over human life. It is a battle over what kind of life both women and men can expect in the future. Are we to advance to a freer life based on the principles of equality and democracy, which this country has traditionally espoused? Or are we to regress to a life based on inequality and coercion, symbolized by the constitutional definition of one-half of humanity not as people but as male-controlled — now also government-controlled — reproduction machines?

Global 2000, the report to the president prepared by the State Department and the Council for Environmental Quality, demonstrates that population growth is the Earth's single most serious problem, not only in terms of global security, natural resources depletion, and environmental problems but in terms of human misery and suffering. For example, of the 134 million children born worldwide in 1978, 22 percent died of starvation. Experts predict that, at current birth rates (30 million per year), 90 million children will die of starvation in the next thirty years alone. And, as population experts keep reiterating, in order to slow down birth rates women *must* be given free access to existing birth control technologies and, just as fundamentally, to equality of opportunity for education, training, jobs, and careers leading to valued and respected non-reproduction-linked life and work roles.

The United States, which now constitutes 6 percent of the world's population, consumes approximately 35 percent of global energy and other natural resources. These resources — such as oil and gas, arable land, clean water and air — are, as we are all too painfully finding out, not infinite nor, for that matter, as we are finding out as demand increases and supply decreases, are they any longer cheap. There is, therefore, little question that American population policies are of national and global significance. What happens in the United States also exerts enormous influence on the population policies of less developed nations, and it is becoming crystal clear that the unbridled population growth of these countries threatens not only global natural resources but American national security as well. . . .

. . . The world's population growth rate would be roughly 50 percent greater if there were no abortions. Beyond that, as former World Bank President Robert McNamara, who considers population growth "the gravest issue that the world faces," put it, equality of opportunity for women is, in simple dollars-and-cents terms, "a very good buy."

There is, of course, another approach to population control: the traditional one of war and famine. Whether or not this approach, coupled with government-enforced restrictions on women — not forcing them to have children, but rather forcing them not to have children — will be the way the population explosion is eventually to be stopped in many ways hinges on the outcome of the current battle over the Human Life Amendment. For there is no question that global population growth rates, now adding a staggering one billion people to the Earth every twelve years,

16. SHOULD ABORTION BE OUTLAWED?

must be halted. The only question is whether this will be done by intelligent and reasoned free choice or by violence, hunger, and coercion.

In the battle over the Human Life Amendment, the American people and their representatives have the opportunity to carefully examine that question — and the overarching question of freedom versus repression in our future — and to make a fateful decision. For those firmly committed to the American tradition of individual freedom, it is also an opportunity to unmask a strategy ominously reminiscent of the doublethink and doublespeak of Orwell's *1984*. For HLA, being merchandised as "pro-life," is a measure that on all accounts threatens the quality of human life. Being promoted by those proclaiming they "just want to get government off our backs," it is also an unparalleled governmental invasion of the privacy and rights of the American individual.

• • •

POSTSCRIPT

SHOULD ABORTION BE OUTLAWED?

Perhaps never before in our history have moral issues been given more prominent attention in American political life, and no moral issue arouses as much passionate partisanship as does that of abortion. Why is this so? Why has the issue emerged as one of the most divisive political questions of the 1980s?

In part this is the result of the Supreme Court's 1973 decisions which overturned state laws forbidding or sharply limiting abortions. The inevitable controversy over those decisions was heightened by the rise of new political forces. The feminist movement supporting the Equal Rights Amendment and its liberal allies have been the staunchest supporters of the right of abortion. The Moral Majority and other often church-related groups have been the most ardent opponents.

Can the issue be debated on its merits or must it be considered in the context of other moral and social issues? While John Noonan and Riane Eisler do disagree on the specific scientific and moral issues, Eisler goes further to argue that anti-abortion views are closely correlated with conservative positions on other issues, such as capital punishment. (Studies suggest, however, that no statistical difference exists between pro- and anti-abortion activists on capital punishment.) Certainly, there is a New Right which shares certain moral positions. On the other hand, political attitudes on economic issues are often quite independent of the fundamentally moral questions.

If dispassionate debate on the abortion issue is possible at all, it is possible only if we distinguish among several questions. Is there a scientific basis for defining the beginning of human life? Should the state legislate to enforce moral principles which are not nearly universally shared? If a ban on abortions were reinstated, would it be enforceable, or would it spawn illegal abortion clinics?

As if these questions were not difficult enough, congressional debate on proposed amendments and bills to bar abortion reveal that we must also consider the constitutional consequences of either overturning a Supreme Court decision or bypassing the Court by eliminating its appellate jurisdiction in such cases.

Among the recent books opposing abortion, the most persuasive are Bernard N. Nathanson, ABORTING AMERICA (Doubleday, 1979), by a doctor who had once favored abortion, and James T. Burtchaell, RACHEL WEEPING AND OTHER ESSAYS ON ABORTION (Andrews and McMeel, 1981). The right to abortion is strongly advocated in Lawrence Lader, ABORTION II: MAKING THE REVOLUTION (Beacon Press, 1973).

ISSUE 17

SHOULD WE ALLOW PRAYER IN THE PUBLIC SCHOOLS?

YES: Martha Rountree, from Hearings on the "School Prayer" Bill, July 29, 1981

NO: M. William Howard, from Hearings on the "School Prayer" Bill, July 29, 1981

ISSUE SUMMARY

YES: Lobbyist and conservative activist, Martha Rountree, argues that America is a religious nation, and that voluntary school prayer should be made available to those who want it.

NO: Religious leader, M. William Howard, echoes Thomas Jefferson's view that when government and religion mix, both suffer, and freedom is lessened.

The United States has more members (well in excess of one hundred million) of more churches (more than 300,000) than any other country in the world. More than ninety-five percent of all Americans profess a belief in God. Recently, the growth of so-called "cult" religions and the increasing visibility of "born-again" Christians suggest that religion remains a powerful force in American society. Inevitably, religion and the state intersect.

For the past thirty years the United States Supreme Court has been examining and handing down judgments on some of the more controversial intersections. The controversies have included the right of a state to reimburse parents of children attending parochial schools for the cost of bus transportation (which the Court has approved), the right to conduct classes in religious instruction on public school property (which the Court has denied), the right of schoolchildren to release time from public school in order to attend religious instruction on public school property (denied), the right of schoolchildren to release time from public school in order to attend religious instruction outside of public school property (approved), and, what has proven to be the most controversial church-state issue of them all, the right of children and teachers to start their school day with a prayer. In the case of *Engel v. Vitale* (1962), these twenty-two words, recited daily in a number of public schools throughout the state of New York, became the center of a national controversy:

Almighty God, we acknowledge our dependence upon Thee, and we beg Thy blessings upon us, our parents, our teachers and our country.

The prayer, composed by the New York State Board of Regents, was intended to be nondenominational. It was also voluntary, at least in the sense that the children were not required to recite it and could leave the room during the time in which it was recited. Nevertheless, the Court declared it unconstitutional, and in subsequent cases it also outlawed Bible reading and the Lord's Prayer. Its reason for doing so is bound up with its interpretation of the First Amendment's "establishment" clause: "Congress shall make no law respecting an establishment of religion." Does this clause mean that the state may have nothing to do with religion? Or is its meaning restricted to prohibition of a national church of one denomination? America is by tradition and practice a religious nation and our Founders did not mean the state to be utterly indifferent to religion. On the other hand, those who favor complete separation of church and state point to Thomas Jefferson's famous metaphor about the necessary "wall of separation" between church and state. They remind us of the practical difficulty of providing benefits impartially to all churches.

Seventy-five percent of Americans want a restoration of school prayers. Public opinion does not decide constitutional issues or moral ones, and these issue is surely both. But public opinion can lead to legal change, and there is a distinct possibility that this can happen in the 1980s.

The most direct way to reverse the Court's rulings on school prayer would be to adopt a Constitutional amendment permitting it. This, however, is easier said than done. In 1966 the Senate voted 49-37 for such an amendment, but the vote was nine short of the constitutionally required two-thirds majority. In 1971 the House of Representatives voted 240-162 for a similar amendment, but this fell 28 votes short of the necessary two-thirds. More recently, on May 6, 1982, President Reagan, at a special Rose Garden ceremony, proposed an amendment permitting voluntary prayer.

There remains another strategy for restoring public school prayers. This would be to withdraw from the jurisdiction of Federal courts the whole issue of school prayer, leaving it up to the states to resolve. Since this could be done by ordinary legislation, it would not be necessary to muster the two-thirds majority of both houses which an amendment requires. However, it is constitutionally questionable (see Issue 7) and vulnerable to being declared unconstitutional by the very courts whose rulings it seeks to curb.

The following selections are concerned with the substantive question of prayers in public schools, though their immediate focus is on the legislation sponsored by Senator Jesse Helms of North Carolina in 1980 (S. 450) which would withdraw the issue of school prayer from the jurisdiction of Federal courts. In their statements before a congressional subcommittee, Martha Rountree outlines her view that the right of school prayer is integrally tied to all that is best in the American tradition, while M. William Howard contends that such prayers violate freedom and degrade religion.

YES

Martha Rountree

SCHOOL PRAYER IS AN AMERICAN TRADITION

School prayer has become one of the most controversial issues in the Nation's history. Even though national polls, as well as State polls and referendums have shown that the overwhelming majority of Americans want voluntary prayer back in our public schools, Congress, for the most part has blatantly ignored the wishes of their constituents. Why? After all, the members of Congress are servants of the people and dependent upon the vote of the people to hold public office. Their power, under the Constitution, is derived from the people.

Perhaps the real problem lies in the fact that the issue has been fought out emotionally rather than constitutionally. If we go back into history and review the early debates that preceded the drafting of the Constitution, we can have no doubt but that freedom was key. The first 13 States called the shots. Before they would even consider the formation of a Union they gave grave consideration to the problem of protecting their rights, their freedoms and their sovereignty. Sovereignty was a big concern. They had many reservations as history shows. Religious freedom was the cornerstone of their hard won rights in America. The Declaration of Independence clearly defines their belief and dependence upon God. The Constitution was their contract with the new Government they were forming and they weighed each and every word carefully. They spelled out those powers which they were willing to give to the Federal Government and made it clear that any and all powers not delegated to the Government remained with the States (see article 10 in the Bill of Rights).

So concerned were they about their States rights, their sovereignty and their freedom, that even after the Constitution had been meticulously hammered out word by word, reviewed, debated and rewritten many times before being executed, they still were uneasy. As a result they felt the need to clarify their intent as demonstrated in the amendments to the Constitution. Still fearful of

From, *Hearings on the "School Prayer" Bill,* July 29, 1980.

any misinterpretation, they wrote the Bill of Rights. They took every precaution to see that the Constitution provided a system of checks and balances in the three branches of Government, the judicial, the executive and the legislative.

Especially fearful of judicial usurpation of power they made it clear in article 3, section 2 of the amendments that the appellate jurisdiction of the Court is subject to, "Such exceptions and such regulations as the Congress shall make."

Under article 3, section 2, the Congress was given the power by a simple majority vote of both Houses to limit the Supreme Court's appellate jurisdiction.

It was on these constitutional grounds that Senator Jesse Helms introduced legislation in the U.S. Senate to: Limit the jurisdication of the Supreme Court of the United States and of the Federal courts to enter any judgment, decree, or order denying or restricting, as unconstitutional, voluntary prayer in any public school, bill (S. 450).

On April 9, 1979 the Helms' legislation based on the Constitution, was passed in the U.S. Senate by a vote of 51 to 40. This was a big victory for the majority of the American people who support voluntary school prayer. For over 18 years many amendments and bills had been introduced in the House and Senate only to die. After this victory in the Senate, bill S. 450, as required by the Constitution, was sent to the Judiciary Committee of the House of Representatives for final consideration.

The antiprayer groups' favorite arguments are: We have heard them here this morning and they are being stepped up. "What kind of prayer would you have the children say in school?"

Let us stop here and answer this question.

First: We are not talking about mandatory school prayer. We are talking about voluntary prayer in the schools.

Second: We are not talking about religion. Religion is a doctrine or a denomination. We are talking about Almighty God, Creator of the Universe, of everyone regardless of denomination, doctrine, language or belief. We are talking about the rights of the people and the rights of the States, as set forth in the Constitution. We are talking about the right of the people to decide for themselves if they want their children in public schools to acknowledge God.

People have become so accustomed to having the Federal Government tell them what to do, they find it hard to imagine their right or their State's right to make decisions. The opponents of school prayer will tell you that children who do not believe in God will be embarrassed. Statistics show that only a minute percentage of the population are atheists. Certainly no child is an atheist unless they are taught atheism. If there was ever need for any legal redress, the local and State civil courts would be empowered to handle the matter as has always been the case until the Supreme Court usurped the judicial power of the States in 1962.

The purpose of the first amendment was to protect the people from the establishment of a state church, such as the Church of England and to insure the rights of the people to the free exercise of whatever form of religion they should choose.

Nowhere in the Constitution, the amendments to the Constitution or in the Bill of Rights, are the courts given the right to make binding laws. Nowhere in the Constitution is there written or suggested that any branch of the Government shall have the right to deny those powers which have not been given them in the Constitution.

17. SHOULD WE ALLOW PRAYER IN PUBLIC SCHOOLS?

There again I refer to article 10 of the Bill of Rights.

In 1957 the Supreme Court handed down a ruling in the case of *Reed v. Covert* acknowledging that: "The United States is entirely a creature of the Constitution. Its power and authority have no other source. It can only act in accordance with all the limitations imposed by the Constitution."

Opponents of school prayer quote the first amendment by saying, "Congress shall make no law respecting the establishing of religion," and there they stop. They do not complete the sentence, "or prohibiting the free exercise thereof." It is important to be familiar with the background and the wording of the Constitution and its amendments and the Bill of Rights to arrive at an understanding of the rights of the American people.

The first amendment was intended to protect the States from an imposed state church and to maintain the rights of the States to exercise whatever form of religion they chose. They were referring to the Church of England, which taxed everyone and no one dared to rebel in fear of heavy penalties or even their lives. Anyone who has studied history or constitutional law cannot argue this point.

You will hear the opponents of school prayer refer to the 14th amendment in an attempt to back up their antischool prayer position. Nowhere in the 14th amendment is religion mentioned.

When the opponents of school prayer bemoan the loss of Federal jurisdiction they ignore the fact that the Federal courts are creatures of the Congress and dependent upon Congress for appropriations to keep them in business.

Let us go back to that little school house in New Hyde Park, N.Y., where prayer in the school was first attacked. That was a very simple little prayer, nondenomina-

tional. The prayer was "Almighty God we acknowledge our dependence upon thee and we beg thy Blessings upon us, our parents, our teachers and our Country." A beautiful prayer that was not denominational or doctrinal.

It is interesting to note the Supreme Court that handed down the decision in 1962 which resulted in taking prayer out of the schools, opens each session with the following prayer: "God save the United States and this Honorable Court." The Senate and the House of Representatives, as you know, both open each day's session with a prayer by their chaplain.

In one school where the Civil Liberties Union challenged the board of education on not adhering to the Supreme Court's decision, they were using the same prayer that was given in the U.S. Congress.

Madalyn O'Hair, who is credited with leading the fight against school prayer which resulted in the Supreme Court's ruling in 1962, has a son named William Murray. She brought her son up to be an atheist and it was because of her son that she fought school prayer. Today Bill Murray apologizes for the part he played in the removal of school prayer. He says:

> I believe I can give a great deal of insight for the need of passing bill (S. 450) into law. The passage of (S. 450) would reverse the effect of the suit titled *William J. Murray* vs. *Curlett, et al.* decided upon by the Supreme Court in 1963. This suit, which I was a principal to, in effect stopped involuntary and voluntary prayer in public schools nationwide. The Court decision caused great harm to the moral fiber of our youth and therefore to our Nation. Grave damage to the foundation of the republic itself was done.

There is much that can be said in favor of school prayer. An awareness of God is very reassuring thing to human beings and especially to children, it can mold their characters and give them a faith and awareness that will stand them in good stead throughout their lives. We do not suggest that all the problems with children today stem from the removal of prayer in the schools 18 years ago.

However, as a result of this trend, we are losing a most effective source of moral and ethical conditioning of our youth. Crime among school-age juveniles has increased dramatically. Vandalism in school and churches and against private property is rampant. A drug culture permeates the scene. Juvenile theft is taken for granted; and arson, murder, muggings, and rape are high on the list. It is significant to note that this moral decline among the youth of America has taken place during the 18 years since prayer was first taken out of the schools. What kind of leaders can we expect in future years? How could we have let this happen? Appeals to the high courts have been fruitless. The alternative has to be congressional action. . . .

These are the questions which we are being bombarded with daily, through the mails and over the long distance telephones.

These questions reflect real concern for the fate of S. 450 because it is the first time in 18 years there has been such a real chance to restore the people's rights to decide if they want voluntary prayer in the schools. . . . I know that millions of Americans are praying for this. If this, the issue of restoring voluntary school prayer were to be put to a popular vote there is no doubt but what there would be a landslide victory for voluntary school prayer.

In conclusion: S. 450 does not make school prayer mandatory. It restores the constitutional right of the people to decide for themselves in their States, if they want

their children to acknowledge Almighty God.

MR. KASTENMEIER. Thank you, Mrs. Rountree. . . . The gentleman from California, Mr. [George E.] Danielson.

MR. DANIELSON. Thank you, Mr. Chairman. Thank you, Ms. Rountree.

First of all, I want to commend you for taking a deep enough interest in our country, in our Government, in our society, to do the tremendous amount of work which you have done in this field. One thing that causes us to suffer in this country is that not enough people take a profound enough interest in what we are doing, and that is one criticism that cannot be made of Martha Rountree, I can assure you.

I understand that you are the prime mover, spark plug, whatever you want to call it, behind the literally thousands of postcards printed in brown ink that I have been receiving for a year. That is a lot of work.

MS. ROUNTREE. I will tell you, Mr. Chairman, what we do, we research and poll women, our members, affiliated groups and organizations throughout the country, and we tell them what the situation is. We don't tell them what to do, but if they want help we tell them how to do it and we respond to their wishes and we have taken this on as an issue in this respect that we want to tell people what they can do if they want prayer back in the schools.

MR. DANIELSON. I understand, ma'am, and I would say if anybody wants an example of what is the meaning of that provision of the Constitution which says that people shall have the right to petition their Congress, they should see Martha Rountree, because without a doubt, she has set a new standard for the world in that field.

I speak lightheartedly but that is not a lack of respect, it happens to be a fact. I think the world ought to know it.

I have one question and it has been asked, but I am not sure I fully perceived the answer. I have this in mind. You speak of voluntary prayer in the context, of course, of this Helms amendment, that is what is before us. That is what is on our table here today.

Whose voluntariness could you perceive to be affected by this, and I will state it in another context to try to sharpen my question. Do you mean that the prayer, the participation in the prayer, shall be voluntary on the part of the pupil in school, or do you mean that it is to be voluntary as to the school district or State or community as to whether or not they have voluntary prayer?

MS. ROUNTREE. It would be voluntary legally, as I understand it, it would be voluntary from the standpoint of whether the States want it and their districts wanted it. If they didn't want it, it would not be mandatory.

MR. DANIELSON. The voluntariness is an adjective which describes what action the governmental entity would have. A State could prescribe prayer in school or not so under the Helms amendment. Is that what you have in mind?

MS. ROUNTREE. Voluntary school prayer means I think just what it says. You see, the whole thing is——

MR. DANIELSON. Yes, ma'am, I have to take my time back because we are wandering astray here. My point is this: Do you mean, let's say we have a classroom with 30 pupils, do each of the 30 pupils have a right to give his or her own individual prayer in this period of prayer, or does the schoolteacher say pupils, it is voluntary prayer time, and this is our prayer for today. How do you approach it?

MS. ROUNTREE. I thought I had covered that in my testimony here and——

MR. DANIELSON. I didn't fully get it.

MS. ROUNTREE. I don't blame you for not listening to all of that. We sit here—and really with all due respect, we sit here trying to figure what the States are going to decide they want to do. We have been told we have had, the Government has had to figure out so long what people are going to do and everybody has become a number and everybody has been told what to do and we can't possibly understand why a State would have a right to make up their own mind. It is not up to me to decide that, I don't think.

MR. DANIELSON. You feel that it is up to the State or the school board, as the case may be?

MS. ROUNTREE. Absolutely.

MR. DANIELSON. To decide?

MS. ROUNTREE. Yes, sir.

MR. DANIELSON. And they could either say that the kids could each give his own prayer, for example, or today is the prayer, whatever it is, nondenominational prayer?

MS. ROUNTREE. There again, you are trying to say what they are going to do. I don't know.

MR. DANIELSON. Your point is they should have a right to decide what it is going to be?

MS. ROUNTREE. I am talking about the right, the constitutional right of people to decide.

MR. DANIELSON. We have to get down to the final analysis because the Helms amendment simply says the Supreme Court will not have appellate jurisdiction.

MS. ROUNTREE. You have civil courts.

MR. DANIELSON. Now, assuming that this became law, I am sure you wouldn't say that they wouldn't have jurisdiction over compulsory prayer?

MS. ROUNTREE. My contention sir, is just as it was in the start, that if such legislation is enacted in this session of Congress, which would limit the appellate jurisdiction of the Court in the area of the right of the

States to decide what they want, it would go back to them.

MR. DANIELSON. Ma'am, the Helms amendment says in the area of voluntary prayer. It doesn't treat compulsory prayer, it only treats the voluntary prayer, am I not right? It only treats the voluntary prayer. So if a State should prescribe compulsory prayer, this would not take that jurisdiction away.

MS. ROUNTREE. No, I have to read you the bill. That is not what the legislation says.

MR. DANIELSON. Just read the words there.

MS. ROUNTREE. Anyway, it keeps the Supreme Court from denying or restricting.

MR. DANIELSON. Here it is. It says "which relates to voluntary prayers in public schools and buildings." The word voluntary is here. So, since we are talking about voluntary prayer, obviously we are not talking about compulsory or involuntary prayer. Now, if that is the case, somebody is going to have to decide whether a given prayer is voluntary or involuntary. Who is going to decide that?

MS. ROUNTREE. The people are going to decide that. That is what the Constitution is all about.

MR. DANIELSON. The Supreme Court would have a right, any court would have a right to.

MS. ROUNTREE. I know you are trying to push me in a corner. I can't answer your question.

MR. DANIELSON. You know more about this than anybody else.

MS. ROUNTREE. Beg your pardon?

MR. DANIELSON. You know more about this than anybody else. You are absolutely the most profoundly learned person on Earth on this subject, I think.

MS. ROUNTREE. You embarrass me. That isn't true. I didn't mean to be rude. I can't answer the question on a presumption that I don't accept because my knowledge of law is limited.

MR. DANIELSON. I thank you, but frankly, one of the things that worries me very much is who is going to decide whether a given prayer is voluntary or not voluntary.

MS. ROUNTREE. I just hope the American people have the chance because they really would like to have prayer back in the school.

MR. DANIELSON. Thank you very much.

MR. KASTENMEIER. The gentleman from Kentucky.

MR. MAZZOLI. Thank you.

Thank you for your help. We have this vote, Mr. Chairman. I think my questions have all been asked, so I would thank the gentlelady for her attention and help.

MR. KASTENMEIER. The gentleman from Virginia.

MS. ROUNTREE. You throw some tough questions but it was good to have a chance to speak for the women of America.

• • •

NO

M. William Howard

SCHOOL PRAYER VIOLATES FREEDOM

This is the fifth time in 17 years that major religious bodies of the Nation have come to Washington to resist attempts to reverse the rulings of the Supreme Court which held that it is not the business of Government to institute prayers for the Nation's children to recite in public schools.

There was the Becker amendment in 1964, followed by two Dirksen amendments in the 1960's, the Wylie amendment in the early 1970's and now the Helms amendment in 1980. Whereas the previous four attempts sought to reshape the first amendment to the U.S. Constitution by straight-forwardly following the amending process set forth in the Constitution, the Helms amendment seeks to achieve the same effect without submitting the issue to the necessary two-thirds majority vote of both Houses of Congress and the ratification by three-quarters of the States.

The amendment in question undertakes to withdraw the subject of prayer from the jurisdiction of the U.S. Supreme Court and relegate it to jurisdiction of State authorities. This tactic is fraught with problems that reach far beyond the issue of prayer itself. If Congress can eliminate from the purview of the Supreme Court any issues on which its decision displeases a portion of the electorate, what implication will this have for the entire Bill of Rights? If this can happen by way of a mere majority vote of both Houses of Congress, without ratification by the States, is this not a way of amending the Constitution without regard for the safeguards which shield our Nation's highest laws and principles from capricious attack?

To say the very least, it is appalling that one should propose to put outside the purview of the Supreme Court the protection of the basic rights of Americans guaranteed by the Bill of Rights in any area, let alone the sensitive and intimate area of religion. . . .

Once more we must reiterate the arguments for a new generation, and we do so gladly.

From, *Hearings on the "School Prayer" Bill,* July 29, 1980.

One, public school prayers are an injustice to those children and their families who belong to minority religions or to no religious group. Persons in this category, because of their religious views, can be made to feel out of place and less than equals in public institutions. Such persons are told they are free to excuse themselves from prayers which offend their religious beliefs. I suppose that is what is meant by voluntary prayer.

But do we really expect the impressionable and vulnerable children to separate themselves from the rest of their peers, thus branding themselves as "oddballs"? Do we expect them to excuse themselves from activities that are sanctioned by their school, in which all the other children are joining? Mr. Chairman, having a difference in religious belief should not be a stigma for our children. In our increasingly pluralistic society, we must not subject youngsters of religious minorities to the queries, taunts, and jeers of uncomprehending classmates. Instead we must leave way for the children, with ease, to be true to the religious tutelage, or the lack of it, that is propagated in their families. This does not even begin to address the problem of religiously pluralistic teaching and administrative staffs who would presumably be responsible for leading such prayers.

Two, public school prayers are a disservice to true religion. The other reason we are opposed to prayer in public schools is that we believe prayer is too important, too sacred, too intimate to be scheduled or administered by Government. It is the responsibility of the family, the home, the religious institution, not the public school, to provide religious education and experience. Children attend public schools under force of law. They come from many religious and ethnic backgrounds and, therefore, should not find their school experience demeaning to their religious heritage.

We are told that the prayers could be "nonsecretarian," or that they could be offered from various religious traditions in rotation. I believe such a solution is least acceptable to those most fervently devoted to their own religion. Furthermore, I believe they do not want least-common-denominator prayers addressed "to whom it may concern." Even less do they wish to engage in the prayer-forms peculiar to religious traditions other than their own or to have to show their colleagues the discourtesy of nonparticipation.

In our view, there is simply no such thing as "nonsectarian" prayer, and if there were, it would be of little value to either committed Christians or adherents of the other religious traditions. Whenever prayer is presented in a group gathered for other purposes—such as a public school classroom—the question cannot be avoided: "Whose prayer is it"? And all too often it will be either the prayer form of the majority—imposed on the minorities—or a nearly meaningless prayer belonging to no historic religion. In the latter case, the exercise is likely to be offensive to devout members of all religions.

We are told that there are many children in public schools who would have no other contact with prayer and religion than what they might gain from public schools.

We think it odd that this argument comes most often from those who otherwise are highly resistant to governmental interference in family life. It suggests a curious willingness to condone governmental imposition of religious practices on children contrary to their own parents' choices for them. We oppose any effort to allow the Government to intrude in this most sacred of parental responsibilities, even if the parents have chosen to give

17. SHOULD WE ALLOW PRAYER IN PUBLIC SCHOOLS?

their children no religious training. This is their right. If it is not, then religious freedom in this Nation has lost an essential part of its meaning.

We are told that the current proposal is not designed to overturn the Supreme Court's decisions barring prayer from public schools. We are told that it is meant only to restore the matter to the States for the future. What can this mean other than a return to the "local option" which prevailed before the Supreme Court's decision on this issue? During the days of local option, children were actually subjected to corporal punishment for refusing to participate in public school prayers that were contrary to their own religious practice.

"Local option" is unlikely to be very pluralistic. Though this Nation is highly pluralistic, taken as a whole, its pluralism tends not to be very local. A map showing the religious complexion of the counties of the United States was submitted by Prof. Martin Marty in the 1964 hearings showing that the vast majority of the counties in the United States have more than 51 percent of their population affiliated with one particular denomination; Lutherans in the North Central States, Baptists in the Southeast, Roman Catholics in the Northeast and Southwest, et cetera. In those counties it would be surprising if the majority religion did not dominate the prayer practices in the public schools.

We are told that 70 percent of our people responding to public opinion polls favor restoring prayer to public schools, and that may indeed be the case. But the rights protected by the Bill of Rights, I am pleased to say, are not at the mercy of public opinion polls. As the U.S. Supreme Court said in words that undergird the rights of every one of us:

The very purpose of the Bill of Rights was to withdraw certain subjects from the vicissitudes of political controversy, to place them beyond the reach of majorities and officials and to establish them as legal principles to be applied by the courts. One's right to life, liberty, and property, to free speech, a free press, freedom of worship and assembly, and other fundamental rights may not be submitted to vote; they depend on the outcome of no election.

Our experience over the past 20 years has been that when people are asked point-blank, "Do you think there should be prayer in public schools," their impulse may be to reply, "Why, yes, I guess so." But if they study the issues, all their ramifications, for a while, they often come to the opposite conclusion. That has happened in the governing body of the NCCC when it considered this issue in 1963. It happened in the United Presbyterian Church and in one after another of our major member denominations.

That is the kind of consideration that we believe this important matter deserves. We do not believe these issues can be properly understood without in-depth study and reflection on the issues and their widest implications. So we welcome the hearings being undertaken by this committee. We are confident that all sides will be fully considered and that a deeper understanding of this fundamental issue of civil liberty will be attained by all.

The churches of the National Council of Churches believe deeply in prayer, contrary to what some of our critics may think. We open all of our sessions with prayer and worship. But we are a church body, and a public school is not. We do not think we should look to the public schools to keep alive our religious faith. Let us leave his very vital need to be fulfilled by families and religious organizations, but certainly not public institutions.

Whatever Congress and the several governments across the land may decide we will ultimately take our counsel on how to pray from the Lord of our faith, who said:

> Beware of practicing your piety before men in order to be seen by them . . . When you pray, you must not be like the hypocrites, for they love to stand and pray in the synagogues and at the street corners, that they may be seen by men. Truly, I say to you that they have their reward. But when you pray, go into your room and shut the door and pray to your father who is in secret; and your Father who sees in secret will reward you. (Matt. 6:1, 5-6.)

The Supreme Court has not forbidden anyone to follow the instruction I have just read. It could not if it tried. Any child can pray to God, anytime, anywhere, in school or out. The effort to make the prayer an oral, collective one is apparently intended to accomplish something else.

We are told it is necessary to "put God back into the public schools" in order to remedy delinquency, restore discipline, reduce violence, eliminate alcohol and drug addiction, and increase respect for authority. They are laudable goals, and I confess if school prayers would change them then I might be for it. But it is a farce to suppose that they can be achieved by the recitation of a 2-minute prayer at the beginning of the public schoolday.

The disorganization and deterioration of public schools has many causes, deep and of long development, which will not be rectified by simplistic measures. Imposing formalized, routine prayer recitations on teachers and pupils, who may not be motivated by the true and free devotion of

the heart is too simplistic a measure. And while it will not be the answer to certain current crises, it will undo the foundation of our civil rights for all time. . . .

MR. KASTENMEIER. I compliment you on a most eloquent statement. The gentleman from North Carolina, Mr. [Lamar] Gudger?

MR. GUDGER. Thank you, Mr. Chairman. Mr. Howard, I've observed in the statement attached to your testimony, this observation:

> The public schools have an obligation to help individuals develop an intelligent understanding and appreciation of the role of religion in the life of the people of this Nation.

Would that not be consistent with Bible reading in the public schools?

MR. HOWARD. I think this is probably meant to mean the examination, from an academic standpoint, of the Nation's history and the role of religious institutions in the evolution of that history from a historical standpoint. At which——

MR. GUDGER. Doesn't the Old Testament meet that case? Doesn't the Old Testament certainly meet that case?

MR. HOWARD. In the same policy statement we affirm the use of the Bible insomuch as it assists in the explanation of our religious heritage. We do not believe, on the other hand, that Bible reading should be used in a devotional context.

MR. GUDGER. So, really, your remarks here relate to prayer rather than Bible readings? Or do I misunderstand?

MR. HOWARD. Well, the remarks that I have given, yes. I have tried to stick to the proposed amendment.

MR. GUDGER. How do you feel about prayer in the opening sessions of the Senate and the House of Representatives?

17. SHOULD WE ALLOW PRAYER IN PUBLIC SCHOOLS?

MR. HOWARD. We would be inclined to regard the position taken by adults in a house of Congress quite differently from those that we would regard as, you know, the position of impressionable children.

MR. GUDGER. How about secondary educational institutions such as the State-supported universities? Would you favor bible readings and prayers in those institutions since they are serving adults? Those over 18?

MR. HOWARD. According to the statement of the Council, I would state that we would oppose any systematic imposition of prayer reading in any public institution. We do not oppose the voluntary agreement by adults to adhere to a particular religious practice. But the decision by the State to have it, as a part of the regular organized procedure of a State institution, I think we would have to oppose.

MR. GUDGER. And I take it that you do not perceive that there is any responsibility on the part of the public schools system in any context whatever to enhance the knowledge and education of its students in the ways of prayer or in the ways of the history of our religious faiths?

MR. HOWARD. I think it is possible to teach—and by the way, I'm a student of the history of religions—I believe it is possible to teach about a particular people's religious heritage without propagating that particular heritage. And I would say we would be for the former and not the latter.

MR. GUDGER. All right, sir. You have a very interesting statement on page 4 of your testimony in which you say: "Instead, we must leave way for the children, with ease, to be true to the religious tutelage, or the lack of it, that is propagaged in the families."

Do you not feel that as a minister of the gospel you have some responsibility to encourage the enlightenment of children to religious history and faith? Particularly where they have been deprived of it in their families? Or do you really perceive that it is your duty, as a minister of the gospel, to encourage adherence of children to the faith of their parents, as you say in this statement?

MR. HOWARD. As a Baptist preacher from Georgia, I would reserve the right to buttonhole a child as they leave the schoolyard and share the essence of my faith. But I think what we have been talking about here is a very important civil liberty.

We talk in the testimony about children being required by law to attend school. And I would certainly want to stand steadfastly against the imposition of my own faith on those children who may be from a different religious tradition.

● ● ●

POSTSCRIPT

SHOULD WE ALLOW PRAYER IN PUBLIC SCHOOLS?

One of Howard's most telling points is his jibe about the "to whom it may concern" quality of so-called "non-denominational" prayers. The prayer struck down in the *Engel* case, which is cited in the introduction to this issue, is a good example of this kind of vacuous compromise. But has Howard proven that such prayers are necessarily unconstitutional? Rountree contends that the "establishment" clause has to be balanced off against the "free exercise" clause of the First Amendment. Suppose that the prayer were truly voluntary, free from even the subtle psychological pressures to which Howard refers, and suppose that all wished to say it. Would it still be an "establishment of religion" for all to say it? Would it violate the "free exercise" clause if they were prevented from saying it? Such questions may never be raised in a courtroom, for who would bring the suit if all wanted the prayer? There are indications, in fact, that prayers are still being said in some public schools around the nation.

The issue of school prayer is part of the larger issue of church-state relations in America. A thoughtful exploration of this question from the perspective of liberal Catholicism is John Courtney Murray's WE HOLD THESE TRUTHS (Doubleday Image, 1964). Leo Pfeffer's CREEDS IN COMPETITION (Greenwood, 1978, originally published in 1958) proceeds from the Jeffersonian premise that there must be a "wall of separation between Government and religion." Will Herberg's classic PROTESTANT-CATHOLIC-JEW (Doubleday, 1955) is a sensitive study of the relationship between America's three major creeds. The "religious right" has been a much-discussed topic in recent years. In the "Reporter at Large" section of the May 18, 1981 *New Yorker*, Frances Fitzgerald views it with alarm. A critique of her view is supplied by Nathan Glazer in the Summer 1982 issue of *This World*, a new periodical which explores the relevance of religion to public affairs.

ISSUE 18

IS DETENTE POSSIBLE?

YES: George F. Kennan, from THE CLOUD OF DANGER: CURRENT REALITIES OF AMERICAN FOREIGN POLICY (Boston, Massachusetts, 1977)
NO: Aleksandr Solzhenitsyn, from "Misconceptions About Russia Are a Threat to America," *Foreign Affairs,* Spring 1980

ISSUE SUMMARY

YES: Former State Department officer Kennan is persuaded that there are no differences between the U.S. and the Soviet Union which are worth the devastation that would result from confrontation between the superpowers.
NO: Nobel prize Laureate Solzhenitsyn is adamant in his belief that there can be no such thing as peaceful co-existence between democracy and communism, and that detente only serves to weaken us for the inevitable struggle.

Ever since British Prime Minister Chamberlain appeased Adolf Hitler in 1938 and consented to the dismemberment of Czechoslovakia in the hope of thus averting war (which came the following year, because Hitler's appetite for more territory remained unappeased), a foreign policy of appeasement has had a bad name.

Appeasement was the charge hurled against those who sought to negotiate trade, disarmament or peace with the Soviet Union in the "cold war" era following World War II. Non-appeasement meant "standing up to the Soviets," "calling the Communist bluffs," and preparing for the war which some thought was inevitable and others thought likely if we betrayed weakness.

This tough approach to Soviet expansionism received its most influential expression in an article entitled "The Sources of Soviet Conduct," published in 1947 in the magazine *Foreign Affairs* and signed by "Mr. X." Mr. X it was soon learned was George Kennan, head of the State Department's Policy Planning Staff, then and for many years one of the major shapers of American foreign policy toward the Soviet Union. The Soviet press almost invariably called Kennan "the architect of the cold war," whose strategy seemed to be summed up in Kennan's call for:

the adroit and vigilant application of counter-force at a series of constantly shifting geographical and political points, corresponding to the shifts and maneuvers of Soviet policy.

By the mid-1960s the notion of a monolithic Communist conspiracy to conquer the world had lost much of its credibility. The Soviet Union was no longer the unchallenged leader of world communism. The deep rift that developed between Communist China and the Soviet Union served not only to allay fears of their alliance against the West but also to dispel myths of Soviet invulnerability. Soviet bloc Communist nations and Communist parties elsewhere displayed increasing independence. "Third World" countries grew in number and influence, and neither the U.S. nor the U.S.S.R. could take their support for granted. Moreover, Soviet non-intervention in Vietnam appeared to belie the belief in their designs for world conquest.

The most dramatic symbolic expression of a changed American attitude toward communism came in President Nixon's trips to Moscow and Peking to meet with the Russian and Chinese heads of state. Gradually the cold war seemed to thaw, and Henry Kissinger, first an influential foreign policy adviser and then Secretary of State under Presidents Nixon and Ford, helped to fashion a foreign policy of detente, or relaxation of tension. The policy embodied a conviction that the two super-powers could negotiate to their mutual advantage such grave matters as nuclear arms limitations and foreign trade. The first SALT (Strategic Arms Limitation Treaty) and American wheat grain sales to Russia were among the fruits of detente. If the policy was seen as a major step toward lasting peace by its advocates, its critics castigated it as merely another form of appeasement.

The Soviet invasion of Afghanistan, the repression of political dissidents within the Soviet Union, and the encouragement of revolutionary movements abroad led many analysts of Soviet behavior to reassess the policy of detente. A second SALT treaty was at least temporarily abandoned by President Carter while it was still pending in the Senate, the government embargoed Soviet grain sales, the United States withdrew its participation from the Summer Olympics in Moscow in 1980, and the President and Congress seemed more inclined to sharply increase the military budget. Out of office, Kissinger no longer sounded like the conciliatory spokesman for detente. But George Kennan, denying that he had ever believed that the Russians constituted a serious threat to our survival, counselled moderation and conciliation.

Those who believe today that both detente and Kennan are wrong include many of the leading political figures in both parties. No one expresses that opposition more passionately or persuasively than Aleksandr Solzhenitsyn, the Nobel Prize-winning Russian novelist, who was compelled to leave the Soviet Union in 1974 and has lived in the United States since 1975. The context in which foreign policy is viewed is subject to change, but the fundamental choice—detente or deterrence, rapprochement or resistance— is likely to remain the same for years to come.

YES
George F. Kennan

THE CLOUD OF DANGER

"DETENTE" AND ITS MISINTERPRETATION

Some years ago, towards the end of the 1960s, for a variety of reasons, among which Russia's relations with China and the consolidation of the authority of the Brezhnev regime played a prominent part, prospects improved for an effort by the U.S. government to reach a better understanding with the Soviet government on a limited but important group of questions. These included outstandingly those of the control of strategic nuclear weaponry—also, those of the possible extension and improvement of exchanges and facilities for collaboration in various commercial and cultural fields. . . .

All this soon became known, for some reason, by a special name: *detente*. The name itself was not new, but its use in just this connection caught on mightily with the press and promptly became attached to the efforts just described, as though *they* were something wholly new. To many people the name soon came to signify a general change in Soviet-American relations—a basic turning of the corner, distinguishing this phase of the relationship from all that had gone on before. This impression was then deepened by the histrionics of the various summit meetings. Neither of the two governments concerned (though in each case for different reasons) was averse to letting the impression stand that what was involved here was a major and historical change, promising a new era in the relations between the two countries and between Russia and the West, generally. The press, of course, loved all this, systematically over-dramatized it, and magnified it, in its usual fashion, to several times life size.

The pursuit and conclusion by Messrs. Nixon and Kissinger of useful agreements between the two governments in several specific areas was not in itself unfortunate; what *was* unfortunate was the misimpression conveyed to the public of the significance of what was done. These efforts did not, actually, fall outside the long-established pattern of American policy. There had always been ups and downs in this relationship, defining at each juncture the limits of the possible in the way of their improvement; and the United States government had naturally been concerned, at all times except possibly at the height of the Cold War in the early 1950s, to take advantage of the more favorable opportunities.

It may well be that the early 1970s were a uniquely favorable time for progress in certain directions. But the change was one of degree, not of substance. And the fields in question remained limited. The Soviet authorities never gave reason to suppose that they were willing to depart significantly from their established policies and practices in the suppression of political opposition within the Soviet Union, or in the encouragement of pseudo-Marxist "national liberation movements" in the Third World, or in the continued development of their armed forces in areas not covered by specific arms-control agreements. That government was prepared to conclude agreements with us in specific and limited areas. It reserved its freedom of action in areas not covered by the respective agreements, and gave us no serious reason to assume that its conduct in those other areas would be significantly affected by what people sometimes called "the atmosphere of detente." For the contrary impression we had our own press, and the confusing euphoria of summitry, to thank.

Both governments, perhaps, could be held at fault for not moving to correct the growing impression that some all-pervasive change had occurred by virtue of which the Soviet government would now cease to behave like the Soviet government. But the United States government had no reason to deceive itself on this score. Nor did media of communications

commanding such great resources as those of the United States have any excuse for peddling an impression which, as the most rudimentary study of the historical facts would have shown, had no foundation in fact.

Nevertheless, by the time of Watergate, the damage had been done. Large parts of American opinion had been led to expect something that was not to be. And the reaction was not long coming. The achievements of "detente," once the vertigo induced by the summit meetings had passed and the press had turned its magnifying glass on other events, now began to appear insignificant (more so, actually, than was deserved); whereas the continued pursuit by the Soviet authorities of practices in other fields that were disagreeable in American eyes caused displeasure in some American circles and disillusionment in others. This, in turn, was happily seized upon by numbers of people who had never wanted improved relations with the Soviet Union in the first place.

These last were a varied but numerous and vociferous band. Their ranks included those who had an interest of one sort or another in military expenditures; those whose long-standing dream had been to see the United States committed to the overthrow of Soviet power; and those for whom a ringing show of anti-Communist belligerence and vigilance was the stock of political trade. It included others who were wholly unselfish and dedicated in motive but who had a highly bipolar view of international problems and whose suspicions of the Soviet leadership, and hopes for the establishment of American military superiority, were such that they were inclined to see great and dangerous chinks in any arms agreement to which the Soviet government was likely to set its signature; they thus preferred to see us go the path of all-out military preparation rather than that of negotiation for arms control. To all this there was added, as the election of 1976 approached, the fact that the apparent breach between the promises of detente and its demonstrable results provided one more convenient weapon for criticism of the outgoing administration. The Soviet government made its own contribution to this reaction by its action in Angola, demonstrating its newly acquired ability to project its military presence to distant and peripheral points.

Out of all this was brewed, then, a powerful current of opinion in the United States, and to some extent in Western Europe, that professed to see Soviet intentions and actions as more menacing than ever before and advocated not only greatly heightened military expenditures and preparations but the adoption by the United States government, in particular, of a hostile, defiant, and challenging attitude towards the Soviet government—an attitude designed to compel the latter, in the end, to change its policies in the direction of ones more suitable to Western interests. . . .

The principal argument for the thesis that detente was a failure and has brought us into a dangerous position is that which is based on the alleged developing disbalance between the Soviet armed forces and defense preparations and our own. . . .

Closely connected with this, but with a somewhat different focus of emphasis, is the supporting charge that these allegedly menacing defense preparations are only part of a general effort on the part of the Soviet leadership to move out of the position of great and unanswerable regional power that they have so long enjoyed and to challenge the United States for influence and supremacy on a global basis. . . .

The Soviet Union has endeavored for many years to acquire influence with one or another of the factions competing for power in Third World countries. It is an effort not foreign to the practice of great powers generally, including ourselves. What strikes one about these efforts on the Soviet side, particularly in Africa, is not their success but the lack of it. . . .

SOVIET INTENTIONS

On examining these various warnings of heightened Soviet aggressiveness and determination to achieve military superiority, one is struck by certain implicit assumptions that seem to run through them concerning the nature and intentions of the Soviet leadership. These might be summarized as follows:

(a) That the Soviet leadership has not significantly changed since the days of the Cold War and is still primarily inspired by a desire, and intention, to achieve world domination.

(b) That the Soviet leadership views a military showdown with the United States as the inevitable outcome of the ideological and political conflict between the two powers, and looks only for an opportunity to attack the United States and its NATO allies successfully, or to confront them with such overpowering military force that they will "surrender" and place themselves in its power.

(c) That for this reason, the Soviet armed forces serve, in the eyes of the leaders, primarily aggressive rather then defensive purposes.

Supplementing these views there seems to be an assumption on the part of the spokesmen of this thesis, themselves, that the differences of aim and outlook between the Soviet Union and the United States are indeed of such a nature that no peaceful resolution of them is conceivable—that they can be resolved only by war or by the achievement of an unanswerable military superiority by the one party or the other.

I hope to be able, in the following chapter, to treat this question of Soviet intentions at greater length and more adequately. But there are one or two things about these assumptions that ought to be said at this point.

First: When people suggest or imply that there is no significant difference between the Soviet Union we knew at the close of the Stalin era, a quarter of a century ago, and that which we have before us today, this is a sign that those same people have not looked very attentively or deeply at either the composition or the situation of the Soviet regime. Actually, even Stalin, in his final years, seems to have accepted the inevitability, or probability, of an eventual military showdown not because he himself wanted it or thought it necessary from the Soviet standpoint, but rather because he thought the Western powers were determined to push things to that point. But whatever he may then have thought, there is not reason to suppose that the present leadership would see things precisely as he did.

Certainly, if all this could be achieved bloodlessly, without upsetting repercussions at home and without increased responsibilities for the Soviet Union abroad, the leadership of that country would no doubt be pleased—but only within limits—to see such things as abandonment of the Western position in Berlin, a clear Soviet military ascendancy all the way from the Atlantic to the Chinese frontier, and heightened Soviet prestige the world over. Whether they would really like to see a dismantling of American military power in Western Europe is questionable. But that this leadership would wish to see all this achieved by war, even if this could be done with only a relatively moderate amount of military damage to the Soviet Union, is highly doubtful. I must dismiss, as unworthy of serious attention, the suggestion that the Soviet leaders would be prepared to accept a loss of several tens of millions of the Soviet population in a nuclear encounter if it could thereby expect to establish a military superiority over the United States. The memories and trauma of World War II are far more active in Russia than people in the West seem generally to realize. Wars, particularly ones waged at distance from the center of Russian power and for purposes that did not seem to include the defense of the heartland, have always been politically dangerous in modern times to Russian governments. And there are other, more subjective reasons for such hesitations on the part of the present leadership, which it will be more useful to treat in the next chapter.

But beyond this, the people who profess to see some sort of a military showdown as inevitable, allegedly because the Soviet leaders are determined to have it, seem themselves to be only too ready to accept that same thesis for themselves, as something flowing from the logic of the conflict of aims and ideals between the two countries. This is perhaps the most dangerous of all the elements in their thinking. For competitive military preparations, pursued over a long period of time, conduce insensibly to the assumption that a military conflict so long and intensively prepared for must at some point take place. People tend, then, to forget that perhaps there was nothing in the actual interests and needs of the respective peoples to justify a war in the first place. . . .

There is no political or ideological difference between the Soviet Union and the United States—nothing which either side would like, or would hope, to achieve at the expense of the other—that would be worth the risks and sacrifices of a military encounter. Given a realistic appreciation of the limitations of great-power imperialism, and particularly of Russian imperialism, in the modern age, it would be cheaper, safer, and less damaging over the long term for either side to yield on any of the points of difference between them rather than to accept the disaster which modern war would spell. This has been repeatedly demonstrated by recent history. It is evident, for example, that in 1916, in the middle of World War I, either side could have accepted the maximum terms of the other side for ending the war and have been better off than it was by continuing the war for another two years. (To observe this is not to make a plea for political surrender. It is merely to urge that we get our thinking straight.)

While there are no doubt individuals in the Soviet hierarchy of power who do not understand this, there is abundant evidence that the Soviet leadership as a whole does. War, consequently, or even the risk of it that would be implied in any all-out effort to achieve military superiority, is not their favored means of achieving such of their objectives as seem to be in conflict with those of the United States. Nor do any of these objectives, insofar as we can observe them— particularly in Eurasia—seem to be of such a nature as to challenge any vital

interest of ours—the only possible exception being Berlin. There appear, however, most unfortunately, to be numbers of Americans to whom none of this is apparent.

It has been noted above that the tendency of the American military mind, when confronted with the argument that the Soviet leaders are perhaps neither determined to do, or even desirous of doing, to us all the dreadful things of which we are now being warned, is to say: "We cannot make assumptions about Soviet intentions. The evidence is too vague and too complex. We must assume them desirous of doing anything injurious to us which they have the capability of doing."

Does it never occur to these people, one wonders, that in taking that position they are themselves making a sweeping assumption about Soviet intentions— namely, the most extreme, most pessimistic, least sophisticated, and most improbable assumption they could make— the assumption, namely, that these, their political opponents, lack all the normal attributes of humanity and are motivated by nothing but the most blind and single-minded urge of destruction towards the peoples and substance of the United States and its allies?

This effort at the dehumanization of the opponent—the insistence on seeing him as the embodiment of all evil, unaffected by motives other than the desire to wreak injury upon others—has bedeviled the leaders of American opinion in two world wars. There should be no place for it in the assessment of another great power in peacetime, and particularly not of one with whom our political differences are not such as to require or justify a war for their settlement. Particularly should there be no place for it in an age when war between great nuclear-armed powers has become mortally dangerous to all participants— as well as nonparticipants.

If the United States is to behave, in the face of the problem of Soviet power, in a manner conducive to its own present security and that of future generations, it has no choice but to put this sort of childishness behind it and consent to look at that power soberly and carefully, for what it is, not for what would fit best into the dialectics of theoretical military planning. . . .

THE INTERNAL SITUATION

No Western policy towards the Soviet Union that fails to take into account the nature and situation of the present Soviet leadership can be a sound one. Much of the discussion of Soviet-American relations on the alarmist side is cast in terms indistinguishable from those that were being used at the height of the Cold War, around the time of the death of Stalin. One would suppose, to read this material, that no significant change of any sort had taken place since Stalin's death—that the men now in power presented precisely the same problem from our standpoint as their predecessors of a quarter of a century ago. Actually, this is far from being the case.

The present Soviet leadership is, as governing groups in great countries go, an exceptionally old one The average age of the top five or six figures is well over seventy. . . . The advanced age of the senior leadership in the Soviet Union is a fact well known to all students of Soviet affairs.

This does not mean that the men in question are ineffectual or lacking in the capacity for hard work. It does mean that they are men who have had long and sobering governmental experience. Men of this age and this experience are not normally given to adventuristic policies or to moves likely to impose enormous additional strains and uncertainties upon themselves and upon the system of power they head. . . .

Many of the more alarmist visions of Soviet behavior, as now voiced in the United States, seem to reflect a view of the top Soviet leadership as a group of men who, having all internal problems effectively solved and nothing to do but to plot our destruction, sit at the pinnacle of a structure of power whose blind and unquestioning obedience resembles that of a tremendously disciplined military force, poised for the attack and only awaiting superior orders. This is unrealistic even from the standpoint of the actual relations between that leadership and its own bureaucracy. It is even more unrealistic when applied to the relationship of that leadership with the leaders of the Eastern European satellite regimes. And it disregards another factor commonly regarded in the West as insignificant in the case of Russia, namely: public opinion within the country. Public opinion in Russia naturally does not play the same role in Russia that it plays under a democratic system; but it is not wholly without importance in the eyes of the regime, if only because it affects political and labor morale. The reactions of common people, too, are something the regime has to think about before it launches on abrupt and drastic changes of policy. All this has relevance, of course, to the fears expressed in the West about a sudden Soviet attack on Western Europe, for it affects the ability of the regime to take full advantage of the element of surprise. . . .

The Soviet leadership must be seen, then, as an old and aging group of men,

307

commanding—but also very deeply involved with—a vast and highly stable bureaucracy. This bureaucracy is very much a creature of habit. It is effective in governing the country, but it would not be a very flexible instrument for sudden or abrupt changes. This does not preclude a certain amount of conspiratorial activity on the part of the secret intelligence services and of those sections of the Party which deal with clandestine operations in foreign countries. It does mean that the Soviet apparatus of power is not one that can suddenly be turned around and switched, in the course of a few days, from the normal governing of the country to the huge and wholly abnormal exertions of a major war.

All of the above would be true even if the main concerns of this top leadership were ones addressed primarily to foreign affairs, and specifically to thoughts of aggressive expansion at the expense of other powers. Actually, there is no reason to suppose that this last is the case. The overwhelming weight of evidence indicates that there has never been a time since the aftermath of the recent war when the main concerns of the Soviet leadership have not been ones related to the internal problems that face them: first, the preservation of the security of their own rule within the country, and secondly, the development of the economic strength of a country which, although considerably greater than the United States in area and population, has only roughly one half of the latter's gross national product.

With respect to the first of these concerns the leadership faces a number of problems—not immediately crucial ones, but ones that give it no small measure of puzzlement and anxiety. One of these is the general indifference, among the population, towards the ideological pretensions of the regime, and the curious sort of boredom and spiritlessness that overcome so much of Soviet society in the face of the insistence of the regime that nothing but that same stale and outdated ideology must find expression in either public utterance or organized activity. This has a number of negative consequences which the regime cannot ignore. Not the least of these is the appalling growth of alcoholism in all echelons of the population but particularly among the working youth. Another one is the continuing vitality of religious faith under a regime which has always held religion in contempt and created its own ideology as a replacement for it. . . .

Then there is, of course, the problem of dissent among the intellectuals. . . . Like the problem of the dissidents, . . . national restlessness in the constituent republics is not a serious short-term problem for the regime, but it is a hard one to cope with; for both tolerance and repression tend to enhance rather than to dispel it. . . .

Added to these concerns, and probably more important than any of them in the claims they place on the attention of the leaders, are the various continuing problems of the economic development of the country. . . .Chief among these, of course, is the persistent inadequacy of Soviet agriculture to meet the needs of a growing population. . . .

THE EXTERNAL SITUATION

Just as the security (not the expansion) of their own power is the prime consideration for the Soviet leaders when they face their own country, so it is when they face the outside world.

This means for them, first of all, no premature or unsettling relaxation of

Soviet authority over the Eastern European satellite area. The Soviet leadership could possibly accommodate itself, in time, to a greater degree of independence on the part of one or another of the countries concerned (to a certain extent it has already done so), but only if this does not change the military-political balance in Europe in a manner too detrimental to Soviet military security or prestige, and only if it does not set up liberationist ripples that would carry into the Soviet Union itself. This last is a greater danger than it would have been before 1939, because the extension of the Soviet borders so far to the west during World War II had the effect of bringing into the Soviet Union peoples who are more sensitive to happenings elsewhere in Eastern and Central Europe than are the Russians themselves.

The first requirement of Soviet foreign policy is thus the preservation of the present delicate balance of forces in Europe and, in the absence of any satisfactory arrangements with the Western powers for mutual disengagement or withdrawal in Central Europe, the assurance of the integrity of Soviet hegemony in that region. This, the reader will note, is a strongly defensive consideration.

The second requirement, not addressed to relations with "capitalist" countries, but one which nevertheless belongs in the category of foreign policy, is the protection of the image of the Soviet Union as the central bastion of revolutionary socialism throughout the world, and of the Soviet Party leadership as a uniquely wise and prestigious body of men, endowed with a profound understanding of Marxist principles and enjoying great experience in their application—hence, an indispensable source of guidance for Commmunist and national-liberationist forces everywhere.

This, obviously, is the ideal, not the complete present-day reality. It is an ideal which has been steadily eroded in recent years, and is still under severe attack by the Chinese and others. But it is not wholly devoid of political substance. It is the pretense, if not the reality, and it must, in the eyes of the men in the Kremlin, be defended at all costs.

Why defended? Because the forfeiture or serious undermining of this image would spell for the leadership the most dangerous sort of isolation and insecurity: isolation between a capitalist world which has not fully accepted it, and could not fully accept it, and a Communist world that had lost confidence in it and rejected it; insecurity, because the loss of this image would throw into question the legitimacy of the regime at home. The posture of moral and political ascendancy among the Marxist and national-liberationist political forces of the world is essential to the justification of the dictatorship exercised over, and the sacrifices demanded of, the peoples of the Soviet Union for more than half a century. Having once forfeited the plausibility of this external posture, it would be hard to maintain the internal one. . . .

If these considerations have any validity, the position of the Soviet leadership might be summed up somewhat as follows:

This is an aging, highly experienced, and very steady leadership, deeply involved with a structure of power, and particularly a higher bureaucracy, that would not easily lend itself to the implementation of policies of that nature. It faces serious internal problems, which constitute its main preoccupation.

18. IS DETENTE POSSIBLE?

As this leadership looks abroad, it sees more dangers than inviting opportunities. Its reactions and purposes are therefore much more defensive than aggressive. It has no desire for any major war, least of all for a nuclear one. It fears and respects American military power even as it tries to match it, and hopes to avoid a conflict with it. Plotting an attack on Western Europe would be, in the circumstances, the last thing that would come into its head.

The most active external concerns of this leadership relate, today, to the challenge to its position within the world Communist movement now being mounted by the Chinese and others. It will consider itself fortunate if, in the face of this challenge, it succeeds in preserving its pre-eminence within the Communist sector of the world's political spectrum, in avoiding a major war which, as it clearly recognizes, would be the ruin of everyone involved, itself included, and in ending its own days peacefully—its members going down in history as constructive leaders who contributed, much more than Stalin and at least as much as Khrushchev, to the advancement of the glory of the Soviet Union and the cause of world communism.

●   ●   ●

NO   Aleksandr Solzhenitsyn

MISCONCEPTIONS ABOUT RUSSIA ARE A THREAT TO AMERICA

Anyone not hopelessly blinded by his own illusions must recognize that the West today finds itself in a crisis, perhaps even in mortal danger. One could point to numerous particular causes or trace the specific stages over the last 60 years which have led to the present state of affairs. But the ultimate cause clearly lies in 60 years of obstinate blindness to the true nature of communism.

I am not concerned here with those who cherish, glorify and defend communism to this day. To such people I have nothing to say. Yet there are many others who are aware that communism is an evil and menace to the world, but who have nevertheless failed to grasp its implacable nature. And such individuals, in their capacities as policy advisors and political leaders, are even now committing fresh blunders which will inevitably have lethal repercussions in the future.

Two mistakes are especially common. One is the failure to understand the radical hostility of communism to mankind as a whole—the failure to realize that communism is irredeemable, that there exist no "better" variants of communism; that it is incapable of growing "kinder," that it cannot survive as an ideology without using terror, and that, consequently, to coexist with communism on the same planet is impossible. Either it will spread, cancer-like, to destroy mankind, or else mankind will have to rid itself of communism (and even then face lengthy treatment for secondary tumors).

The second and equally prevalent mistake is to assume an indissoluble link between the universal disease of communism and the country where it first seized control—Russia. This error skews one's perception of the threat and cripples all attempts to respond sensibly to it, thus leaving the West disarmed. This misinterpretation is fraught with tragic consequences; it is imperiling every nation, Americans no less than Russians. One will not have to await the coming of future generations to hear curses flung at those who have implanted this misapprehension in the public awareness. . . .

From, "Misconceptions About Russia are a Threat to America," *Foreign Affairs*, Spring 1980. ©1980, Aleksandr Solzhenitsyn. Reprinted by permission.

18. IS DETENTE POSSIBLE?

By means of his essays, public statements, and words of advice, all of which are supposedly rooted in a profound understanding of Soviet life, George Kennan has for years had a major detrimental influence upon the shape and direction of American foreign policy. He is one of the more persistent architects of the myth of the "moderates" in the Politburo, despite the fact that no such moderates have ever revealed themselves by so much as a hint. He is forever urging us to pay greater heed to the Soviet leaders' pronouncements and even today finds it inconceivable that anyone should mistrust Brezhnev's vigorous denials of aggressive intent. He prefers to ascribe the seizure of Afghanistan to the "defensive impulses" of the Soviet leadership. Many Western diplomats have abandoned painstaking analysis in favor of incurable self-delusion, as we can see in such a veteran of the political arena as Willy Brandt, whose "Ostpolitik" is suicidal for Germany. Yet these ruinous ventures are the very ones honored with Nobel Prizes for Peace.

I would note here a tendency which might be called the "Kissinger syndrome," although it is by no means peculiar to him alone. Such individuals, while holding high office, pursue a policy of appeasement and capitulation, which sooner or later will cost the West many years and many lives, but immediately upon retirement the scales fall from their eyes and they begin to advocate firmness and resolution. How can this be? What caused the change? Enlightenment just doesn't come that suddenly! Might we not assume that they were well aware of the real state of affairs all along, but simply drifted with the political tide, clinging to their posts?

Long years of appeasement have invariably entailed the surrender of the West's positions and the bolstering of its adversary. Today we can assess on a global scale the achievement of the West's leading diplomats after 35 years of concerted effort: they have succeeded in strengthening the U.S.S.R. and Communist China in so many ways that only the ideological rift between those two regimes (for which the West can take no credit) still preserves the Western world from disaster. In other words, the survival of the West already depends on factors which are effectively beyond its control.

These diplomats still fall back on their precarious assumptions about an imaginary split within the Soviet Politburo between nonexistent "conservatives" and "liberals," "hawks" and "doves," "Right" and "Left," between old and young, bad and good—an exercise of surpassing futility. Never has the Politburo numbered a humane or peace-loving man among its members. The communist bureaucracy is not constituted to allow men of that caliber to rise to the top—they would instantly suffocate there.

Despite all this, America continues to be fed a soothing diet of fond hopes and illusions. Hopes have been expressed of a split in the Politburo, with one particular version claiming that it was not in fact Brezhnev who occupied Afghanistan! Or else leading experts have offered the fancy that "the U.S.S.R. will meet its Vietnam," be it in Angola, Ethiopia or Afghanistan. (These experts and their readers may rest assured that the U.S.S.R. is at present quite capable of gobbling up five more such countries, swiftly and without choking.) And again and again we are asked to set our hopes on detente despite the trampling of yet another country. (There is indeed no cause for alarm here, for even after Afghanistan the Soviet leaders will be only too happy to restore detente to the status quo ante—an opportunity for them to purchase all that they require in between acts of aggression.)

It goes without saying that America will never understand the U.S.S.R. or fully grasp the danger it poses by relying on information from diplomats such as these. . . .

But even a humbled, defeated and despoiled nation continues to exist physically, and the aim of the communist authorities (whether in the U.S.S.R., in China or in Cuba) is to force the people to serve them unfailingly as a work force or, if need be, as a fighting force. However, when it comes to war, communist ideology has long since lost all its drawing power in the U.S.S.R.; it inspires no one. The regime's intention is thus obvious: to take that same Russian national sentiment which they themselves have been persecuting and to exploit it once more for their new war, for their brutal imperialistic ambitions; indeed to do so with ever greater frenzy and desperation as communism grows ideologically moribund, in a bid to derive from national sentiments the strength and fortitude they lack. This is certainly a real danger.

The informants discussed earlier see this danger, indeed they recognize nothing *but* this danger (rather than the true aspirations of the national spirit). Hence, at their bluntest they abuse us in advance as chauvinists and fascists, while at their most circumspect they argue as follows: since you can see that any religious and national renascence of the Russian people may be exploited by the Soviet authorities for their own vile purposes, you must renounce not only this renascence but any national aspirations whatever.

But then the Soviet authorities also try to exploit the Jewish emigration from the U.S.S.R. in order to fan the flames of anti-Semitism, and not without success. ("See that? They're the only ones allowed to escape from this hell, and the West sends goods to pay for it!") Does it follow that we are entitled to advise Jews to forego the quest for their spiritual and national origins? Of course not. Are we not all entitled to live our natural life on the earth and to strive toward our individual goals, without heed for what others may think or what the papers may write, and without worrying about the dark forces that may attempt to exploit those goals for their own ends?

And why should we speak only about the future? We have our recent past to draw on. In 1918-22 throughout Russia, throngs of peasants with pitchforks (and even in some recorded cases bearing only icons) marched in their thousands against the machine guns of the Red Army; in bolshevism they saw a force inimical to their very existence as a nation. And in their thousands they were slaughtered.

And what of 1941–45? It was then that communism first succeeded in saddling and bridling Russian nationalism: millions of lives were affected and it took place in full view of the rest of the world; the murderer saddled his half-dead victim but in America or Britain no one was appalled; the whole Western world responded with unanimous enthusiasm, and "Russia" was forgiven for all the unpleasant associations her name aroused and for all past sins and omissions. For the first time she became the object of infatuation and applause (paradoxically, even as she ceased being herself), because this saddle horse was then saving the Western world from Hitler. Nor did we hear any reproaches about this being the "supreme danger," although that is in fact precisely what it was. At the time the West refused even to entertain the thought that the Russians might have any feelings other than communist ones.

But what were the real feelings of the peoples under Soviet dominion? Here is how it was. June 22, 1941 had just reverberated into history, Old Man Stalin had sobbed out his bewildered speech, and the entire working population of adult age and of whatever nationality (not the younger generation, cretinized by Marxism) held its breath in anticipation: Our bloodsuckers have had it! We'll soon be free now. This damned communism is done for! Lithuania, Latvia and Estonia gave the Germans a jubilant welcome. Byelorussia, the Western Ukraine and the first occupied Russian territories followed suit. But the mood of the people was demonstrated most graphically of all by the Red Army: before the eyes of the whole world it retreated along a 2,000-kilometer front, on foot, but every bit as fast as motorized units. Nothing could possibly be more convincing than the way these men, soldiers in their prime, voted with their feet. Numerical superiority was entirely with the Red Army, they had excellent artillery and a strong tank force, yet back they rolled, a rout without compare, unprecedented in the annals of Russian and world history. In the first few months some three million officers and men had fallen into enemy hands!

That is what the popular mood was like—the mood of peoples some of whom had lived through 24 years of com-

munism and others but a single year.* For them the whole point of this latest war was to cast off the scourge of communism. Naturally enough, each people was primarily bent not on resolving any European problem, but on its own national task—liberation from communism.

Did the West see this catastrophic retreat? It could not do otherwise. But did it learn any lessons from it? No; blinded by its own pains and anxieties it has failed to grasp the point to this very day. Yet if it had been unflinchingly committed to the principle of *universal* liberty it should not have used Lend-Lease to buy the murderous Stalin's help, and should not have strengthened his dominion over nations which were seeking their own freedom. The West should have opened an independent front against Hitler and crushed him by *its own* efforts. The democratic countries had the strength to achieve this, but they grudged it, preferring to shield themselves with the unfortunate peoples of the U.S.S.R.

After 24 years of terror no amount of persuasion could have enabled communism to save its skin by saddling Russian nationalism. But as it turned out (deprived of outside information in the hermetically sealed communist world we had no way of anticipating this) another similar scourge was bearing down on us from the West, one, moreover, with its own special anti-national mission: to annihilate the Russian people in part and to enslave the survivors. And the first thing the Germans did was to restore the collective farms (whose members had

Translator's note. A number of countries and territories were annexed by the U.S.S.R. in 1939-40. These included Western Ukraine and Western Byelorussia (carved out of Poland in 1939), Estonia, Latvia, Lithuania, Northern Bukovina and Bessarabia.

scattered in all directions) in order to exploit the peasantry more efficiently. Thus the Russian people were caught between hammer and anvil; faced with two ferocious adversaries they were bound to favor the one who spoke their own language. Thus was our nationalism forced to don the saddle and bridle of communism. At a stroke communism seemed to forget its own slogans and doctrines, remaining deaf to them for several years to come; it forgot Marxism, whereas phrases about "glorious Russia" never left its lips; it even went so far as to restore the Church—but all this lasted only until the end of the war. And so our victory in this ill-starred war served only to tighten the yoke about our necks.

But .there was also a Russian movement that sought a third path: attempting to take advantage of this war and in spite of the odds to liberate Russia from communism. Such men were in no sense supporters of Hitler; their integration into his empire was involuntary and in their hearts they regarded only the Western countries as their allies (moreover they felt this sincerely, with none of the duplicity of the communists). For the West, however, anyone who wanted to liberate himself from communism in that war was regarded as a traitor to the cause of the West. Every nation in the U.S.S.R. could be wiped out for all the West cared, and any number of millions could die in Soviet concentration camps, just as long as it could get out of this war successfully and as quickly as possible. And so hundreds of thousands of these Russians and Cossacks, Tatars and Caucasian nationals were sacrificed; they were not even allowed to surrender to the Americans, but were turned over to the Soviet Union, there to face reprisals and execution.

Even more shocking is the way the British and American armies surrendered into the vengeful hands of the communists hundreds of thousands of peaceful civilians, convoys of old men, women and children, as well as ordinary Soviet POWs and forced laborers used by the Germans—surrendered them against their will, and even after witnessing the suicide of some of them. And British units shot, bayonetted and clubbed these people who for some reason did not wish to return to their homeland. Yet more amazing still is the fact that not only were none of these British and American officers ever punished or reprimanded, but for almost 30 years the free, proud and unfettered press of these two countries unanimously and with studied innocence kept its silence about their governments' act of treachery. For 30 years not a single honest pen presented itself! Surely this is the most astonishing fact of all! In this single instance the West's unbroken tradition of publicity suddenly failed. Why?

At the time, it seemed more advantageous to buy off the communists with a couple of million foolish people and in this way to purchase perpetual peace.

In the same way—and without any real need—the whole of Eastern Europe was sacrificed to Stalin.

Now, 35 years later, we can sum up the cost of this wisdom: the security of the West today is solely dependent upon the unforeseen Sino-Soviet rift.

The selfish and ruinous mistake that the West committed during World War II has since been repeated time and time again, always in the fervent hope of avoiding a confrontation with communism. The West has done its utmost to ignore communist mass murder and aggression. It promptly forgave East Berlin (1953) as well as Budapest and Prague. It hastened to believe in the peaceful intentions of North Korea (which will yet show its true worth) and in the nobility of North Vietnam. It has allowed itself to be shamefully duped over the Helsinki agreement (for which it paid by recognizing forever all the communist takeovers in Europe). It seized on the myth of a progressive Cuba (even Angola, Ethiopia and South Yemen have not sufficed to disenchant Senator McGovern), and put its faith in the alleged key to salvation represented by Eurocommunism. It solemnly participated in the interminable sessions of the sham Vienna Conference on European Disarmament. And after April 1978, it tried for two years not to notice the seizure of Afghanistan. Historians and future observers will be amazed and at a loss to explain such cowardly blindness. Only the appalling Cambodian genocide has exposed to the West the depth of the lethal abyss (familiar to us, who have lived there for 60 years), but even here, it seems, the Western conscience is already becoming inured and distracted.

It is high time for all starry-eyed dreamers to realize that the nature of communism is one and the same the whole world over, that it is everywhere inimical to the national welfare, invariably striving to destroy the national organism in which it is developing, before moving on to destroy adjacent organisms. No matter what the illusions of detente, no one will ever achieve a stable peace with communism, which is capable only of voracious expansion. Whatever the latest act in the charade of detente, communism continues to wage an incessant ideological war in which the West is unfailingly referred to as the enemy.

Communism will never desist from its effort to seize the world, be it through direct military conquest, through subversion and terrorism, or by subtly undermining society from within.

Italy and France are still free, but they have already allowed themselves to be corroded by powerful communist parties. Every human being and any society (especially a democracy) tries to hope for the best, this is only natural. But in the case of communism there is simply nothing to hope for: no reconciliation with communist doctrine is possible. The alternatives are either its complete triumph throughout the world or else its total collapse everywhere. The only salvation for Russia, for China and for the entire world lies in a renunciation of this doctrine. Otherwise the world will face inexorable ruin.

The communist occupation of Eastern Europe and East Asia will not come to an end; indeed, there is an imminent danger of a takeover in Western Europe and many other parts of the world. The prospects for communism in Latin America and Africa have already been clearly demonstrated; in fact any country that is not careful can be seized. There is of course the hope that things will turn out differently: that the communist aggressors will ultimately fail, like all agressors in the past. They themselves believe that their hour of world conquest has arrived and, scenting victory, they unwittingly hasten—to their doom. But to achieve such an outcome in a future war would cost mankind billions of casualties.

In view of this mortal danger, one might have thought that American diplomatic efforts would be directed above all toward reducing the threatening might of these imperialistic "horsemen," to ensuring that they will never again succeed in bridling the national feelings of any country and drawing upon the vitality of its people. Yet this path has not been followed; in fact, the opposite course of action has been pursued.

American diplomacy over the last 35 years presents a spectacle of sorry bumbling. The United States, only recently the dominant world power, the victor in World War II and the leader in the United Nations, has seen a steady, rapid and often humiliating erosion of its position at the U.N. and in the world at large. It has continually declined vis-a-vis the U.S.S.R. a process which even its Western allies have come to condone. Things have reached the point where American senators make apologetic visits to Moscow in order to ensure that the debates in the Senate are not taken amiss in the Kremlin. The whole thrust of American diplomacy has been directed to postponing any conflict, even at the cost of progressively diminishing American strength.

The lesson of World War II is that only desperate, pitiless circumstances can bring about any cooperation between communism and the nation it has enslaved. The United States has not learned this lesson: the Soviet and Eastern European governments have been treated as the genuine spokesmen of the national aspirations of the peoples they have subjugated, and the false representatives of these regimes have been dealt with respectfully. This amounts to a rejection—in advance, and in a form most detrimental to American interests—of any future alliance with the oppressed peoples, who are thereby driven firmly into the clutches of communism. This policy leaves the Russian and the Chinese people in bitter and desperate isolation—

something the Russians already tasted in 1941.

In the 1950s an eminent representative of the postwar Russian emigration submitted to the U.S. Administration a project for coordinating the efforts of Russian anti-communist forces. The response was formulated by a high-ranking American official: "We have no need of any kind of Russia, whether future or past." A conceited, mindless and suicidal answer as far as American interests are concerned. The world has now come to the point where without the rebirth of a healthy, national-minded Russia, America itself will not survive, since all would be annihilated in the bloody clash. In that struggle it would be ruinous for America to fail to distinguish, in theory and in practice, between the communist aggressors and the peoples of the U.S.S.R. so tragically drawn into the conflict. It would be disastrous to fight "the Russians" instead of communism and thereby force a repetition of 1941, when the Russians will again grasp at freedom and find no helping hand.

The day-to-day implementation of current American foreign policy has served to support this perverse and pernicious surrender of the Russian national consciousness to its communist taskmaster. And now, after 35 years of failure, American diplomacy has gambled on another shortsighted, unwise—indeed mad—policy: to use China as a shield, which means in effect abandoning the national forces of China as well, and driving them completely under the communist yoke. (In the interests of this policy it was even deemed acceptable to contribute Taiwan as a down payment.)

This act of betrayal is a blow to the national feelings of both Chinese and Russians. ("America is openly supporting

18. IS DETENTE POSSIBLE?

our totalitarian oppressors and equipping them against us!")

I hardly dare ask where that leaves the principles of democracy. Where is the vaunted respect for the freedom of all nations? But even in purely strategic terms this is a shortsighted policy: a fateful reconciliation of the two communist regimes could occur overnight, at which point they could unite in turning against the West. But even without such a reconciliation, a China armed by America would be more than a match for America. . . .

Today Afghanistan, yesterday Czechoslavakia and Angola, tomorrow some other Soviet takeover— yet even after all this, how good it would be to go on believing in detente! Could it really be over? "But the Soviet leaders haven't repudiated it at all! Brezhnev was quite clear about that: it was in *Pravda!*" (Thus Marshall Shulman and other like-minded experts.)

The West simply does not want to believe that the time for sacrifices has arrived; it is simply unprepared for sacrifices. Men who go on trading right until the first salvo is fired are incapable of sacrificing so much as their commercial profits: they have not the wit to realize that their children will never enjoy these gains, that today's illusory profits will return as tomorrow's devastation. The Western allies are maneuvering to see who can sacrifice the least. Behind all this lies that sleek god of affluence which is now proclaimed as the goal of life, replacing the high-minded view of the world which the West has lost.

Communism will never be halted by negotiations or through the machinations of detente. It can be halted only by force from without or by disintegration from within. The smooth and effortless course of the West's long retreat could not go on forever, and it is now coming to an end: the brink may not have been reached, but it is already the merest step away. Since the outlying borders were never defended, the nearer ones will have to be held. Today the Western world faces a greater danger than that which threatened it in 1939.

It would be disastrous for the world if America were to look upon the Beijing leadership as an ally while regarding the Russian people as no less a foe than communism: by so doing she would drive both these great nations into the maw of communism and plunge in after them. She would deprive both great peoples of their last hope of liberation. The indefatigable denigrators of Russia and all things Russian are forgetting to check their watches: all of America's mistakes and misconceptions about Russia might have been purely academic in the past but not in the swift-moving world of today. On the eve of the global battle between world communism and world humanity, would that the West at least distinguished the enemies of humanity from its friends, and that it sought an alliance not of foes but of friends. So much has been ceded, surrendered and traded away that today even a fully united Western world can no longer prevail except by allying itself with the captive peoples of the communist world.

● ● ●

POSTSCRIPT
IS DETENTE POSSIBLE?

George Kennan, an American who has spent most of his adult life studying the Soviet Union, and Aleksandr Solzhenitsyn, who lived most of his life within the Soviet Union and was sent into involuntary exile by it, are actually in agreement on an interesting point: the Soviet Union's policies are not subject to erratic and frequent change. On the contrary, where many other observers see sharp swings from territorial conquest to peaceful coexistence, both Kennan and Solzhenitsyn observe a long-range consistency in Soviet goals. Yet they arrive at diametrically opposed conclusions with regard to the possibility of detente. Most Americans thought that an American President's visits to the Soviet and Chinese capitals constituted a turning-point in our relations with the Communist world, and that perhaps the Soviet invasion of Afghanistan constituted another kind of turning, away from mutual coopera-tion. Although Kennan's book was written in 1977, he has indicated that the invasion of Afghanistan does not alter his thesis.

Kennan is the author of a number of highly regarded historical studies of Soviet foreign relations and Soviet-American relations. Henry Kissinger's thinking as Secretary of State is probably best expressed in the collection of his addresses, AMERICAN FOREIGN POLICY, Expanded Edition (Norton, 1974). J. William Fulbright, who was the influential Chairman of the Senate Committee on Foreign Relations and a critic of American involvement in Vietnam, outlined his foreign policy views in THE CRIPPLED GIANT: AMERICAN FOREIGN POLICY AND ITS DOMESTIC CONSEQUENCES (Vintage, 1972). Much foreign policy debate invokes national ideals; more than thirty years ago Hans Morgenthau argued that a nation's foreign relations must always be based upon its self-interest. That view is applied to American foreign policy in the recent past in Morgenthau's A NEW FOREIGN POLICY FOR THE UNITED STATES (Praeger, 1969). Many of the most insightful analyses of foreign relations appear in two scholarly publications, *Foreign Affairs,* the older and more establishment-oriented, and *Foreign Policy,* more likely to contain sharply critical studies.

Prophesying whether we are leaving a period of detente and entering into another era of cold war is foolhardy. Leaders change, events change, and the course of our relations with the Soviet Union will change. But two such divergent views as those of Kennan and Solzhenitsyn urge steadfastness and consistency in our foreign policy, and both offer the constants, albeit quite different constants, by which we should set our course. Given the surprises of recent decades—the Sino-Soviet split, American recognition of China, detente, the oil crisis—we may continue to expect the unexpected in our foreign relations.

ISSUE 19

IS NUCLEAR DETERRENCE IRRATIONAL?

YES: Jonathan Schell, from THE FATE OF THE EARTH (Knopf, 1982)

NO: Charles Krauthammer, from "The Real Way to Prevent Nuclear War," *The New Republic,* April 28, 1982

ISSUE SUMMARY

YES: In arguing for an end to the nuclear arms race, Jonathan Schell, staff writer for the *New Yorker,* offers a view of the consequences of nuclear war and its implications for the human race and the Earth itself.

NO: Charles Krauthammer, Senior Editor of the *New Republic,* does not dispute the terror of nuclear war, but argues that this very balance of terror is what prevents war from occurring.

The Cold War between the two superpowers and their allies which has existed since the end of World War II, has spurred the new technology and the stockpiling of more and more weapons of greater destructive power. As each of the two superpowers succeeded in either deploying a new weapon or surpassing the output of the other in an old one, it was seen as necessary for the lagging power to catch up or get ahead.

By the early 1960s, the doctrine of Mutual Assured Destruction (for which the acronym MAD seems fitting) was well entrenched. It argued the importance of deterrence for both sides. As long as the U.S. and its allies on the one hand, and the Soviet Union and its allies on the other, believed that the other side had a military capacity sufficient to counterattack with force adequate to wreak nearly equal, if not superior, injury upon the other in the event of attack (what military planners call second strike capability), both sides shared the conviction that whichever side started the war, it would end in mutual assured destruction.

This provided all the assurance needed that rational leaders would not undertake a preemptive first strike against the other side. But, the advocates of increased arms argued, maintenance of deterrence requires improved technology and newer weapons so that our side will not fall behind, as well as sheer quantitative increases to keep up with our adversary. They point to Soviet superiority in the number of submarine-launched ballistic missiles and the greater firepower of Soviet nuclear warheads. Employing these arguments, President Reagan in 1981 requested a military build-up that if carried to execution would cost in excess of $1.5 trillion by 1986.

Critics of increased arms expenditures countered that both sides already had stockpiled more than 50,000 nuclear bombs. These possessed more than one million times the force of the bomb that had been dropped on Hiroshima, and more than one hundred times the explosive power necessary to destroy all of the large cities on Earth. In the words of one scientist: "The targeters would run out of targets and victims long before they ran out of bombs." What is needed, in the view of critics of American nuclear policy, is a radical reduction of nuclear weapons and the adoption of effective controls that would prevent any of the following possibilities: the proliferation of nations possessing the nuclear weapons, their possession by terrorists or others who might employ them recklessly, their mistaken or accidental use which might trigger a nuclear war, or the escalation of a conventional war into a nuclear conflict.

How can we prevent such a disaster? A nuclear freeze? President Reagan has said that a freeze doesn't go far enough, and opponents of his military policy would be the first to agree. Disavow first use? We might be skeptical of any nation's respecting such a pledge if facing defeat in so-called conventional war. Nuclear arms reduction? Some analysts point out that nuclear weapons make the superpowers nearly equal, while conventional weapons are "destabilizing," because one side is bound to be superior to the other. Mutual disarmament? Assuming effective enforcement (a major stumbling block in disarmament negotiations), the problem remains as to how disarmament policy can be imposed upon nations which are not signatories to such a pact. Unilateral disarmament? Better Red than dead is an unacceptable policy to nearly all Americans and our allies.

The debate in American society is not likely to be resolved soon. While California Senator Alan Cranston warns that we will not survive a nuclear war, nuclear scientist Edward Teller maintains that we will not survive a nuclear freeze. In a spate of books arguing against postwar military policy, Jonathan Schell's THE FATE OF THE EARTH has won the widest public attention for its advocacy of nuclear disarmament. Charles Krauthammer's defense of the policy of nuclear deterrence is also an explicit rebuttal of Schell's analysis and of the contemporary "freeze" movement.

On no issue of contemporary society are the stakes higher. We cannot afford to be paralyzed by fear. In Herman Kahn's phrase, we must learn to think about the unthinkable.

YES
Jonathan Schell

THE CHOICE

. . . One way to begin to grasp the destructive power of present-day nuclear weapons is to describe the consequences of the detonation of a one-megaton bomb, which possesses eighty times the explosive power of the Hiroshima bomb, on a large city, such as New York. Burst some eighty-five hundred feet above the Empire State Building, a one-megaton bomb would gut or flatten almost every building between Battery Park and 125th Street, or within a radius of four and four-tenths miles, or in an area of sixty-one square miles, and would heavily damage buildings between the northern tip of Staten Island and the George Washington Bridge, or within a radius of about eight miles, or in an area of about two hundred square miles. A conventional explosive delivers a swift shock, like a slap, to whatever it hits, but the blast wave of a sizable nuclear weapon endures for several seconds and "can surround and destroy whole buildings" (Glasstone). People, of course, would be picked up and hurled away from the blast along with the rest of the debris. Within the sixty-one square miles, the walls, roofs, and floors of any buildings that had not been flattened would be collapsed, and the people and furniture inside would be swept down onto the street. (Technically, this zone would be hit by various overpressures of at least five pounds per square inch. Overpressure is defined as the pressure in excess of normal atmospheric pressure.) As far away as ten miles from ground zero, pieces of glass and other sharp objects would be hurled about by the blast wave at lethal velocities. In Hiroshima, where buildings were low and, outside the center of the city, were often constructed of light materials, injuries from falling buildings were often minor. But in New York, where the buildings are tall and are constructed of heavy materials, the physical collapse of the city would certainly kill millions of people. The streets of New York are narrow ravines running between the high walls of the city's buildings. In a nuclear attack, the walls would fall and the ravines would fill up. The people in the buildings would fall to the street with the debris of the buildings, and the people in the street would be crushed by this avalanche of people and buildings. At a distance of two miles or so from ground zero, winds would reach four hundred miles an hour, and another two miles away they would reach a hundred and eighty miles an hour. Meanwhile, the fireball would be growing, until it was more than a mile wide, and rocketing upward, to a height of over six miles. For ten seconds, it would broil the city below. Anyone caught in the open within nine miles of ground zero would receive third-degree burns and would probably be killed; closer to the explosion, people would be charred and killed instantly. From Greenwich Village up to Central Park, the heat would be great enough to melt metal and glass. Readily inflammable materials, such as newspapers and dry leaves, would ignite in all five boroughs (though in only a small part of Staten Island) and west to the Passaic River, in New Jersey, within a radius of about nine and a half miles from ground zero, thereby creating an area of more than two hundred and eighty square miles in which mass fires were likely to break out.

If it were possible (as it would not be) for someone to stand at Fifth Avenue and Seventy-second Street (about two miles from ground zero) without being instantly killed, he would see the following sequence of events. A dazzling white light from the fireball would illumine the scene, continuing for perhaps thirty seconds. Simultaneously, searing heat would ignite everything flammable and start to melt windows, cars, buses, lampposts, and everything else made of metal or glass. People in the street would immediately catch fire, and would shortly be reduced to heavily charred corpses. About five seconds after the light appeared, the blast wave would strike, laden with the debris of a now nonexistent midtown. Some buildings might be crushed, as though a giant fist had squeezed them on all sides, and others might be picked up off their foundations and whirled uptown with the other debris. On the far side of Central Park, the West Side skyline would fall from south to north. The four-hundred-mile-an-hour wind would blow from south to north, die down after a few seconds, and then blow in the reverse direction with diminished intensity. While these things were happening, the fireball would be burning in the sky for the ten seconds of the thermal pulse. Soon huge, thick clouds of dust and smoke would envelop the scene, and as the mushroom cloud rushed overhead (it would have a diameter of about twelve miles) the light from the sun would be blotted out, and day would turn to night. Within minutes, fires, ignited both by the thermal pulse and by broken gas mains, tanks of gas and oil, and the like, would begin to spread in the darkness, and a strong, steady wind would begin to blow in the direction of the blast. As at Hiroshima, a whirlwind might be produced, which would sweep through the ruins and radioactive rain, generated under the meteorological conditions created by the blast, might fall. Before long, the individual fires would coalesce into a mass fire, which, depending largely on the winds, would become either a conflagration or a firestorm. In a conflagration, prevailing winds spread a wall of fire as far as there is any combustible material to sustain it; in a firestorm, a vertical updraft caused by the fire itself sucks the surrounding air in toward a central point, and the fires therefore converge in a single fire of extreme heat. A mass fire of either kind renders shelters useless by burning up all the oxygen in the air and creating toxic gases, so that anyone inside the shelters is asphyxiated, and also by heating the ground to such high temperatures that the shelters turn, in effect, into ovens, cremating the people inside them. In Dresden, several days after the firestorm raised there by Allied conventional bombing, the interiors of some bomb shelters were still so hot that when they were opened the inrushing air caused the contents to burst into flame. Only those who had fled their shelters when the bombing started had any chance of surviving. (It is difficult to predict in a particular situation which form the fires will take. In actual experience, Hiroshima suffered a firestorm and Nagasaki suffered a conflagration.)

In this vast theatre of physical effects, all the scenes of agony and death that took place at Hiroshima would again take place, but now involving millions of people rather than hundreds of thousands. Like the people of Hiroshima, the people of New York would be burned, battered, crushed, and irradiated in every conceivable way. The city and its people would be mingled in a smoldering heap. And then, as the fires started, the survivors (most of whom would be on the periphery of the explosion) would be driven to abandon to the flames those family members and other people who were unable to flee, or else to die with them. Before long, while the ruins burned, the processions of injured, mute people would begin their slow progress out of the outskirts of the devastated zone. However, this time a much smaller proportion of the population than at Hiroshima would have a chance of escaping. In general, as the size of the area of devastation increases, the possibilities for escape decrease. When the devastated area is relatively small, as it was at Hiroshima, people who are not incapacitated will have a good chance of escaping to safety before the fires coalesce into a mass fire. But when the devastated area is great, as it would be after the

detonation of a megaton bomb, and fires are springing up at a distance of nine and a half miles from ground zero, and when what used to be the streets are piled high with burning rubble, and the day (if the attack occurs in the daytime) has grown impenetrably dark, there is little chance that anyone who is not on the very edge of the devastated area will be able to make his way to safety. In New York, most people would die wherever the blast found them, or not very far from there.

If instead of being burst in the air the bomb were burst on or near the ground in the vicinity of the Empire State Building, the overpressure would be very much greater near the center of the blast area but the range hit by a minimum of five pounds per square inch of overpressure would be less. The range of the thermal pulse would be about the same as that of the air burst. The fireball would be almost two miles across, and would engulf midtown Manhattan from Greenwich Village nearly to Central Park. Very little is known about what would happen to a city that was inside a fireball, but one would expect a good deal of what was there to be first pulverized and then melted or vaporized. Any human beings in the area would be reduced to smoke and ashes; they would simply disappear. A crater roughly three blocks in diameter and two hundred feet deep would open up. In addition, heavy radioactive fallout would be created as dust and debris from the city rose with the mushroom cloud and then fell back to the ground. Fallout would begin to drop almost immediately, contaminating the ground beneath the cloud with levels of radiation many times lethal doses, and quickly killing anyone who might have survived the blast wave and the thermal pulse and might now be attempting an escape; it is difficult to believe that there would be appreciable survival of the people of the city after a megaton ground burst. And for the next twenty-four hours or so more fallout would descend downwind from the blast, in a plume whose direction and length would depend on the speed and the direction of the wind that happened to be blowing at the time of the attack. If the wind was blowing at fifteen miles an hour, fallout of lethal intensity would descend in a plume about a hundred and fifty miles long and as much as fifteen miles wide. Fallout that was sublethal but could still cause serious illness would extend another hundred and fifty miles downwind. Exposure to radioactivity in human beings is measured in units called rems—an acronym for "roentgen equivalent in man." The roentgen is a standard measurement of gamma- and X-ray radiation, and the expression "equivalent in man" indicates that an adjustment has been made to take into account the differences in the degree of biological damage that is caused by radiation of different types. Many of the kinds of harm done to human beings by radiation—for example, the incidence of cancer and of genetic damage—depend on the dose accumulated over many years; but radiation sickness, capable of causing death, results from an "acute" dose, received in a period of anything from a few seconds to several days. Because almost ninety per cent of the so-called "infinite-time dose" of radiation from fallout—that is, the dose from a given quantity of fallout that one would receive if one lived for many thousands of years—is emitted in the first week, the one-week accumulated dose is often used as a convenient measure for calculating the immediate harm from fallout. Doses in the thousands of rems, which could be expected throughout the city, would attack the central nervous system and would bring about death with-

in a few hours. Doses of around a thousand rems, which would be delivered some tens of miles downwind from the blast, would kill within two weeks everyone who was exposed to them. Doses of around five hundred rems, which would be delivered as far as a hundred and fifty miles downwind (given a wind speed of fifteen miles per hour), would kill half of all exposed able-bodied young adults. At this level of exposure, radiation sickness proceeds in the three stages observed at Hiroshima. The plume of lethal fallout could descend, depending on the direction of the wind, on other parts of New York State and parts of New Jersey, Pennsylvania, Delaware, Maryland, Connecticut, Massachusetts, Rhode Island, Vermont, and New Hampshire, killing additional millions of people. The circumstances in heavily contaminated areas, in which millions of people were all declining together, over a period of weeks, toward painful deaths, are ones that, like so many of the consequences of nuclear explosions, have never been experienced....

The central proposition of the deterrence doctrine—the piece of logic on which the world theoretically depends to see the sun rise tomorrow—is that a nuclear holocaust can best be prevented if each nuclear power, or bloc of powers, holds in readiness a nuclear force with which it "credibly" threatens to destroy the entire society of any attacker, even after suffering the worst possible "first strike" that the attacker can launch. Robert McNamara, who served as Secretary of Defense for seven years under Presidents Kennedy and Johnson, defined the policy, in his book "THE ESSENCE OF SECURITY," published in 1968, in the following terms: "Assured destruction is the very essence of the whole deterrence concept. We must possess an actual assured-destruction capability, and that capability also must be

325

credible. The point is that a potential aggressor must believe that our assured-destruction capability is in fact actual, and that our will to use it in retaliation to an attack is in fact unwavering." Thus, deterrence "means the certainty of suicide to the aggressor, not merely to his military forces, but to his society as a whole." Let us picture what is going on here. There are two possible eventualities: success of the strategy or its failure. If it succeeds, both sides are frozen into inaction by fear of retaliation by the other side. If it fails, one side annihilates the other, and then the leaders of the second side annihilate the "society as a whole" of the attacker, and the earth as a whole suffers the consequences of a full-scale holocaust, which might include the extinction of man. In point of fact, neither the United States nor the Soviet Union has ever adopted the "mutual-assured-destruction" doctrine in pure form; other aims, such as attempting to reduce the damage of the adversary's nuclear attack and increasing the capacity for destroying the nuclear forces of the adversary, have been mixed in. Nevertheless, underlying these deviations the concept of deterring a first strike by preserving the capacity for a devastating second strike has remained constant. The strategists of deterrence have addressed the chief issue in any sane policy in a nuclear-armed world—the issue of survival—and have come up with this answer: Salvation from extinction by nuclear weapons is to be found in the nuclear weapons themselves. The possession of nuclear weapons by the great powers, it is believed, will prevent the use of nuclear weapons by those same powers. Or, to put it more accurately, the threat of their use by those powers will prevent their use. Or, in the words of Bernard Brodie, a pioneer in nuclear strategy, in "THE ABSOLUTE WEAPON: ATOMIC POWER AND

WORLD ORDER," a book published in 1946: "Thus far, the chief purpose of our military establishment has been to win wars. From now on its chief purpose must be to avert them. It can have almost no other useful purpose." Or, in the classic, broad formulation of Winston Churchill, in a speech to the House of Commons in 1955: "Safety will be the sturdy child of terror, and survival the twin brother of annihilation."

This doctrine, in its detailed as well as its more general formulations, is diagrammatic of the world's failure to come to terms with the nuclear predicament. In it, two irreconcilable purposes clash. The first purpose is to permit the survival of the species, and this is expressed in the doctrine's aim of frightening everybody into holding back from using nuclear weapons at all; the second purpose is to serve national ends, and this is expressed in the doctrine's permitting the defense of one's nation and its interests by threatening to use nuclear weapons. The strategists are pleased to call this clash of two opposing purposes in one doctrine a paradox, but in actuality it is a contradiction. We cannot both threaten ourselves with something and hope to avoid that same thing by making the threat—both intend to do something and intend not to do it. The head-on contradiction between these aims has set up a crosscurrent of tension within the policies of each superpower. The "safety" that Churchill mentions may be emphasized at one moment, and at the next moment it is the "terror" that comes to the fore. And since the deterrence doctrine pairs the safety and the terror, and makes the former depend on the latter, the world is never quite sure from day to day which one is in the ascendant—if, indeed, the distinction can be maintained in the first place. All that the world can know for certain is that at any moment the fireballs may arrive. I have said that we do not have two earths, one to blow up experimentally and the other to live on; nor do we have two souls, one for reacting to daily life and the other for reacting to the peril to all life. But neither do we have two wills, one with which we can intend to destroy our species and the other with which we can intend to save ourselves. Ultimately, we must all live together with one soul and one will on our one earth.

. . . The policy of deterrence does not contemplate doing anything in defense of the homeland; it only promises that if the homeland is annihilated the aggressor's homeland will be annihilated, too. In fact, the policy goes further than this: it positively requires that each side leave its population open to attack, and make no serious effort to protect it. This requirement follows from the basic logic of deterrence, which is that safety is "the sturdy child of terror." According to this logic, the safety can be only as great as the terror is, and the terror therefore has to be kept relentless. If it were to be diminished—by, for example, building bomb shelters that protected some significant part of the population—then safety would be diminished, too, because the protected side might be tempted to launch a holocaust, in the belief that it could "win" the hostilities. That is why in nuclear strategy "destruction" must, perversely, be "assured," as though our aim were to destroy, and not to save, mankind.

In strategic terms, the requirement that the terror be perfected, and never allowed to deteriorate toward safety, translates into the requirement that the retaliatory force of both sides be guaranteed—first, by making sure that the retaliatory weapons cannot be destroyed in a first strike, and, second, by making sure that the society of

the attacking power *can* be destroyed in the second strike. And since in this upside-down scheme of things the two sides will suffer equally no matter which one opens the hostilities, each side actually has an interest in maintaining its adversary's retaliatory forces as well as its own. For the most dangerous of all the configurations of forces is that in which one side appears to have the ability to destroy the nuclear forces of the other in a first strike. Then not only is the stronger side theoretically tempted to launch hostilities but—what is probably far more dangerous—the other side, fearful of completely losing its forces, might, in a crisis, feel compelled to launch the first strike itself. If on either side the population becomes relatively safe from attack or the retaliatory strike becomes vulnerable to attack, the temptation to launch a first strike is created, and "stability"—the leading virtue of any nuclear balance of power—is lost. As Thomas Schelling, the economist and noted nuclear theorist, has put it, in "THE STRATEGY OF CONFLICT," a book published in 1960, once instability is introduced on either side, both sides may reason as follows: "He, thinking I was about to kill him in self-defense, was about to kill me in self-defense, so I had to kill him in self-defense." Under deterrence, military "superiority" is therefore as dangerous to the side that possesses it as it is to the side that is supposedly threatened by it. (According to this logic, the United States should have heaved a sigh of relief when the Soviet Union reached nuclear parity with it, for then stability was achieved.) All these conclusions follow from the deterrence doctrine, yet they run so consistently counter to the far simpler, more familiar, and emotionally more comprehensible logic of traditional military thinking—not to mention instinct and plain common sense, which rebel against any such notion as "assuring" our own annihilation—that we should not be surprised when we find that the deterrence doctrine is constantly under challenge from traditional doctrine, no matter how glaringly at odds with the facts traditional doctrine may be. The hard-won gains of deterrence, such as they are, are repeatedly threatened by a recrudescence of the old desire for victory, for national defense in the old sense, and for military superiority, even though every one of these goals not only would add nothing to our security but, if it should be pursued far enough, would undermine the precarious safety that the deterrence doctrine tries to provide.

If the virtue of the deterrence policy lies in its acceptance of the basic fact of life in the nuclear world—that a holocaust will bring annihilation to both sides, and possibly the extinction of man as well—its defect lies in the strategic construct that it erects on the foundation of that fact. For if we try to guarantee our safety by threatening ourselves with doom, then we have to mean the threat; but if we mean it, then we are actually planning to do, in some circumstance or other, that which we categorically must never do and are supposedly trying to prevent—namely, extinguish ourselves. This is the circularity at the core of the nuclear-deterrence doctrine; we seek to avoid our self-extinction by threatening to perform the act. According to this logic, it is almost as though if we stopped threatening ourselves with extinction, then extinction would occur. Brodie's formula can be reversed: if the aim of having nuclear forces is to avert annihilation (misnamed "war" by him), then we must cling for our lives to those same forces. Churchill's dictum can be reversed, too: If safety is the sturdy child of terror, then terror is equally the sturdy child of safety.

But who is to guarantee which of the children will be born? And if survival is the twin brother of annihilation, then we must cultivate annihilation. But then we may *get* annihilation. By growing to actually rely on terror, we do more than tolerate its presence in our world: we place our trust in it. And while this is not quite to "love the bomb," as the saying goes, it decidedly is to place our faith in it, and go give it an all-important position in the very heart of our affairs. Under this doctrine, instead of getting rid of the bomb we build it ever more deeply into our lives. . . .

Yet the deterrence policy in itself is clearly not the deepest source of our difficulty. Rather, as we have seen, it is only a piece of repair work on the immeasurably more deeply entrenched system of national sovereignty. People do not want deterrence for its own sake; indeed, they hardly know what it is, and tend to shun the whole subject. They want the national sovereignty that deterrence promises to preserve. National sovereignty lies at the very core of the political issues that the peril of extinction forces upon us. Sovereignty is the "reality" that the "realists" counsel us to accept as inevitable, referring to any alternative as "unrealistic" or "utopian." If the argument about nuclear weapons is to be conducted in good faith, then just as those who favor the deterrence policy (not to speak of traditional military doctrine) must in all honesty admit that their scheme contemplates the extinction of man in the name of protecting national sovereignty, so must those who favor complete nuclear and conventional disarmament, as I do, admit that their recommendation is inconsistent with national sovereignty; to pretend otherwise would be to evade the political question that is central to the nuclear predicament. The terms of the deal that the world has now struck with itself must be made clear. On the one side stand human life and the terrestrial creation. On the other side stands a particular organization of human life—the system of independent, sovereign nation-states. Our choice so far has been to preserve that political organization of human life at the cost of risking all human life. We are told that "realism" compels us to preserve the system of sovereignty. But that political realism is not biological realism; it is biological nihilism—and for that reason is, of course, political nihilism, too. Indeed, it is nihilism in every conceivable sense of that word. We are told that it is human fate—perhaps even "a law of human nature"—that, in obedience, perhaps, to some "territorial imperative," or to some dark and ineluctable truth in the bottom of our souls, we must preserve sovereignty and always settle our differences with violence. If this is our fate, then it is our fate to die. But must we embrace nihilism? Is there nothing we can do? I do not believe so. Indeed, if we admit the reality of the basic terms of the nuclear predicament—that present levels of global armament are great enough to possibly extinguish the species if a holocaust should occur; that in extinction every human purpose would be lost; that because once the species has been extinguished there will be no second chance, and the game will be over for all time; that therefore this possibility must be dealt with morally and politically as though it were a certainty; and that either by accident or by design a holocaust can occur at any second—then, whatever political views we may hold on other matters, we are driven almost inescapably to take action to rid the world of nuclear arms. Just as we have chosen to live in the system of sovereign states, we can choose to live in some other system. To do so would, of course, be unprecedented, and in many

ways frightening, even truly perilous, but it is by no means impossible. Our present system and the institutions that make it up are the debris of history. They have become inimical to life, and must be swept away. They constitute a noose around the neck of mankind, threatening to choke off the human future, but we can cut the noose and break free. To suppose otherwise would be to set up a false, fictitious fate, molded out of our own weaknesses and our own alterable decisions. We are indeed fated by our acquisition of the basic knowledge of physics to live for the rest of time with the knowledge of how to destroy ourselves. But we are not for that reason fated to destroy ourselves. We can choose to live.

[I] have not sought to define a political solution to the nuclear predicament—either to embark on the full-scale re-examination of the foundations of political thought which must be undertaken if the world's political institutions are to be made consonant with the global reality in which they operate or to work out the practical steps by which mankind, acting for the first time in history as a single entity, can reorganize its political life. I have left to others those awesome, urgent tasks, which, imposed on us by history, constitute the political work of our age. Rather, I have attempted to examine the physical extent, the human significance, and the practical dimensions of the nuclear predicament in which the whole world now finds itself. This predicament is a sort of cage that has quietly grown up around the earth, imprisoning every person on it, and the demanding terms of the predicament—its durability, its global political sweep, its human totality—constitute the bars of that cage. However, if a description of the predicament, which is the greatest that mankind has ever faced, cannot in itself reveal to us how we can escape, it can, I believe, acquaint us with the magnitude and shape of the task that we have to address ourselves to. And it can summon us to action. . . .

In supposing for a moment that the world had found a political means of making international decisions, I made a very large supposition indeed—one that encompasses something close to the whole work of resolving the nuclear predicament, for, once a political solution has been found, disarmament becomes a merely technical matter, which should present no special difficulties. And yet simply to recognize that the task is at bottom political, and that only a political solution can prepare the way for full disarmament and real safety for the species, is in itself important. The recognition calls attention to the fact that disarmament in isolation from political change cannot proceed very far. It alerts us to the fact that when someone proposes, as President Carter did in his Inaugural Address, to aim at ridding the world of nuclear weapons, there is an immense obstacle that has to be faced and surmounted. For the world, in freeing itself of one burden, the peril of extinction, must inevitably shoulder another: it must assume fully responsibility for settling human differences peacefully. Moreover, this recognition forces us to acknowledge that nuclear disarmament cannot occur if conventional arms are left in place, since as long as nations defend themselves with arms of any kind they will be fully sovereign, and as long as they are fully sovereign they will be at liberty to build nuclear weapons if they so choose. And if we assume that wars do break out and some nations find themselves facing defeat in the conventional arena. Then the reappearance of nuclear arms, which would prevent such defeat, becomes a strong likelihood. What nation, once having entrusted its fortunes to the force of arms, would permit itself to be conquered by an enemy when the means of driving him back, perhaps with a mere threat, was on hand? And how safe can the world be while nations threaten one another's existence with violence and retain for themselves the sovereign right to build whatever weapons they choose to build? This vision of an international life that in the military sphere is restricted to the pre-nuclear world is, in fact, thoroughly implausible. If we are serious about nuclear disarmament—the minimum technical requirement for real safety from extinction—then we must accept conventional disarmament as well, and this means disarmament not just of nuclear powers but of all powers, for the present nuclear powers are hardly likely to throw away their conventional arms while non-nuclear powers hold on to theirs. But if we accept both nuclear and conventional disarmament, then we are speaking of revolutionizing the politics of the earth. The goals of the political revolution are defined by those of the nuclear revolution. We must lay down our arms, relinquish sovereignty, and found a political system for the peaceful settlement of international disputes.

The task we face is to find a means of political action that will permit human beings to pursue any end for the rest of time. We are asked to replace the mechanism by which political decisions, whatever they may be, are reached. In sum, the task is nothing less than to reinvent politics: to reinvent the world. However, extinction will not wait for us to reinvent the world. . .

Two paths lie before us. One leads to death, the other to life. If we choose the first path—if we numbly refuse to acknowledge the nearness of extinction, all the while increasing our preparations to bring it about—then we in effect become the allies of death, and in everything we do our attachment to life will weaken; our vision, blinded to the abyss that has opened at our feet, will dim and grow confused; our will, discouraged by the thought of trying to build on such a precarious foundation anything that is meant to last, will slacken; and we will sink into stupefaction, as though we were gradually weaning ourselves from life in preparation for the end. On the other hand, if we reject our doom, and bend our efforts toward survival—if we arouse ourselves to the peril and act to forestall it, making ourselves the allies of life—then the anesthetic fog will lift: our vision, no longer straining not to see the obvious, will sharpen; our will, finding secure ground to build on, will be restored; and we will take full and clear possession of life again. One day—and it is hard to believe that it will not be soon—we will make our choice. Either we will sink into the final coma and end it all or, as I trust and believe, we will awaken to the truth of our peril, a truth as great as life itself, and, like a person who has swallowed a lethal poison but shakes off his stupor at the last moment and vomits the poison up, we will break through the layers of our denials, put aside our fainthearted excuses, and rise up to cleanse the earth of nuclear weapons.

● ● ●

NO

Charles Krauthammer

HOW TO PREVENT NUCLEAR WAR

"Safety will be the sturdy child of terror, and survival the twin brother of annihilation." That was Winston Churchill's description of what he called "The balance of terror." Each superpower has the ability to incinerate the defenseless population of the other many times over; each refrains from attacking because it fears retaliation in kind; each knows that aggression is tantamount to suicide. That is deterrence. Sometimes deterrence is called MAD, mutual assured destruction. By whatever name, deterrence has prevented the outbreak of nuclear war, indeed any war, between the United States and the Soviet Union for a generation.

Living in a world of deterrence is very uncomfortable. Every American and Soviet city dweller knows that he is targeted for destruction by nuclear weapons five thousand miles away. But the physical danger is only part of the problem. The world of deterrence is a world of paradoxes. Weapons are built in order never to be used. Weapons purely for defense of helpless populations, like the antiballistic missile systems, become the greatest threat to peace. Weapons aimed at people lessen the risk of war; weapons aimed at weapons, increase it.

The strains of living in such a world are enormous. A vast antinuclear movement is now rising in the U.S., animated principally by weariness and revulsion with this arrangement. Why now? Ronald Reagan is much of the answer. He helped defeat the SALT II treaty before his election, and has been reluctant to engage the Soviets in strategic arms talks since. For the first time in more than a decade, the U.S. and the Soviet Union are not engaged in negotiations to control strategic nuclear weapons. Worse, Mr. Reagan and some of his advisers have spoken in frighteningly offhand ways about "limited nuclear war" and nuclear warning shots. The Carter Administration's mobile MX plan played a part, too. It appeared such an enormously cumbersome and expensive contrivance that people began to wonder if the experts had not lost touch with reality. So millions of Americans have decided it is time for them to take the problem into their own hands, and an antinuclear grass-roots crusade has emerged.

Like all crusades, it has its bible: Jonathan Schell's just published THE FATE OF THE EARTH and its banner: "the freeze." Recently it even acquired an auxiliary brigade, four members of the American foreign policy establishment who opened a wholly new front by calling for a U.S. renunciation of any first use of nuclear weapons. The bible, the banner, and the brigade approach the nuclear dilemma from different directions, but they all challenge the established doctrines of deterrence. The brigade wants to limit deterrence; the freeze proponents want to ignore it; and Jonathan Schell wants to abolish it. Each deserves the closest scrutiny.

Jonathan Schell flatly rejects deterrence. That is the source of his originality. Otherwise his three-part thesis is unremarkable. Part I restates, albeit elegantly, the awful details of a nuclear holocaust, and concludes that it would lead to the extinction of the human race. (That is the view of some scientists, though not of the National Academy of Sciences' study which Schell used in reaching many of his conclusions.) Part II, an interminable rumination on the meaning of human extinction, comes to the unsurprising conclusion that extinction would be monstrous.

"From the foregoing it follows," Schell writes, after delivering his message in a reiterative style that constitutes its own kind of overkill, "that there can be no justification for extinguishing mankind." The real interest in Schell's book lies in Part III, "The Choice." Here he argues that traditional approaches to nuclear peril, like strategic arms limitation treaties, are mere gestures, aspirin given to a dying patient. He argues that deterrence is a logical fraud because the leaders of a country that had sustained a first strike would have no reason to retaliate, indeed, no country in whose name to retaliate.

What Schell refuses to acknowledge is that any potential aggressor would be deterred—and for over thirty years has been deterred—from striking first because he must anticipate not only the logical responses of the victim, but all possible human responses. Revenge, for example, is one motive to launch a second strike. Paul Warnke, President Carter's arms control chief, gives another. He argues that "our moral commitment" would "require that the leaders who had perpetrated this enormity not be allowed to inherit the earth and bend its people to their will." Soviet leaders reading Warnke (a nuclear dove and a supporter of the freeze) are highly unlikely to calculate that a first strike would meet with no response because that would be "illogical." Furthermore, no one knows what would happen in the confused, unimaginably strained atmosphere of a nuclear crisis. To act—to attack—under the assumption that the other side is constrained to follow purely "logical" courses of action is itself totally illogical. It is precisely because of these calculations that nuclear deterrence has succeeded in preventing nuclear war. That is not to say that deterrence can never fail, but the argument from history is a powerful one. An even more powerful one is the absence of an alternative.

Not that Schell shies away from providing one: a world graced by total disarmament (nuclear and conventional), the abolition of violence, the eradication of national boundaries, the renunciation of sovereignty, and the founding of a new world political order for the peaceful settlement of international disputes. How does he propose to bring this about? That is a detail he could not work into his 231-page treatise. That "awesome, urgent task," he graciously concedes, "I have left to others."

Although he does not explain how we are to bring about a lion-and-lamb scenario which even Isaiah had the audacity only to predict and not to mandate, he does give us a clue as to what the operating principle of his post-messianic world will be. Here we come directly to the critical center of Schell's thinking, to the force that not only underlies his passion today but will save mankind tomorrow—fear. In his world, Schell writes, "Fear would no longer dictate particular decisions, such as whether or not the Soviet Union might place missiles in Cuba; rather, it would be a moving force behind the establishment of a new system by which every decision was made. And, having dictated the foundation of the system, it would stand guard over it forever after, guaranteeing that the species did not slide back toward anarchy and doom." I have my doubts.

Fear is not just the saving principle of Schell's new world order; it is the animating force behind a new mass movement— the freeze campaign. The movement demands a mutual halt in the development, production, and deployment of all nuclear weapons, "because," as the campaign slogan puts it, "no one wants a nuclear war." Like Schell, freeze pro-

ponents are deeply concerned, and rightly so, about the prospect of living in a world in which we have the capacity to blow ourselves to bits at any moment. The freeze crusade has enlisted hundreds of thousands of Americans by showing what happens if the Sword of Damocles ever drops. Thus the graphic skills of Hiroshima victims and the maps with concentric circles radiating from ground zero in everyone's hometown. Schell recognizes that removing this sword requires renunciation not just of overkill, but of minimal deterrence, of the simple capacity to destroy the other side *once*. But very few freeze proponents advocate reducing levels below "sufficiency," because they recognize that in a pre-messianic world this would destabilize the nuclear balance and increase the chances of war. Under a freeze— indeed, under even the most radical of arms proposals, such as former Ambassador George Kennan's proposal to cut nuclear levels in half—the superpowers would still retain the capacity for the total destruction of the other society. Insofar as people support the freeze because they can't stand the thought of being a target for Soviet missiles, they have joined the wrong movement. The freeze offers no solution to that problem. They should be with Jonathan Schell's total disarmament movement, working on the "awesome, urgent task" of remaking human nature.

Some might argue that there is another way, short of universal brotherhood, to remove the Sword of Damocles. That is unilateral disarmament. But quite apart from the fact that such a move would mean the surrender of our values, it would do little to secure our survival. The historical record does not support the proposition that helplessness is a guarantee of safety. There has been one nuclear war on record; in it a nonnuclear Japan lost Hiroshima and Nagasaki. So far there has been only one biological war, the one going on today in Laos and Cambodia. These weapons, now used against helpless tribesmen, were never used against American troops fighting the same Vietnamese forces in the same place. The Hmong, unlike the Americans, lack the capacity to retaliate in kind.

The freeze is not unilateralist, nor do many of its advocates reject deterrence. They say they reject overkill. "Enough is enough," they say. "Why waste billions on useless weapons if all they will do, as Churchill said, is to make the rubble bounce?" (It is sometimes also argued, somewhat anomalously, that having useless, rubble-bouncing weapons is at the same time dangerous.)

The problem is that in their zeal to curb overkill, freeze advocates ignore the requirements of deterrence and, in particular, the requirement for survivability of the deterrent. Our weapons must be able to withstand a first strike and penetrate Soviet defenses in a retaliatory strike (and vice versa). If either side finds the survivability of its weapons systems declining, the world becomes less safe. In an international crisis, each side, particularly the more vulnerable side, has incentive to strike first: the invulnerable side to use its advantage, the vulnerable side to strike before it is too late.

What would happen under a freeze? The U.S. retaliatory capacity depends on the three legs of its strategic triad: the land-based ICBMs, the bomber force, and submarines. Because of the increasing accuracy, power, and numbers of Soviet missiles, the U.S. landbased missile force will soon become vulnerable to a first strike. (It is precisely to eliminate that vulnerability that President Carter proposed hiding the MX in multiple shelters, a scheme now abandoned.) That leaves the

bomber and submarine forces. The bomber force consists of aging B-52s that are increasingly vulnerable to attack while still on the ground, and to being shot down while trying to penetrate Soviet air space. Hence President Carter's decision to deploy air-launched cruise missiles, which would be better able to penetrate Soviet defenses and would allow the B-52s to remain outside Soviet air space. The freeze proposal would prevent deployment of these missiles. It would also prevent production and development of a new bomber, either the B-1 or the Stealth, which would be better able to elude destruction on the ground and Soviet defenses in the air. Note that the B-1 or the Stealth would not be any more destructive than the B-52. They would not make the rubble bounce any higher. They would simply be more likely to get the target, and therefore present the Soviets with a very good reason never to launch a first strike.

That leaves the submarine force, which the U.S. is now in the process of modernizing to make more survivable. The new Tridents are quieter than existing subs, and because they have longer-range missiles they can hide in larger areas of the ocean. The freeze would stop their deployment.

The freeze, a proposal devised for its simplicity, does not deal very well with paradox. It is one of the paradoxes of deterrence that defensive weapons (the ABM, for example) can be more destabilizing and therefore more dangerous to peace than offensive weapons. The freeze fixates on nuclear weapons because they appear more terrible than others. And indeed they are. But they are not necessarily more destabilizing. As former Under Secretary of the Navy James Woolsey points out, the freeze does nothing to prevent nonnuclear antisubmarine and antiaircraft advances, which weaken deterrence. But it does prevent modernization of nuclear systems designed for survivability, which enhances deterrence.

What exactly does it mean to say that if survivability declines, war becomes more likely? One quick fix for a vulnerable deterrent is to adopt a policy of launch-on-warning: as soon as we detect enemy missiles leaving their silos, we launch our missiles before they can be destroyed. (Some officials unsuccessfully urged President Carter to adopt launch-on-warning as an alternative to building the mobile MX.) But this creates a hairtrigger situation, where the time for the world's most important decision is not a matter of minutes but of seconds, too short to check out a faulty radar reading or a misinterpretation of data. That's the price of ignoring the deterrence.

This analysis looks simply at what would happen if the freeze were already a reality. But however fervently American citizens may wish it, they cannot vote a "mututal verifiable freeze" into existence. Unfortunately, that must be negotiated with the Soviets. And bad as a freeze would be as an end point, it would be worse as a U.S. negotiating position—which is exactly what it would be if, say, the Kennedy-Hatfield amendment were adopted. First, it is certain to delay other arms control initiatives. The freeze appeals to American voters because of its simplicity, but a mutual freeze would involve complex negotiations with the Soviets. What exactly would be frozen? At what stage? How would it be verified? The production, stockpiling, and qualitative upgrading of nuclear weapons cannot be detected by satellite, and the Russians have always refused on-site inspection. That problem alone turns the freeze into either a nonstarter or a source of interminable negotiation.

Ironically, there does exist an arms control proposal which, though very complicated, poorly understood by the American people, and unsuited for two-hour ratification by town meetings, is very well understood by the Soviets: SALT II. They have already signed it. If the aim of the freeze movement is a quick, simple, bold move in arms control that would allow us to proceed to real reductions, then the answer is not a freeze, but SALT II. Representative Les Aspin has already pointed out with dismay the American penchant for reinventing the arms control wheel every four years. In 1977 President Carter rejected the Vladivostok Accords negotiated by President Ford and proposed drastic reductions instead. The Soviets rejected his proposal out of hand. It took more than two years to renegotiate SALT II on the original lines of Vladivostok. President Reagan in turn rejected SALT II and called for as yet unspecified START talks. The freeze proponents are doing precisely the same thing. It simply makes no sense to propose a freeze that would require years of negotiations when SALT II is at hand, has already been approved by the Soviets, and could be adjusted in small details and ratified quickly. Of course, SALT is not as catchy a slogan as the freeze. But it is certainly a better, quicker, and more serious path to arms control.

Another aim of the freeze campaign is to move to real reductions. But to arm a U.S. negotiating team with a freeze offer is to ensure that it will have no leverage with which to bargain the Soviets into reductions. We will have unilaterally announced our willingness to forgo all our modernization programs, like the Trident, the cruise missile, and the Stealth bomber. The theory is that this gesture will elicit from the Soviets a more conciliatory negotiating position. The theory is in conflict with history. The Soviets do not have a good record of responding to unilateral gestures. At the Glassboro Summit in 1967, President Johnson tried to interest Premier Kosygin in ABM negotiations. Kosygin demurred. A year later, the Senate defeated an amendment to deny funds for an American ABM system. Three days later Soviet Foreign Minister Andrei Gromyko announced the Soviets' willingness to negotiate arms control. Eventually they agreed to an almost total ban on ABMs. We are using the same strategy today in Geneva, offering systems that we propose to build as bargaining chips. We offer to forgo deployment of the Pershing II and ground-launched cruise missiles in Europe if the Soviets dismantle their SS-20s. Under a freeze, our position in Geneva would collapse and the SS-20s would remain in place. (Brezhnev calls *that* arrangement a freeze.) In strategic arms talks, any attempts on our part to, say, bargain away one of our new systems against the Soviets' destabilizing silo-killing ICBMs would fail.

The freeze is not a plan; it is a sentiment. Montana's proposed freeze resolution, for example, opposes, "the production, development and deployment of nuclear weapons by any nation." It will unfortunately not be binding on President Zia of Pakistan.) The freeze reflects the deeply felt and wholly laudable wish of millions of Americans that something be done to control nuclear weapons. But when taken seriously as a plan, the freeze continually fails on its own terms. It seeks safety, but would jeopardize deterrence; it seeks quick action, but would delay arms control; it seeks real reductions, but removes any leverage we might have to bring them about.

Finally, it mistakes the most likely cause of an outbreak of nuclear war. In its fixation on numbers, the freeze assumes that somehow high weapons levels *in themselves* make war more likely. True, an uncontrolled arms race breeds suspicion between the superpowers and can increase the risk of war, but arms control measures (like SALT I or II) can allow higher levels, and still decrease the risk of building confidence on both sides and letting each know precisely what the other is doing. If nuclear war even comes, it most likely will be not because the weapons fire themselves, but because some national leader, in order to preserve some national interest, orders them fired. When did we come closest to nuclear war in the last thirty-six years? In October 1962, when President Kennedy decided to threaten Khrushchev with war unless he obeyed our ultimatum on the Cuban missiles. In 1962 the level of nuclear arms was much lower than it is today. And when was the chance of nuclear war smallest? Probably at the height of detente, during the Apollo-Soyuz love fest, when U.S.-Soviet relations were good, even though each side had the capacity for multiple overkill.

The absolute level of nuclear weapons is only one factor, and a relatively small one at that, in determining the likelihood of nuclear war breaking out. (It is certainly less important than the balance of vulnerabilities on each side, i.e., the stability of deterrence.) The most likely source of nuclear war is from a regional conflict between the superpower, where one or the other has important interests, but finds itself at a conventional disadvantage. That is the American situation today in Europe and in the Persian Gulf. To prevent the Soviets from taking advantage of their superiority in conventional arms, the U.S. has reserved the option of using nuclear weapons to respond to a nonnuclear Soviet attack. This policy of extending nuclear

19. IS NUCLEAR DETERRENCE IRRATIONAL?

deterrence to conventional conflicts has kept the peace. But it is dangerous. It blurs the line between conventional and nuclear war, and by threatening "limited" nuclear war it opens the door to a nuclear holocaust, since no one knows whether a limited nuclear war can be kept limited. The most effective way to eliminate that danger, and thus eliminate the greatest risk of nuclear war, is to make this kind of extended deterrence unnecessary: to right the conventional balance by radically bolstering allied forces, particularly on the West European frontier. NATO could then deter a conventional attack without having to threaten to wage nuclear war.

One of Schell's dictums is that compared to the peril of a nuclear holocaust, all other human values pale into insignificance, indeed, lose their meaning because they lose their context. If the antinuclear crusaders really believe that, they should be clamoring for increased conventional forces to reduce the European imbalance. They aren't. The reason is that the freeze crusade, which springs from deeply felt antiwar and antiarmament sentiments, is not comfortable with the thought that preventing nuclear war may require a radically enlarged conventional defense. Furthermore, one of the major appeals of the antinuclear movement is the promise to halt the economic drain caused by "useless" nuclear weapons and to redirect resources to human needs. But a shift away from strategic to conventional weapons would be very expensive. Our reliance on nuclear weapons—and the current conventional balance in Europe—results in large part from a desire to *reduce* defense spending. In the 1950s we decided to buy defense in Europe on the cheap. Rather than match the vast armies and tank forces of the Warsaw Pact, we

decided to go nuclear, because, as John Foster Dulles put it, it offered "more bang for the buck."

But the European defense balance has become more unstable since Dulles's day. In the 1950s the U.S. threatened "massive retaliation." If the Soviets crossed into Western Europe, we would attack the Russian homeland with a strategic nuclear strike. When the Russians acquired the same capacity against the U.S., that threat lost its credibility. The Kennedy Administration adopted a new policy of "flexible response," a euphemism for a limited nuclear war. Under the new doctrine, the U.S. reserved the right to use theater nuclear weapons on the battlefield to thwart a conventional Soviet attack. That has been our policy ever since. (Ronald Reagan did not invent it, although he had the habit of throwing it around more casually and publicly than other Presidents.) This doctrine has troubled many Americans, but as long as the U.S. was not prepared to challenge the Soviet conventional superiority in Europe, nor prepared to abandon its European allies, there seemed no other choice.

Enter the auxilliary brigade of the antinuclear movement: four former high Administration officials, two of whom, under President Kennedy, gave us "limited nuclear war" (Robert McNamara and McGeorge Bundy); one of whom gave us "containment" (George Kennan); and one of whom gave us SALT I (Gerard Smith). Two weeks ago they opened an entirely new front in the crusade. They called for the adoption of a "no-first-use" policy of nuclear weapons. It was a renunciation of "flexible response" and of "extended deterrence." (They would retain extended deterrence in one restricted sense: as retaliation for a Soviet *nuclear* attack of Western Europe, an unlikely possibili-

338

since the Soviets are prepared to renounce first use, and since with their conventional advantage they have no reason to attack with nuclear weapons.)

The problem with folding our nuclear umbrella, as the four wise men themselves acknowledged, is that, unaccompanied by conventional rearmament, it means the end of the Western alliance and the abandonment in particular of West Germany to Soviet intimidation and blackmail. The other problem with a no-first-use policy is that it might paradoxically increase the chances of nuclear war. Today a war between the U.S. and the Soviets is deterred at its origin: since even the slightest conventional conflict between them carries the threat of escalating into a nuclear one, neither happens. The no-first-use policy moves the "firebreak" from the line dividing war from peace to the line dividing conventional war from nuclear war. It trades the increased chance of conventional war (because now less dangerous and more "thinkable") for a decreased chance of such a war becoming nuclear. But no one can guarantee that in extremis, faced with a massive Soviet invasion of Western Europe, the U.S. would stick to its no-first-use pledge. Thus, by making a European war thinkable, this policy could, whatever its intentions, lead to a nuclear war.

Unless, that is, we have the conventional forces to preserve the original firebreak between war and peace. Thus, to prevent both political and (possibly) nuclear calamity, a no-first-use pledge must be accompanied, indeed preceded, by a serious conventional buildup of Western forces on the European frontier. The problem with McNamara et al is that although they acknowledge this need, they treat it very casually—certainly with nothing like the urgency with which they call for abandoning extended deterrence. They speak only vaguely of the need for "review" and "study" of conventional military needs, of whether the political will exists in the West for such a build-up, and of "whether we Americans have a durable and effective answer to our military manpower needs in the present all-volunteer active and reserve forces" (they cannot quite bring themselves to say the word "draft"). Their eagerness to be the first off the blocks with a no-first-use policy is obvious. Their reluctance to urge on their antinuclear allies the only responsible and safe (and costly) means of achieving it is lamentable. The result of their highly publicized, grossly unbalanced proposal is predictable: another support in the complex and high vulnerable structure of deterrence has been weakened. The world will be no safer for it.

Despite the prophesies of Schell, the pandering of the freeze-riding politicians, and the posturing of the four wise men—and the good intentions of millions of concerned Americans caught up in the antinuclear maelstrom—there is no need to reinvent nuclear policy. There is a need for arms control: SALT II is the best transition to real reductions. There is a need to avoid limited nuclear war: rebuilding our conventional strength and perhaps reintroducing the draft would reduce that risk. These proposals are neither new nor exciting. Unlike Schell's crusade, they don't promise to restore "the wholeness and meaning of life." They don't suggest that "the passion and will that we need to save ourselves would flood into our lives. Then the walls of indifference, inertia, and coldness that now isolate each of us from others, and all of us from the past and future generations, would melt, like snow in the spring." They don't promise to set right "our disordered instinctual life." That is because working to reduce the chances of nuclear war is not an exercise in psychotherapy. It is not a romance. It is mundane work in pursuit of mundane objectives: a modest program of nuclear modernization, SALT II, and a bigger conventional defense. These measures will not cure anomie, but will help to maintain deterrence, that difficult abstraction on which our values and our safety depend.

● ● ●

POSTSCRIPT

IS NUCLEAR DETERRENCE IRRATIONAL?

The lines are sharply drawn between Jonathan Schell, who rejects the doctrine of nuclear deterrence, and Charles Krauthammer, who believes that nuclear deterrence is the surest preventive of nuclear war. The anti-nuclear slogans of "nuclear freeze" and "no first use" similarly seem to separate those who favor nuclear weapons from those who oppose them.

Surely this is too simple. No one wants nuclear war. The question is whether we are more likely to prevent this terrible occurrence by preparing for it—and thus, in the judgment of its advocates, making it less likely that the other side will use the weapons for fear of retaliation, or whether we are more likely to prevent such a disaster by adopting appropriate anti-nuclear policies now. Perhaps the correct question is whether any of these policies is more likely to prevent the outbreak of any general war between the superpowers. If war did break out between the United States and the Soviet Union, it seems likely that a "freeze" would thaw and pledges of "no first use" would not be honored.

The proliferating literature on nuclear warfare is unbalanced because the anti-nuclear works tend to focus upon the issue while those analyses that support nuclear armaments place such forces in the context of national defense and deterrence. Nigel Calder, NUCLEAR NIGHTMARES: AN INVESTIGATION INTO POSSIBLE WARS (Viking, 1979) argues for negotiated disarmament, beginning with a superpower disavowal of first use. Solly Zuckerman, NUCLEAR ILLUSION AND REALITY (Viking, 1982) argues for nothing less than total abolition of nuclear weapons. The defense of nuclear weapons was given its first full statement in Henry Kissinger, NUCLEAR WEAPONS AND FOREIGN POLICY (Harper, 1957). More recently American nuclear armament has been defended in General Maxwell D. Taylor, PRECARIOUS SECURITY (W.W. Norton, 1976), and Norman Podhoretz, THE PRESENT DANGER (Simon and Schuster, 1980). Podhoretz's subtitle raises the question often asked by advocates of increased nuclear armament in the U.S.: "Do we have the will to reverse the decline of American power?"

Other divisive issues have high stakes, but on the resolution of this issue may depend the survival of civilization. What policy regarding nuclear weapons is most likely to assure that survival?

ISSUE 20

HUMAN RIGHTS: BETTER "AUTHORITARIANISM" THAN COMMUNISM?

YES: Jeane Kirkpatrick, from "Human Rights and American Foreign Policy: A Symposium," *Commentary,* November 1981

NO: Charles William Maynes, from "Human Rights and American Foreign Policy: A Symposium," *Commentary,* November 1981

ISSUE SUMMARY

YES: Jeane Kirkpatrick, Ambassador to the U.N., suggests that we are injuring our own interests while doing nothing to promote human rights by failing to distinguish between "authoritarian" and "totalitarian" forms of government.

NO: Charles Maynes, editor of *Foreign Policy* magazine, points to our history of concern for human rights and argues that we ignore violations at our peril, no matter what form of government commits them.

The concept of "human rights" is, at least potentially, an explosive idea. Though its philosophical underpinnings can be traced back to early Christianity and Roman Stoicism, its first appearance as a full-blown political program came during the age of revolution in the late eighteenth-century. Our Declaration of Independence begins with its famous trinity of "unalienable" human rights, goes on to list all the infractions of these rights by King and Parliament, and concludes that Americans have the right and even the duty to overthrow such an oppressive government. The French Revolution, which turned out to be far more violent and far-reaching, began with a similar theme of "The Rights of Man and of Citizens."

The doctrine of human rights has its critics, and by no means are all of them people who favor repression or autocracy. Edmund Burke, the great British statesman and political thinker of the eighteenth century, was an outspoken supporter of conciliation with America, but he bitterly opposed the French Revolution for trying to re-make society from a blueprint of "the rights of man." Liberty and self-government, Burke said, are gradually built up over centuries on the basis of precedent and tradition. The attempt to force change overnight on the basis of abstract, "metaphysic" principles will only result in fanaticism and chaos. Burke's chief opponent was Thomas Paine, whose writings helped to inspire the American Revolution. Paine defended the French Revolution and criticized Burke's emphasis on precedent. "Government by precedent, without any regard to the principle of the precedent, is one of the vilest systems that can be set up."

Echoes of the Burke-Paine debate can still be heard in some of the more recent controversies over the role "human rights" should play in American foreign policy. When Jimmy Carter came into office, he contended that an "inordinate fear of Communism" had sometimes blinded American administrations to right-wing repression. Carter declared that henceforward he would let the chips fall where they may by opposing human rights violations in *any* country, whether ruled by the "right" or the "left." Andrew Young, Carter's U.N. ambassador, carried the logic of universalism to its conclusion by denouncing racism everywhere, including Sweden and Queens, New York.

If Young's approach sometimes breathed the spirit of Thomas Paine's famous credo ("My country is the world, and my religion is to do good"), Jeane Kirkpatrick, Ronald Reagan's U.N. ambassador, sounds more like Edmund Burke. In an article she wrote in *Commentary* two years before the Reagan administration came into office, Kirkpatrick reminded her readers of the long maturation period needed before liberal and democratic regimes can appear. "Decades, if not centuries, are normally required for people to acquire the necessary disciplines and habits." Her criticism of the Carter approach was that by trying to force autocratic but friendly regimes to suddenly become "moderate," it would destabilize them, making them vulnerable to revolution. Since our own political system is the result of a revolution, many Americans might ask why we need to worry if a revolution does break out. Her answer, an opinion generally shared by Reagan policymakers, rests upon the implications of a term which did not exist in Edmund Burke's day. The term is "totalitarianism."

Although the terms are sometimes used interchangeably, Reagan officials insist that "totalitarian" regimes are radically different from "authoritarian" ones. Adapting to their own policy ends a school of thought that goes back to the 1940s and '50s, Reagan's policymakers suggest at least three differences between the two. First, totalitarianism is far more lethal to human freedom than is authoritarianism. Second, it is possible to find authoritarian regimes friendly to the United States, but totalitarian regimes are almost invariably hostile. Third, history demonstrates that authoritarian regimes can be gradually liberalized, while totalitarian ones remain so. The conclusion of Kirkpatrick and other Reagan officials is as follows. By constantly criticizing authoritarian but friendly regimes, such as those in Nicaragua and Iran, Carter helped to destabilize them and pave the way toward their replacement by totalitarian regimes. Today, their subjects have fewer "human rights" than ever, and we have some new enemies among the nations of the world.

The Kirkpatrick philosophy has many critics, among them Charles W. Maynes, who develops the thesis that she ignores America's own liberal heritage.

YES
Jeane Kirkpatrick

THE LESSER EVIL OVER
THE GREATER EVIL

The human-rights debate of recent years to which this symposium is directed is not really about which should play the most important role in U.S. foreign policy: human rights or the national interest. It is rather a debate about *which* policies promote human rights, *which* regimes threaten them most gravely, *which* policies actually serve the national interest and how the U.S. national interest should be conceived anyway. Some of us believe that because they seek by violent, repressive means total control over the societies they govern, establish great armies, and pursue aggressive and expansionist foreign policies, Marxist-Leninist states constitute the gravest threat to human rights in the contemporary world. Others, including the human-rights establishment of the Carter period, believe that because authoritarian regimes such as those found in Chile, Argentina, and Uruguay tolerate social injustice and sometimes use violence arbitrarily, they perpetrate the gravest offenses against human rights. Involved here are different assessments of practices (which type of regime in fact imprisons, enslaves, tortures, kills most people?); different assessments of the future (which type of regime is most susceptible of liberalization and democratization?); different views of the U.S. national interest (is the establishment of new Marxist-Leninist regimes compatible with our national interest?); different views about the relation of U.S. strength to human rights (is freedom safer if we are strong, or does that matter?); and perhaps most basic of all, different views about the relations between state and society.

All of these questions must be considered if we are to confront seriously *Commentary's* questions. The first of these questions is the easiest: not only should human rights play a central role in U.S. foreign policy, no U.S. foreign policy can possibly succeed that does not accord them a central role. The nature of politics and the character of the United States alike guarantee that this should be the case.

Politics is a purposive human activity which involves the use of power in the name of some collectivity, some "we," and some vision of the collective good. The collective may be a nation, class, tribe, family, or church. The vision of the public good may be modest or grand, monstrous or divine, elaborate or simple, explicitly articulated or simply "understood." It may call for the restoration of the glory of France; the establishment of a Jewish homeland; the construction of a racially pure one-thousand-year Reich; the achievement of a classless society from which power has been eliminated. The point is that government act with reference to a vision of the public good characteristic of a people. If they are to command popular assent, important public policies must be congruent with the core identity of a people. In democracies the need for moral justification of political action is especially compelling—nowhere more so than in the United States. The fact that Americans do not share a common history, race, language, religion gives added centrality to American values, beliefs, and goals, making them the key element of our national identity. The American people are defined by the American creed. The vision of the public good which defines us is and always has been a commitment to individual freedom and a conviction that government exists, above all, for the purpose of protecting individual rights. ("To protect these rights," says the Declaration of Independence, "governments are instituted among men.") Government, in the American view, has no purpose greater than that of protecting and extending the rights of its citizens. For this reason, the definitive justification of government policy in the U.S. is to protect the rights—liberty, property, personal security—of citizens. Defending these rights or extend-ing them to other peoples is the only legitimate purpose of American foreign policy.

From the War of Independence through the final withdrawal from Vietnam, American Presidents have justified our policies, especially in time of danger and sacrifice (when greatest justification is required), by reference to our national commitment to the preservation and/or extension of freedom—and the democratic institutions through which that freedom is guaranteed. Obviously, then, there is no conflict between a concern for human rights and the American national interest as traditionally conceived. Our national interest flows from our identity, and our identity features a commitment to the rights of persons. (Conventional debate about whether foreign policy should be based on "power" or morality is in fact a disagreement about moral ends and political means.)

It is true that the explicit moral emphasis on presidential pronouncements on U.S. foreign policy had declined in the decade preceding Jimmy Carter's candidacy, partly because of the diminishing national consensus about whether protecting human rights required (or even permitted) containing Communism even through war, and partly because of concern that moral appeals would excite popular passions and complicate the task of limiting the war in Vietnam. It is also true that Jimmy Carter shared this reticence and only reluctantly—and in response to pressure from Senator Henry Jackson—incorporated the human-rights theme into his presidential campaign.

Almost immediately, however, it became clear that the human-rights policies expounded and implemented by Jimmy Carter were different in their conception and their consequences from those of his predecessors. The cultural revolution that had swept through American cities, campuses, and news rooms, challenging basic beliefs and transforming institutional practices, had as its principal target the morality of the American experience and the legitimacy of American national interests. It was, after all, a period when the leading columnist of a distinguished newspaper wrote: "The United States is the most dangerous and destructive power in the world." It was a time when the president of a leading university asserted: "In twenty-six years since waging a world war against the forces of tyranny, fascism, and genocide in Europe we have become a nation more tyrannical, more fascistic, and more capable of genocide than was ever conceived or thought possible two decades ago. We conquered Hitler but we have come to embrace Hitlerism." It was the period when a nationally known cleric said: "The reason for the paroxysm in the nation's conscience is simply that Calley is all of us. He is every single citizen in our graceless land."

If the United States is "the most destructive power in the world," if we are "capable of genocide," if we are a "graceless land," then the defense of our national interest could not be integrally linked to the defense of human rights or any other morally worthy cause.

The cultural revolution set the scene for two redefinitions: first, a redefinition of human rights, which now became something very different from the freedoms and protections embodied in U.S. constitutional practices; and second, a redefinition of the national interest which dissociated morality and U.S. power.

As long as the United States was perceived as a virtuous society, policies which enhanced its power were also seen as virtuous. Morality and American power were indissolubly linked in the traditional conception. But with the U.S. defined as an essentially immoral society, pursuit of U.S. power was perceived as immoral and pursuit of morality as indifferent to U.S. power. Morality now required transforming our deeply flawed society, not enhancing its power.

In the human-rights policies of the Carter administration, the effects of the cultural revolution were reinforced, first, by a secular translation of the Christian imperative to cast first the beam from one's own eye, and, second, by a determinist, quasi-Marxist theory of historical development. The result was a conception of human rights so broad, ambiguous, and utopian that it could serve as the grounds for condemning almost any society; a conception of national interest to which U.S. power was, at best, irrelevant; and a tendency to suppose history was on the side of our opponents. (Of course, the Carter administration did not invent these orientations, it simply reflected the views of the new liberalism that was both the carrier and the consequence of the cultural revolution.)

Human rights in the Carter version had no specific content, except a general demand that societies provide all the freedoms associated with constitutional democracy, all the economic security promised by socialism, and all the self-fulfillment featured in Abraham Maslow's psychology. And it assumed that governments were responsible for providing these. Any society which did not feature democracy, "social justice," and self-fulfillment—that is, any society at all—could be measured against these standards and found wanting. And where all are "guilty," no one is especially so.

The judicial protections associated with the rule of law and the political freedoms associated with democracy had no special priority in the Carter doctrine of human rights. To the contrary, the powerful inarticulate predisposition of the new liberalism favored equality over liberty, and economic over political rights; socialism over capitalism, and Communist dictatorship over traditional military regimes. These preferences, foreshadowed in Carter's Notre Dame speech, found forthright expression in the administration's human-rights policy. UN Ambassador Andrew Young asserted, for example: "For most of the world, civil and political rights . . . come as luxuries that are far away in the future," and he called on the U.S. to recognize that there are various equally valid concepts of human rights in the world. The Soviets, he added, "have developed a completely different concept of human rights. For them, human rights are essentially not civil and political but economic. . . ." President Carter, for his part, tried hard to erase the impression that *his* advocacy of human rights implied an anti-Soviet bias. "I have never had an inclination to single out the Soviet Union as the only place where human rights are being abridged," he told a press conference on February 23, 1977. "I've tried to make sure that the world knows that we're not singling out the Soviet Union for criticism." In Carter's conception of the political universe, strong opposition to Marxist-Leninist totalitarianism would have been inappropriate because of our shared "goals." On April 12, 1978, he informed President Ceausescu of Romania that "our goals are also the same, to have a just system of economics and politics, to let the people of the world share in growth, in peace, in personal freedom.

It should not be supposed that under Carter no distinction was made between totalitarian and authoritarian regimes—for while the Carter administration was reluc-

tant to criticize Communist states for their human-rights violations (incredibly, not until April 21, 1978 did Carter officials denounce Cambodia for its massive human-rights violations), no similar reticence was displayed in criticizing authoritarian recipients of U.S. aid. On the basis of annual reports required by a 1976 law, the Carter administration moved quickly to withhold economic credits and military assistance from Chile, Argentina, Paraguay, Brazil, Nicaragua, and El Salvador, and accompanied these decisions with a policy of deliberate slights and insults that helped delegitimize these governments at the same time it rendered them less open to U.S. influence.

President Carter's 1977 decision to support the mandatory UN arms embargo against South Africa; Secretary Vance's call, before a meeting of the Organization of American States in June 1979, for the departure of Nicaragua's President Somoza; the decision in 1979 to withhold U.S. support from the Shah of Iran; and President Carter's decision, in June 1979, not to lift economic sanctions against the Muzorewa government in Zimbabwe Rhodesia expressed the same predilection for the selective application of an "absolute" commitment to human rights.

Why were South American military regimes judged so much more harshly than African ones? Why were friendly autocrats treated less indulgently than hostile ones? Why were authoritarian regimes treated more harshly than totalitarian ones? Part of the reason was the the curious focus on those countries that received some form of U.S. assistance, as though our interest in human rights were limited to the requirements of the 1976 Foreign Assistance Act; and part of the reason was the exclusive concern with violations of human rights by governments. By definition, guerrilla murders did not qualify as violations of human rights, while a government's efforts to eliminate terrorism qualified as repression. This curious focus not only permitted Carter policy-makers to condemn government "repression" while ignoring guerrilla violence, it encouraged consideration of human-rights violations independently of their context.

Universal in its rhetoric, unflagging in its pursuit of perceived violations—"I've worked day and night to make sure that a concern for human rights is woven through everything our government does, both at home and abroad" (Jimmy Carter, December 15, 1977)—the Carter human-rights policy alienated non-democratic but friendly nations, enabled anti-Western opposition groups to come to power in Iran, and totalitarians in Nicaragua, and reduced American influence throughout the world.

The Carter administration made an operational (if inarticulate) distinction between authoritarianism and totalitarianism and preferred the latter. The reason for its preference lay, I believe, not only in the affinity of contemporary liberalism for other secular egalitarian development-oriented ideologies (such as Communism) but also in the progressive disappearance from modern liberalism of the distinction between state and society. The assumption that governments *can* create good societies, affluent economies, just distributions of wealth, abundant opportunity, and all the other prerequisites of the good life creates the demand that they should do so, and provokes harsh criticism of governments which fail to provide these goods. The fact that primitive technology, widespread poverty, gross discrepancies of wealth, rigid class and caste structures, and low social and economic mobility are characteristic of most societies which also feature authoritarian governments is ground enough for the modern liberal to hold the existing governments morally responsible for having *caused* these hardships.

The same indifference to the distinction between state and society also renders the new liberals insensitive to the pitfalls and consequences of extending the jurisdiction and the coercive power of government over all institutions and aspects of life in society. It is, of course, precisely this extension of government's plans and power over society, culture, and personality that makes life in totalitarian societies unbearable to so many. Authoritarian governments are frequently corrupt, inefficient, arbitrary, and brutal, but they make limited claims on the lives, property, and loyalties of their citizens. Families, churches, businesses, independent schools and labor unions, fraternal lodges, and other institutions compete with government for loyalties and resources, and so limit its power.

Authoritarian governments—traditional and modern—have many faults and one significant virtue: their power is limited and where the power of government is limited, the damage it can do is limited also. So is its duration in office. Authoritarian systems do not destroy all alternative power bases in a society. The persistence of dispersed economic and social power renders those regimes less repressive than a totalitarian system and provides the bases for their eventual transformation. Totalitarian regimes, to the contrary, in claiming a monopoly of power over all institutions, eliminate competitive, alternative elites. This is the reason history provides not one but numerous examples of the evolution of authoritarian regimes into democracies (not only Spain and Portugal, but Venezuela, Peru, Ecuador, Bangladesh, among others) and *no* example of the democratic transformation of totalitarian regimes.

Authoritarian governments have significant moral and political faults, all the worst of which spring from the possession of arbitrary power. But compared to totalitarian governments, their arbitrary power is limited. Only democracies do a reliable job of protecting the rights of all their citizens. That is why their survival must be the first priority of those committed to the protection of human rights.

The restoration of the subjective conviction that American power is a necessary precondition for the survival of liberal democracy in the modern world is the most important development in U.S. foreign policy in the past decade. During the Vietnam epoch that subjective link between American power and the survival of liberal democratic societies was lost. Its restoration marks the beginning of a new era.

The first implication of that fact is that human-rights policies should be and, one trusts, will be, scrutinized not only for their effect on the total strategic position of the United States and its democratic allies—not because power is taking precedence over morality, but because the power of the U.S. and its allies is a necessary condition for the national independence, self-determination, self-government, and freedom of other nations. The human-rights policy of the Reagan administration has

not been fully articulated, but the myriad concrete decisions made so far suggest that it will manifest the following characteristics:

First, clarity about our own commitment to due process, rule of law, democratic government and all its associated freedoms.

Second, aggressive statements in information programs and official pronouncements of the case for constitutional democracy. As the party of freedom we should make the case for freedom by precept as well as by example.

Third, careful assessment of all relevant aspects of any situation in another country in which we may be tempted to intervene, symbolically, economically, or otherwise. In Poland as in El Salvador we should be careful neither to overestimate our power to shape events according to our own preference, nor to underestimate the potential negative consequences of our acts.

Finally, a steady preference for the lesser over the greater evil.

Such policies will not make a perfect world, but at least they will not make the lives of actual people more difficult or perilous, less free than they already are. Conceivably, they might leave some people in some places more secure and less oppressed than they are today.

● ● ●

NO

Charles William Maynes

AMERICA'S LIBERAL TRADITION

Much of the angry debate over U.S. human-rights policy overlooks one obdurate fact: America is a liberal country. It is not liberal in the sense that conservatives always lose elections. Numerous elections, including those in 1980, have shown that to be false. America is liberal in the sense that even conservative administrations are under pressure to pursue liberal political values.

America's behavior throughout the 20th century demonstrates just how strong the American liberal tradition is. Repeatedly, the country has been willing to sacrifice quite concrete commercial or security interests in order to respond to its liberal tradition. In 1911, when big business dominated American political life in a way it has seldom done since, the United States nonetheless abrogated its commercial treaty with Czarist Russia because of American outrage over the regime's treatment of its Jewish population. In the early 1920's, the vehemently anti-Communist Harding administration undertook a massive food program to feed the starving Russian people even though that move helped to save the new and hated Bolshevik regime. Under President Carter, although the U.S. relationship with Vietnam was one of intense hostility, the United States provided food to millions of starving Cambodians, a step that meant propping up the Vietnamese-supported puppet regime in Phnom Penh.

The existence of the liberal tradition does not mean that the U.S. always has liberal policies. It does mean that a foreign policy that is in flagrant conflict with that tradition is in trouble. The Reagan administration has recognized this point by shifting its stance on human rights. Although it earlier attempted to draw a distinction between human-rights abuses committed by authoritarian regimes and those committed by totalitarian regimes, it now contends it will have a single standard for all countries.

From, "Human Rights and American Foreign Policy: A Symposium," *Commentary*, November, 1981. Copyright, 1981. Reprinted by permission of Commentary and the author.

In short, the American liberal tradition of interest in the human rights of others is deeply rooted in the American body politic. It has manifested itself repeatedly throughout our history in both Republican and Democratic administrations. It is in this regard that Americans—whether conservative or radical—are in the end liberal.

Even the heated debates over the U.S. human-rights policy that have taken place in *Commentary* are a tribute to the strength of the U.S. liberal tradition. Many of *Commentary's* authors want policy results different from those suggested by that tradition. But they are reluctant to call openly for a departure from that tradition. To defend unpopular recommendations, they are forced to argue counter-intuitively that in the Third World the best way to pursue democratic liberties is not to strike out for them directly but to support authoritarian regimes that allegedly will evolve in a democratic direction. Even if the immediate policy recommended violates the American liberal tradition, in other words, the underlying message is that the final result will conform to that liberal tradition.

The traditional American attitude toward human rights has acquired a new contemporary potency, however. The reason is modern-day ethnic politics. Today there is scarcely a nation on earth without some of its citizens or their descendants living in the United States. And in our system of government, with its checks and balances and with the unique power our Congress enjoys in the field of foreign policy, the more significant groups have had and will continue to have a major voice in the development of American foreign policy. In particular, they will be very concerned about the degree of political and economic welfare of their former countrymen or coreligionists. Inevitably, they will seize on the emotive power of the American liberal tradition and its support for democracy and the human rights that flow from that system of government to buttress their concern. Convincing other Americans that the issue is not simply a form of tribal loyalty to Israel or Cyprus or black South Africans but a form of liberal concern for democracy, self-determination, or common decency can only broaden the base of national support.

Can this approach lead to a conflict with U.S. national interest? The answer depends on the time-frame through which one is viewing the national interest. Certainly in the short run the conflict can be severe. The U.S. concern with human rights in the Soviet Union has troubled sensitive negotiations with that country in recent years. When non-Jewish Americans have based their support for Israel on the issue of self-determination and democracy, U.S. relations with oil-producing Arab states have been affected. Relations with South Africa have become increasingly strained because of U.S. attitudes toward the inhumane treatment of blacks in that country. Our bases in Turkey were closed down temporarily because we opposed Turkish suppression of self-determination in democratic Cyprus. Our influence with Argentina has fallen because of opposition to government-sanctioned slaughter of dissidents, real and imagined, in that country.

But those who shake their heads at this price in the American approach to foreign policy should ask themselves: what kind of foreign policy would we end up with over the long run if we were to follow the approach of clear-headed *Realpolitik* they advocate? Isn't our aim a policy that serves our interests and that commands popular support? And in that regard can one imagine the American people over the long run ever supporting a policy toward the

Soviet Union that overlooks completely the fate of communities inside the Soviet Union that have so many ties to communities inside the United States? As long as we have a free press, could a policy of *Realpolitik* toward South Africa or Guatemala long survive the continued shocks of the expose of one human-rights outrage after another? Could any relationship with the Arab world be healthy that did not reflect the strong American support for a Jewish people expressing its democratic right of self-determination?

The reality for American foreign-policy "realists" is that their fellow citizens will not support a foreign policy over the long run that offends too frontally the American liberal tradition. Indeed, this is why the Begin government's attitude toward the Palestinians is so critical. For it is not clear that the traditionally warm relationship between the United States and Israel can survive the incorporation into Israel proper of the West Bank, with permanent political repression or expulsion of the Arab majority living there.

Given the American attitude, how should the U.S. handle the hard realities of international politics? In the short run the U.S. should deal on a pragmatic basis with both totalitarian and authoritarian regimes to protect U.S. security and welfare. It should buy key minerals from authoritarian South Africa. It should assist totalitarian China, at least with economic aid, to stand up to the Soviet Union. But over the long run it must be opposed to the political system of both authoritarian and totalitarian regimes, and it should not hesitate to say so. Our people will reject any short-run policy that ignores this long-run American preference. Foreign policy is basically the effort to manage the resulting tension between short-run policy needs and long-run policy preferences.

This observation about tension in any foreign policy is relevant to the contention that somehow authoritarian governments are better than totalitarian governments. Viewed closely, some of the distinctions drawn between the two seem weak at best. For example, it is not at all clear that one is more likely than the other to evolve in directions that we would like to see. There have been repeated efforts to gain political freedom in totalitarian Eastern Europe. Is it not likely that one day they will succeed? Would they not have succeeded already except for the intervention of the Soviet army, which may not be able to move so easily into non-contiguous areas?

Nor are all totalitarian states always more bloody than all authoritarian states. Few places have been more bloody than Guatemala in recent years.

Another major problem with the asserted distinction between authoritarianism and totalitarianism is that both labels cover too vast a spectrum of countries to be meaningful. Is Mexico, authoritarian but relatively benign, to be placed in the same category as authoritarian El Salvador, in which political opponents are hunted down like some tagged member of the animal kingdom? If we accept, as many who draw this distinction do but I would not, that Communist states cannot change and remain forever totalitarian, then are we comfortable with the fact that we must place Yugoslavia and North Korea in the same pigeonhole? If we are forced to group such wildly different countries under the two labels, is the distinction not useless for policy purposes?

Nor is it always true—certainly in the longer run—that right-wing dictatorships serve U.S. interests better than left-wing dictatorships. Did Somoza of Nicaragua serve U.S. interests? As a right-wing foreign minister from a major Latin American country once explained to the Carter administration, Somoza's main achievement was to develop a plantation and to lose a country.

There is, however, one condition under which the distinction between authoritarianism and totalitarianism might acquire new significance, or at least be viewed in a new light. Suppose that the United States were now effectively at war with the Soviet Union. In wartime a country cannot always be overly selective in its choice of allies. Survival becomes the key issue and at virtually any price. Finland, after the Soviet attack in 1939, later accepted the support of Nazi Germany in an attempt to regain its territory. The Western allies did not hesitate to join hands with Stalin, a dictator of comparable moral degradation, in their effort to crush Hitler.

Are we at war? Some, including the editor of *Commentary,* Norman Podhoretz, in effect argue that we are. The Soviet Union is seen as "exactly" like Nazi Germany. It is seen as posing precisely the same kind of threat to American security and welfare. Whether intended or not, the equation of the Soviet Union with Nazi Germany is incendiary in its policy implications. Given our collective memory of World War II and the lessons we all believe we learned from the history of the 1930's, the evocation of Nazi Germany can only suggest inevitable and fairly immediate conflict. Negotiations begin to seem foolish. Even preemptive war might be in order. We would not want to make the mistake we made in the 1930's of letting the aggressor power choose the time and place of the inevitable attack. In any event, we should join with any allies we can find in combating this new menace, whose appetite, like that of Nazi Germany, cannot be sated. Against such a threat, some would also take action at home. The new chairman of the Senate Judiciary Committee has stated that Senator Joseph McCarthy was doing the right thing, only in the wrong way.

Few would deny that the Soviet Union poses a severe challenge to American interests worldwide. Indeed, were the Soviet Union to invade Poland, the international situation would begin to resemble the summer of 1914 in its tensions and dangers. Vigorous military and diplomatic measures would become even more pressing than they are now. But even viewing the Soviet Union today in the way the rest of Europe viewed Imperial Germany in the summer of 1914 is very different from viewing the Soviet Union as the modern-day equivalent of Nazi Germany. In the former case, there could still remain some hope that through logic, diplomacy, and appeals to common interest catastrophe could be avoided. The margin of maneuver would be small but it would still allow some room for attention to be given to longer-run considerations. In the latter case, the margin for maneuver disappears altogether. The only value is survival, and the sole test of a foreign-policy relationship is whether it contributes to the pressing goal of survival.

Among the prominent supporters of the Reagan administration there are some who do see American options in the single blinding light of "the present danger" that now transfixes many of the contributors to *Commentary* in its high beam. These supporters would drive the administration to court South Africa, to embrace reaction in Central America, and to condone human-rights abuses so long as they are committed by our friends. They might even nod their heads approvingly when *New York Times* columnist William Safire writes: "What is 'winning' [in El Salvador]? Is it a military junta that kills the opposition but by its repressive nature produces more opposition that it becomes necessary to kill? If need be, yes—considering the aggressive totalitarian alternative. . . ."

The problem for those who espouse such a policy is that their fellow citizens will not accept it. The American people remain adherents to the liberal tradition. They fear the Soviet Union but they are not so terrified that they are willing to abandon long-standing American values. For that reason they have already rejected decisively the administration's initial hard-line and callous policy toward El Salvador. They will reject similar policies elsewhere. The Reagan administration would save itself much political gain if it acknowledged that there are some things that it cannot change and one of them is the basic liberal character of the country it governs.

• • •

POSTSCRIPT

HUMAN RIGHTS: BETTER "AUTHORITARIANISM" THAN COMMUNISM?

It can be seen that one of the basic issues that divides Kirkpatrick and Maynes is the question of national self-interest. Kirkpatrick stresses it, because she suggests that the atmosphere in America during the Carter years came close to national self-hatred and that Carter's version of "human rights" tended to reflect that spirit. To get the nation back on course she favors a reassertion of "realism" in foreign policy, in which policymakers ask not so much whether a regime tolerates dissent but whether it supports America. Maynes's response is that this approach will itself prove contrary to our long-range self-interest. Both sides to the debate should cause us to ponder whether American mistakes in foreign policy result from an excess of idealism, or from narrow-minded *realpolitik,* or even possibly from both.

A useful general work on the theory and practice of human rights internationally is Vernon Van Dyke's HUMAN RIGHTS, THE UNITED STATES, AND THE WORLD COMMUNITY (Oxford, 1970). Valery Chalidze, one of the founders of the Moscow Human Rights Committee, who was told not to return to his country while on a speaking tour of the United States, recounts his own experiences and tells what goes on in "corrective labor" camps and "psychiatric" wards of the U.S.S.R. in TO DEFEND THESE RIGHTS (Random House, 1974). As for repression in "friendly" autocracies, Jacobo Timermann, in PRISONER WITHOUT A NAME, CELL WITHOUT A NUMBER (Knopf, 1981), writes of his imprisonment and torture in Argentina.

The fragility of America's "friendship" with Argentina was dramatically demonstrated in the spring of 1982, after Argentina invaded the Falkland Islands. Following an unsuccessful attempt to mediate, the United States sided with Great Britain. Not long afterward, American television viewers were startled to see film of Argentina's foreign minister embracing Fidel Castro. The crisis was embarassing to the Reagan Administration but not fatal to the Kirkpatrick doctrine, for once the crisis ended the administration moved quickly to repair to damage. The work was made easier by a palace revolt which replaced the government whose rhetoric was beginning to sound distinctly anti-"Gringo."

CONTRIBUTORS
TO THIS VOLUME

EDITORS

GEORGE MC KENNA was born in Chicago in 1937. He attended high school in the city and received his bachelor's degree from the University of Chicago in 1959, an M.A. from the University of Massachusetts in 1962, and a Ph.D. from Fordham University in 1967. He has been teaching political science at City College of New York since 1963. He edited, with his introduction and notes, AMERICAN POPULISM (Putnam, 1974), wrote a textbook, AMERICAN POLITICS: IDEALS AND REALITIES (McGraw-Hill, 1976), and has written articles in the fields of American government and political theory. He has edited other volumes in the TAKING SIDES series, including the first edition of this volume.

STANLEY FEINGOLD was born in New York City in 1926. He attended high school in the city and received his bachelor's degree from the City College of New York. He received a graduate education at Columbia University and taught political science at City College. From 1970 to 1974 he was given a special appointment as Visiting Professor of Politics at the University of Leeds, England. At present he is Visiting Professor at Westchester Community College, a unit of the State University of New York. He edited, with George McKenna, the first two editions of this book.

AUTHORS

DAVID L. BAZELON has been Chief Judge of the U.S. Court of Appeals for the District of Columbia circuit since 1962.

JERRY J. BERMAN is legislative council for the American Civil Liberties Union.

WALTER BERNS is professor of political science at the University of Toronto. Among other works, Professor Berns is the author of THE FIRST AMENDMENT AND THE FUTURE OF AMERICAN DEMOCRACY.

BARRY BRUCE-BRIGGS is a historian and policy analyst, who has written several books, including THE WAR AGAINST THE AUTOMOBILE (1977) and THE NEW CLASS? (1978).

ROBERT B. CARLESON is Special Assistant to President Reagan for policy development.

JOHN CHAFEE is U.S. Senator from Rhode Island.

HARRY M. CLOR is professor of political science at Kenyon College and the author of OBSCENITY AND PUBLIC MORALITY. Professor Clor has also edited THE MASS MEDIA AND MODERN DEMOCRACY.

CARL COHEN is professor of philosophy at the Residential College of the University of Michigan. He is author of DEMOCRACY and of CIVIL DISOBEDIENCE.

BARRY CRICKMER is a senior editor of *Nation's Business,* a monthly magazine published by the Chamber of Commerce of the United States.

WILLIAM J. CROTTY is a professor of political science at Northwestern University. He was a consultant to the McGovern-Fraser Commission on Party-Structure and Delegate Selection. Professor Crotty is the author of POLITICAL REFORM AND THE AMERICAN EXPERIMENT.

RIANE EISLER is a lawyer, liberal political activist and author of THE EQUAL RIGHTS HANDBOOK.

SAM FIELDS is the Field Director of the National Coalition to Ban Handguns, an umbrella coalition of religious, educational and public interest organizations.

The late JEROME FRANK was a Judge of the U.S. Court of Appeals for the Second Circuit, and before that a federal commissioner. Judge Frank was the author of COURTS ON TRIAL and other books.

ANDREW GREELEY, a Catholic priest and professor of sociology at the University of Arizona, is also a program director at the National Opinion Research Center in Chicago. Among his books is THE AMERICAN CATHOLIC: A SOCIAL PORTRAIT.

MORTON H. HALPERIN is a former Defense Department and National Security Council official who now directs the Center for National Security Studies of the American Civil Liberties Union. He is the author of several books, including LIMITED WAR IN THE NUCLEAR AGE.

KEVIN R. HOPKINS is Special Assistant to President Reagan, specializing in economic affairs.

M. WILLIAM HOWARD is president of the National Council of the Churches of Christ.

IRVING LOUIS HOROWITZ is a professor of social and political theory at Rutgers University; Editor-in-Chief of *Society* magazine; and author of IDEOLOGY AND UTOPIA IN THE UNITED STATES: 1956-1976.

IRVING KAUFMAN is a Judge of the United States Court of Appeals for the Second Circuit.

STEVEN KELMAN teaches public policy at the Kennedy School of Government at Harvard University.

GEORGE F. KENNAN has spent long careers in both the U.S. Foreign Service and university teaching. His books on foreign relations and Soviet policy, which include AMERICAN DIPLOMACY, 1900-1950 and RUSSIA AND THE WEST UNDER LENIN AND STALIN, have won many awards including the Pulitizer and Bancroft Prizes.

JEANE KIRKPATRICK is U.S. Ambassador to the United Nations.

CHARLES KRAUTHAMMER is the Senior Editor of *The New Republic,* a liberal weekly journal of opinion.

EVERETT CARLL LADD, Jr. is professor of political science and director of the Social Science Data Center at the University of Connecticut. He is the author of many books, including IDEOLOGY IN AMERICA and, with Charles D. Hadley, TRANSFORMATIONS OF THE AMERICAN PARTY SYSTEM.

DONAL E.J. MACNAMARA is a criminologist and director of corrections programs at the John Jay College of Criminal Justice in New York. He is the author of CORRECTIONS and other books and articles.

EDWARD MAGNUSON is a senior writer for *Time* magazine.

THURGOOD MARSHALL is an Associate Justice of the United States Supreme Court.

CHARLES WILLIAM MAYNES is the editor of *Foreign Policy* magazine.

GEORGE MC GOVERN is a former U.S. Senator from North Dakota.

JOHN T. NOONAN, Jr. is professor of law at the University of California, Berkeley law school, and author of several works including three books on contraception and abortion.

MICHAEL NOVAK is the Executive Director of EMPAC (Ethnic Millions Political Action Committee). Besides ELECTING OUR KING, from which the selection in this book is taken, he has written extensively on American culture and institutions.

GARY ORFIELD is a staff member of The Brookings Institution, engaged in basic research in governmental affairs. He is the author of CONGRES-SIONAL POWER: CONGRESS AND SOCIAL CHANGE, from which the selection in this book was taken.

WILLIAM PALEY is the Chairman of the Columbia Broadcasting System (CBS).

MICHAEL PARENTI was recently a visiting fellow at the Institute for Policy Studies. His most recent books are DEMOCRACY FOR THE FEW and POWER AND THE POWERLESS.

KEVIN P. PHILLIPS, a newspaper columnist, once served as special assistant to the campaign manager of the Nixon for President Committee. Among his books are THE EMERGING REPUBLICAN MAJORITY and MEDIACRACY.

MARTHA ROUNTREE is president of the Leadership Foundation which lobbies on behalf of school prayer.

JONATHAN SCHELL is a staff writer for the *New Yorker* magazine, and has written other books, including THE MILITARY HALF and TIME OF ILLUSION.

PHYLLIS SCHLAFLY publishes a monthly newsletter, and is well-known as a conservative political activist who led the Stop ERA movement.

ALEKSANDR SOLZHENITSYN, the author of THE FIRST CIRCLE, CANCER WARD, THE GULAG ARCHIPELAGO and other works, was awarded the Nobel Prize for Literature in 1970.

THEODORE SORENSEN, former Special Assistant to President Kennedy, is the author of DECISION-MAKING IN THE WHITE HOUSE and WATCH-MEN IN THE NIGHT, which is exerpted in this book.

TAD SZULC, a journalist and commentator, is author of many works on Latin America, foreign affairs, and American politics. His latest book is THE ILLUSION OF PEACE.

JAMES Q. WILSON is professor of government at Harvard University and the author of THE AMATEUR DEMOCRAT, NEGRO POLITICS, and VARIETIES OF POLICE BEHAVIOR.

INDEX

Brodie, Bernard, 326
Brown v. Board of Education of Topeka,
122, 201, 211
Bruce-Briggs, B: on gun control, 190-197;
on handgun theft, 187; on self-protective
value of firearms, 185
Budget Reform Plan, of Reagan administration, 219, 221
Burch, Dean, 52
business: as elite group in United States, 16,
17; strategic position with government, 16
Business Government, and the Public
(Weidenbaum), 111
Business Roundtable, 49
busing, and Supreme Court, 114, 119, 121,
124

Califano, Joseph, 229
Cambodia, 91, 316
Camus, Albert, 166
capital punishment: and abortion voting,
282; ten arguments against, 173-180;
defense of and arguments against, 166-
180; number of executions in recent
decades, 164, 165; opinions of Americans
on, 169, 170; and concept of retribution,
167
Carleson, Robert B., on Reagan rationale of
welfare reform, 218-225
Carlucci, Frank, 262
Carter administration, support of intelligence identities protection, 254
Carter, Jimmy, 27, 38, 41, 46, 64, 66, 67,
81, 116, 118
Casey, William, 254
censorship: of books by government, 242;
and free speech, 234-259; under obscenity statute, 241-242; fear of prosecution
as, 241-242; by public opinion vs government, 242
Central Intelligence Agency (CIA) officers:
danger involving publication of names of,
254-259; listed in publically available
sources, 261, 262
Chafee, Zechariah, 255
Challenge of Crime in a Free Society, 163
Chamber of Commerce, as a powerful special interest group, 49, 50
Charter Commission, 32

"Chicago welfare queen," Reagan's denun-
ciation of, 227
Chief of State, and separation of presidency
into two functions, 86, 87, 88, 92, 93
China, *see* Communist China
Choosing the President (Barber), 43
Christian Voice, 280
Churchill, Winston, 326, 327, 332, 335
Civil Aeronautics Board, 96
civil rights, and presidential power vs con-
gressional power, 73
Civil Rights Act of 1857, 209, 210
Civil War Amendments, Supreme Court's
interpretation of, 210
Clark, Dick, 46
"classics," as exceptions to obscenity, 241
Clor, Harry M., on censorship and free
speech, 244-259
Coase, Ronald, 139
Cohen, Carl, on racial classifications as
unconstitutional, 200-207
Cohens v. Virginia, 127
COINTELPRO, 263
cold war, 300
Cole, Michael, 51
Colt. 45 Peacemakers, as first handgun, 184
*Commission on Obscenity and Porno-
graphy,* 251
Committee for the Survival of a Free
Congress, 49
Committee to Reelect the President
(CREEP), 40
Common Cause, as special interest group,
47, 51, 56, 58
common situs picketing bill, 50
Communications Act of 1934, 144
communications industry, in past, 135
communism: effect of negotiations on half of,
318; possibility of peaceful co-existence
with, 302-318; distinguished from "the
Russians," 317-318; Western blindness to
nature of, 311-318
Communist China, rift with Soviet Union,
301, 312, 315
compensatory justice, racial proportionality
as, 203-204
conflagration, from nuclear blast, 323, 324
Congress: and balancing power with presi-

Fourteenth Amendment: 124, 165, 168; effect of Human Life Amendment on, 280; racial civil rights, 211-212, 214; and prohibition of racial classifications, 200, 205
Freedmen's Bureau, 209
freeze campaign: vs. deterrence concept, 335-337; and nuclear war, 333, 334
Frank, Judge Jerome, on protection of obscenity as free speech, 234-243
Franklin, John Hope, 209
freedom of expression, see free speech
Freedom of Information Act, 261
free speech: First Amendment protection of obscenity as, 236-243; intelligence identities legislation as violation of, 255, 256, 260-266
Free Speech in the United States (Chafee), 255
Fulbright, J. William, 89

Gannett Co. v. DePasquale, 143
Gardiner, John, as founder of Common Cause, 51, 56
General Electric, 49
General Motors, 49
genetic engineering, government directed, 280
Gerard, Jules, 117, 118, 119
Gilder, George, 231
global political organization, as prerequisite for disarmament, 328-331, 334
Global 2000, 283
Gorin v. United States, 265
Governing America (Herbers), 55
government: relationship with business, 16; in a pluralistic society, 15, 16; responsibility to poor, 227; unrest of poor as threat to, 225, 227; role in transfer of income, 219
"Government affairs specialists," 48
Governmental Process, The (Truman), 61
governmental regulation: American attitudes concerning, 104, 105; of broadcast media, 144; controversy over, 98-110; criticism of, 97; vs. profit incentive, 101; public interest in, 97; cost vs. benefit of social, 108, 109; failures of social, 98-102; success of social, 106, 107; and social regulatory agencies, 105, 106

Great Society, 73, 76
Greeley, Andrew M., on elitism in America, 20-24
Griffin, Robert, 118
ground zero, 322, 323
Gudger, Lamar, 297, 298
gun control: 188-189; Bruce-Briggs on, 190-196; deterrence as method of, 190; existing, 192-193; interdiction as method of, 191, 193-194; international experience with, 194-195; licensing as method of, 192-193; lack of research on, 190

Hamilton, Alexander, 80, 123
Hand, Judge Learned, 127, 264
handguns: federal vs. state controls on, 188, 196; use of in crime, 185-186, 192; number of deaths attributable to, 184; problems with licensing, 192-193; as a menace to society, 184-189; number in United States, 185; origin of, 184; self-protective value of, 185-186, 188, 191-192; theft of, 187
Harlan, Justice, dissent on Civil Rights Cases, 210
Harriman, Averell, 88
Harris v. McRae, 114
Hart, Henry, 129
Hayden, Tom, 55
head of state, and separation of presidency into two functions, 86, 87, 88, 92, 93
health and safety regulations, see government regulations
Helsinki agreement, 316
Helms Amendment, 282, 289, 292, 294
Helms, Jesse, 289
Hennings, Thomas C., 127
Higher Circles, The (Domhoff), 25
Hiram Johnson Acts of 1934, 118
Hiroshima, 323, 324
Hitler, Russian nationalism revived to fight, 313-315
Holmes, Justice Oliver Wendell, 255
Hopkins, Kevin R., on Reagan rationale of welfare reform, 218-225
Horowitz, Irving Louis, on lobbying endangering democracy, 54-60

Howard, M. William, on voluntary school prayer, 294-298
Hughes, Richard, 31
Human Life Amendment (HLA): 278; catholic support for, 280; unintended consequences of, 280; effect on Fourteenth Amendment, 280; dangerous implications of, 279-280; women's opposition to, 279; as threat to quality of, 278-284
Human Life Bill (HLB), 278
human-rights: policies of Carter Administration, 345-346; role of in United States foreign policy, 344-355
Humphrey, Hubert H., 28
Hustler magazine, as obscenity, 235
Hyde Amendment, 282

immiserization, 15
"Imperial Judiciary," 114, 115, 117
"Imperial Presidency," definition, 114
"implied constitutional authority," and the presidency, 91
income equality vs. welfare, 219-220
income taxes, and federal transfer programs, 219-220
indeterminate sentencing, 159
individualized justice, need for, 160
infanticide, abortion as, 277
inflation, 15, 17
in-kind benefits, 222
Intelligence Identities Protection Act of 1981: adequacy of, 261, 262; constitutionality of, 255-256, 260-266; definition of covert agent in, 262-263; dangers of, 258-259, 266-267; as First Amendment issue, 262-264; purpose of, 254; section 601(c), 256, 258, 260-266
intelligence officers: governmental protection of identities of, 254-259; listed in publically available sources, 261, 262
interdiction, as method of gun control, 191, limitations of, 193-194
interest groups, *see* special interest groups
interest group politics, and the media, 57
Interstate Commerce Commission, 105
intra-amniotic instillation, description of abortion by, 274

Jacobs, Andy, 51
Jahoda, Marie, 238, 239

Jesse Helms Amendment, 118
Jim Crow laws, 211
Johnson, Andrew, 75
Johnson, Lyndon B., 37, 73, 81, 91
judges, and sentence discretion, 160, 162
Judges Bill of 1925, 128
judicial power, lack of limitations on, 114-120
juvenile delinquency: causes of, 239; effect of obscenity on, 238-240

Kaufman, Irving R., Congress vs. the Supreme Court, 121-130
Kelman, Steven, on government regulations, 104-110
Kennedy, Edward, 46
Kennedy, John F., 17, 81, 116
Kennan, George F., on importance of detente between U.S. and Soviet Union, 300-310; influence on U.S. foreign policy, 312
Key Resource People, 50
King, Martin Luther, 83
Kinsman, Richard, 256
Kirkpatrick, Jeanne, on human-rights debate, 344-349
Kissinger, Henry, 301, 302
"Kissinger syndrome," 312
"kitchen cabinet," 94
knowledge industry, as a "new class," 135
Kristol, Irving, and knowledge industry as a "new class," 135
Kuh, Richard H., 251

labor unions, and special interest lobbies, 47, 51
Ladd, Everett Carll, Jr., on controversy over success of party reform, 37-42
Laffer, Arthur, 231
Landmark Communications, Inc. v. Virginia, 264
Laski, Harold, 173
Laxalt, Paul, 50, 97
Liberals, and party reform, 26
licensing, of hand guns, 192-193
life, impact of abortion laws on meaning, 275; beginning at fertilization, 278, 279
life tenure, dangers of and Supreme Court, 115, 116, 117, 124

litmus test, and appointment of Federal Court judges, 119

lobbies, *see* special interest groups

lobbyists: and Big Business, 48, 49; changes in nature of Congress and effect on, 48; conservative, 50; function of, 59, 60; increased complexity of job, 48; and labor, 51; need for, 59; *see also* special interest groups

MacAvoy, Paul, 101

MacNamara, Donal E.J., arguments against capital punishment, 173-180

Madison, James: 127; and special interest groups, 44, 45, 61

Magnuson, Edward, on lobbying endangering democracy, 46-53

mandatory sentencing, 159, 160

Manson, Charles, 166

Marbury v. Madison, 123

Mars, Inc., 51

Marshall, Thurgood: 169; affirmative action as compensatory racial justice, 208-214

Maynes, Charles William, on American attitude toward human rights, 350-355

McCarthy, Eugene, 83

McGovern, George: 27, 29, 39, 41; criticism of Reagan's cutbacks in welfare programs, 226-232; on right wing, 281

McGovern-Fraser Commission: criticism of, 41, 42; and party reform, 30-33, 39

McKevitt, James, 49

McNamara, Robert, 325

Mead, Margaret, 88

media: impact on Congress, 137-138; effect on government regulatory programs, 100; and interest group politics, 57; political impact of, 136-137; controversy over power of, 134-146; regulation of, 139-140; *see also,* specific types of media

mediacracy, 134, 136

Mikulski commission, 30

Mills, C. Wright, and elitist groups, 22

Milton, John, 238, 240

minorities: lobbies for, 55; constitutionality of preferential admission programs for, 200-207

"Missouri Plan," 117

"Mr. X," George Kennan as, 300

Mobil Oil, 49

moral leadership, and presidency, 82, 87

Moral Majority, 280

"moral police," 242, 243

Morbid Snatch, The, 245, 247

Morris, Norval, 162

Murray, William, 290

mutually assured destruction (MAD), as center of deterrence doctrine, 325-329, 332, 333-337

Nader, Ralph, 47, 51, 56

Nagasaki, 324

"Naming Names" section of Covert Action Information Bulletin, 256, 257

Nathanson, Bernard, 275

National Association of Manufacturers, 49

National Coalition to Ban Handguns, 189

National Council of Churches, on voluntary school prayer, 294-298

National Highway Traffic Safety Administration, 97, 99, 105

national press, *see* Press

Natural Resources Defense Council, 54

National Rifle Association (NRA): 58; lobby against handgun control, 52, 189, 191

national sovereignty, vs. disarmament, 328-329

Negro, *see* blacks

New Class: 42; knowledge industry as, 135

New Deal, 227

New Liberalism, 42

New York City, consequences of detonation of nuclear bomb over, 322-325

New York Times v. United States, 264

1984 (Orwell), 284

Nixon, Richard, 28, 37, 40, 48, 70, 73, 75, 76, 79, 81, 86, 89, 91, 92, 116, 301, 302

"no-first-use" policy on nuclear weapons, 338-339

Noonan, John T., Jr., on issue of abortion, 270-277

Norris-LaGuardia Act of 1932, 118

Novak, Michael: and controversy over power of presidency, 82-88; criticism of reforms proposed by, 92, 93, 94

nuclear parity, importance of to deterrence concept, 327-329

nuclear war: most probable cause of, 337;

conventional forces to avoid, 338-339; deterrence concept for avoiding, 325-329, 332; freeze concept for avoiding, 333-337; "limited," 333, 338; need for SALT II, 339-340

nuclear weapons: rise of antinuclear movement in U.S., 332; and deterrence concept, 325-329, 333-337; effect of detonation over New York City, 322-325; criticism of freeze proposal for, 333-337; need for global political organization for disarmament of, 328-331, 334; "no-first-use" policy on, 338-339; destructive power of, 322; need for SALT II, 339-340

Nuremberg, German researchers convicted at, 272-273

obscenity: in adult book shop magazines, 245; effect on adult conduct, 237-238; impact on cultural and moral environment, 249; in exploitation films, 245-246; as free speech, 234-259; and human dignity, 248; and the law, 249-250; in paperback novelettes, 246; in press advertisements, 240; and violence, 246; effect on young, 238-240

Obscenity and Public Morality (Clor), 251

Occupational Safety and Health Administration, 97,100, 102, 105, 107, 109

O'Connor, Sandra, 116

O'Hair, Madalyn, 290

O'Hara, James, 39

O'Hara Commission, and party reform, 30, 32

O'Neill, Thomas P., 66, 118

"open" convention, as response to Democratic Convention of 1968, 28

Orfield, Gary, controversy over power of Congress, 70-78

Orgiasts, The, 246, 247

overpressure, 322 (def.)

Paley, William, and controversy over power of media, 142-146

Parenti, Michael, on controversy over elitists ruling America, 14-19

Party reform, *see* reforms, reforms movement

Pelzman, Sam, and failure of social regulations, 99

Perle, Richard, 66

Phillips, Kevin, and controversy over power of media, 134-141

plea bargain, 160

Plessy v. Ferguson, 210, 214

pluralism: and distribution of benefits, 14, 15; criticism of, 23; definition of, 14; existence of in America, 20-24; nonexistence of in America, 14-19; and distribution of power, 14, 15, 18, 20, 21; and public policy, 14, 15

pluralistic democracy, 15

pluralists, special interest groups as, 45

Politburo, myth of "moderates" in, 312

political action committees (PACs), effect on Congress, 67

political monism, 45

political parties: reaction to Democratic convention of 1968, 28; weakening of through reforms, 37, 38, 39, 40

political system, United States as having dual, 16

politico-economic system, effect of elitist groups on, 17, 18, 19

politics: impact of media on, 136-137; effect of television on, 136

Politics, Position and Power (Seidman), 111

pollution, 15

poor: impact of abortion laws on, 276; budget cuts for not truly needy, 221; government responsibility to, 227; difficulty establishing truly needy, 228; unrest of as threat to government, 225, 227

population control: 283-284; lobbies for, 55

population growth, as Earth's most serious problem, 283

postal law, on obscenity, 235

"poverty level," problems with, 221

power: of media, 134-136; and pluralism in America, 14, 15, 18, 20, 21, 23, 24; presidential, 63, 73-78, 80-94; lack of limits on Supreme Court, 114-120

Power Elite (Mills), 25

power, rearrangement of in Democratic Party reforms, 30, 31

and capital punishment, 170, 171
rightest-fundamentalist alliance, and Human
  Life Amendment, 280-281
Road to the White House (Wayne), 43
Rockefeller III, John D., 88
Roe v. Wade, 114, 278
Rogers, Paul, 52
Roman Catholic Church, 20, 25
Roosevelt, Franklin, 116
Roosevelt, Theodore, 17
Rose, Gerhard, 272
Rostker v. Goldberg, 114
Roth v. U.S., 234
Rountree, Martha, on voluntary school
  prayer, 288-293
Russian nationalism, 314, 315
Russians, as distinguished from communism,
  317-318

S. 391, *see* Intelligence Identities Protection
  Act
S. 450, on voluntary school prayer, 288-293
SALT I, 301
SALT II, 336, 339-340
Schell, Jonathan: criticism of, 333, 334; on
  deterrence doctrine for avoiding nuclear
  war, 322-331
Schelling, Thomas, 327
Schlafly, Phyllis, on reforming the Supreme
  Court, 114-120
Schlesinger, Arthur, Jr., 95
school lunch subsidies, fraud in, 221
school prayer: and Bill of Rights, 296; and
  civil liberty, 294-298; constitutionality of,
  290-293; problems with local option of,
  296; National Council of Churches on,
  294-298; "nonsectarian," 295; public
  desire for, 288, 291, 296; attempt to
  reinstate, 288-293; and states' rights, 292-
  293; and Supreme Court, 114, 119, 121,
  122, 124; impact of on declining youth
  morality, 291
Section 601(c) of Intelligence Identities
  Protection Act of 1981, 256, 258, 260-
  266
segregation, post-Civil War to twentieth
  century, 210-211

self-protection, and handguns, 185-186,
  188, 191-192
Selzer, Richard, 274
seniority system, breaking down of Congressional, 48
sentencing discretion, 160, 162
sentencing reform, to curb crime, 148-157
separation of church and state: 295; and
  Human Life Amendment, 279
"sexual revolution," 244
Shelley v. Kraemer, 205
Sherman Antitrust Act 1890, 96
Simpson v. Vance, 261
single interest groups, and effect on government regulatory programs, 100
single-issue groups: 47; impact of on political
  system, 57, 58
Sino-Soviet rift, 301, 312, 315
Slaughter-House Cases, 209
slavery, protection of in Constitution, 208-
  209
"Sleight of Mind" (Tobin), 231
socialism, 20
social regulations, *see* government regulations
social security student benefits, cuts in, 221
social-welfare: lobbies for, 55; *see also*,
  welfare
society, influence of president on attitudes
  of, 83, 84
Solzhenitsyn, Aleksandr: criticism of Kennan's views on Soviet Union, 312-313; on
  possibility of peaceful co-existence between U.S. and Soviet Union, 300, 311-
  318
Sorensen, Theodore, and controversy over
  power of presidency, 89-94
Soviet-American relations: importance of
  detente in, 302-310; role of press in selling
  detente in, 302-303; and war as inevitable,
  304-306
Soviet grain sales, embargo on, 301
Soviet Union: in Angola, 304; bureaucracy
  of, 308; rift with Communist China, 301,
  312, 315; economic problems within,
  308; external concerns of, 309-310; recent history of, 313; intentions of, 304-